VOLT

ink.

VOLT ink.

BRYAN VOLTAGGIO & **MICHAEL VOLTAGGIO**
PHOTOGRAPHS BY ED ANDERSON

OLIVE PRESS

BRYAN

For my wife, Jennifer; my son, Thacher, and my baby girl, Piper. For my mother, father, family, friends, and mentors who have all been there to support and embrace the life of a chef. I will be forever grateful.

MICHAEL

To my daughters Olivia and Sophia, you are my inspiration and I thank god for creating the recipe that made us family.

OLIVE PRESS

Olive Press is an imprint of Weldon Owen, Inc. and Williams-Sonoma, Inc.

Weldon Owen, Inc., is a division of Bonnier Corporation.
415 Jackson St, Ste 200, San Francisco, CA 94111

Library of Congress Control Number: 2011931849

ISBN 978-1-61628-161-8

www.weldonowen.com
www.williams-sonoma.com

Color separations by Mission Productions

Printed and bound in China by
Toppan-Leefung Printing Limited

First printed in 2011
10 9

INGREDIENT FAMILIES

On Family and Food

JOSÉ ANDRÉS When the Voltaggio brothers asked me to contribute something to their first cookbook, I was very moved. I remember when I met Michael Voltaggio for the first time. I was opening a restaurant in Los Angeles, the Bazaar by José Andrés. But it wasn't just any restaurant opening. It was going to be my most ambitious project to date. I had this vision of a bazaar, of a place that was different every time you ate there. It was a grand project, and I needed to hire a chef to run it.

A friend recommended I talk to Michael Voltaggio. "Bryan Voltaggio? He is leaving Charlie Palmer?" I asked. "No, no, Michael. His brother," my friend replied. So I met Michael. I of course knew his brother Bryan, a young chef whom I first met when he was Charlie Palmer's protégé in Washington, D.C. Bryan was to me a very all-American guy—tall, blond, big.

Michael was something different. Where Bryan seemed very methodical, very measured, reserved, even formal, the younger brother, Michael, was a quieter, extremely intense guy with many tattoos, very rock and roll. He did share one thing with his brother: he was a terrific cook. I liked his energy, too, so I hired him to work with me on the Los Angeles project.

I like to think of the people with whom I work in terms of family. These people are my family. We spend a lot of time together, we strive toward common goals, and every success I have I share with them. Very quickly Michael became a key member of that family—my work family—while we toiled together to create my dream restaurant. Within a few months of opening, thanks in large part to Michael's hard work and dedication, we earned four stars from the *Los Angeles Times*.

A few months later, Michael came to me and said he wanted to leave to be on the TV show "Top Chef." I thought he was crazy to walk away from Bazaar. "José, my brother is doing it. I have to go," he told me. I could see he was torn; he was so proud of what we were doing together at The Bazaar. We talked back and forth, but he knew what he had to do. Michael's love and respect for his older brother (and, yes, his need to compete with him!) are so strong that they pulled him away. All of us who watched them on the program witnessed how close they are, how different they are, how they encourage each other, and ultimately, how they push each other to be better.

It does not surprise me that the Voltaggios chose to write this book together. The bond between these very different two brothers is very powerful and a very beautiful thing. As one of several boys in my family, I understand that. The relationship with your sibling is inevitably strange and compelling. No one knows you better, and no matter how different you grow up to be or how much distance separates you, your sibling understands you like no one else does. Unlike most brothers, the connection between Bryan and Michael has the added layer of their connection through the kitchen. Both of them are amazing and talented cooks, among the best I know.

Even here the brothers cannot resist the temptation to compete! In the following pages, each offers his recipes for a given ingredient within a family of related ingredients, a format that showcases their own familial dynamic. The approach is appropriate, for food and cooking find their truest expression within the boundaries of family.

A Fusion of Culinary Talents

CHARLIE PALMER Considering America's current love affair with food, there has never been a better time to be a chef in this country, and there are no better examples of kitchen craftsmen in our exciting culinary era than the Voltaggio brothers.

I feel lucky to say that for a time, Bryan and Michael ran the kitchens in two of my own restaurants, one on the east coast, the other on the west—and not because I felt I had to separate them by a continent. No matter what you might have seen on their successful season of "Top Chef," battling competition is not the electric charge between the brothers. They're more like a pair of skilled raconteurs who set out to tell the same story, but each in a very personal, very prideful way. As such, being a judge on the Top Chef Vegas episode when they faced off against each other was a difficult thing for me—one of the hardest things I've ever done. Because honestly, creating cuisine isn't really about the "best." It's about imagination, about interpretation, about the journey from the idea to execution. That's why the differences between Bryan and Michael Voltaggio aren't nearly as important as their similarities—and in those connections lays their bond.

You see, the Voltaggio brothers are neo-traditionalists at heart. But, because you have to know the rules before you can bend (let alone break) them, the Voltaggio brothers first committed themselves to formal culinary training and "staged" under numerous mentors to become truly skilled, damn good cooks. During his reign over the kitchen at Charlie Palmer Steak in Washington DC, Bryan exhibited remarkable confidence in his ability to give a classic steak house menu a thrilling twist. He utilized the best offerings from the Chesapeake Bay and Mid-Atlantic regions that he knows so well and where he has rightfully made a name for himself in his support of all things local—particularly heritage breed animals and sustainable seafood. While at Dry Creek Kitchen in Healdsburg, California, Michael reveled in the culinary hothouse that is Sonoma County, hell bent on changing, pushing and tweaking the mainstream conception of what constitutes "fine dining." As a chef, Michael is restless on the plate; never satisfied.

Their diversity of style doesn't make them competitors, it makes them colleagues and at their core, the Voltaggio brothers are remarkably allied. They are earthy in their approach to sourcing ingredients, cerebral in their use of those ingredients, and theatrical in the presentation of their final dishes. It's a devastatingly effective fusion of talents that they have successfully translated for the home cook in this, their first book.

I'm enormously proud of Bryan and Michael. Over the years, I have watched them grow both as men and as chefs. I've been challenged by their food: amused, inspired and, at times, even a little afraid. But bored? Never.

ink

A Note From Bryan

A CHEF'S CAREER begins in childhood. Your family influences your palate in countless ways, which becomes the starting point for a life in the kitchen. I remember my brother, Michael, sitting at the table for hours fighting with the Brussels sprouts on his plate. Mom would keep the battle going and eventually he would give in. I have seen some of the same behavior in my son, Thacher, who has not yet developed a strong liking for most foods. But because I also see the excitement in his eyes when he walks into my kitchen, I know that eventually that love of food will happen.

Memories of my childhood are punctuated by holiday meals, the aroma of cinnamon coffee cake baking in the oven, the smell of charcoal embers in the barbecue, the sight of mom's sauce for spaghetti simmering in a crockpot, and neighborhood gatherings at our house at which a bushel of crabs and a huge pot of creamed corn are on the menu. I also remember our backyard fruit and vegetable garden where my two siblings and I had decided it was okay to snack straight from the source. Although we got in trouble from time to time for eating ingredients before our mother could get to them, our petty thievery proved a harbinger of things to come: we were already seeking out the best ingredients before we could actually cook them.

All of those early experiences helped to make me the food nerd I am today. I love to discover new and intriguing ways to create, to teach about, and to share food. For this book, I was fascinated by the idea of studying the various food families to see how the members of each one might interact with one another. Michael and I chose which families to focus on based on our respective repertoires and our passion for specific ingredients, and then each contributed two recipes to each family. Interestingly, chefs typically cook within a family of ingredients without realizing it. For example, the nightshade family includes peppers, potatoes, eggplants, and tomatoes, ingredients that are classically paired together in different cuisines and in many variations. Or, coriander, cumin, and fennel, all part of the parsley family, prove equally complementary in countless dishes.

Michael and I share a lot of the same passions when it comes to our craft. In both our kitchens, ingredients are the primary focus, and spending time at our respective local farmers' markets helps drive our creative forces. Foragers find their way to the back doors of our kitchens and we immediately restructure the night's menu. We examine every ingredient and carefully choose the best way to showcase it without compromising its integrity. And although our approach and flavor combinations may differ, our love and respect for food is the same. Naturally, we see contrasts and similarities in our cuisines, which make us both the best supporters and the toughest critics of each other's creative process. We trust each other not to sugarcoat our opinions, which has helped us to propel each other to the next level. Ours is the ideal familial relationship: we are always there for each other, freely sharing ideas and criticisms.

My extended family is made up of the people who are part of what happens every day at VOLT. I learned how important a restaurant family is when I worked in the kitchens of my mentors—the chefs who taught me how to be a chef. Becoming a cook and being part of a team is more than mastering techniques and understanding how to treat ingredients and pair flavors. The chefs for whom I worked taught me that a kitchen crew is a family, and that the success of that family, like all families, depends on trust and support. I trust my staff to execute my vision, to work as a team, and to take pride in what we do every day. In turn, they trust me to teach them the ways of a professional kitchen, to share my creative vision, and to help them become better cooks. That kind of positive exchange means that everyone, from the executive chef to a lowly apprentice, feels free to share his or her ideas in a way that breeds an atmosphere of creativity.

But that creative environment would not have been possible without one more family: my wife, Jennifer, and our children, Thacher and Piper. They have been the inspiration behind my quest to create a kitchen family that works for everyone in it.

A Note From Michael

CHEFS ARE IN THE BUSINESS of emotion. We create emotions in others through the dining experience, and we use food as a means to express our own emotions. Our work is our passion, our passion is food, and our craft is to cook. But cook what? Cook how? These are the questions I often ask myself. Perhaps I'll never be able to answer them, but for more than fifteen years, I have had fun trying to do just that.

The reason these questions are so difficult to answer is because working with food offers endless possibilities. Add a little of this and a little of that and in seconds you have given birth to a new flavor, texture, aroma, and, if you are lucky, a visual masterpiece. Of course, your handiwork is destined to be admired for only seconds before it is deconstructed, briefly investigated, and then consumed promptly by the diner, hopefully leaving a fond memory or evoking a past one in its wake.

But eating is much more than a transitory consumption of calories. My mother made the entire family sit down together at the dinner table every day to share a meal. Unfortunately, many people take this ritual for granted, not realizing that food has the power to bring us together—that it is more than just the fuel that keeps the body going for life's adventures.

Indeed, family is the underlying theme in this book. According to my Merriam-Webster dictionary, family is both "a group of persons of common ancestry" and "a closely related series of elements." This book fits both definitions: my brother, Bryan, and I, wrote it together, and we organized the recipes into twenty families of ingredients.

But food and family are also connected in another important way. The people we work with in our kitchens are family. Kitchen workers spend long hours together, learn from each other, support one another, and, just like every family, they argue and fight. The restaurant kitchen is a constantly evolving environment in which lasting friendships are formed and great ideas are hatched.

This volume is a scrapbook of sorts that tells the story of our kitchens and the dishes we created in them during the past two years. To put this book together, Bryan and I have drawn on our "common ancestry," on a score of closely related ingredient groups, and on the creativity that flourishes in our respective kitchen staffs—three distinctly different families working as one.

AVIAN

SQUAB
QUAIL
CHICKEN

Birds have graced our tables almost as far back as we can trace our culinary history and have much to offer at the table: crisp skin, juicy meat, tender bits of offal; even the bones and feet make for wonderful broths and sauces. Domestically raised birds such as chickens, ducks, and turkeys are readily available and part of almost everyone's culinary repertoire. Farmers' markets and specialty purveyors stock more exotic specimens like quail, pheasant, and guinea hen. But the squab is perhaps the most prized game bird among chefs, famous for its rich meat and savory flavor. Whether it's wild or domestic, we believe that a happy bird makes a better meal, so we always obtain birds from responsible sources.

MAIN INGREDIENTS

4½ cups (1000 g) water

½ cup (106 g) firmly packed light brown sugar

¼ cup (72 g) salt

1 teaspoon (6.8 g) pink curing salt (see sources)

1 tablespoon (7 g) black peppercorns

½ bunch fresh thyme

3 fresh bay leaves

6 whole cloves

4 cloves garlic, crushed

1 teaspoon (2 g) juniper berries

6 pigeons (squabs), 12–14 ounces (350–400 g) each

1 tablespoon (14 g) rendered duck fat

Pigeon-Rye Broth (below)

Sauerkraut Noodles (below)

1 tablespoon (14 g) unsalted butter

Spiced Pastrami Syrup (below)

Gruyère Cracker (below)

Petite mustard greens

Equipment

thermal immersion circulator

smoking gun and applewood shavings

vacuum sealer and vacuum bags

6-quart (5.7-l) pressure cooker

masticating vegetable juicer

high-speed blender

plastic food syringe

plastic tubing, about 24 inches (60 cm) long (see sources)

combi-oven (optional)

food dehydrator (optional)

deep fryer (optional)

Serves 12 as a first course

››

MICHAEL Here's my unconventional take on the classic Reuben sandwich. The flavors in the broth—the mild sweetness of molasses and the distinctive aroma of caraway—are like rye bread in liquid form. The gamy, spice-rubbed pigeon mimics the Reuben's traditional pastrami, while the noodles deliver the familiar flavor of sauerkraut but in a more subtle way. Finally, the crispy, puffed Gruyère cracker is both the melted Swiss and the side of chips in a single bite.

Pigeon Pastrami, Sauerkraut, Swiss, Rye

To make a brine, in a saucepan, bring the water to a boil over high heat. Add the sugar, salt, and curing salt and stir until everything dissolves. Remove from the heat and add the peppercorns, thyme, bay leaves, cloves, garlic, and juniper berries. Let the mixture stand at room temperature until completely cool to develop the flavor. Strain the brine through a fine-mesh sieve into a lidded container, cover, and refrigerate until cold, about 30 minutes. (The brine may be stored in the refrigerator for up to 1 week.)

Remove the giblets (if present) from the pigeons and save for another use or discard. Rinse the birds under cold running water. Pat them dry with paper towels. Remove the breasts from the pigeons, keeping the skin intact. Reserve the legs and thighs of each bird for the sauce. Put the pigeon breasts in a large lock-top bag, pour in the brine, and seal the bag, squeezing out as much excess air as possible. Put the bag in a bowl and refrigerate for 12 hours.

Preheat the circulating water bath to 129°F (54°C).

Remove the pigeon breasts from the brine and discard the brine. Pat them dry and lay them in a single layer in a baking dish. Cover the dish tightly with plastic wrap, and then poke the tube of the smoking gun through the plastic. Fill the chamber with applewood shavings, light the gun, and discharge the smoke into the container. Once the smoke dissipates, leave the tube in the dish, refill the chamber, light the smoking gun, and smoke the breasts again. Repeat one more time.

Divide the breasts between 2 vacuum bags, 6 breasts to each bag. Divide the duck fat evenly between the bags, and vacuum seal on full power. Cook the pigeon breasts in the circulating water bath for 30 minutes. Remove the bags from the water bath and let cool down at room temperature for 15 minutes. Meanwhile, prepare an ice bath. When the breasts have cooled down, transfer the bags to the ice bath and let the breasts cool completely, about 2 hours. (The breasts may be stored in their bags in the refrigerator for up to 3 days.)

PIGEON-RYE BROTH

Leg-thigh portions from 6 pigeons (above)

4½ cups (1000 g) Chicken Stock (page 319)

1 carrot, peeled and cut into medium dice

1 onion, halved and seared on cut sides

2 celery ribs, cut into medium dice

1 whole clove

1 whole allspice berry

½ cup plus 2 tablespoons (50 g) caraway seeds

1 whole star anise

1 fresh bay leaf

¼ cup plus 2 teaspoons (100 g) blackstrap molasses

SAUERKRAUT NOODLES

35¼ ounces (1000 g) sauerkraut

12 grams agar (see sources)

Extra-virgin olive oil

SPICED PASTRAMI SYRUP

5 tablespoons plus 2 teaspoons (156 g) liquid glucose (see sources)

5 tablespoons (62.5 g) water

3 tablespoons (37.5 g) granulated sugar

¾ teaspoon (1.25 g) allspice berries

½ tablespoon (3.5 g) black peppercorns

1¼ teaspoons (1.9 g) pink peppercorns

3 tablespoons (10.5 g) coriander seeds

¼ teaspoon (1.5 g) fine sea salt

1½ tablespoons (12 g) yellow mustard seeds, soaked in water for 20 minutes and drained

GRUYÈRE CRACKER

2½ ounces (70 g) Gruyère cheese, coarsely grated, plus more for sprinkling

1 cup (130 g) tapioca starch (see sources)

¼ teaspoon (1.5 g) fine sea salt

6 tablespoons (85 g) water

Canola oil for deep-frying

To serve, preheat the broiler. If the pigeon breasts have been refrigerated, bring them to room temperature. Pour the pigeon-rye broth into a small saucepan, place over medium-high heat, and cook until reduced by half, 30–45 minutes. Keep warm.

Remove the pigeon breasts from the bags and discard the liquid. Place a large nonstick sauté pan over medium-high heat. When it is hot, add the pigeon breasts, skin side down, and cook until the skin is crisp and golden brown, 2–3 minutes. Transfer the breasts, skin side up, to a warmed plate and let them rest in a warm spot on the stove top.

Remove the sauerkraut "noodles" from their juice. Divide the noodles into 12 equal portions, lay the portions on a sheet pan, and place under the broiler to warm. Drizzle the noodles with the olive oil. Stir the butter into the hot reduced broth to make a sauce. Cut each squab breast crosswise into 4 slices. Place 4 slices on each of 12 serving plates. Top each with a portion of the noodles, and drizzle with the sauce. Using a small spoon, put a circle of pastrami syrup about the size of a nickel on the plate and several dollops of syrup on the squab. Garnish plates with a Gruyère cracker and a few fresh mustard greens.

PIGEON-RYE BROTH

In the pressure cooker, combine the pigeon bones, stock, carrot, onion, celery, clove, allspice, caraway seeds, star anise, bay leaf, and molasses. Following the manufacturer's instructions, lock the lid in place, bring up to high pressure, and cook for 30 minutes. Let the pressure dissipate naturally, then remove the lid. Strain the stock through a colander, and then through a fine-mesh sieve into a saucepan. Place over medium-high heat and cook, skimming any foam or impurities that rise to the surface, until reduced to 1 cup (225 g), about 1 hour. Remove from the heat and set aside.

SAUERKRAUT NOODLES

Drain the sauerkraut in a fine-mesh sieve placed over a bowl. Reserve the liquid. Juice the sauerkraut in a masticating vegetable juicer, then add the juice to the reserved liquid. Measure 2¼ cups (500 g) of the liquid, and pour into a small saucepan. Place over medium-high heat and cook until reduced by half, 30–45 minutes. Measure another 1 cup plus 2 tablespoons (250 g) of the liquid and add it to the pan. Continue to cook over medium-high heat until reduced to 1 cup plus 2 tablespoons (250 g) total.

Pour the hot liquid into the blender and turn the blender on low speed. Slowly increase the speed until a vortex forms in the center of the liquid. Sprinkle in the agar and blend for 15 seconds to disperse the agar fully. Transfer the mixture to a small, clean saucepan, place over medium heat, and bring the liquid to a boil. Boil the mixture for a full 5 minutes, stirring constantly with a whisk to hydrate the agar.

Prepare an ice bath. Fill a plastic food syringe with the hot agar mixture and release it into the 24-inch (60-cm) length of narrow plastic tubing. When the tubing is full, immerse it in the ice bath and let stand until the mixture has set, about 5 minutes. Use the empty syringe to blow air into the tubing to extract the gel in the shape of a long noodle. Repeat the process until all of the sauerkraut mixture has been used.

Place the finished noodles in a lidded container with the remaining sauerkraut liquid and refrigerate until serving. They will keep for up to 3 days.

SPICED PASTRAMI SYRUP

In a saucepan, combine the glucose, water, and sugar, place over high heat, and bring to a full boil. Cook until the mixture reaches 215°F (102°C), then remove from the heat. As the syrup stands, the temperature will continue to rise to about 225°F (106°C). Let the syrup cool at room temperature until it reaches 110°F (43°C), about 30 minutes.

Meanwhile, put the allspice in a spice grinder and grind to a medium-coarse texture. Pour into a bowl. Put the black peppercorns, pink peppercorns, and coriander seeds in the spice grinder and grind to a medium-coarse texture. Add the ground spices and the salt to the bowl with the allspice. Add the drained soaked mustard seeds and cooled pastrami syrup to the bowl and stir to mix well. (The cooled syrup may be stored in a lidded container at room temperature for up to 1 week.)

GRUYÈRE CRACKER

Preheat a combi-oven to 212°F (100°C), or prepare a large steamer.

In a food processor, combine the 2½ ounces (70 g) cheese, the tapioca starch, and the salt and pulse until blended but still chunky. With the machine running, add the water and continue to process until the mixture forms a uniform dough. Turn the dough out onto a sheet of plastic wrap and divide it in half. Put one-half on a large sheet of plastic wrap, and cover with another large sheet of plastic wrap. Using a rolling pin, roll out as thinly as possible in a roughly rectangular shape that will fit into both your combi-oven or steamer and the food dehydrator. Wrap it securely in plastic wrap, keeping it as flat as possible. Repeat the rolling and wrapping with the remaining dough half.

Place the wrapped dough in the combi-oven or steamer and steam until translucent, 10–12 minutes. Transfer the dough, still wrapped, to a work surface and let cool completely, about 30 minutes. Line the dehydrator tray or a sheet pan with a silicone mat. Unwrap each rectangle of dough, and place it on the silicone mat. Place in the dehydrator set at 150°F (65°C) or an oven preheated to 175°F (80°C) until the dough is no longer sticky to the touch, about 1½ hours. Gently pull away the silicone mat, then flip the dough rectangle over back onto the mat. Return the dough to the dehydrator or oven until it is dry to the touch but still flexible, about 1½ hours more (3 hours total).

Pour the canola oil into a deep fryer to the fill line or into a high-sided saucepan to a depth of 2½ inches (6 cm) and heat to 375°F (190°C).

Break each dough rectangle into 6 pieces, each roughly 2 by 1 inch (5 by 2.5 cm). Add the pieces to the hot oil and fry until they are puffed and golden, 15–20 seconds. Using a skimmer, quickly transfer them to a paper towel–lined plate. Using a Microplane grater, finely grate a thin layer of Gruyère over the crackers. Break the second dough rectangle into 6 pieces and deep-fry the same way. The crackers are best used fresh, but leftovers may be stored in an airtight container at room temperature for up to 3 days.

THE CRISPY PUFFED GRUYÈRE IN THIS MODERN TAKE ON A PASTRAMI SANDWICH IS BOTH THE MELTED SWISS AND SIDE OF CHIPS IN ONE BITE

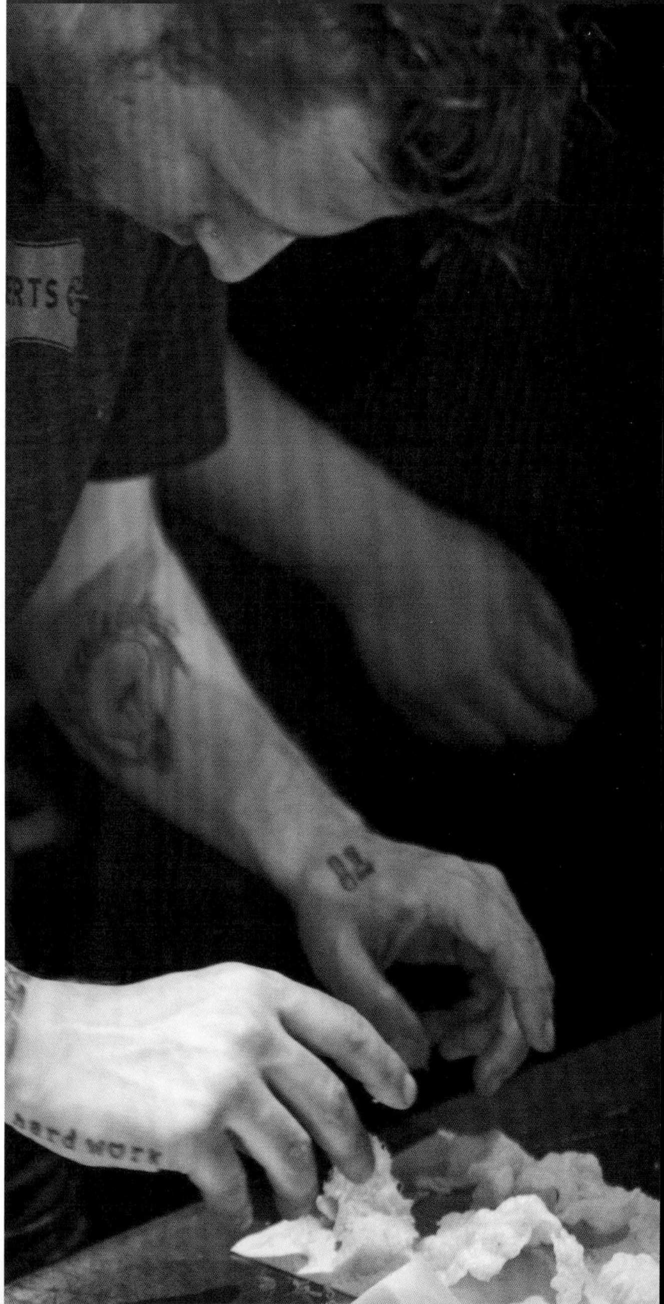

BRYAN Squab is one of my favorite birds to cook. I like the texture of the crisped skin and the liverlike flavor of the meat. The accompaniments—here, Brussels sprouts, chanterelles, and salsify—can change with the seasons, but cooking the birds sous vide is a constant. In fact, the vacuum sealer does double duty in the kitchen: it is a great way to preserve the freshness of squabs in storage and it ensures a consistent result at the table.

Whole Roasted Squab, Brussels Sprouts, Chanterelle Mushrooms, Salsify Variations

MAIN INGREDIENTS

4 squabs, about 1 pound (450 g) each
Fine sea salt
Cracked coriander seeds
Fennel seeds
Ground long pepper (see sources)
1 cup (225 g) rendered duck fat
Leaves from 1 fresh sage sprig
Leaves from 1 fresh rosemary sprig
Leaves from 2 fresh tarragon sprigs
Leaves from 2 fresh thyme sprigs
1¾ cups (500 g) fine sea salt
1 cup (200 g) sugar
Finely grated zest of 1 navel orange
2 juniper berries
Salsify Purée (below)
Petite Brussels Sprouts (below)
3 tablespoons (42 g) canola oil
3 fresh lemon thyme sprigs
½ clove garlic, smashed
Brussels Sprout Purée (below)
Caramelized Salsify (below)
Chanterelle Mushrooms (below)
Squab Sauce (below)
Fried Salsify (below)

Equipment

thermal immersion circulator
vacuum sealer and vacuum bags
food dehydrator (optional)
high-speed blender
deep fryer (optional)

Serves 4 as a main course

Preheat the circulating water bath to 142°F (61.5°C).

Remove the giblets (if present) from the squabs and save for another use or discard. Rinse the birds under cold running water. Pat them dry with paper towels. Cut off the heads and necks, reserving the necks for the squab sauce. Remove the legs from the body, leaving the drumstick and thigh attached to each another. Cut the muscles around the base of each drumstick so that it will contract around the top of the bone as it cooks. Remove the thighbone. Set the legs aside for curing.

Leave the breast meat on the bone and season lightly with salt, coriander seeds, fennel seeds, and long pepper. Put the breasts and ⅔ cup (150 g) of the duck fat in a vacuum bag and vacuum seal. Cook the breasts in the circulating water bath for 30 minutes. Meanwhile, prepare an ice bath. When the breasts are ready, transfer the bag to the ice bath to cool completely, replenishing the ice as needed, about 2 hours. Refrigerate the breasts in the bag until you are ready to finish the dish, up to 3 days.

To prepare the squab legs, in a food processor, combine the sage, rosemary, tarragon, thyme, salt, sugar, orange zest, and juniper berries and process until a uniform purée forms. Put the squab legs in a bowl, add the purée, and turn the legs to coat evenly with the seasoning mixture. Cover and refrigerate for 30 minutes to cure.

Preheat the circulating water bath to 147°F (64°C). Rinse the seasoning mixture off the legs under cold running water and pat dry. Put the legs and the remaining ⅓ cup (75 g) duck fat in a vacuum bag and vacuum seal. Cook the legs in the circulating water bath for 2 hours. Meanwhile, prepare an ice bath. When the legs are ready, transfer the bag to the ice bath to cool completely, replenishing the ice as needed, about 60 minutes. Refrigerate the legs in the bag until you are ready to finish the dish, up to 3 days.

When ready to serve, preheat the oven to 350°F (180°C).

››

SALSIFY PURÉE

1 cup (320 g) diced, peeled black salsify

1 cup (240 g) heavy cream

1 clove garlic, smashed

.5 gram xanthan gum (see sources)

Fine sea salt and freshly ground black pepper

PETITE BRUSSELS SPROUTS

12 petite Brussels sprouts

5½ tablespoons (77 g) cold unsalted butter

¼ cup (56 g) Chicken Stock (page 319)

››

In a small saucepan, heat the salsify purée over medium-low heat, stirring occasionally, just until the purée is steaming. Keep in a warm spot on the stove until ready to serve.

Bring a large pot of water to a simmer over high heat. Drop the bag of petite Brussels sprouts into the simmering water and cook until heated through, about 5 minutes. Put the stock in a small saucepan over medium heat and bring to a simmer. Dice the remaining 4 tablespoons (56 g) butter, then whisk into the stock to thicken slightly.

In an ovenproof sauté pan, heat 1 tablespoon (14 g) of the canola oil over medium heat until it begins to shimmer but not smoke. Remove the squab legs from the vacuum bag and place them, skin side down, in the hot oil. Place the pan in the oven to heat the legs through, 8–10 minutes.

Meanwhile, in a large sauté pan, heat the remaining 2 tablespoons (28 g) canola oil over medium heat until it begins to shimmer but not smoke. Put the breasts, skin side down, in the pan and let them cook for a few minutes. Once the breasts begin to brown, flip them over and, using a wide, flat, large metal spoon, baste the meat with the hot oil. Add the lemon thyme and garlic to the pan and continue to baste until the breasts are well browned all over and just heated through, about 4 minutes. Transfer the breasts to a cutting board and let them rest for 3 minutes.

Remove the legs from the oven, checking to be sure they are heated through. Transfer them to a warmed plate to rest along with the breasts.

Using a wide spatula, put the salsify purée on each of 4 warmed plates, then top with the squab breasts. Add dollops of the Brussels sprout purée around the plate, and spoon on the petite Brussels sprouts. Place the caramelized salsify around the purée; lay the legs on 1 piece of the caramelized salsify. Scatter the Brussels sprout leaves and chanterelle mushrooms around the plate. Finally, add a small amount of the squab sauce and fried salsify to each plate and serve.

SALSIFY PURÉE

In a saucepan, combine the salsify, cream, and garlic, place over medium heat, and bring to a simmer. Cook until the salsify is tender enough to purée, about 30 minutes. Remove from the heat and transfer to the blender. Turn on the blender to low speed, then slowly increase the speed until a vortex forms in the center of the liquid. Sprinkle in the xanthan gum and continue to process until it is completely absorbed, a full 5 seconds, then turn off the blender. Strain the purée through a fine-mesh sieve. Season to taste with salt and pepper. (The salsify purée may be made ahead and chilled over an ice bath until serving. Or, it may be stored in a lidded container in the refrigerator for up to 3 days.)

PETITE BRUSSELS SPROUTS

Preheat the circulating water bath to 189°F (87°C). Trim off the ends of all of the petite sprouts and remove any browning leaves. Put the sprouts, 1½ tablespoons (21 g) of the butter, and a pinch each of salt and pepper into a vacuum bag and vacuum seal. Cook in the circulating water bath until just tender to the touch, about 15 minutes. Meanwhile, prepare an ice bath. When the sprouts are ready, transfer the bags to the ice bath to cool

A VACUUM SEALER DOES DOUBLE DUTY

PRESERVING THE FRESHNESS OF THE BIRD DURING STORAGE

AND HELPING IT TO COOK EVENLY

completely, 5–10 minutes. (The Brussels sprouts may be stored in their bags in the refrigerator for up to 3 days.) Reserve the sprout leaves, stock, and the remaining 4 tablespoons (56 g) butter for assembly.

BRUSSELS SPROUT PURÉE

In a large pot, bring the water to a boil over medium-high heat. While the water is heating, prepare an ice bath. Add the salt and then the Brussels sprouts to the boiling water and cook until tender and the color has set, 3–5 minutes. Add the parsley and cook just until bright green, 30–40 seconds. Scoop out the sprouts and parsley and immerse in the ice bath. Measure out ¾ cup (170 g) of the blanching water into a container, and place the container in the ice bath. Let stand until the contents gel and are firmly set, 30–45 minutes.

Remove the Brussels sprouts and the parsley leaves from the ice bath, and squeeze out the excess liquid. Place in the clean blender and process until mixture is smooth and a vortex forms in the center of the liquid. Add the xanthan gum to the vortex and continue to process until fully incorporated, about 5 seconds. If needed, use the reserved blanching water to loosen the purée to the desired consistency. The purée may be stored in a lidded container in the refrigerator for up to 3 days.

CARAMELIZED SALSIFY

Preheat the circulating water bath to 189°F (87°C).

Peel the salsify, rinse under cold running water, and pat dry. Place the salsify and butter in a vacuum bag and vacuum seal. Cook the salsify in the circulating water bath until the surface feels just tender when pressed but the stalks are still firm, about 20 minutes. Meanwhile, prepare an ice bath. When the salsify is ready, transfer the bag to the ice bath to cool completely, about 10 minutes.

Remove the salsify from the bag and cut into rounds ¼ inch (6 mm) thick. In a sauté pan, heat the canola oil over medium heat until it begins to shimmer but not smoke. Add the salsify rounds to the hot oil and cook, flipping them as needed so they brown evenly on the top and bottom. When they are nicely browned, add the stock and thyme and bring the stock to a simmer. Cook until the stock reduces slightly and the salsify is glazed, 8–10 minutes. Keep the pan in a warm spot on the stove top until ready to serve.

CHANTERELLE MUSHROOMS

Using the tip of a paring knife, carefully peel the stems of the mushrooms. Cut the larger mushrooms into halves or quarters to create equal-sized pieces. In a large sauté pan, melt 2 tablespoons (28 g) of the butter over medium heat. Cook until the butter starts to brown, about 30 seconds. Add the mushrooms to the pan and cook, stirring, until they begin to release some liquid, 3–5 minutes. Continue to cook until they dry out and start to brown, 5–8 minutes longer. Add the shallot and cook, stirring constantly to prevent browning, until tender, 2–3 minutes. (At this point, the mushrooms may be cooled, then stored in a lidded container in the refrigerator for up to 3 days before continuing.)

Add the stock to the pan and bring it to a simmer, then turn off the heat. Dice the remaining 2 tablespoons (28 g) butter and stir into the hot stock to thicken it and create a butter fondue. Add the thyme and season to taste with salt and pepper. Keep the pan in a warm spot until ready to serve.

SQUAB SAUCE

In a large saucepan, heat the canola oil over medium-high heat until it begins to shimmer but not smoke. Add the squab bones and necks and cook, stirring occasionally, until golden brown, 8–10 minutes. Add the shallots, reduce the heat to medium, and cook, stirring. As the shallots release their liquid, use it to deglaze the pan, scraping up the browned bits. Add the honey and cook, stirring constantly, until it just begins to darken and caramelize, about 30 seconds. Add the long pepper, coriander seeds, and stock, bring to a simmer, and cook, uncovered, for 45 minutes.

Strain the sauce through a fine-mesh sieve into a saucepan and discard the contents of the sieve. Place the pan over medium-high heat and continue to reduce the sauce, skimming off any foam and impurities that form on the surface, until it is smooth and syrupy, about 30 minutes. Meanwhile, prepare an ice bath. When the sauce is ready, transfer the pan to the ice bath and let stand, stirring occasionally, until the sauce is cool, about 10 minutes. The sauce may be stored in a lidded container in the refrigerator for up to 3 days.

FRIED SALSIFY

Pour canola oil into a deep fryer to the fill line or into a high-sided saucepan to a depth of 2½ inches (6 mm) and heat to 350°F (175°C).

Peel the salsify and then use a mandoline to cut it into long, very thin strips. Add the strips to the hot oil and fry until crisp and golden brown, a few seconds. Transfer to a paper towel–lined plate, season lightly with salt, and set aside until serving.

BRUSSELS SPROUT PURÉE

- 8½ cups (1913 g) water
- 2 tablespoons plus 1 teaspoon (40 g) salt
- 12 ounces (350 g) green Brussels sprouts (12 sprouts)
- ½ bunch fresh flat-leaf parsley
- .5 gram xanthan gum (see sources)

CARAMELIZED SALSIFY

- 2 black salsify stalks, about 5½ ounces (160 g) total weight
- 4 tablespoons (56 g) unsalted butter
- 2 tablespoons (28 g) canola oil
- ¼ cup (56 g) Chicken Stock (page 319)
- 1 fresh thyme sprig

CHANTERELLE MUSHROOMS

- 3 ounces (85 g) chanterelle mushrooms
- 4 tablespoons (56 g) unsalted butter
- 1 shallot, minced
- ½ cup (113 g) Chicken Stock (page 319)
- Fine sea salt and freshly ground black pepper
- 1 teaspoon fresh thyme leaves

SQUAB SAUCE

- ¼ cup (56 g) canola oil
- Bones and necks reserved from butchering squabs (above)
- 6 shallots, thinly sliced
- 3 tablespoons (49 g) honey
- 1 long pepper (see sources)
- 2 teaspoons (2.4 g) toasted cracked coriander seeds
- 1½ cups (338 g) Chicken Stock (page 319)

FRIED SALSIFY

- 1 black salsify stalk
- Canola oil for deep-frying
- Fine sea salt

MAIN INGREDIENTS

4½ cups (1000 g) water

7 tablespoons (93 g) firmly packed dark brown sugar

2 tablespoons (36 g) fine sea salt

1 teaspoon (6.8 g) pink curing salt (see sources)

About 2 ounces (60 g) Art of Tea Chocolate Monkey tea

4 quail, about 6 ounces (128 g) each

Extra-virgin olive oil

Canola oil for deep-frying

Arugula-Tarragon Gelée (below)

2 bananas

1 tablespoon (14 g) unsalted butter

20 pieces Sylvetta arugula or other petite arugula

Maldon sea salt

Banana Polenta (below)

Truffle Bolognese (below)

Equipment

thermal immersion circulator

vacuum sealer and vacuum bags

deep fryer (optional)

high-speed blender

Serves 8 as a first course

ARUGULA-TARRAGON GELÉE

2¼ cups (500 g) water

1 teaspoon (6 g) fine sea salt

1 ounce (30 g) fresh tarragon leaves

5½ ounces (160 g) arugula leaves

2½ tablespoons (35 g) olive oil

2 grams agar (see sources)

2 sheets silver-grade leaf gelatin (see sources)

››

MICHAEL This dish came about through a sequence of small connections. I like to brine quail to keep them juicy, so I tried a chocolate-and-banana-flavored tea for the brine base. From there, bananas made me think of green bananas, which gave me the idea of using arugula and tarragon, hence, the gelée. I was intrigued by pairing the scents of truffle and banana, which led to the banana polenta and the truffle sauce. Each small leap led to the birth of this beautiful dish.

Chocolate Tea Roasted Quail, Banana Polenta, Truffle Bolognese

In a saucepan, combine the water, brown sugar, sea salt, and curing salt, place over high heat, and bring to a boil. Put the tea in a heatproof container large enough to hold all of the liquid. Pour the boiling liquid over the tea and cover with plastic wrap. Let the mixture cool to room temperature, about 15 minutes. Remove the plastic wrap and strain the liquid through a fine-mesh sieve into a lidded container. Cover and refrigerate until needed. The mixture will keep for up to 24 hours.

Rinse the quail under running cold water and pat dry. Submerge the quail in the tea brine, cover with plastic wrap, and refrigerate for 24 hours.

Preheat the circulating water bath to 140°F (60°C).

Remove the quail from the brine and pat dry with paper towels. Place 1 quail and 1 teaspoon (5 g) of the extra-virgin olive oil in a vacuum bag and vacuum seal. Repeat with the remaining 3 quail, sealing each one with 1 teaspoon (5 g) oil in a vacuum bag. Cook the quail in the circulating water bath for 1 hour. When the quail are done, remove the bags from the water bath and let cool down at room temperature for 10 minutes. Meanwhile, prepare an ice bath. When the quail have cooled down, transfer the bags to the ice bath and let the quail cool completely, replenishing the ice as needed, about 30 minutes. The quail may be stored in their bags in the refrigerator for up to 3 days.

When ready to serve, pour canola oil into a deep fryer to the fill line or into a high-sided saucepan to a depth of 2½ inches (6 cm) and heat to 375°F (190°C).

Remove the quail from their bags. Working with 1 or 2 at a time, add the quail to the hot oil and fry until the skin is golden brown and crispy, 1–2 minutes. Using a large skimmer or slotted spoon, transfer the quail to a paper towel–lined sheet pan and let the quail rest for 2–3 minutes. Using a sharp paring knife, remove the breasts and full leg and thigh portions from each quail. Set aside 1 breast and 1 leg-thigh portion for each serving. Using the same knife, remove the skin and tissue down to the joint where the wing and leg meet to french the leg. Keep the quail in a warm spot on the stove top or in a low oven.

THIS DISH CAME ABOUT THROUGH A SEQUENCE OF SMALL CONNECTIONS AND AS WE ADDED NEW ELEMENTS IT LED TO THE BIRTH OF A BEAUTIFUL DISH

Using a paring knife and a straight edge, cut the arugula-tarragon gelée into 2½-inch (6-cm) squares. Using a small offset palette knife, lift the gelée squares from the pan. Cut the bananas into 2-inch (5-cm) pieces; you need a total of 16 pieces. Use a ¾-inch (19-mm) round cutter to cut out the cores of the banana pieces. Put the butter in a medium sauté pan set over medium heat. When the butter begins to froth, add the banana "cores" and sauté, gently rolling the pieces in the pan, until golden brown, 3–4 minutes. Put the arugula leaves in a small bowl and dress lightly with crushed Maldon salt and about 1 teaspoon (5 g) olive oil.

Lay 2 squares of gelée, slightly offset one another, at the top and bottom of the center of each plate. Lay one quail breast vertically in the center of the plate so that the top and bottom tips touch the squares of gelée. Tuck 1 banana core underneath the breast on the left side. Lean the leg up against the breast at the top so that the leg bone is pointing up into the air and use the other banana core to hold the leg in place. Put a spoonful of polenta on the lower piece of gelée. Put a generous spoonful of truffle bolognese sauce over the breast. Garnish with the dressed arugula leaves. Serve right away.

ARUGULA-TARRAGON GELÉE

In a small saucepan, combine the water and salt, place over high heat, and bring to a boil. Add the tarragon and arugula and boil until both greens are fully cooked and the color is set, about 10 seconds. Transfer the leaves to the blender and process on high speed until completely smooth, about 10 seconds. With the blender running, slowly drizzle in the olive oil until it has emulsified into the purée. Transfer the mixture to a wide, shallow container and put in the refrigerator to cool, about 30 minutes. Strain the cooled tarragon-arugula mixture through a fine-mesh sieve into a small bowl and let stand for 1 hour. Do not push or stir the mixture; capture only the liquid that falls through

naturally. Measure 7 tablespoons plus 1 teaspoon (200 g) of the liquid and add it to the clean blender. Turn the blender on to low speed. Slowly increase the speed until a vortex forms in the center of the liquid. Sprinkle in the agar and blend for a full 5 seconds to hydrate the agar. Transfer the mixture to a small saucepan, place over medium heat, and bring to a boil. Boil for 5 minutes. Meanwhile, put the gelatin sheets in a small bowl of ice water and let soak until softened, about 5 minutes. Lift out the gelatin sheets and squeeze out the excess water. Add the softened gelatin to the hot agar mixture and stir gently to dissolve. Pour the mixture into an 8-inch (20-cm) square glass baking dish, forming a layer about 1⁄16 inch (1.5 mm) thick. Let cool completely, about 30 minutes. Cover the dish and refrigerate until the gelée is firmly set, at least 30 minutes. (The gelée may be stored in the refrigerator for up to 3 days.)

BANANA POLENTA

In a small saucepan, combine the milk and butter, place over medium heat, and bring to a simmer, being careful not to scorch the milk. Whisk in the polenta and the banana and cook, whisking constantly, until the polenta begins to thicken and set up, about 20 minutes. Stir in the salt and continue to cook, stirring occasionally, until the polenta is fully cooked and smooth, about 20 minutes longer. Remove from heat and stir in the mascarpone and Parmigiano-Reggiano. Keep warm until ready to serve.

TRUFFLE BOLOGNESE

In a small saucepan, heat the canola oil over medium-low heat. Add the carrot, celery, and onion and cook, stirring occasionally until the onion and celery are translucent and the carrot is tender, 5–8 minutes. Carefully add the brandy to the pan, stir to scrape up the browned bits on the pan bottom, and let cook until the liquid has reduced by half, about 5 minutes. Add the truffle juice and stock and bring to a simmer. Add the cream and simmer until the mixture is reduced by half, about 30 minutes. Whisk in the xanthan gum until fully incorporated. Add the chives and tomato, stir to mix, and remove from the heat. Whisk in the butter and keep the sauce warm until ready to serve. Just before serving, add the chopped fresh truffles (if using) and the vinegar to the sauce and stir well. Serve right away.

BANANA POLENTA

¾ cup (200 g) whole milk
1 tablespoon (14 g) unsalted butter
¼ cup (40 g) Italian fine polenta
2 ounces (55 g) banana, chopped
¼ teaspoon (1.5 g) fine sea salt
4 teaspoons (20 g) mascarpone cheese
2½ tablespoons (15 g) grated Parmigiano-Reggiano cheese

TRUFFLE BOLOGNESE

2 tablespoons (28 g) canola oil
1¾ ounces (50 g) carrot, cut into brunoise
1¾ ounces (50 g) celery, cut into brunoise
1¾ ounces (50 g) yellow onion, cut into brunoise
7 tablespoons (100 g) brandy
¾ cup plus 2 tablespoons (200 g) truffle juice (see sources)
¾ cup plus 2 tablespoons (200 g) Chicken Stock (page 319)
2 tablespoons (30 g) heavy cream
.5 gram xanthan gum (see sources)
¾ ounce (20 g) fresh chives, finely sliced
1¾ ounces (50 g) tomato, peeled, seeded, and finely diced
4 teaspoons (20 g) cold unsalted butter, diced
7 ounces (200 g) fresh black Perigord truffle, chopped (optional)
1 teaspoon (4 g) Banyuls vinegar

BRYAN Charlie Palmer always prepared a wonderful roasted chicken with truffles. Inspired by his recipe, I wanted to make an equally delicious roasted bird that was not time sensitive. Partially cooking the chicken sous vide allows you to have it on hand and ready to roast when you need it. That leaves you plenty of time to cook some stone-milled grits with the flavor of smoke and creamed spinach with a rye crust for serving alongside the bird—a perfect menu for a family-style meal.

Roasted Chicken, Preserved Truffle, Walla Walla Onions, Bacon

MAIN INGREDIENTS

1 chicken, 6 pounds (2.75 kg)

1 tablespoon (18 g) fine sea salt, plus more to season

Freshly ground black pepper

One 12-ounce (350-g) can preserved black truffles in cooking liquid

1¼ cups (280 g) cold Chicken Stock (page 319)

8 ounces (225 g) Newsom's or other high-quality hickory-smoked slab bacon, cut crosswise into 1-inch (2.5-cm) pieces

8 young Walla Walla onions, each about 3 inches (7.5 cm) in diameter

Creamed Spinach (below)

Smoked Grits (below)

Equipment

thermal immersion circulator

vacuum sealer and vacuum bags

6-quart (5.7-l) pressure cooker

high-speed blender

Serves 4 as a family-style main course

CREAMED SPINACH

1 cup (100 g) fresh rye bread, cut into small dice

1 pound (453.6 g) spinach

¾ cup (172.5 g) ricotta cheese

Finely grated zest of ½ lemon

1 teaspoon (5 g) lemon juice

1 large egg

¼ teaspoon (.5 g) Espelette pepper

1 teaspoon (6 g) fine sea salt

¼ teaspoon (.25 g) freshly grated nutmeg

1 tablespoon (14 g) unsalted butter, melted

2 tablespoons (28 g) extra-virgin olive oil

¼ cup (25 g) grated Parmigiano-Reggiano cheese

SMOKED GRITS

½ cup (95 g) stone-milled grits, cold-smoked for 1 hour

4 cups (1040 g) whole milk

½ teaspoon (3 g) fine sea salt

½ cup (50 g) finely grated smoked Cheddar cheese

Preheat the circulating water bath to 162.5°F (72.5°C).

Remove the giblets (if present) from the chicken and save for another use or discard. Season the chicken inside and outside with the 1 tablespoon (18 g) salt, then dust the chicken evenly inside and out with the pepper. Truss the bird with cotton butcher's twine.

Open the truffle can and remove the truffles. You should have 7.83 ounces (221 g) truffles. Set the truffles aside in a covered container in the refrigerator. Measure 7 tablespoons (100 g) of the truffle liquid. Put the chicken, the truffle liquid, and the stock in a vacuum bag and vacuum seal. Cook the chicken in the circulating water bath for 4 hours.

Just before the chicken is ready, prepare a cool water bath. When the chicken is done, transfer the bag to the cool water bath to cool down for 15–20 minutes. Prepare an ice bath, and when the chicken has cooled down, transfer the bag to the ice bath. Let the chicken cool until very cold, replenishing the ice as needed, about 1 hour. (If desired, the chicken can be refrigerated in the bag for up to 1 week before serving.) If using right away, lift the chicken out of the bag, taking care to reserve all of the cooking liquid in a separate container. Pat the chicken dry with paper towels.

Preheat the oven to 375°F (190°C). Put the chicken in a 6-quart (5.7-l) Dutch oven, cover, and place in the oven for 15 minutes. Remove the lid, raise the oven temperature to 400°F (200°C), and roast the chicken until golden brown, 12–15 minutes. Meanwhile, put the bacon pieces in a large sauté pan, place over medium heat, and let cook undisturbed until they begin to render their fat. Once they begin to sizzle, cook, stirring occasionally, until browned, 8–10 minutes. Using a slotted spoon, transfer to a paper towel–lined plate. Drain off all but about 1 tablespoon (14 g) of the fat from the pan. Return the pan to medium heat, add the onions, and sauté until they are translucent and the sugars begin to caramelize, 5–8 minutes. Season lightly with salt and pepper and remove from the heat. Dice the reserved truffles and add to the onions along with the bacon. Stir to mix well.

Remove the chicken from the oven. Distribute the bacon-onion mixture in an even layer around the chicken and return the chicken to the oven until the skin is golden and crisp, about 10 minutes. Remove the chicken from the oven and let stand for 10–15 minutes before serving. Using a slotted spoon, transfer the bacon-onion mixture to a serving bowl. Spoon the pan juices over the chicken and serve right away, carving the chicken at the table. Set out the bacon-onion mixture, creamed spinach, and smoked grits for serving family style.

CREAMED SPINACH

Put the rye bread on a sheet pan lined with parchment paper and let it dry out at room temperature for 24 hours.

Set a large pot of generously salted water over high heat and bring it to a boil. In batches, blanch the spinach for 5–10 seconds, until the color sets, and then use a metal skimmer to transfer it to an ice bath. Once all of the spinach has been cooled, squeeze it dry and divide it in half by volume. Put half of the blanched spinach in the blender with the ricotta cheese, lemon zest, lemon juice, egg, and Espelette pepper. Purée on high speed until completely smooth. Finely chop the remaining spinach and put it in a medium bowl. Pour the puréed spinach over the chopped spinach and fold them together using a silicone spatula. Season with ½ teaspoon (2.5 g) of the salt and the nutmeg. Transfer to a prepared casserole dish that is 6-by-6-inches (15.25-by-15.25-cm) and 2–3 inches (5–7.5 cm) deep.

Preheat the oven to 375°F (190°C). Fill a large tea kettle and set over medium-low heat.

Put the rye bread cubes in a food processor and pulse a few times to form coarse crumbs; you should end up with about ½ cup (50 g). In a small bowl, combine the bread crumbs, melted butter, olive oil, cheese, and remaining ½ teaspoon (2.5 g) salt and mix well. Sprinkle evenly over the spinach.

Put the casserole dish in a larger roasting pan. Pour boiling water from the tea kettle around the casserole dish, coming halfway up the sides. Cover with the lid and bake for 20 minutes. Uncover the casserole dish and bake for an additional 10 minutes or until the crust is crisp and nicely browned. Remove from the oven and let the casserole rest on the stove top for 5 minutes.

SMOKED GRITS

Put the grits, milk, and salt in a heatproof bowl that fits inside a 6-quart (5.7 l) pressure cooker and stir to mix well. Put the bowl in the pressure cooker and pour water around it to a depth of 2–3 inches. Following the manufacturer's instructions, lock the lid in place and cook at high pressure for 15 minutes. Let the pressure dissipate naturally. When you open the lid, the milk should have just begun to caramelize on top and the grits will have separated to the bottom of the bowl. Use an immersion blender to purée the grits back into the milk and transfer them to a saucepan set over medium heat. Bring to a simmer and adjust the heat to very low and cook for 45 minutes, stirring occasionally, until the grits have the consistency of porridge. Add the cheese, stirring to blend it into the grits, and then transfer to a serving dish.

INSPIRED BY **CHARLIE PALMER**

THIS FAMILY-STYLE RECIPE LETS YOU PARTIALLY COOK THE BIRD SOUS VIDE

SO THAT IT IS READY TO ROAST JUST BEFORE YOU ARE READY TO EAT

BUCKWHEAT

BUCKWHEAT FLOUR
SORREL
BUCKWHEAT GROAT
RHUBARB

People think of buckwheat as the dark flour with an earthy nutty flavor. In fact, there is a small family of buckwheat ingredients encompassing buckwheat (flour and groats), rhubarb, and garden sorrel. Buckwheat groats are the hulled seeds of the buckwheat plant; they have a nutty flavor that intensifies when they are roasted. Rhubarb is one of spring's first vegetables, a tart harbinger of things to come in the garden. The stems, cooked or raw, add brightness and acidity to any preparation. Sorrel comes in several beautiful varieties. Their leaves are known for their lemony flavor. Tiny, tender specimens make for a delicate salad or an herbal garnish, while larger, heartier leaves can be wilted or puréed into a flavorful soup.

MICHAEL This is a take-off on a dish I made with Arnaud Berthelier, the chef who introduced me to fine dining. Roasted bird and chestnut soup is not new. But adding buckwheat groats delivers a surprising toasty nuttiness to a familiar combination. The guinea hen gives the dish its structure and richness, while the fried buckwheat pasta provides texture, much like the addition of fried noodles or tortilla strips to other soups. The result is a luxurious and satisfying dish.

MAIN INGREDIENTS

1 guinea hen, 3–4 pounds (1.3–1.8 kg)
Whole milk, as needed
Fine sea salt and freshly ground white pepper
5 tablespoons plus 1 teaspoon (75 g) rendered bacon fat, cold enough to spread
4 fresh thyme sprigs
Canola oil for deep-frying
Mustard Gelée (below)
1 tablespoon (14 g) unsalted butter
Chestnut Milk (below)
Buckwheat Pasta (below)
12 peeled chestnuts
2 tablespoons (32 g) chestnut honey
Date Purée (below)
Petite sorrel leaves

Equipment

thermal immersion circulator
vacuum sealer and vacuum bags
deep fryer (optional)
high-speed blender
plastic squeeze bottle
pasta machine
food dehydrator (optional)

Serves 4 as a first course or a light main course

››

Guinea Hen, Chestnut Milk, Crispy Buckwheat, Date, Mustard

Preheat the circulating water bath to 140°F (60°C).

Remove the liver and heart from the cavity of the guinea hen, put them in a lidded container with milk to cover completely, and refrigerate overnight. Using a boning knife, remove the breasts from the body of the hen, keeping the skin intact. Using a cleaver, chop the remaining parts of the hen, including the legs and bones, into small pieces and set them aside for the chestnut milk.

Season the breasts with salt and pepper. Spread half of the bacon fat all over each breast, then top with 2 thyme sprigs. Lay 1 breast, skin side down, on a large sheet of plastic wrap, and roll it up horizontally in the plastic wrap, forming a log; the skin will be on the outside of the log. Holding the plastic wrap at each end of the log, roll the log toward you a few times to make sure the plastic is tight and there is even pressure along the length of the log. Tie each end securely with cotton butcher's twine. Repeat with the second breast. Place the logs in a large vacuum bag and vacuum seal. Cook in the circulating water bath for 45 minutes. Just before the breasts are ready, prepare an ice bath. Then, when the breasts are done, transfer the bag to the ice bath and let cool completely, replenishing the ice as needed, about 15 minutes. The breasts may be stored in the bag in the refrigerator for up to 2 days.

To serve, preheat the circulating water bath to 60°F (15.5°C). Pour the canola oil into a deep fryer to the fill line or into a tall-sided saucepan to a depth of 2½ inches (6 cm) and heat to 350°F (180°C).

Warm up the guinea hen breasts in the circulating water bath for 10 minutes. Meanwhile, remove the mustard gelée from the refrigerator and, using a small offset spatula, unmold it onto a work surface. Cut the gelée into ½-inch (12-mm) cubes.

Remove the hen breasts from their bag and unwrap them. Place a sauté pan over high heat and add the butter. When the butter foams, add the breast logs, skin side down, and sear until the skin renders and becomes golden brown, 4–5 minutes. Transfer the logs, skin side up, to a warmed plate and let rest.

DON'T BE DAUNTED BY THIS DISH'S COMPLEXITY

MOST OF THE ELEMENTS CAN BE MADE FAR AHEAD OF TIME AND WARMED JUST BEFORE SERVING

Leave the oil on. In a saucepan, bring the chestnut milk to a bare simmer. Add 8 strips of the dried buckwheat pasta to the hot oil and deep-fry until golden and crisp, 5–10 seconds. Using a skimmer, transfer to a paper towel–lined plate and season lightly with salt. Add the chestnuts to the hot oil and fry until golden brown, about 30 seconds. Transfer to a bowl and drizzle with the honey. Toss until thoroughly coated and season lightly with salt.

Put 3 cubes of mustard gelée into each of 4 shallow bowls. Cut the hen breasts crosswise into 4 slices each, and arrange them, skin side up, in each bowl. Lay the pieces of fried pasta over the breasts. Divide the chestnuts among the bowls. Squeeze a few dots of date purée into each bowl. Garnish the bowls with the sorrel leaves. Set a bowl in front of each diner. Carefully pour the warm chestnut milk into the bowls one at a time, dividing it evenly.

MUSTARD GELÉE

Put the gelatin sheets in a small bowl of ice water and let soak until softened, about 5 minutes. In the blender, combine the mustard, water, sugar, agar, and glucose and process until smooth. Transfer to a small saucepan, place over medium heat, and bring to a boil. Let the mixture boil gently for 5 minutes, then transfer to a clean blender. Lift the gelatin sheets from the ice water, squeeze out the excess water, and add to the blender. Process until the mixture is smooth. Pour the mixture into an 8-inch (20-cm) square glass baking dish, forming a layer about ½ inch (12 mm) thick. Cover the dish and refrigerate until the gelée is firmly set, about 2 hours. The gelée may be stored in the refrigerator for up to 1 week.

CHESTNUT MILK

Preheat the oven to 350°F (180°C). Lay the reserved chopped hen and bones in a single layer on a sheet pan and roast, stirring once halfway through the cooking time, until golden brown, 20–30 minutes. Remove from the oven.

Place an 8-quart (7.5-l) stockpot over medium-high heat. When it is hot, add the bacon fat, chestnuts, and buckwheat groats and cook, stirring constantly, until the chestnuts are evenly caramelized, 8–10 minutes. Using a slotted spoon, transfer the chestnuts and groats to a bowl. Add the onion, carrots, and celery to the pot and cook, stirring occasionally, until the vegetables are golden brown on all sides, about 5 minutes. Drain the heart and liver, discarding the milk, and pat them dry. Add them to the pot and sear on both sides.

Add the roasted chopped hen and bones and caramelized chestnuts and buckwheat groats to the pot, and then pour in the brandy and stir to scrape up the browned bits on the pot bottom. Cook until the liquid reduces and just glazes the contents of the pot, about 30 minutes. Add the stock, milk, cream, and honey to the pot and bring to a bare simmer. Reduce the heat to medium-low and let the mixture simmer, skimming away any foam that forms on the surface, for 1½ hours for maximum flavor development.

In batches, transfer the contents of the pot, including the bones, to the clean blender and process until the mixture is the consistency of a thick tomato sauce, leaving it a little chunky and somewhat coarsely textured. Strain the mixture first through a colander and then through a fine-mesh sieve. Transfer the strained mixture to a clean blender and process until completely smooth. Season to taste with salt. The chestnut milk may be cooled and stored in a lidded container in the refrigerator for up to 3 days.

BUCKWHEAT PASTA

In a food processor, combine the all-purpose flour, buckwheat flour, eggs, egg yolks, milk, and olive oil and process until a smooth, uniform dough forms, 10–15 seconds. Transfer the dough to a vacuum bag and vacuum seal, or wrap the dough in plastic wrap. Let the dough rest at room temperature for 1 hour.

Put a large pot of generously salted water over high heat and bring to a boil. Meanwhile, roll out the dough. Set the rollers on a pasta machine to the widest setting. Roll the dough through the rollers twice, taking care that the dough remains flat as you roll it. Reset the rollers one width narrower and again pass the dough through the rollers twice. Repeat the process, resetting the rollers one width narrower and rolling the dough twice through each setting until you reach the narrowest setting. After rolling the dough twice through the narrowest setting, lay the dough sheet flat on a work surface. Cut it into 8 strips, each 5 inches (13 cm) long and ½ inch (12 mm) wide.

Prepare an ice bath. Add the dough strips to the boiling water and cook until tender, about 40 seconds. Using a skimmer, quickly transfer the dough strips to the ice bath. Let the strips cool briefly in the ice bath, then transfer them to paper towels to dry. Lay the dry pasta strips out on a dehydrator tray or sheet pan. Place in the dehydrator set at 155°F (65°C) or in an oven preheated to 175°F (80°C) until completely dry, about 1 hour. The dried pasta sheets may be covered and stored at room temperature for up to 3 days before frying.

DATE PURÉE

In a small saucepan, heat the olive oil over medium heat until it begins to shimmer but does not smoke. Add the shallot and cook, stirring occasionally, until translucent and tender, about 5 minutes. Do not allow to brown. Add the dates, port, red wine, and sorrel and cook until the dates are completely tender, about 10 minutes. Transfer to the clean blender and process until smooth. Let the purée cool to room temperature, then transfer to the squeeze bottle and refrigerate until ready to serve.

MUSTARD GELÉE

2½ sheets silver-grade leaf gelatin (see sources)
1 cup plus 2 tablespoons (250 g) Dijon mustard
1 cup plus 2 tablespoons (250 g) water
1½ teaspoons (6.25 g) sugar
5 grams agar (see sources)
¼ cup (110 g) liquid glucose (see sources)

CHESTNUT MILK

Reserved chopped guinea hen
2 tablespoons (28 g) rendered bacon fat
14 ounces (400 g) peeled, frozen chestnuts
3½ ounces (100 g) buckwheat groats
1 yellow onion, cut into medium dice
2 large carrots, cut into medium dice
2 celery ribs, cut into medium dice
Liver and heart from the guinea hen soaked in milk
1 cup (225 g) brandy
4 cups (900 g) Chicken Stock (page 319)
3 cups plus 7 fl oz (1000 g) whole milk
7 ounces (200 g) heavy cream
2 tablespoons (30 g) chestnut honey
1½ teaspoons (9 g) fine sea salt

BUCKWHEAT PASTA

2⅔ cups (400 g) all-purpose flour
¾ cup plus 4 teaspoons (100 g) buckwheat flour
4 large eggs
2 large egg yolks
3 tablespoons (50 g) whole milk
1 tablespoon (14 g) extra-virgin olive oil
Fine sea salt

DATE PURÉE

2 teaspoons (10 g) olive oil
1 shallot, peeled and sliced
16 Medjool dates, pitted and chopped
¾ cup plus 2 tablespoons (200 g) port
¾ cup plus 2 tablespoons (200 g) dry red wine
4 ounces (113 g) sorrel leaves

BRYAN The partridge unites all of the elements here. Cooking the legs in a pressure cooker yields both the braised leg meat and a flavorful stock for cooking the buckwheat groats. The creaminess and brightness of the sorrel pudding contrasts with the tartness of the quince and heartiness of the groats, which are laced with the skin, leg meat, and livers of the birds. And completing the flavor circle is the mildly acidic, bitter endive—the perfect counterpoint to the richness of the meat.

Partridge, Braised Endive, Quince, Sorrel Pudding

MAIN INGREDIENTS

3 partridges with feet, 16–18 ounces (450–500 g) each

7 tablespoons (125 g) plus 1 teaspoon (6 g) fine sea salt, plus more to season

4 tablespoons (56 g) unsalted butter

¼ cup (53 g) firmly packed light brown sugar

Finely grated zest of ½ Cara Cara orange

1 juniper berry

¼ whole clove, smashed with the side of a chef's knife

¼ cup (55 g) sorrel leaves

2 tablespoons (28 g) canola oil, or as needed

1 carrot, cut into ½-inch (12-mm) rounds

½ yellow onion, cut into large dice

4 cloves garlic, 3 thinly sliced and 1 smashed

2 cups plus 3½ tablespoons (500 g) water

¼ cup (56 g) dry red wine

¼ cup (56 g) soy sauce

Quince Stock (below)

Quince-Braised Endive (below)

Simmered Buckwheat Groats (below)

Sorrel Pudding (below)

½ shallot, sliced

2 fresh thyme sprigs

Equipment

thermal immersion circulator

vacuum sealer and vacuum bags

6-quart (5.7-l) pressure cooker

Serves 6 as a main course

››

Remove the livers from the partridge cavities and reserve. Remove and discard any other giblets (if present). Remove the legs from each bird, keeping the skin, drumstick, and thigh intact. Cut the foot from each leg and reserve. Remove the neck and wings from each body, keeping the breasts intact and leaving them attached to the bird's ribcage. Reserve the necks and wings.

Preheat the circulating water bath to 143°F (61.5°C).

Season the 3 whole partridge breasts with ½ teaspoon (3 g) of the salt. Put each breast and 1 tablespoon (14 g) of the butter into a vacuum bag and vacuum seal. Cook the breasts in the water bath for 20 minutes. Transfer the bags to an ice bath and let the breasts cool completely, replenishing the ice as needed, about 2 hours. The partridge breasts may be stored in their bags in the refrigerator for up to 3 days.

In a food processor, combine the 7 tablespoons (125 g) salt, the brown sugar, orange zest, juniper berry, clove, and sorrel and process to form a uniform curing mixture, about 30 seconds. Season each leg-thigh portion with 1 tablespoon (20 g) of the curing mixture. Put the portions in a vacuum bag and vacuum seal. Let the legs cure for 20 minutes. Remove the legs from the bag and rinse off the cure under running cold water. Pat dry and keep covered in the refrigerator until ready to use.

In a large sauté pan, heat 1 tablespoon (14 g) of the canola oil over medium heat until it shimmers but does not smoke. Season the legs very lightly with salt, place in the hot oil, and cook, turning them every so often to brown evenly, until they are seared on both sides, 5–7 minutes. Transfer the legs to a plate. Add the wings to the pan and sear them on both sides in the same manner. Repeat to brown the feet and necks, adding a bit more oil to the pan if necessary to encourage browning.

In the pressure cooker, combine the carrot, onion, sliced garlic, water, wine, soy sauce, and partridge wings, feet, and necks. Top with the leg-thigh portions. Following the manufacturer's instructions, lock the lid in place, bring up to high

QUINCE STOCK

8 cups (1800 g) plus 6 cups (1350 g) water

18 grams citric acid (see sources)

6 quinces

2 allspice berries

Juice of 2 Cara Cara oranges (about ¾ cup/170 g)

⅓ cup plus 1 tablespoon (100 g) sorghum molasses

1¼ teaspoons (7.5 g) fine sea salt

QUINCE-BRAISED ENDIVE

6 cups (1350 g) Quince Stock (above)

1 tablespoon (14 g) canola oil

3 shallots, sliced paper-thin on a mandoline

6 heads Belgian endive

Quince dice from Quince Stock (above)

SIMMERED BUCKWHEAT GROATS

1 cup (125 g) buckwheat groats

2 cups (450 g) reserved partridge stock

1 cup (225 g) water

Chicken Stock (page 319), if needed

½ teaspoon (3 g) fine sea salt

SORREL PUDDING

2 large eggs

8 ounces (225 g) sorrel

¼ teaspoon (1.5 g) fine sea salt

.3 gram xanthan gum (see sources)

pressure, and cook for 15 minutes. Let the pressure dissipate naturally, then uncover. Set aside the leg-thigh portions on a plate. Strain the stock through a fine-mesh sieve and discard the contents of the sieve. Remove the leg and thigh meat from the bones with your fingers, breaking it into bite-sized pieces, reserving the skin but discarding the bones. Put the meat in a small container, add ½ cup (113 g) of the strained stock, and cover tightly. Pour the remaining stock into a separate lidded container. Store both containers in the refrigerator until needed. If not continuing right away, store the reserved skin in a separate container in the refrigerator.

To serve, preheat the circulating water bath to 143°F (61.5°C).

Reheat the partridge breasts in the circulating water bath for 10 minutes. Dice the reserved skin. Heat a sauté pan over medium heat. When it is hot, add the skin and cook, stirring constantly, until the skin pieces are brown and crisp, 5–8 minutes. Using a slotted spoon, transfer to a paper towel–lined plate and season lightly with salt. Season the livers lightly with salt and add them to the same pan over medium heat. Cook, turning occasionally, until golden brown on both sides but still pink in the center, about 5 minutes. Transfer the livers to a plate and let rest for 5 minutes.

Cut the braised endives in half lengthwise. Place in a saucepan, add one-fourth of the liquid from the bag, and bring to a simmer over medium heat. In another saucepan, combine the quince dice with its cooking liquid and bring to a simmer over medium heat. Lift off and reserve the fat that has solidified on top of the reserved partridge stock. Dice the livers, place them in a saucepan, and add the simmered buckwheat groats, the fat from the partridge stock, the crispy skin, and the leg meat and the stock that it was stored in. Put the sorrel purée in a small saucepan over medium heat to gently warm; do not let it boil.

In a large sauté pan, heat the remaining 1 tablespoon (14 g) canola oil over medium-high heat until it shimmers but does not smoke. Add the partridge breasts and sear until the skin is golden brown. Add the smashed garlic clove, the shallot, the thyme sprigs, and the remaining 1 tablespoon (14 g) butter to the pan. Using a wide, flat, large metal spoon, rapidly baste the breasts on both sides until the butter stops foaming, 1–2 minutes. Transfer the breasts to a plate and let them rest for 5 minutes. Remove the partridge tenderloins and set aside. Slice the breasts from the bone, being careful to leave the skin attached.

Put a spoonful of the buckwheat groats in the center right of the bottom half of each plate. Arrange the breast meat vertically along the right side of the plate, fanning the slices slightly from top to bottom over the groats. Cut the endive into julienne and arrange a spoonful to the left of the sliced breast meat. Put a small spoonful of sorrel pudding in a circular drop at the top and bottom of the endive. Lay the tenderloin diagonally across the endive. Scatter the quince dice around the meat and serve.

QUINCE STOCK

In a large bowl, whisk together the 8 cups (1800 g) water and citric acid. Divide evenly between 2 containers. Peel and core the quinces, reserving the peels, cores, and other trimmings; discard the seeds. Put the trimmings in one container and set aside at room temperature. Cut the quinces into ½-inch (12-mm) dice. Put the diced quince into the other container. The diced quince may be covered and stored with the liquid in the refrigerator for up to 24 hours. Drain the quince trimmings. In the pressure cooker, combine the trimmings, allspice, orange juice, sorghum, salt, and the remaining 6 cups (1350 g) water. Following the manufacturer's instructions, lock the lid in place, bring up to high pressure, and cook for 10 minutes. Let the pressure dissipate naturally, then uncover. Strain the stock through a fine-mesh sieve and let cool. The stock may be stored in a lidded container in the refrigerator for up to 1 week.

QUINCE-BRAISED ENDIVE

In a saucepan, bring the quince stock to a boil over high heat. Reduce the heat to medium-low and simmer, skimming off any foam that forms on the surface, until the liquid is reduced by half and syrupy, about 45 minutes. Meanwhile, prepare an ice bath. When the stock is syrupy, pour it into a metal bowl. Set the bowl over the ice bath and let cool to 104°F (40°C), 5–10 minutes. Divide the syrup into 2 equal portions.

Preheat the circulating water bath to 194°F (90°C).

In a sauté pan, heat the canola oil over medium heat until it begins to shimmer but does not smoke. Add the shallots, reduce the heat to low, and cook, stirring occasionally, until translucent, 8–10 minutes. Transfer the shallots to a vacuum bag, add the endives, and half of the quince syrup, and vacuum seal. Cook in the circulating water bath until the endives are tender but still firm to the touch, about 20 minutes. Meanwhile, prepare an ice bath. When the endives are ready, transfer the bag to the ice bath and let cool completely, replenishing the ice as needed, about 20 minutes. The endives can be stored in their bag in the refrigerator for up to 3 days.

Drain the reserved quince dice. In a saucepan, combine the remaining quince syrup and the quince dice and bring to a bare simmer over medium-high heat. Simmer gently until the quince is just tender when pierced with a paring knife, about 10 minutes. Remove from the heat and let cool in the cooking liquid.

SIMMERED BUCKWHEAT GROATS

Preheat the oven to 350°F (180°C).

Spread out the groats on a sheet pan and roast in the oven until aromatic, about 12 minutes. Let the groats cool to room temperature, then transfer to a saucepan. Measure 2 cups (450 g) of the reserved partridge stock; if you do not have enough, supplement it with chicken stock. Add the stock, water, and salt to the pan, place over medium-high heat, and bring to a simmer. Reduce the heat slightly and continue to simmer gently until the groats are tender and almost dry, 15–18 minutes. Keep warm until ready to serve, up to 10 minutes.

SORREL PUDDING

Preheat the circulating water bath to 167°F (75°C).

Cook the eggs in the circulating water bath for 13 minutes. Meanwhile, prepare an ice bath. When the eggs are ready, transfer them to the ice and let cool completely, about 10 minutes. Crack the eggs into the clean blender. Add the sorrel, salt, and xanthan gum and purée until completely smooth, about 15 seconds. Strain the mixture through a fine-mesh sieve. Use right away.

PRESSURE-COOKING THE PARTRIDGE ALLOWS YOU TO BRAISE THE MEAT AND MAKE THE FULL-FLAVORED SAUCE AT THE SAME TIME

BRYAN Each spring, I anxiously await the arrival of long, slender stalks of rhubarb in the market. They symbolize a change in both the season and in my eating habits. It is the time of the year when not only rhubarb but also ramps, morels, and asparagus battle for attention in my kitchen. Staying seasonal is important when shopping for every ingredient, including the spring halibut I use here, which is sustainably caught in the cold waters off Alaska.

Halibut, White Asparagus, Ginger, Rhubarb, Cardamom Shoots

MAIN INGREDIENTS

4 cups (900 g) water
7½ teaspoons (45 g) fine sea salt
6 West Coast halibut fillet portions, 4 ounces (113 g) each
2 tablespoons (28 g) extra-virgin olive oil
Braised White Asparagus (below)
Rhubarb Compote (below)
White Asparagus Risotto (below)
18 oyster leaves (see sources)
Pickled Cardamom Shoots (below)
Crisp Ginger (below)
Petite opal basil leaves

Equipment

thermal immersion circulator
vacuum sealer and vacuum bags
food dehydrator (optional)

Serves 6 as a main course

Preheat the circulating water bath to 126°F (52°C).

To make a brine, in a container, whisk together the water and salt until the salt dissolves. Add the fish fillets and let soak for 10 minutes. Remove the fillets from the brine and discard the brine. Pat the fillets dry with paper towels. Put the fillets and olive oil in a vacuum bag large enough for all of them to lie flat in a single layer and vacuum seal. (Or, use 2 bags, dividing the fillets and oil evenly between them.) Cook in the circulating water bath for 15 minutes. Meanwhile, in a small saucepan, combine the braised white asparagus tips with the reserved ½ cup (113 g) asparagus stock. Place over low heat and bring just to a simmer to warm through.

To serve, put a spoonful of rhubarb compote on the left side of each plate in a vertical line 2 inches (5 cm) wide. Lay the fish on the compote. Put a spoonful of risotto beside the fish without touching it, and garnish with a few oyster leaves. Lay 2 asparagus tips horizontally below the risotto and garnish with opal basil and crisp ginger. Garnish the fish with crisp ginger, opal basil leaves, and pickled cardamom shoots. Serve right away.

BRAISED WHITE ASPARAGUS

1 pound (450 g) white asparagus
1 tablespoon (14 g) grape seed oil
½ yellow onion, thinly sliced
¼-ounce (7-g) piece fresh ginger
6 cups (1350 g) water
1 bay leaf
2 fresh thyme sprigs
Finely grated zest of 1 lemon
2 tablespoons (25 g) sugar
1 tablespoon (18 g) fine sea salt

Cut off the bottom 3 inches (7.5 cm) of each asparagus spear, then peel off the outer layer of skin from just below the tip to the bottom. Set the peeled asparagus aside, and reserve the trimmings. In a saucepan, heat the grape seed oil over medium heat until it begins to shimmer but not smoke. Add the onion and ginger and sauté until tender but not brown, 4–6 minutes. Add the water, bay leaf, thyme, lemon zest, and 1 tablespoon (12.5 g) of the sugar. Bring just to a simmer, then immediately remove from heat. Add the asparagus peelings and stalk bottoms, cover the pan, and let steep for 20 minutes to make a stock. Strain the stock into a 10-inch (25-cm) sauté pan. Add the reserved peeled asparagus spears, the remaining 1 tablespoon (12.5 g) sugar, and the salt and place the pan over medium-high heat. Bring to a low simmer, adjust the heat to maintain the simmer, and cook gently until the spears are tender, about

››

STRAWBERRY SYRUP

½ cup (113 g) water

½ cup (120 g) dry Riesling

¼ cup (50 g) sugar

¼ teaspoon (1.5 g) fine sea salt

1 pound (450 g) fresh strawberries, cored

RHUBARB COMPOTE

¼ cup (70 g) verjus

¼ cup (60 g) Strawberry Syrup (above)

½ cup (130 g) diced yellow onion (medium dice)

1 cup (220 g) diced rhubarb (medium dice)

1 green cardamom pod

¼ teaspoon (.5 g) ground coriander

¼ cinnamon stick

WHITE ASPARAGUS RISOTTO

4 cups (900 g) reserved asparagus stock (from Braised White Asparagus, above)

4 tablespoons (56 g) unsalted butter

2 tablespoons (28 g) extra-virgin olive oil

¼ medium yellow onion, minced

1 cup (200 g) risotto rice, preferably Gli Aironi Vialone Nano (see sources)

1 cup (240 g) dry white wine

2½ ounces (70 g) Parmigiano-Reggiano cheese, grated

Spears from Braised White Asparagus (above)

Fine sea salt and freshly ground black pepper

PICKLING LIQUID

1 tablespoon (14 g) grape seed oil

10 shallots, sliced

6 cloves garlic, smashed

2 cups (480 g) dry white wine

1 cup (280 g) rice vinegar

½ cup (100 g) sugar

1 tablespoon (18 g) fine sea salt

2 tablespoons (12.8 g) Pickling Spice (page 318)

2 fresh mint sprigs

3 fresh cilantro sprigs

30 minutes. Remove from the heat and let cool in the stock to room temperature, about 30 minutes.

Strain the stock through a fine-mesh sieve, reserving both the asparagus and the stock. Reserve the stock for reheating the asparagus for serving and for the white asparagus risotto (below). Cut the 2-inch (5-cm) tips off the asparagus. Cut the remaining portion of the spears into slices ½ inch (12 mm) thick. Store the tip sections and spear slices in separate lidded containers. They will keep in the refrigerator for up to 2 days.

STRAWBERRY SYRUP

In a saucepan, combine the water, Riesling, sugar, and salt over medium-high heat and bring to a simmer. Cook until the liquid is reduced by one-third, about 10 minutes. Add the strawberries, bring the liquid back to a simmer, cover, and remove from the heat. Let the fruit steep in the syrup for 20 minutes. Place a fine-mesh sieve over a small saucepan, and strain the syrup through the sieve without pressing on the solids. Place the pan over medium heat and bring to a simmer. Cook until the liquid is reduced to ¼ cup (60 g), then remove from the heat. The strawberry syrup may be stored in a lidded container in the refrigerator for up to 3 days.

RHUBARB COMPOTE

In a small saucepan, combine the verjus and strawberry syrup and bring to a simmer over medium heat. Reduce the heat slightly to maintain a low simmer and then cook until the liquid is reduced by half, 10–12 minutes. Remove from the heat. In a large, dry sauté pan, cook the onion over medium heat, stirring constantly, until it caramelizes and turns golden brown, 8–10 minutes. Add the rhubarb and cook, stirring, until just tender, about 5 minutes. Fold in the cardamom, coriander, cinnamon, and the strawberry-verjus mixture. Use immediately or let cool to room temperature and store in a lidded container in the refrigerator for up to 5 days.

WHITE ASPARAGUS RISOTTO

Set aside ½ cup (113 g) of the asparagus stock. Put the remaining stock in a saucepan over medium-high heat and bring to a simmer. Reduce the heat to keep the stock at a bare simmer. In another saucepan, melt 2 tablespoons (28 g) of the butter with the olive oil over medium-high heat. Add the onion and sauté until it is tender but not brown, about 6 minutes. Add the rice and stir well to coat thoroughly with the fat. Sauté until a nutty aroma begins to rise off the toasted rice, about 6 minutes. Add the wine and simmer, stirring slowly, until almost all of the wine has evaporated. Add one-third of the hot stock and cook, stirring constantly, until almost all of the stock has been absorbed by the rice. Add half of the remaining stock and continue to stir slowly until the stock is absorbed. Add the remaining stock and cook, stirring, until absorbed. Stir in the cheese and remaining butter and then taste for seasoning. Fold in the reserved asparagus slices and keep the risotto warm until ready to plate.

PICKLING LIQUID

In a saucepan, heat the grape seed oil over medium heat until it begins to shimmer but does not smoke. Add the shallots and cook, stirring, until

translucent and tender, about 5 minutes. Add the garlic and cook, stirring, until it becomes aromatic, about 30 seconds. Add the wine, vinegar, sugar, salt, pickling spice, mint, and cilantro and bring just to a simmer. Remove from the heat, cover, and let steep for 30 minutes. Meanwhile, prepare an ice bath. When the liquid has steeped, pour it through a fine-mesh sieve into a metal bowl. Set the bowl over the ice bath and let cool until very cold, about 15 minutes. The pickling liquid may be stored in a lidded container in the refrigerator for up to 1 week.

PICKLED CARDAMOM SHOOTS

In a small saucepan, bring the pickling liquid to a simmer over medium heat. Meanwhile, prepare an ice bath. Put the cardamom shoots in a small metal bowl and pour the hot liquid over them. Set the bowl over the ice bath and let the shoots steep for 10 minutes. Drain the shoots, discarding the liquid. The shoots may be stored in a lidded container in the refrigerator for up to 1 week.

CRISP GINGER

Peel the ginger and then slice it paper-thin on a mandoline. Put the ginger slices in a small saucepan, add cold water to cover, place over medium heat, and bring to a boil. Drain, then repeat the procedure 2 more times. Set aside. In a small saucepan, combine the 1 cup (225 g) water and the sugar over medium heat and bring to a simmer. Add the star anise and the blanched ginger slices and simmer for 5 minutes, stirring until the sugar dissolves. Remove from the heat, cover, and let steep for 20 minutes. Drain the ginger and arrange the slices in a single layer on a food dehydrator tray or a sheet pan. Place in the dehydrator set at 95°F (35°C) or an oven preheated to 175°F (80°C) until crisp, about 10 hours. Let cool to room temperature. The ginger may be stored in an airtight container at room temperature for up to 3 days.

PICKLED CARDAMOM SHOOTS

½ cup (225 g) Pickling Liquid (above)
6 cardamom shoots (see sources)

CRISP GINGER

1 knob fresh ginger, about 1½ ounces (42 g)
1 cup (225 g) water
½ cup (100 g) sugar
½ whole star anise

MICHAEL Foie gras and brioche go hand in hand. Here, I borrowed the idea of iSi canister–leavened cakes from Ferran and Albert Adrià and created one-minute buckwheat-flour brioche. As the dish developed, I looked to balance the sweetness of the berries, and sorrel provided the acidity I needed. The "nori" came about because the dark green of the oxidized sorrel leaves reminded me of the seaweed, so I dried the puréed sorrel into look-alike sheets.

Foie Gras, Wild Strawberry, Wild Sorrel "Nori," Aerated Buckwheat Brioche

MAIN INGREDIENTS

1 pound (450 g) foie gras cubes and pieces or "butter" (see sources)

3 tablespoons (40 g) sweet sake

1 teaspoon (6 g) fine sea salt

20 grinds of black pepper

2 pounds (900 g) strawberries, cored and quartered lengthwise

½ cup (100 g) sugar

4 grams agar (see sources)

3 sheets (7 g) silver-grade leaf gelatin (see sources)

1 tablespoon plus 1 teaspoon (17.5 g) yuzu juice (see sources)

6 pieces Aerated Buckwheat Brioche (below)

1 pint (240 g) red and white frais de bois

1 cup (50 g) petite ribbon sorrel

Extra-virgin olive oil

Maldon sea salt

1 sheet Wild Sorrel "Nori" (below)

Equipment

thermal immersion circulator

vacuum sealer and vacuum bags

tamis

high-speed blender

liquid nitrogen (optional)

small Styrofoam cooler (optional)

6-inch bamboo skewers (optional)

chocolate-dipping fork (optional)

iSi canister with 3 N_2O chargers (1-quart/.95-l canister)

six 1-cup paper coffee cups

food dehydrator (optional)

Serves 6 as a first course

››

Preheat the circulating water bath to 158°F (70°C).

Put the foie gras cubes and pieces in a bowl and pick out any apparent veins, blood spots, and blemishes. Add the sake, salt, and pepper and stir to coat the foie gras evenly with the seasonings. Put the foie gras and all of the seasonings in a vacuum bag and vacuum seal. Cook the foie gras in the circulating water bath for 11 minutes. Meanwhile, prepare an ice bath. When the foie gras is ready, transfer the bag to the ice bath to cool, replenishing the ice as needed, until the liver and its fat are solid all the way through, about 1 hour.

Remove the bag from the ice bath, and remove the foie gras and its fat from the bag. Slice the foie gras into small pieces. In a food processor, combine the foie gras pieces and the fat and process until the mixture is airy and mousselike, about 2 minutes. Using a plastic bench scraper, pass the mixture through the tamis. Put it in 1 large or 2 small vacuum bags and vacuum seal. Use a rolling pin to roll out the mixture in the bag so that it is spread from corner to corner and has a uniform thickness of about ¼ inch (6 mm). Put the bag(s) on a sheet pan, cover with another sheet pan pressed directly against the bag(s) and add 2 bags of flour or other heavy weights to the top of the pan. Freeze until frozen solid, at least 4 hours.

Preheat the circulating water bath to 185°F (85°C). Line a sheet pan with parchment paper and have it ready in the refrigerator.

Put the strawberries and sugar in a large vacuum bag and vacuum seal. Cook in the circulating water bath until the strawberries have released their juices, about 15 minutes. (Alternatively, combine the berries and sugar in the top of a double boiler set over barely simmering water until the juices are released.)

Open the bag and pour the berries and juice into a fine-mesh sieve set over a bowl. You can gently stir the strawberries in the sieve, but do not push them through. Measure out 3 cups plus 2 tablespoons (700 g) strawberry juice (the rest can be saved for another use) and transfer to a blender. Turn on the blender to low speed, then slowly increase the speed until a vortex forms in the center

THE ADDITION OF BUCKWHEAT FLOUR ADDS NUTTINESS AND STRUCTURE TO A "MINUTE BRIOCHE" THAT IS ACTUALLY BAKED IN A MICROWAVE

of the liquid. Sprinkle in the agar and continue to process until it is completely absorbed, a full 15 seconds. Transfer the mixture to a saucepan and place over medium-high heat. Bring to a boil and cook for 5 minutes.

Meanwhile, put the gelatin sheets in a small bowl of ice water and let soak until softened, about 5 minutes. Lift out the gelatin sheets, squeeze out the excess water, and put them in the blender. Carefully pour the hot strawberry-agar mixture over the gelatin, turn on the blender to low speed, and process for 1 minute. Add the yuzu juice and blend on low speed for 20 seconds.

Pour the strawberry liquid into a deep container with no more than 1-quart (.95-l) capacity. Pour the liquid nitrogen into a small Styrofoam cooler, filling it about half full. Take the foie gras sheets out of the freezer. Remove the foie gras from the bag(s) and use your hands to break it into rough 2-inch (5-cm) pieces that resemble irregular paving tiles. Insert a 6-inch (15.25-cm) bamboo skewer into each of the fois gras pieces like a Popsicle stick. Carefully dip one piece into the nitrogen bath, submerging it completely and holding it there for a full 10 seconds. Transfer the piece to the container with the strawberry mixture, submerge it completely, and hold it there for 2 seconds. Dip the strawberry-coated foie gras piece back into the liquid nitrogen bath for 1 full second, and then dip it back into the strawberry mixture for 2 seconds. Put the coated foie gras piece on a parchment-lined sheet pan in the refrigerator. Repeat the dipping and coating process until all of the foie gras pieces have been coated with strawberry mixture and are in the refrigerator. Refrigerate for a minimum of 1 hour before serving. The coated foie gras will keep in the refrigerator for up to 3 days.

Alternatively, freeze the foie gras mixture in the bags for a minimum of 8 hours. Cool the strawberry mixture until it is just warm and still liquid. Remove the foie gras from the bag(s) and use your hands to break it into rough 2-inch (5-cm) pieces that resemble irregular paving tiles. Use a chocolate-dipping fork to carefully submerge a foie gras piece into the strawberry-yuzu liquid and hold it there for 1 minute. Lay the coated foie gras piece on a sheet pan lined with a silicone sheet. Refrigerate coated foie gras pieces for at least 6 hours so that the centers have time to melt before serving.

To serve, arrange 3 foie gras pieces on each plate. Using scissors, cut the aerated brioche apart and place a couple of natural-looking chunks on each plate. In a bowl, toss together the frais de bois and petite ribbon sorrel, drizzle lightly with olive oil, and season lightly with crushed Maldon salt. Put individual pieces of the berries and petite sorrel around and on the foie gras. Garnish with torn pieces of the wild sorrel "nori" and serve right away.

AERATED BUCKWHEAT BRIOCHE

Crack the eggs into a bowl and whisk until well blended. Measure 3/4 cup (175 g) of the beaten eggs and discard the remainder. In a blender, combine the eggs, milk, buckwheat flour, all-purpose flour, butter, sugar, and salt and process until completely smooth. Using a funnel, transfer the mixture to the iSi canister and, following the manufacturer's instructions, charge 3 times with the nitrous oxide chargers. Using a paring knife, poke 4 holes in a 1-cup paper coffee cup,

1 hole on the bottom and 3 holes evenly spaced around the sides of the cup. Spray the inside of the cup with nonstick cooking spray. Repeat with the remaining 5 paper cups.

Extrude the brioche batter into 1 prepared cup, filling it three-fourths full. Place the cup in a microwave and cook on high power until the batter puffs up in the cup, 30–60 seconds. Every microwave is different, so the timing will vary. Remove the cup from microwave, invert it onto a plate, and leave it upside down for 1 minute so the brioche will steam in the cup and finish cooking. Tap the cup gently on a counter top to loosen the brioche and remove it from the cup. Repeat to make 5 more brioches. Use right away.

WILD SORREL "NORI"

In a saucepan, combine the water and salt over high heat and bring to a boil. Add the sorrel and then scoop it out with a skimmer after 1–2 seconds, stirring it briefly just before removing it. Transfer to a blender and process until smooth. Line a food dehydrator tray or a sheet pan with a silicone mat. Using an offset spatula, spread the sorrel onto the mat as evenly as possible, forming a layer about 1/4 inch (6 mm) thick. Place in the dehydrator set at 155°F (68°C) or an oven set at 175°F (80°C) until most of the moisture is removed and the texture is reminiscent of nori, about 1 hour. The nori can be stored in an airtight container at room temperature for up to 1 week.

AERATED BUCKWEAT BRIOCHE

4 large eggs

3 tablespoons (50 g) whole milk

1/4 cup plus 4 teaspoons (50 g) buckwheat flour

2 tablespoons (20 g) all-purpose flour

3 tablespoons plus 1 teaspoon (50 g) unsalted butter

2 tablespoons plus 1 teaspoon (30 g) sugar

1/2 teaspoon (3 g) fine sea salt

Nonstick cooking spray

WILD SORREL "NORI"

8 1/2 cups (1913 g) water

5 teaspoons (30 g) fine sea salt

3 1/2 ounces (100 g) sorrel

CITRUS

YUZU CLEMENTINE BLOOD ORANGE KUMQUAT

This varied family includes members as small as a kumquat and as large as a grapefruit. What they all have in common is a bright floral aroma and an appealing balance of tart and sweet, qualities that we like to explore in our recipes. For example, the soft sweetness of a clementine contrasts beautifully with dark chocolate, the tartness of a lemon heightens the delicacy of sea scallops. We use the zests as well, grating or charring them for seasoning, and we bruise the leaves when we want just a hint of citrus. Color plays an important role, too, whether it's the pale yellow of a lemon purée, the bright orange of candied kumquats, or the rosy pink of grapefruit sorbet.

MICHAEL Hearts of palm and citrus (here, yuzu) are natural partners. I wanted to make a beef-flavored ponzu, which I achieved by concentrating the flavors of flank steak in a pressure cooker and then mixing the resulting stock with yuzu to make a gelée. The steak becomes quite stringy in the process and can be pulled into threads. When you dehydrate the threads and fry them, you end up with wisps of beef jerky that contrast well with the gelée and the shaved palm hearts.

Raw Beef, Beef Threads, Ponzu, Palm Hearts

MAIN INGREDIENTS

1 tablespoon (14 g) canola oil
1 pound (450 g) flank steak
Fine sea salt
1 yellow onion, diced
1¾ ounces (50 g) kombu
5 tablespoons (100 g) soy sauce
4 pieces fresh heart of palm, each 4 inches (7.5 cm) long
8½ cups (1913 g) water
1 sheet silver-grade leaf gelatin (see sources)
2 teaspoons (10 g) yuzu mitsu (see sources)
1 teaspoon (5 g) yuzu shibori (see sources)
1 jalapeño chile
1 pomelo
1 Oro Blanco or Ruby Red grapefruit
2 tablespoons (28 g) extra-virgin olive oil, plus more to dress the greens
2 tablespoons (20 g) Maldon sea salt
4 ounces (113 g) Wagyu rib eye
Shaved Hearts of Palm (below)
Flank Steak Threads (below)
Jalapeño Salt (below)
Baby greens such as mixed petite cress, mustard greens, or shiso

Equipment

6-quart (5.7-l) pressure cooker
kitchen blowtorch
food dehydrator (optional)
deep fryer (optional)
vacuum sealer and vacuum bags

Serves 8 as a first course

SHAVED HEARTS OF PALM

1 fresh heart of palm, peeled
1 tablespoon (14 g) extra-virgin olive oil
Fine sea salt

FLANK STEAK THREADS

Reserved flank steak (from above)
Canola oil for deep-frying
Fine sea salt

JALAPEÑO SALT

1 jalapeño chile
3 tablespoons (30 g) Maldon sea salt

In the pressure cooker, heat the canola oil over medium-high heat until it begins to shimmer but does not smoke. Season the steak generously with salt, add to the hot oil, and cook until seared on one side, 3–4 minutes. Turn the steak over, add the onion, and cook until the steak is seared on the second side, 3–4 minutes. Add the kombu, soy sauce, hearts of palm, and water. Following the manufacturer's instructions, lock the lid in place, bring up to high pressure, and cook for 25 minutes. Let the pressure dissipate naturally, and then uncover the pot.

Remove the flank steak from the pressure cooker and reserve for making the flank steak threads. Remove the hearts of palm from the pressure cooker and let cool to room temperature, about 15 minutes. Store in a covered container in the refrigerator until ready to serve. Strain the cooking liquid through a fine-mesh sieve into a clean container. Put the gelatin sheet in a small bowl of ice water and let soak until softened, about 5 minutes. Measure ⅔ cup (150 g) of the cooking liquid into a bowl. Lift out the gelatin sheet, squeeze out the excess water, and add to the bowl. Whisk until fully dissolved. Whisk both yuzu juices into the gelatin mixture to make the ponzu gelée. Pour the liquid into a small bowl and put it, uncovered, in the refrigerator until cool and set. The gelée may be covered and stored in the refrigerator for up to 3 days.

To serve, thinly slice the jalapeño into rings and soak the rings in a small bowl of ice water to cover for 30 minutes.

Cut a thin slice off the top and bottom of the pomelo to expose the flesh. Stand the fruit upright on a cutting board and, using a sharp knife, slice off the peel and pith, cutting downward and following the contour of the fruit. Holding the fruit over a bowl, cut along each side of the membrane between the segments, releasing the segments into the bowl. Using your fingers, break each pomelo segment apart to separate them into individual "cells." Set aside.

Following the instructions for the pomelo, cut the grapefruit into individual segments. Cut each segment in half crosswise, and lay the segment halves out on the cutting board. Using a blowtorch, lightly caramelize the top surface of each segment half. Put the caramelized segments in a small bowl, sprinkle with 1 tablespoon (14 g) of the olive oil and 1 tablespoon (10 g) of the Maldon salt, and mix gently.

Cut the rib eye into strips 1½ inches (4 cm) long and ¼ inch (6 mm) wide. Put the beef strips in a bowl, season with the remaining 1 tablespoon (14 g) olive oil and 1 tablespoon (10 g) Maldon salt, and stir to mix.

Cut each palm heart piece in half lengthwise, creating 2 long pieces from each palm heart. Center 1 piece, flat side up, in the center of each plate. Spoon the ponzu gelée on top of the hearts of palm. Arrange the raw beef ribbons over the gelée and top with the shaved hearts of palm. Garnish with jalapeño rings and beef threads, and sprinkle with the pomelo cells. Put one piece of caramelized grapefruit on the top right of each plate and one piece directly below the beef ribbons. Season the dish lightly with jalapeño salt. Lightly dress the greens with olive oil and use them to garnish the plates.

SHAVED HEARTS OF PALM

Thinly slice the palm heart and poke out the center core. Place in a bowl, add the olive oil, sprinkle lightly with salt, and toss well.

FLANK STEAK THREADS

Using your fingers, pull apart the flank steak into very fine threads along the natural grain of the meat. Line a food dehydrator tray or a sheet pan with a silicone mat. Place in the dehydrator set at 155°F (68°C) or an oven preheated to 175°F (80°C) until the threads are completely dry, about 1½ hours.

Pour the oil into a deep fryer to the fill line or into tall-sided saucepan to a depth of 2½ inches (6 cm) and heat to 350°F (180°C). Working in batches, add the dried beef threads to the hot oil and fry until crisp, about 3 seconds. Using a skimmer, transfer the beef threads to a paper towel–lined sheet pan. Season lightly with salt.

JALAPEÑO SALT

Cut the chile lengthwise into quarters, put the chile quarters into a vacuum bag with the salt, vacuum seal, and refrigerate overnight.

The next day, pour the contents of the vacuum bag into a shallow bowl. Remove and discard the jalapeño flesh and any seeds. Line a food dehydrator tray or a sheet pan with a silicone mat, and pour the salt onto the mat. Place in the dehydrator set at 155°F (68°C) or an oven preheated to 175°F (80°C) until completely dry, about 2 hours. The salt will keep in an airtight container at room temperature for up to 1 week.

TAKING ADVANTAGE OF THE NATURAL TEXTURE OF FLANK STEAK I PULL IT INTO THREADS DEHYDRATE THEM AND FRY THEM TO MAKE JERKY

BRYAN I like to take my likes and transform them, in this case a clementine and a chocolate bar, into something new. In fact, before you make this dish, sit down and eat a clementine and a chocolate bar to enjoy them the way that I do. Then, when you taste the finished dish, you will have a sense of its origin. Much of this recipe grew out of my love affair with liquid nitrogen, which allows chefs to do things, like powdering sorbet, that were never possible before.

Caramelized White Chocolate Goat Cheese Cakes, Clementine Sorbet, Chocolate "Rocks"

MAIN INGREDIENTS

3½ ounces (100 g) white chocolate, chopped
½ cup (120 g) heavy cream
½ cup (113 g) fresh goat cheese
¾ cup plus 4 teaspoons (175 g) sugar
3 ounces (85 g) cream cheese
1 teaspoon (6 g) salt
2 large eggs
1 large egg yolk
2 tablespoons plus 1 teaspoon (35 g) sour cream
¼ teaspoon (1.5 g) pure vanilla extract
1 tablespoon plus ¾ teaspoon (45 g) all-purpose flour, sifted
Chocolate "Rocks" (below)
Clementine Sorbet (below)
Petite mint leaves

Equipment

iSi canister with 2 N_2O chargers (1-quart/.95-l canister)
liquid nitrogen (optional)
small Styrofoam cooler (optional)
ice-cream maker
high-speed blender

Serves 12 as a dessert

››

Preheat the oven to 250°F (120°C). Put the chopped white chocolate in a heatproof bowl and put it in the oven for 45–60 minutes, stirring occasionally. The chocolate will caramelize and turn golden brown. Remove from the oven and use immediately, or let cool, wrap in plastic wrap, and store at room temperature for up to 1 week.

Preheat a convection oven to 325°F (165°C) or a standard oven to 350°F (165°C). Line a quarter sheet pan (9½ by 13 inches/24 by 33 cm) with parchment paper, extending it about 1½ inches (4 cm) over the long sides of the pan. Put the pan into a large baking pan. Fill a teakettle with water and bring the water to a boil over high heat. Reduce the heat to maintain a simmer.

Meanwhile, put the cream in a small saucepan, place over medium-high heat, and bring to a simmer. Put the caramelized white chocolate in a heatproof bowl. Pour the hot cream over the chocolate and whisk to blend completely. Set aside to cool. In a stand mixer fitted with the paddle attachment, combine the goat cheese, sugar, cream cheese, and salt. Mix on medium-low speed until light and creamy, about 4 minutes. Add the eggs and egg yolk one at a time, mixing after each addition until fully incorporated. Add the sour cream and vanilla, mixing just until blended. Add the flour and again mix just until blended. Add the white chocolate–cream mixture and mix until fully incorporated. Strain the batter through a fine-mesh sieve into a container with a spout. Pour the mixture into the prepared quarter sheet pan, filling it three-fourths full.

Put the sheet pan in the baking pan on the center rack of the oven, and carefully pour a shallow layer of the simmering water from the teakettle into the bottom of the baking pan. Invert another sheet pan on top of the quarter sheet pan and bake until the center of the cake is set but still jiggles slightly, 25–30 minutes. Remove from the oven, remove the top sheet pan, and let cool in the pan to room temperature, about 1 hour. Gently cover the quarter sheet pan with plastic wrap and refrigerate for at least 12 hours or up to 3 days.

THIS RECIPE GREW FROM A LOVE OF USING LIQUID NITROGEN WHICH ALLOWS US TO DO THINGS LIKE POWDERING SORBET IN A WAY THAT WAS NEVER POSSIBLE BEFORE

To serve, take the loaf pans with the chocolate rocks mixture from the freezer and remove the top layer of plastic wrap. Using the overhang of the plastic wrap lining each pan, lift out the frozen chocolate. Using a meat mallet or the back of a chef's knife, break the chocolate into randomly sized pieces. Pour the liquid nitrogen into a small Styrofoam cooler, filling it half full. Using a skimmer or small sieve, dip the chocolate pieces into the nitrogen bath for 20–30 seconds to firm them up. Transfer the rocks to the freezer while you prepare the sorbet. Alternatively, using a small ice cream scoop, scoop the frozen chocolate out of the pans.

If necessary, add more liquid nitrogen to the cooler to fill it halfway. Using an ice cream scoop, add 4 scoops of the clementine sorbet to the nitrogen bath and leave undisturbed until rock solid, 1–2 minutes. Use the skimmer to transfer the frozen sorbet to the blender. Carefully add a spoonful of the liquid nitrogen from the cooler to the blender and purée to a fine powder, about 30 seconds. Pour into a cold metal bowl and place in the freezer while you freeze and powder the remaining sorbet. Alternatively, leave the sorbet as is and add a scoop or two to the plate when serving.

Run the tip of a paring knife around the inside of the cheesecake pan. Then, using the parchment overhang, lift the cheesecake from the pan. Cut the cake into 12 equal portions, each 3 by 4 inches (7.5 by 10 cm), then cut each portion in half crosswise. Put 2 cake portions on each plate. Scatter a few chocolate rocks on each plate and then add a few spoonfuls of powdered sorbet. Garnish with the petite mint leaves and serve immediately.

CHOCOLATE "ROCKS"

Line two 9-by-5-inch (23-by-13-cm) loaf pans with plastic wrap, allowing the plastic wrap to overhang the long sides.

In a saucepan, whisk together the sugar, milk powder, cocoa powder, cornstarch, salt, cream, and water until well blended. Place the pan over medium heat and bring to a simmer. Put the chocolate and hazelnut paste in a large heatproof bowl. Prepare an ice bath. When the cream mixture begins to simmer, remove from the heat, pour over the chocolate mixture, and whisk until the chocolate is melted and the mixture is smooth. Strain the mixture through a fine-mesh sieve placed over a metal bowl. Set the bowl over the ice bath and let the mixture cool, stirring occasionally and replenishing the ice as needed, until completely cold, about 30 minutes.

Using a funnel, and working in batches if necessary, transfer the cooled chocolate mixture to the iSi canister, filling it half full. Following the manufacturer's instructions, charge 2 times with the nitrous oxide chargers. Extrude the mixture into the prepared loaf pans. There is no need to smooth the rough edges. Cover the pans gently with plastic wrap and place in the freezer for at least 24 hours or up to 1 week.

CLEMENTINE SORBET

Measure 1½ cups plus 2 tablespoons (500 g) of the clementine juice (you can drink any remaining juice). In a saucepan, combine the clementine juice, water, sugar, glucose powder, and salt, place over medium-high heat, and bring to a simmer. Cook for 5 minutes. Remove the pan from the heat and let cool to room temperature, about 20 minutes. Put the juice mixture in a lidded container and chill in the refrigerator for at least 4 hours. Transfer the chilled juice mixture to the ice-cream maker and freeze according to the manufacturer's instructions. Transfer to a freezer container and freeze for at least 2 hours or up to 1 week.

CHOCOLATE "ROCKS"

¼ cup (50 g) sugar

8 tablespoons (40 g) dry milk powder

7 tablespoons (40 g) black cocoa powder (see sources)

3 tablespoons (20 g) cornstarch

1 teaspoon (6 g) fine sea salt

1 cup plus 2 teaspoons (250 g) heavy cream

1 cup plus 5 teaspoons (250 g) water

9 ounces (250 g) 72 percent cacao dark chocolate, finely chopped

¼ cup (50 g) hazelnut paste (see sources)

CLEMENTINE SORBET

Juice of 18 clementines

½ cup plus 1 tablespoon (125 g) water

⅓ cup plus 2 tablespoons (90 g) sugar

¼ cup (50 g) glucose powder (see sources)

⅛ teaspoon (.75 g) fine sea salt

MICHAEL This dish was inspired by the blood orange, which has a different type of acid than any other citrus: softer, sweeter, and more floral. And I wanted to use every bit of the fruit—zest, juice, flesh—in the dish. Because the blood orange is so delicate, it complements, rather than overwhelms, the sweet, gentle flavor of the scallops. Its juice also imparts a natural sweet-and-sour flavor to the shellfish. The pumpkin seeds add a subtle richness and a pleasing crunch.

Scallops, Blood Orange Jam, Pepitas, Green Olive Caviar

MAIN INGREDIENTS

56 Taylor Bay scallops

2 blood oranges

1 green onion, white and tender green tops, thinly sliced

½ teaspoon (1.7 g) Maldon sea salt, lightly crushed

Tiny pinch of Espelette pepper

Blood Orange Jam (below)

Pumpkin seed oil

Pepitas (below)

Green Olive Caviar (below)

Blood Orange Charcoal (below)

Coriander blooms

Equipment

vacuum sealer and vacuum bags

high-speed blender

deep fryer (optional)

masticating vegetable juicer

plastic squeeze bottle

Serves 8 as a first course

BLOOD ORANGE JAM

¾ cup plus 2 tablespoons (200 g) fresh blood orange juice (from 6–7 blood oranges; reserve the spent oranges)

1 cup (200 g) granulated sugar

3 blood oranges, 10½ ounces (300 g) total weight

7 tablespoons (100 g) orange oil

››

If the scallops are still in their shells, slide a paring knife underneath them to cut them out of the shell. Discard the roe sac and the shells. Remove and discard the adductor muscle from each scallop, and then rinse them in cold running water. Pat the scallops dry with paper towels.

To serve, using a Microplane grater, zest 1 of the oranges over a small bowl. Cut a thin slice off the top and bottom of the orange to expose the flesh. Stand the fruit upright on a cutting board and, using a sharp knife, slice off the remaining portion of the peel and all of the pith, cutting downward and following the contour of the fruit. Holding the fruit over the bowl containing the zest, cut along each side of the membrane between the segments, releasing the segments and any juice into the bowl. Cut the segments in half crosswise and return to the bowl. Cut a thin slice off the top and bottom of the remaining orange to expose the flesh. Then, slice off all of the peel and the pith, release the sections into the bowl, and cut the sections in half as for the first orange and put them in the bowl with the other oranges. Squeeze the spent membranes over the bowl to capture more juice and then discard.

Add the scallops and the onion to the bowl holding the orange sections and juice. Season with the Maldon salt and Espelette pepper and stir gently to mix. Put 3 spoonfuls of the blood orange jam, slightly offset from one another, in the center of each serving plate, leaving a slight indentation in the center of each spoonful. Put a few drops of pumpkin seed oil in the center of each pool of jam. Arrange 7 scallops randomly around the jam. Put several halved orange segments around them. Sprinkle a few pepitas on the scallops. Place a few dollops of the green olive caviar around the plate. Garnish the plate and a couple of scallops with small pinches of the blood orange charcoal. Finish with a few coriander blooms.

BLOOD ORANGE JAM

To make a blood orange simple syrup, in a small saucepan, combine the orange juice and sugar over medium-high heat and bring to a boil, stirring to dissolve the sugar. Remove from the heat and let cool to room temperature.

SOFTER, SWEETER
AND MORE FLORAL

BLOOD ORANGES
HAVE A DIFFERENT TYPE OF ACID
THAN ANY OTHER CITRUS

AND COMPLEMENT
THE GENTLE FLAVOR
OF THE SEA

PEPITAS

Canola oil for deep-frying

3 tablespoons (21 g) confectioners' sugar

1 teaspoon (5 g) water

1 cup (65 g) pepitas

Fine sea salt

GREEN OLIVE CAVIAR

1 cup (225 g) grape seed oil

32 ounces (910 g) green Provençal olives in brine

3 grams agar (see sources)

1 sheet silver-grade leaf gelatin (see sources)

BLOOD ORANGE CHARCOAL

Spent oranges reserved from Blood Orange Jam (above)

Lightly pierce the peel of the blood oranges all over with a fork, then put them in a saucepan with water to cover, and bring to a boil over medium-high heat. Drain off the water and repeat the process 2 more times. Cut the oranges into quarters and remove the seeds. Lay the quarters flat in a vacuum bag and vacuum seal. Place the bag in a microwave oven and cook on high power for 2 minutes. Take the bag out of the microwave and let it deflate completely. Repeat the cycle twice. While the oranges are still hot, transfer them to the blender. Measure 5 tablespoons (100 g) of the blood orange simple syrup and add to the blender along with the orange oil. (The remaining simple syrup may be covered tightly and refrigerated for use in drinks or other preparations.) Process until smooth, then strain the purée through a fine-mesh sieve and discard the solids. The jam may be stored in a lidded container in the refrigerator for up to 1 week before using.

PEPITAS

Pour the canola oil into a deep fryer to the fill line or into a tall-sided saucepan to a depth of 2½ inches (6 cm) and heat to 350°F (180°C).

In a bowl, stir together the confectioners' sugar and water. Add the pepitas and stir to coat them evenly with the sugar mixture. Working in batches, add the pepitas to the hot oil and fry until golden brown, 2–3 minutes. Using a skimmer, transfer to a paper towel–lined sheet pan, season lightly with salt, and let cool before using. The fried pepitas are best used right away. Leftovers may be stored in an airtight container at room temperature for up to 3 days.

GREEN OLIVE CAVIAR

Pour the grape seed oil into a 2-cup (480-ml) container, cover, and place in the freezer. Drain the olives, reserving the brine. Weigh out 3½ ounces (100 g) of

brine and save the rest for another purpose or discard. Pit the olives. Juice the olives in a masticating juicer. Weigh out 7 ounces (200 g) of juice and reserve the rest for another purpose or discard. In the clean blender, combine the olive juice, olive brine, and agar and process on low speed for a 5 full seconds to dissolve the agar completely. Pour the contents of the blender into a small saucepan, place over medium heat, and bring to a simmer. Simmer for 5 minutes.

Meanwhile, rinse the blender. Put the gelatin sheet in a small bowl of ice water and let soak until softened, about 5 minutes. Lift the sheet from the ice water, squeeze out the excess water, and add to the clean blender. Pour the hot olive brine over the gelatin and process on low speed until the gelatin dissolves, about 5 seconds. Transfer to the squeeze bottle.

Prepare an ice bath. Remove the grape seed oil from the freezer, uncover the container, and set the container in the ice bath. Squeeze small beads of the olive brine mixture into the cold oil; the beads will solidify when they hit the cold oil and then drop to the bottom. Drain off the grape seed oil and reserve for another use. The green olive caviar may be stored in a lidded container in the refrigerator for up to 3 days before using.

BLOOD ORANGE CHARCOAL

Preheat the oven to 400°F (200°C). Line a sheet pan with parchment paper.

Put the spent oranges from making the blood orange jam on the prepared pan, place in the oven, and bake until jet black and thoroughly dried, about 1 hour. Remove from the oven and let cool to room temperature.

Put the blackened oranges in a food processor and process until reduced to a fine powder. Transfer the powder to an airtight container and store at room temperature until ready to serve. Any extra will keep for up to 1 month.

BRYAN My repertoire is built on the people I have worked for and with over the years. I learned to make lemon curd from Gerry Hayden when I worked at Aureole. But the technique actually belongs to New York pastry chef Richard Leach. The key here is slow cooking. Once you master a technique, you adapt, refine, and explore its boundaries and make it your own. That's what I did with the kumquat curd here, and everything else in the dish grew up around it.

Kumquat, Ruby Grapefruit, Steamed Coconut Meringues

MAIN INGREDIENTS

3 large egg whites
1 cup plus 2 tablespoons (225 g) sugar
1/8 teaspoon (.75 g) fine sea salt
Nonstick cooking spray
Finely grated zest of 4 limes
1/4 cup (50 g) shredded unsweetened coconut
1/2 teaspoon (1.9 g) Maldon sea salt
Passion Fruit Pudding (below)
Kumquat Curd (below)
Ruby Grapefruit Sorbet (below)
Fresh fennel fronds
Candied Kumquats (below)

Equipment

food dehydrator (optional)
high-speed blender
ice cream maker

Serves 6 as a dessert

››

Preheat the oven to 325°F (165°C).

Fill a teakettle with water and bring the water to a boil over high heat. To make the meringues, put the egg whites, sugar, and salt in a heatproof bowl set over (not touching) simmering water in a saucepan. Whisk the mixture constantly by hand or with an electric mixer until the temperature reaches 100°–110°F (38°–43°C). Remove the bowl from the pan and continue to beat until the mixture forms stiff, glossy peaks, 8–10 minutes. Transfer the mixture to a pastry bag fitted with a 1/2-inch (12-mm) plain tip. Spray six 1/2-cup (120-ml) ramekins lightly with nonstick cooking spray. Pipe the mixture into the prepared molds, filling them to the rim.

Put the filled ramekins in a large, shallow baking dish. Set the dish on the middle rack of the oven, and carefully pour boiling water from the teakettle into the dish to come halfway up the sides of the ramekins. Cover the dish with aluminum foil or a tight-fitting lid and bake until the center of each ramekin is set, about 20 minutes. Transfer the ramekins to a cooling rack and let the meringues cool to room temperature, about 1 hour.

Line a food dehydrator tray or a sheet pan with a silicone mat, and spread the lime zest on the mat. Place in the dehydrator set at 145°F (63°C) or an oven preheated to 175°F (80°C) until completely dry to the touch, about 1 hour for the dehydrator or about 45 minutes for the oven. Do not leave the zest in the dehydrator for longer than 1 hour or the color will begin to fade. The zest dries faster in the higher heat of the oven, but it will probably lose its vibrant color. Let the zest cool completely, transfer to a spice grinder, and grind to a fine powder. The lime powder may be stored in a lidded container at room temperature for up to 5 days.

Preheat the oven to 350°F (180°C). Line a sheet pan with parchment paper. Spread the coconut on the prepared pan, place in the oven, and toast, stirring once at the midpoint to ensure even toasting, until lightly golden, 5–7 minutes. Pour onto a plate to cool. Measure 1 tablespoon (12.5 g) of the toasted coconut into

PASSION FRUIT PUDDING

Pulp and seeds from 8 passion fruits

1 cup (200 g) sugar

¼ cup (56 g) water

3 grams agar (see sources)

¼ cup (110 g) liquid glucose (see sources)

½ teaspoon (3 g) fine sea salt

½ lemongrass stalk, bruised

KUMQUAT CURD

Crust

¼ cup plus 2 tablespoons (75 g) sugar

1½ cups (225 g) all-purpose flour

7 tablespoons (100 g) unsalted butter

½ teaspoon (3 g) fine sea salt

1 large egg, lightly beaten

2 tablespoons (30 g) heavy cream

½ teaspoon (3 g) fine sea salt

Nonstick cooking spray

Filling

40 kumquats (about 3 cups/450–500 g), split lengthwise and seeded

1 cup (200 g) plus 3¾ cups (750 g) sugar

1½ cups (350 g) water

12 large eggs

2 pounds (900 g) cold unsalted butter, diced

5 sheets silver-grade leaf gelatin (see sources)

1½ teaspoons (9 g) fine sea salt

RUBY GRAPEFRUIT SORBET

2¼ cups (500 g) fresh Ruby Red grapefruit juice

1 cup (325 g) Sorbet Base (page 319)

½ teaspoon plus ⅛ teaspoon (3.5 g) fine sea salt

CANDIED KUMQUATS

12 kumquats, sliced and seeded

½ cup (100 g) sugar

1 cup (225 g) water

¼ cinnamon stick

1 long pepper (see sources)

¼ teaspoon (1.5 g) salt

a mortar; chop the remainder and reserve for garnish. Add the lime powder and the Maldon salt to the mortar and grind with a pestle to a fine powder. Run a paring knife around the inside of the ramekins holding the meringues and unmold them onto a sheet pan or cutting board. Roll the cooled meringues in the lime-coconut mixture.

To serve, using a small spoon or scoop, remove some of the interior from each meringue. Fill the meringues with the passion fruit pudding, and put 1 meringue on each plate. Run the edge of a paring knife around the inside edge of the pan of kumquat curd. Using a large offset spatula, gently lift the curd from the pan and put it on a cutting board. Cut the curd into 6 rectangles, each 4 by 1¼ inches (7.5 by 12 mm). Cut each of these rectangles lengthwise into two pieces: one ¾ inch (2 cm) wide and one ½ inch (12 mm) wide. Place 2 pieces, one of each size, on the plate on either side of the meringue. Spoon a quenelle of sorbet on top of 1 of the bars. Garnish with the fennel fronds and candied kumquats.

PASSION FRUIT PUDDING

In a saucepan, combine the passion fruit pulp and seeds, ½ cup (100 g) of the sugar, and the water, place over medium-high heat, and bring to a simmer. Cook, stirring constantly, until the sugar dissolves and the fruit pulp starts to break down and liquefy, about 5 minutes. Strain the passion fruit mixture through a fine-mesh sieve placed over a metal bowl. Prepare an ice bath, set the metal bowl over the ice bath, and let cool completely, stirring occasionally, about 20 minutes.

Weigh out 10½ ounces (300 g) of the passion fruit purée and put it a saucepan. Whisk in the agar, the remaining ½ cup (100 g) sugar, the liquid glucose, and the salt. Add the lemongrass, place over medium-high heat, and bring to a simmer. Cook for 5 minutes to hydrate the agar, then remove from the heat and strain through a fine-mesh sieve into a shallow baking dish. Let stand at room temperature until firmly set to the touch, about 1 hour.

Using a silicone spatula, break up the passion fruit gel, transfer to a blender, and process on high speed until completely smooth. Strain the purée through a fine-mesh sieve into a lidded container. Place in the refrigerator until serving time or for up to 3 days.

KUMQUAT CURD

Preheat the oven to 350°F (180°C).

To make the crust, combine the sugar, flour, butter, and salt in stand mixer fitted with the paddle attachment. Mix on low speed until the mixture resembles cornmeal. Add the egg and cream and mix on low speed just until combined. Gather the dough together, wrap it in plastic wrap, and refrigerate for 1 hour.

Line a quarter sheet pan (9½ by 13 inches/24 by 33 cm) with parchment paper. Spray the sides of the pan with cooking spray. On a lightly floured work surface, roll out the dough into a 9½-by-13-inch (24-by-33-cm) rectangle to fit the bottom of the sheet pan precisely, trimming the edges if necessary. Carefully transfer the dough to the prepared sheet pan. Place a second sheet of parchment on top of the dough, and weight down the dough with pie weights or dried beans. Bake until the crust is firm and golden brown, 15–20 minutes. Remove the pan from the oven, remove the weights and parchment, and let the crust cool to room temperature before filling.

To make the filling, in a saucepan, combine the kumquats, the 1 cup (200 g) sugar, and the water over medium-high heat, cover, and bring to a simmer. Reduce the heat to very low and cook until the kumquats are completely tender and falling apart, about 20 minutes. Remove from the heat. Transfer the contents of the pan to a blender and process until completely smooth. Strain the kumquat purée through a fine-mesh sieve into a bowl and let cool to room temperature.

Weigh out 1 pound (450 g) of the kumquat purée, saving any extra for another use, and pour into a heatproof bowl. Add the eggs and the 3¾ cups (750 g) sugar and place the bowl over (not touching) simmering water in a saucepan. Whisk the mixture until it thickens and the temperature reaches 180°F (82°C). Whisk in the salt, then the butter, a piece at a time, until all of it has been absorbed.

Put the gelatin sheets in a small bowl of ice water and let soak until softened, about 5 minutes. Lift out the gelatin sheets, squeeze out the excess water, and place in a microwave-safe bowl. Microwave on high power for 5-second bursts until the gelatin is liquefied and warmed. Add the gelatin to the bowl with the curd and stir to blend thoroughly. Prepare an ice bath, set the bowl of curd over the bath, and let cool, stirring occasionally and replenishing with ice as needed, until completely cold, about 30 minutes.

Position a rack in the middle of the oven and preheat to 325°F (165°C).

Fill a teakettle with water and bring to a boil over high heat. Immediately remove from the heat. Pour the kumquat curd into the prepared crust. Set the sheet pan in a wide, shallow baking dish, and set the dish on the middle oven rack. Pour hot water from the teakettle into the baking dish until it comes halfway up the sides of the sheet pan. Cover the baking dish tightly with aluminum foil and bake until the curd is set, 50–55 minutes. Transfer the sheet pan to a rack and let cool completely. The kumquat curd is best served the day it is made. Leftovers may be covered with plastic wrap and stored in the refrigerator.

RUBY GRAPEFRUIT SORBET

In a bowl, whisk together grapefruit juice, sorbet base, and salt until the salt dissolves. Transfer to a lidded container and store in the refrigerator for at least 2 hours or up to 24 hours to allow the flavors to bloom. Transfer the chilled mixture to the ice-cream maker and freeze according to the manufacturer's instructions. Transfer the sorbet to a freezer container and freeze for at least 2 hours or up to 1 week.

CANDIED KUMQUATS

In a saucepan, combine the kumquats, sugar, water, cinnamon, long pepper, and salt over medium-high heat and bring to a simmer. Remove from the heat, cover, and let the kumquats steep in the liquid for 20 minutes. The kumquats may be stored in their syrup in a lidded container for up to 1 week.

ONCE YOU MASTER A **TECHNIQUE** SUCH AS CITRUS CURD

YOU CAN THEN ADAPT **REFINE** AND EXPLORE ITS

BOUNDARIES TO MAKE IT YOUR OWN

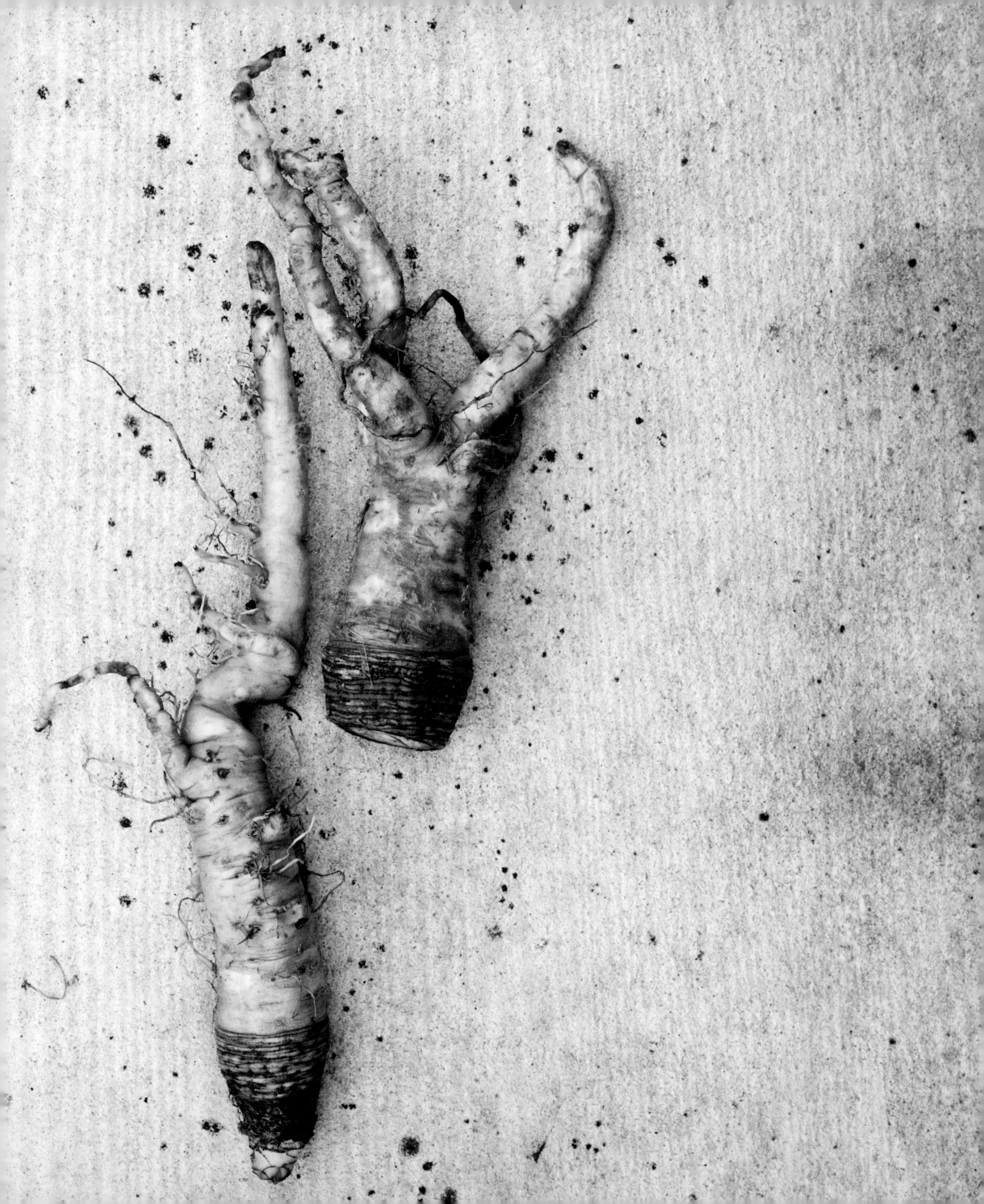

COMPOSITE

ARTICHOKE
SUNCHOKE
SALSIFY
ENDIVE

Endive, chicory, artichoke, sunchoke, salsify—these are just a handful of the many culinary members of this varied family of flowering plants, the largest in the plant kingdom. Many of the edible species of the sprawling composite family have a quality that appeals to the palate but is also a challenge in the kitchen: they taste both sweet and bitter. Chefs often find it difficult to incorporate bitter flavors in a recipe, but when a good balance is achieved, such as in the artichoke and endive preparations in this chapter, they are rewarded with a dish that delivers both complexity and savor.

BRYAN This dish grew out of the idea that every serious cookbook needs to include a recipe for artichokes barigoule. But before you make that iconic dish, you need to know how to clean artichokes, which I explain here. Once you have mastered that technique, you have put in plenty of time and you are ready to begin cooking. I look at preparing artichokes this way as a culinary benchmark. It is a classic that I respect, and I enjoy sharing my version of it.

Chesapeake Striped Bass, Artichokes Barigoule, Chorizo, Opal Basil

MAIN INGREDIENTS
1 tablespoon (14 g) grape seed oil
6 skin-on striped bass fillet portions, each about 3 ounces (85 g) and cut as a thick block
½ teaspoon (3 g) fine sea salt
2 tablespoons (28 g) unsalted butter
Artichoke Cooking Liquid (below)
Artichokes Barigoule (below)
Sous Vide Vegetables (below)
Fennel Purée (below)
Chorizo Vinaigrette (below)
Petite opal basil leaves
Fresh fennel fronds

Equipment
thermal immersion circulator
vacuum sealer and vacuum bags
6-quart (5.7-l) pressure cooker
high-speed blender

Serves 6 as a main course

In a large sauté pan, heat the grape seed oil over high heat until it begins to shimmer but does not smoke. Reduce the heat to medium. Pat the fish pieces dry with paper towels, season with the salt, and immediately put them, skin side down, in the hot oil. Cook for 2–3 minutes (at this point, the skin should not stick to the pan). Using a fish spatula, turn the fillets over and add the butter to the pan. Using a wide, flat, large metal spoon, baste the fish constantly with the butter until the fish is just cooked through, 2–3 minutes more. Transfer to a paper towel-lined plate.

Preheat the circulating water bath to 150°F (65°C).

Put the artichokes barigoule and sous vide vegetables, still in their bags, in the water bath for 10 minutes to reheat.

To serve, put the fennel purée in a small saucepan over medium heat and bring to a bare simmer. Put a dollop of fennel purée on each plate. Lay the fish, skin-side up, on top of the fennel purée. Arrange 3 artichoke pieces, 1 piece of baby fennel, 2 pearl onions, 1 yellow carrot, and 1 orange carrot around the fish. Drizzle the chorizo vinaigrette on the plate. Spoon the broth around the fish. Garnish each plate with a few leaves of petite basil and some fennel fronds.

ARTICHOKE COOKING LIQUID

2 tablespoons (28 g) olive oil
½ yellow onion, cut lengthwise into julienne
2 celery ribs
½ carrot, sliced
¼ fennel bulb, thinly sliced
2 cloves garlic, sliced
1 cup (240 g) dry white wine
¼ cup (60 g) Champagne vinegar
3 cups (675 g) Vegetable Stock (page 319)
2 teaspoons (12 g) fine sea salt

In a saucepan, heat the olive oil over high heat until it begins to shimmer but does not smoke. Add the onion, celery, carrot, fennel, and garlic and cook, stirring constantly, until tender, about 5 minutes. Add the wine and vinegar and cook until reduced by half, about 20 minutes. Add the stock and salt, bring to a simmer, and continue to cook for 20 minutes to develop the flavor. Meanwhile, prepare an ice bath. When the cooking liquid is ready, strain it through a sfine-mesh sieve placed over a metal bowl. Set the bowl over the ice bath and let cool completely, stirring occasionally and replenishing the ice as needed, about 30 minutes. The liquid may be stored in a lidded container in the refrigerator for up to 5 days.

››

ARTICHOKES BARIGOULE

4½ cups (1000 g) water

3 lemons

10 globe artichokes

⅛ teaspoon (2.5 g) red pepper flakes

2 cups (450 g) Artichoke Cooking Liquid (above)

2 spearmint sprigs

2 teaspoons (12 g) fine sea salt

2 tablespoons (28 g) extra-virgin olive oil

SOUS VIDE VEGETABLES

½ cup (120 g) Artichoke Cooking Liquid (above)

¼ cup (56 g) extra-virgin olive oil

1½ teaspoons (9 g) fine sea salt

6 petite fennel bulbs

12 red pearl onions, peeled and trimmed

6 petite yellow carrots, leaves trimmed

6 petite orange carrots, leaves trimmed

FENNEL PURÉE

5⅓ ounces (150 g) fresh fennel, diced

⅛ teaspoon (.75 g) fine sea salt

1¼ cups (280 g) water

.5 gram xanthan gum (see sources)

CHORIZO VINAIGRETTE

2 links Spanish-style cured chorizo, casing removed and cut into small dice

¼ cup (35 g) brunoise-cut red onion

¼ cup (35 g) diced fennel bulb (small dice)

4 cloves garlic, finely julienned

1 tablespoon (2.5 g) ground toasted coriander seeds

1½ cups (360 g) sherry vinegar

1 cup (240 g) extra-virgin olive oil

½ teaspoon (3 g) fine sea salt

ARTICHOKES BARIGOULE

Put the water in a large bowl. Cut each lemon in half, squeeze the juice into the water, and then add the spent fruit. Working with 1 artichoke at a time, use a large knife to cut off 1 inch (2.5 cm) or so from the top. Pull the small leaves from the stems of the artichokes. Then pull away the large outer leaves from the bottom of the artichoke, being careful to leave the tender inner leaves undisturbed. Using a paring knife, and holding the vegetable in your hand, cut from the top down toward the stem to trim away the exterior leaves down to the center light yellow ones. You should be able to see the hairy choke in the center of the vegetable. Using a sharp-edged spoon or a melon baller, remove the choke and discard it. Using a vegetable peeler, trim down the length of the stem to expose the light yellow interior flesh. Trim the base of the stem so the stem is 1 inch (2.5 cm) long. Put the trimmed artichoke in the lemon water and repeat with the remaining artichokes. Once all of the artichokes have been trimmed, cut each artichoke in half lengthwise and return them to the lemon water. Place a clean kitchen towel or plastic wrap directly on the surface of the water to keep the artichokes submerged.

Preheat the circulating water bath to 185°F (85°C). Divide the artichokes between 2 vacuum bags. Combine the red pepper flakes and artichoke cooking liquid and put half in each bag. Add 1 mint sprig, 1 teaspoon (6 g) salt, and 1 tablespoon (14 g) olive oil to each bag. Vacuum seal the bags on full power. Cook the artichokes in the circulating water bath until they feel tender when gently squeezed through the bag, 50–60 minutes. Meanwhile, prepare an ice bath. When the artichokes are ready, transfer the bags to the ice bath to cool completely, replenishing the ice as needed, about 20 minutes. The cooled artichokes may be stored in their bags in the refrigerator for up to 3 days.

SOUS VIDE VEGETABLES

Preheat the circulating water bath to 185°F (85°C). In a bowl, whisk together the artichoke cooking liquid, olive oil, and salt to dissolve the salt. Put each vegetable in its own vacuum bag. Divide the liquid into 4 equal portions, and add a portion to each bag. Vacuum seal the bag on full power. Cook the vegetables in the circulating water bath (this can be done at the same time as the artichokes) until they feel tender when gently squeezed through the bag, 25–35 minutes. Meanwhile, prepare an ice bath. When the vegetables are ready, transfer the bags to the ice bath to cool completely, replenishing the ice as needed, about 15 minutes. The cooled vegetables may be stored in their bags in the refrigerator for up to 3 days.

FENNEL PURÉE

Put the fennel, salt, and ¼ cup (56 g) of the water in a metal bowl that fits inside the pressure cooker. Put the remaining water and a rack in the bottom of the pressure cooker and put the bowl on the rack. Following the manufacturer's instructions, lock the lid in place, bring up to high pressure, and cook for 4 minutes. Let the pressure dissipate naturally, then uncover.

COOKING THE ARTICHOKE **SOUS VIDE** IS A MODERN APPROACH TO THE **CLASSIC** BRAISING TECHNIQUE

THIS IS MY INTERPRETATION OF A **TRADITIONAL** FRENCH RECIPE

Transfer the contents of the bowl to the blender. Prepare an ice bath. Turn on the blender to low speed, then slowly increase the speed until a vortex forms in the center of the liquid. Sprinkle in the xanthan gum and continue to process until it is completely absorbed, a full 5 seconds. Strain the mixture through a fine-mesh sieve into a metal bowl. Set the bowl over the ice bath and stir the purée occasionally until completely cooled, about 10 minutes. The purée may be stored in a lidded container in the refrigerator for up to 3 days.

CHORIZO VINAIGRETTE

Put the chorizo in a saucepan over medium-low heat until some of the fat starts to render. Add the red onion, fennel, and garlic and cook, stirring constantly, until the onion is translucent, about 10 minutes. Add the coriander and cook, stirring, until it is aromatic, about 1 minute. Pour in the vinegar, bring to a simmer, and cook until the liquid has reduced by about one-third, about 20 minutes. Transfer the chorizo mixture with all of its fat to a bowl and let cool to room temperature, about 30 minutes. Whisk in the olive oil and salt and use right away.

MAIN INGREDIENTS

1 cup plus 4 teaspoons (300 g) shelled sunflower seeds

2 cups (500 g) canned young Thai coconut juice

1 lemongrass stalk, cut into 1-inch (2.5-cm) pieces

1 kaffir lime leaf

1 shaved young Thai coconut, pointed top cut off, then flesh scooped out with a spoon, cut into small dice

¾ cup plus 1½ teaspoons (200 g) unsweetened coconut milk

2 Thai chiles, thinly sliced

¾ teaspoon (4.5 g) fine sea salt

Yellow Curry (below)

Sous Vide Sunchokes (below)

Fried Sunchokes (below)

Pan-Roasted Coconut Meat (below)

Marinated Salmon Roe (below)

Fresh sunflower shoots (see sources)

Equipment

6-quart (5.7-l) pressure cooker

masticating vegetable juicer

high-speed blender

thermal immersion circulator

Japanese mandoline-style slicer

vacuum sealer and vacuum bags

deep fryer (optional)

Japanese vegetable sheeter or turning slicer (optional)

tamis

long chef's tweezers

Serves 4 as a first course

YELLOW CURRY

5 tablespoons plus 1 teaspoon (75 g) canola oil

2 ounces (56 g) fresh ginger, peeled and sliced

3½ ounces (100 g) shallots, sliced

1 whole head garlic, separated into cloves, peeled, and green stem ends removed from each clove

››

MICHAEL This dish illustrates the diversity possible with two everyday members of the composite family, sunchokes and sunflower seeds. I cast the sunchokes in the role typically played by boiled potatoes in a traditional curry, while the sunflower seeds stand in for the usual rice accompaniment. I also fry thin sheets of sunchoke, shape them into crisp stacks, and give them a prominent place on the plate. Finally, I use coconut and classic curry spices to complete the curry illusion.

Yellow Curry, Sunchoke, Coconut, Sunflower Seed "Rice"

In the pressure cooker, combine the sunflower seeds, coconut juice, lemongrass, lime leaf, and coconut flesh. Following the manufacturer's instructions, lock the lid in place, bring up to high pressure, and cook for 20 minutes. Quick-release the pressure, then uncover and add the coconut milk, 1 of the chiles, and salt. Stir gently to preserve the texture of the sunflower seed "rice" and keep warm.

To serve, put the sous vide sunchokes in a small saucepan with enough of the yellow curry just to cover the vegetables. Bring to a simmer over medium heat to heat the sunchokes through and glaze them with the sauce. Place a fried sunchoke stack in the center of a wide, flat plate. Place a line of sunflower seed rice horizontally along the center of the plate. Arrange pieces of the sous vide sunchokes and roasted coconut meat alternatingly along the sunflower rice, using 3 pieces of each per plate. Arrange the salmon roe in a horizontal line along the slices of sunchoke and coconut. Garnish one end of the sunflower rice with a chile slice and the other end with a sunflower shoot. Garnish the fried sunchoke stack with more sunflower shoots. Put a few dots of curry sauce in varying sizes around the dish. Serve right away.

YELLOW CURRY

In a small saucepan, heat the canola oil over medium-low heat. Add the ginger, shallots, garlic, lemongrass, and chile and cook slowly, stirring occasionally, until all of the vegetables are tender but not browned, 5–8 minutes. Add the coriander seeds, cumin seeds, and turmeric and cook until the spices begin to toast and become aromatic, 2–3 minutes. Add the tomato and cook, stirring occasionally, until it begins to break down, 3–5 minutes. Add the pepper juice and coconut milk, raise the heat to medium-high, and bring to a simmer. Reduce the heat to medium-low and simmer for 30 minutes to bring all the flavors together. Remove from the heat and stir in the lime juice, fish sauce, and brown sugar. Transfer the mixture to the blender and pulse to break up all of the vegetables. Strain through a fine-mesh sieve into a bowl. Weigh the resulting liquid. Calculate 1.5 percent of the weight of the curry and weigh out that amount of Ultra-Tex 3. Transfer the curry to the clean blender and turn it on low speed.

1 lemongrass stalk, cut into 1-inch (2.5-cm) pieces

1 Thai chile, thinly sliced into rings

2½ tablespoons (9 g) coriander seeds

½ teaspoon (1 g) cumin seeds

1 teaspoon (3 g) ground turmeric

1 ripe yellow tomato, diced

4½ cups (1000 g) yellow pepper juice (from about 6 yellow bell peppers)

¾ cup plus 1½ teaspoons (200 g) unsweetened coconut milk

1 tablespoon (14 g) fresh lime juice

¼ cup (80 g) Asian fish sauce

1 tablespoon (13 g) light brown sugar

Ultra-Tex 3 (see sources)

SOUS VIDE SUNCHOKES

4 large sunchokes, about 6½ ounces (185 g) total weight

1½ cups (340 g) Yellow Curry (above)

FRIED SUNCHOKES

Canola oil for deep-frying

4 large sunchokes, about 6½ ounces (185 g) total weight

1 tablespoon (18 g) fine sea salt

Freeze-dried coconut powder (see sources)

Slowly increase the speed until a vortex forms at the center of the liquid. Sprinkle in the Ultra-Tex 3 and blend at medium speed for 1 full minute to fully disperse the powder. Transfer the mixture to a saucepan, place over medium heat, and bring to a simmer before using. The finished curry can be cooled and stored in a lidded container in the refrigerator for up to 5 days.

SOUS VIDE SUNCHOKES

Preheat a circulating water bath to 185°F (85°C).

Peel the sunchokes. Using the mandoline, cut the sunchokes into slices ⅛ inch (3 mm) thick. Put the sunchokes and yellow curry in a vacuum bag and vacuum seal. Cook in the circulating water bath for 1 hour; they will feel tender when gently squeezed through the bag. Remove the sunchokes from the water bath, cut open the bag, and place them on a cutting board. Using a 1-inch (2.5-cm) round cutter, cut out the sunchokes into 12 rounds. Use immediately.

FRIED SUNCHOKES

Pour the canola oil into a deep fryer to the fill line or into a tall-sided saucepan to a depth of 2½ inches (6 cm) and heat to 350°F (180°C).

Peel and trim the sunchokes. Using the Japanese vegetable sheeter, thinly slice each sunchoke into a long, continuous strip. Alternatively, use a sharp vegetable peeler. One at a time, add the sunchoke sheets to the hot oil and fry until golden brown, 30–45 seconds. Using a skimmer, transfer to a paper towel–lined plate to drain briefly and season with the salt. While the sheets are still hot and pliable, use your fingers to form each sheet into a stack about 2½ inches (6 cm) high and 2½ inches (6 cm) in diameter. Using a fine-mesh sieve, generously dust the fried sunchokes with coconut milk powder. Use immediately.

THIS DISH ILLUSTRATES THE DIVERSITY POSSIBLE WHEN TWO EVERYDAY MEMBERS OF THE COMPOSITE FAMILY ARE COMBINED TO CREATE A VIBRANT AND WILDLY CREATIVE VERSION OF ASIAN CURRY

PAN-ROASTED COCONUT MEAT

Put the coconut flesh on a cutting board. Using a 1-inch (2.5-cm) round cutter, cut the coconut flesh into 12 rounds. Put the oil in a medium sauté pan set over medium-high heat. When the oil begins to shimmer, add the coconut rounds and sear them until golden brown, 2–3 minutes per side. Transfer to a paper towel–lined plate, season lightly with salt, and set aside until serving.

MARINATED SALMON ROE

In a medium bowl, whisk together the water and salt until the salt dissolves completely. Add the salmon roe and stir gently to disperse the eggs without breaking them. Cover and refrigerate for 30 minutes to plump the eggs and loosen their membranes. Pour the roe onto the tamis, discarding the soaking liquid, and shake it gently in a circular motion to remove the skin and membrane from the eggs. Use the tweezers to carefully pick out the clear pieces of membrane that fell off the eggs, leaving the nice, plump eggs behind. Whisk together the mirin and soy sauce. Transfer the eggs to a lidded container and add the mirin mixture. Refrigerate for at least 24 hours or up to 1 week before using.

PAN-ROASTED COCONUT MEAT

2 shaved young Thai coconuts, pointed tops cut off, then flesh scooped out with a spoon

1 teaspoon (5 g) canola oil

Fine sea salt

MARINATED SALMON ROE

2 cups (450 g) water

1 tablespoon (18 g) fine sea salt

4 ounces (112 g) high-quality salmon roe

5 tablespoons (100 g) mirin

½ tablespoon (10 g) soy sauce

BRYAN One day, I sampled an oyster leaf with Graeme Ritchie, my sous chef and right-hand man. Struck by its amazing oyster flavor, we decided to pair it with salsify (aka oyster plant) to re-create the experience of eating its aquatic namesake. When you bite into this mock oyster, it releases a rich, creamy flavor that is perfectly balanced by malt vinegar powder. It takes the taste and texture of a classic—raw oysters with mignonette—and transforms it into something new.

Mock Oyster

In the pressure cooker, combine the salsify, the 1⅓ cups (300 g) water, and the salt. Following the manufacturer's instructions, lock the lid in place, bring up to high pressure, and cook for 5 minutes. Let the pressure dissipate naturally, then uncover the pot.

Prepare an ice bath. Strain the contents of the pressure cooker through a fine-mesh sieve placed over a bowl. Set the bowl over the ice bath and stir the liquid occasionally until completely cooled, about 10 minutes.

Measure out ¾ cup plus 2 tablespoons (200 g) of salsify cooking liquid; reserve the rest for storing the mock oysters. Put the measured liquid into a tall, narrow container and add the milk, gluco, and xanthan gum. Using an immersion blender, blend for a full 5 seconds to dissolve the gluco and xanthan gum. Transfer the salsify milk to a lidded container and store in the refrigerator for at least 2 hours or up to 12 hours so any air bubbles will dissipate.

In the blender, combine the algin and the remaining 4¼ cups (1000 g) water and blend for a full 10 seconds to dissolve the algin completely. Transfer the algin mixture to a lidded container and store in the refrigerator for at least 4 hours or up to 48 hours before using.

Have ready the algin bath, a cold water bath, and the reserved salsify cooking liquid. Using a teaspoon-sized measuring spoon, drop individual portions of the salsify milk into the algin bath. It should drop to the bottom of the bath and then form a sphere. Leave each spoonful undisturbed for at least 1 minute to set. Using a slotted spoon, transfer the sphere to the cold water bath to rinse. Then transfer the sphere to the container with the reserved cooking liquid. Repeat 5 times for a total of 6 mock oysters. Cover the container holding the oysters and refrigerate until ready to serve.

To serve, put each mock oyster in an individual serving spoon and garnish with an oyster leaf and oyster blossom. Season lightly with malt vinegar powder and black sea salt and serve right away.

MAIN INGREDIENTS

1½ cups (300 g) diced, peeled black salsify
1⅓ cups (300 g) plus 4¼ cups (1000 g) water
½ teaspoon (3 g) fine sea salt
2 tablespoons (32.5 g) whole milk
2 grams gluco (see sources)
.25 gram xanthan gum (see sources)
2 teaspoons (5 g) algin (see sources)
6 oyster leaves (see sources)
6 oyster blossoms (see sources)
Malt vinegar powder (see sources)
Black Cyprus sea salt (see sources)

Equipment

6-quart (5.7-l) pressure cooker
high-speed blender

Serves 6 as an amuse-bouche

MAIN INGREDIENTS

5 pig's ears, about 1½ pounds (680 g) total weight

3 quarts (2700 g) water

10 tablespoons plus 2 teaspoons (150 g) sherry vinegar

1 onion

2 bay leaves

7 ounces (200 g) bacon

½ teaspoon (3 g) fine sea salt, plus more to season

Canola oil for deep-frying

Butter-Poached Endive (below)

Smoked Maldon salt

Tangerine Syrup (below)

Tangerine Segments (below)

1 head frisée, white part only, trimmed into bite-sized pieces with scissors

1 teaspoon (4 g) extra-virgin olive oil

Maldon sea salt

Micro chives

Equipment

6-quart (5.7-l) pressure cooker

food dehydrator (optional)

deep fryer (optional)

thermal immersion circulator

vacuum sealer and vacuum bags

Serves 4 as a first course

BUTTER-POACHED ENDIVE

4 heads Belgian endive

1⅓ tablespoons (25 g) fresh lemon juice

1 tablespoon plus 2 teaspoons (24 g) unsalted butter

1½ teaspoons (5 g) sugar

¼ teaspoon (1.5 g) fine sea salt

1½ teaspoons (2.25 g) ground chicory

TANGERINE SYRUP

¾ cup plus 2 tablespoons (200 g) fresh tangerine juice (from about 4 tangerines)

1 tablespoon (27.5 g) liquid glucose (see sources)

TANGERINE SEGMENTS

2 tangerines

MICHAEL Serving fried pig's ears has become pretty common, but I wanted the ear itself to be delicious and tender without having to fry it. I included some fried ears here for texture, but the gelatinous medallion of ear is the most interesting part of the dish. Ground chicory is strongly flavored and, used in moderation, brings an interesting savor to food. Its bitterness cuts through the fattiness of the pig's ear, while the sweet-and-sour tangerine brings balance.

Pig's Ears, Endive, Tangerine

In the pressure cooker, combine the pig's ears, water, vinegar, onion, bay leaves, bacon, and salt. Following the manufacturer's instructions, lock the lid in place, bring up to high pressure, and cook for 45 minutes. Quick-release the pressure and remove the pressure cooker lid.

Line a sheet pan with parchment paper. Remove the pig's ears from the pressure cooker and lay them out on the prepared pan. Cover with a second sheet of parchment and place another sheet pan on top. Add about 10 pounds (4.5 kg) of weights, dispersing the weight evenly on the top pan. Put the weighted pig's ears in the refrigerator overnight. Strain the cooking liquid through a fine-mesh sieve into a lidded container and refrigerate until needed.

Cut a 2-inch (5-cm) square from the center of 4 of the pig's ears, reserving the trimmings. Wrap the 4 squares of pig's ears in plastic wrap and reserve in the refrigerator. Cut the trimmings and the remaining pig's ear into narrow julienne. Line a food dehydrator tray or a sheet pan with a silicone mat, and lay the julienned pig's ears on the mat. Place in a dehydrator set at 150°F (65.6°C) or an oven preheated to 175°F (79°C) until completely dry to the touch, about 2 hours. The dehydrated julienned pig's ears may be stored in an airtight container at room temperature for up to 1 week.

To serve, pour the canola oil into a deep fryer to the fill line or into a high-sided saucepan to a depth of 2½ inches (6 cm) and heat to 400°F (200°C). Preheat the oven to 250°F (120°C).

Remove the endives from their bags, reserving the cooking liquid. Trim the root end of each endive head so it is perfectly flat. Cut each endive crosswise into 3 equal sections; you will have 1 tip and 2 rounds per head. Put the endive sections in a baking dish and pour the cooking liquid over them. Place in the oven and heat until warmed through, about 10 minutes.

Working in small batches, add the julienned pig's ears to the hot oil and fry until they expand and puff up, about 10 seconds. Using a skimmer, transfer to a paper towel–lined plate and season lightly with smoked Maldon salt.

Put 1 pig ear square on each plate. Arrange 2 disks and 1 pointy piece of endive on and around each square. Drizzle the tangerine syrup on and around the pig's ears. Lay a few pieces of the tangerine segments on and around the pig's ears and the endive, and drizzle more tangerine syrup around the outside of the plate. Make a little salad by tossing the frisée with the olive oil and a light sprinkle of Maldon salt. Lay a few pieces of the dressed frisée around the plate. Garnish with a few micro chives.

BUTTER-POACHED ENDIVE

Preheat the circulating water bath to 185°F (85°C).

Peel away any blemished outer layers of the endives, creating 4 perfect barrel-shaped pieces (make a snack salad with the remaining leaves). Put the endives, lemon juice, butter, sugar, salt, and ground chicory in a vacuum bag and vacuum seal. Cook the endives in the circulating water bath until they are tender when gently squeezed through the bag, about 1 hour. Meanwhile, prepare an ice bath. When the endives are ready, transfer the bag to the ice bath and let cool completely, replenishing the ice as needed, about 30 minutes. The endives can be stored in their bag in the refrigerator for up to 3 days.

TANGERINE SYRUP

Strain the tangerine juice through a fine-mesh sieve placed over a bowl. Whisk in the glucose until well blended. Pour into a flat 8-inch (20-cm) square baking pan, creating a thin layer of juice. Put the pan in the food dehydrator set at 140°F (60°C) or in an oven preheated to 175°F (80°C) until the juice becomes a viscous syrup, about 8 hours. The syrup can be stored in a lidded container in the refrigerator until ready to serve, up to 1 week. Bring the syrup back to room temperarature 30 minutes before serving.

TANGERINE SEGMENTS

Cut a thin slice off the top and bottom of the tangerines to expose the flesh. Stand the fruit upright on a cutting board and, using a sharp knife, slice off the peel and pith, cutting downward and following the contour of the fruit. Holding the fruit over a bowl, cut along each side of the membrane between the segments, releasing the segments into the bowl. Lay the sections on a cutting board and cut them into ¼-inch (6-mm) pieces. Store the segments in a lidded container in the refrigerator until serving time, up to 8 hours.

IN MY VERSION OF PIG'S EARS WHICH ARE SEEN ON LOTS OF MENUS THESE DAYS THE GELATINOUS MEDALLION OF MEAT IS THE MOST INTERESTING PART OF THE DISH

CRUSTACEAN

SHRIMP
KING CRAB
LOBSTER
SOFT-SHELL CRAB

All crustaceans share a sweet, succulent flesh protected by a calcium-rich outer shell. Sometimes we highlight those qualities by transforming the flesh into a mousse or sausages; other times we cook it simply and then dress it with a rich sauce that showcases it but does not mask its flavor. Some of our favorite crustaceans, such as the soft-shell crabs harvested off the Maryland coast and the freshwater shrimp raised in the cool waters of Maine, are special in part because they are both seasonal and local, characteristics that inspire us to pair them with seasonal, local vegetables. Precise cooking is the key to preparing any type of crustacean, however. If left over the heat even seconds longer than necessary, the juicy, delicate flesh quickly turns dry and rubbery.

BRYAN The comfort-food standby, chicken and dumplings, is the inspiration here. The dashi is both the cooking medium and the seasoning base for the dumplings. I aerate the shrimp mixture with an iSi canister, which yields an ethereal version of mousse unlike any I have tasted. The crisp shrimp cracker adds texture and contrast, while the quail eggs are like self-contained liquid-filled dumplings. Finally, the yuzu bubbles add a splash of acidity that makes all of the flavors pop.

Shrimp Dumplings, Dashi, Quail Egg, Yuzu

MAIN INGREDIENTS

8½ ounces (250 g) Marvesta Farm shrimp (21–25 count)
Dashi (below)
¼ teaspoon (1.5 g) salt
Dashi Broth (below)
Shrimp Crispies (below)
Quail Eggs (below)
Fine sea salt
Togarashi pepper
Micro lemongrass
Yuzu Bubbles (below)

Equipment

tamis or food mill fitted with the fine grinding disk
iSi canister with 2 N_2O chargers (1-qt/.95-l canister)
induction cooking surface (optional)
high-speed blender
food dehydrator (optional)
deep fryer (optional)
vacuum sealer and vacuum bags
thermal immersion circulator

Serves 6 as a first course

Put the shrimp in a food processor and process until smooth. Add ⅓ cup (70 g) dashi and the salt and process until fully incorporated. To remove any sinew, using a plastic bench scraper, pass the mousse through the tamis or through the food mill fitted with the fine disk into a bowl. Transfer the mousse to the iSi canister and charge twice with nitrous oxide chargers. Refrigerate for at least 3 hours or up to 36 hours before using.

Put 2½ cups (563 g) of the dashi in a stainless-steel pot and use an induction cooking surface to keep the liquid at 180°F (82°C). (Alternatively, you could put the dashi in a stainless steel bowl set into a preheated water bath with a thermal immersion circulator to control the temperature.) Dip a 1-tablespoon measuring spoon in cold water, remove the spoon, and extrude the shrimp mousse into the spoon to fill it. Dip the spoon into the hot dashi to release the mousse and cook it for 1 minute, flipping the mousse with the spoon after 30 seconds so that the mousse cooks evenly. Set aside on a plate. Repeat to make 18 shrimp dumplings total.

To serve, in a saucepan, warm the dashi broth over medium heat. Put 3 shrimp dumplings in each bowl and sprinkle some shrimp crispies over each dumpling. One at a time, crack 2 quail eggs and slip them out of their shells in between the shrimp dumplings. Top the eggs with salt and a tiny pinch of togarashi pepper. Put a few micro lemongrass pieces on each shrimp dumpling. Pour enough dashi broth into the bowl to just cover the bottom of the bowl. Scoop up a spoonful of the yuzu bubbles and put it on one side of the bowl. Serve right away.

DASHI

8½ cups (1913 g) water
1½ ounces (40 g) fresh ginger
1 lemongrass stalk
½ ounce (15 g) kombu
1¾ ounces (50 g) bonito flakes
››

In a saucepan, combine the water, ginger, lemongrass, and kombu, place over medium-high heat, and bring to a boil. Add the bonito flakes, and when the liquid returns to a simmer, remove the pan from the heat, cover, and let steep for 30 minutes. Meanwhile, prepare an ice bath. When the dashi is ready, strain through a fine-mesh sieve placed over a large metal bowl. Set the bowl over the ice bath and let cool completely, stirring occasionally and replenishing the

ice as needed, about 30 minutes. You should have about 8 cups (1800 g). You will need 1⁄3 cup (70 g) for making the shrimp mousse, 2 cups (563 g) for cooking the shrimp dumplings, and 2 1⁄4 cups (506 g) for making the dashi broth. The dashi may be stored in a lidded container in the refrigerator for up to 5 days.

DASHI BROTH

In a blender, combine the dashi, vinegar, and salt. Turn the blender on to low speed. Slowly increase the speed until a vortex forms in the center of the liquid. Sprinkle in the xanthan gum and blend for a full 5 seconds to dissolve the xanthan gum fully. The broth may be stored in a lidded container in the refrigerator for up to 3 days before using.

SHRIMP CRISPIES

Put the shrimp in a food processor and process until smooth. With the processor running, add the dashi and the 3⁄4 teaspoon (4.5 g) salt. Stop the machine, add half of the tapioca starch, and process until the starch is absorbed and the mixture is smooth. With the machine running, slowly sprinkle in the remaining tapioca starch and process until a smooth dough forms. Transfer the dough to a large vacuum bag and vacuum seal. Using a rolling pin, roll out the dough in the bag until it is spread in an even layer and reaches into all corners of the bag. Fill a large pot three-fourths full with water and bring to a boil over high heat. Put the bag in the boiling water and cook until the dough is translucent, about 12 minutes. Meanwhile, prepare an ice bath. When the dough is ready, transfer it, still in the bag, to the ice bath and let cool completely, replenishing the ice as needed, about 20 minutes.

Line a food dehydrator tray or a sheet pan with a silicone mat. Cut the bag open and lay the dough on the mat. Place in the dehydrator set at 150°F (65°C) or the oven preheated to 175°F (80°C) until completely dry, 3–4 hours.

Pour the canola oil into a deep fryer to the fill line or into a tall-sided saucepan to a depth of 2 1⁄2 inches (6 cm) and heat to 400°F (200°C).

Break the shrimp sheet into 1-inch (2.5-cm) pieces. Put the pieces in the food processor and pulse until broken up into coarse crumbs. Working in batches, add the crumbs to the hot oil and fry until puffed and golden, 3–5 seconds. Using a fine-mesh sieve, transfer the crispies to a paper towel–lined plate and season lightly with salt. The crispies may be stored in an airtight container at room temperature for up to 1 day.

QUAIL EGGS

Preheat the circulating water bath to 145°F (63°C).

Cook the quail eggs in the circulating water bath for 45 minutes. Just before the eggs are ready, prepare an ice bath. When the eggs are done, transfer them to the ice bath and let cool completely, about 10 minutes. The cooled eggs may be stored in a lidded container in the refrigerator for up to 3 days before using.

YUZU BUBBLES

In a tall, narrow container, combine the yuzu juice, water, mirin, Sucro, confectioners' sugar, and salt. Blend with an immersion blender for 30 seconds. Use right away.

DASHI BROTH

2 1⁄4 cups (506 g) Dashi (above)
1 tablespoon (14 g) rice vinegar
1⁄2 teaspoon (3 g) fine sea salt
.75 gram xanthan gum (see sources)

SHRIMP CRISPIES

8 Marvesta Farm shrimp (21–25 count)
7 tablespoons (100 g) Dashi (above)
3⁄4 teaspoon (4.5 g) salt, plus more to season
1 1⁄4 cups plus 1 tablespoon (150 g) tapioca starch (see sources)
Canola oil for frying

QUAIL EGGS

12 quail eggs

YUZU BUBBLES

2⁄3 cup (150 g) yuzu juice
3⁄4 cup plus 2 tablespoons (200 g) water
2 tablespoons plus 2 teaspoons (40 g) mirin
1.9 grams Sucro (see sources)
1 teaspoon (5 g) confectioners' sugar
1⁄4 teaspoon (1.5 g) fine sea salt

MICHAEL This is my fresh take on the classic sausage and peppers, with king crab as the centerpiece. The crustacean has a naturally meaty texture, so I knew I wanted just enough binder to bring it together. The fennel pollen and togarashi add the familiar flavors of crushed red pepper and fennel seed found in the original, but the puffed pumpernickel, which remind me of pommes soufflés, was a happy accident that came about when I threw a big piece of bread in the deep fryer.

King Crab, Sausage and Peppers, Hops

MAIN INGREDIENTS

8 ounces (225 g) king crab legs
4 ounces (113 g) peeled and deveined shrimp
1.25 grams Activa RM (see sources)
¼ cup (60 g) heavy cream
½ large egg (whisk 1 egg and divide it in half)
¼ teaspoon (1.5 g) fine sea salt, plus more to season
½ teaspoon (.75 g) fennel pollen
½ teaspoon (1 g) togarashi pepper
Smoked Maldon salt
Red Pepper–Garlic Sauce (below)
Pumpernickel Hemispheres (below)
Red Pepper Confit (below)
Whipped Hops (below)
Espelette pepper

Equipment

thermal immersion circulator
vacuum sealer and vacuum bags
masticating vegetable juicer
deep fryer (optional)

Serves 8 as a first course

GARLIC OIL

25 cloves garlic, peeled but left whole
1 cup plus 4 teaspoons (250 g) cold extra-virgin olive oil

RED PEPPER–GARLIC SAUCE

¼ cup (56 g) extra-virgin olive oil
1 yellow onion, julienned
6 cloves garlic, thinly sliced

››

Preheat the circulating water bath to 138°F (59°C).

Using kitchen scissors, cut the crab legs open and carefully remove the meat. Remove any cartilage from the meat. Separate out the nice thick pieces of crabmeat and set them aside. Shred the cluster meat from the tops of the legs and the small pieces of leg meat. Squeeze the water from the shredded meat by pressing it in a colander.

In a food processor, combine the shrimp and Activa RM and pulse until the shrimp meat is roughly minced. Add the cream, egg, ¼ teaspoon (1.5 g) salt, the fennel pollen, and togarashi and pulse again until mixture is smooth. Transfer the shrimp mixture to a bowl and fold in the shredded crabmeat.

Divide the reserved crabmeat into 5 equal portions. Scoop the crab-shrimp mixture into a pastry bag fitted with a ¾-inch (2-cm) plain tip. Lay a large sheet of plastic wrap on a work surface. Pipe the mixture into a log about 10 inches (25 cm) long on the plastic wrap near the edge of the sheet. Gently press 1 portion of the reserved crabmeat onto the top of the shrimp-crab log. Roll the log up tightly in the plastic wrap so the crabmeat is at the center of the rolled tube and tie each end securely with cotton butcher's twine to ensure the log holds its shape. Put the wrapped crab "sausage" in a vacuum bag and vacuum seal. Repeat 4 times to make a total of 5 individually wrapped sausages, vacuum sealing each one in a bag.

Cook the crab sausages in the circulating water bath for 20 minutes. Meanwhile, prepare an ice bath. When the sausages are ready, transfer the bags to the ice bath and let cool completely, replenishing the ice as needed, about 30 minutes. The cooled crab sausages may be stored in the vacuum bags in the refrigerator for up to 2 days.

To serve, remove the sausages from the bags. Cut 4 of the sausages into 2-inch (5-cm) pieces; reserve the remaining sausage for another use. In a saucepan, bring the red pepper–garlic sauce to a bare simmer over medium heat. Add the crab sausage pieces and heat them through, about 5 minutes. Place 2 sausage pieces in each bowl, saving any extras for the chef to have as a snack. Arrange 3 pumpernickel hemispheres around the sausages. Put 1 piece of red pepper

¾ cup plus 2 tablespoons (200 g) red bell pepper juice (from about 4 large peppers)

1 teaspoon (4 g) sugar

4 teaspoons (20 g) cold Garlic Oil (above)

.4 gram xanthan gum (see sources)

Fine sea salt

PUMPERNICKEL HEMISPHERES

Sponge

2 cups plus 3½ tablespoons (500 g) water heated to 110°F (43°C)

2 tablespoons plus 1 teaspoon (19.6 g) active dry yeast

3 cups plus 3 tablespoons plus 1 teaspoon (480 g) bread flour

Dough

1 cup less 1 tablespoon *each* (140 g) bread flour and whole-wheat flour

1½ cups plus ½ tablespoon (160 g) light rye flour

4 teaspoons (10.8 g) black cocoa powder (see sources)

5½ tablespoons (75 g) blackstrap molasses

1 tablespoon plus ¼ teaspoon (19.5 g) fine sea salt

2 tablespoons plus 1 teaspoon (30 g) sugar

3½ tablespoons (50 g) unsalted butter, at room temperature

2 large eggs plus 1 large egg yolk

Canola oil

2 tablespoons (28 g) Garlic Oil (above)

Maldon sea salt

RED PEPPER CONFIT

2 flat-sided red bell peppers

1 teaspoon (4 g) sugar

½ teaspoon (3 g) fine sea salt

¾ cup plus 2 tablespoons (200 g) extra-virgin olive oil

2 cloves garlic, thinly sliced

2 fresh thyme sprigs

WHIPPED HOPS

1½ cups (340 g) hoppy beer such as Sierra Nevada Extra IPA

3 tablespoons (42 g) fresh lemon juice

1½ tablespoons (25 g) honey

8 grams Versawhip (see sources)

2 grams xanthan gum (see sources)

confit on each piece of sausage. Place a spoonful of hops to the side of the other elements on the plate. Sprinkle a touch of Espelette pepper over the whipped hops and serve right away.

GARLIC OIL

Preheat the circulating water bath to 149°F (65°C).

In a saucepan, combine the garlic and ¾ cup (170 g) of the olive oil over medium-low heat and cook until the garlic is translucent and very aromatic, 3–5 minutes. Remove from the heat and add the remaining ¼ cup plus 4 teaspoons (80 g) olive oil to the pan. Transfer the mixture to a vacuum bag and vacuum seal. Cook in the circulating water bath for 2 hours. Just before the oil is ready, prepare an ice bath. Then, when the oil is ready, transfer the bag to the ice bath and let cool completely, replenishing the ice as needed, about 20 minutes. Open the bag and strain the garlic oil through a fine-mesh sieve placed over a lidded container. The oil may be stored in the refrigerator for up to 3 days before using.

RED PEPPER–GARLIC SAUCE

In a small saucepan, heat the olive oil over medium heat until it begins to shimmer but does not smoke. Add the onion and garlic and cook, stirring, until translucent, about 5 minutes. Add the pepper juice and bring to a boil. Add the sugar, reduce the heat to maintain a low simmer, and cook for 10 minutes. Remove the pan from the heat, cover, and let the mixture steep for 10 minutes.

Strain through a fine-mesh sieve placed over a clean saucepan, and use a wooden spoon to press every last bit of the liquid through. Using an immersion blender, process until a vortex forms in the center of the liquid. Sprinkle in the xanthan gum and blend for a full 5 seconds to dissolve the xanthan gum fully. Season to taste with salt. Set the pan over medium heat and bring the liquid to a boil. Add the garlic oil and blend with the immersion blender until the mixture emulsifies. Once the emulsion has formed, remove from the heat and serve right away.

PUMPERNICKEL HEMISPHERES

To make the sponge, put the warm water in the bowl of a stand mixer and stir in the yeast. Once the yeast has dissolved, mix in the bread flour to form a paste. Cover the bowl loosely with plastic wrap and let the sponge rise at room temperature for 1 hour. It should roughly double in size.

To make the dough, place the bowl containing the sponge on the mixer stand and add the additional bread flour, the whole-wheat flour, rye flour, cocoa powder, molasses, salt, sugar, butter, eggs, and egg yolk. Fit the mixer with the dough hook, turn on the mixer to the second-lowest setting, and mix until the dough forms a ball. Oil another bowl with little canola oil, transfer the dough to the bowl, cover the bowl with plastic wrap, and let the dough rise at room temperature until it doubles in size, about 1 hour.

Pour the canola oil into a deep fryer to the fill line or into a tall-sided saucepan to a depth of 2½ inches (6 cm) and heat to 375°F (190°C).

While the oil is heating, turn the dough out onto a lightly floured work surface. Using a rolling pin, roll out the dough into a rough rectangle about ⅛ inch (3 mm) thick. Using a ring mold about 1 inch (2.5 cm) in diameter, cut out small rounds. You will need at least 24. Any extra dough can be cut and fried as a side garnish or used for another purpose.

When the oil is ready, working in batches, add the rounds to the oil and fry until puffed into balls, 2–3 minutes. Using a skimmer, transfer to paper towel–lined sheet pans. Brush each pumpernickel hemisphere with the garlic oil and season with Maldon salt. Serve right away.

RED PEPPER CONFIT

Preheat the oven to 200°F (95°C).

Set up a steamer on the stove top. Using a vegetable peeler, peel the outer skin from the peppers. Cut off the top and bottom from each pepper. Make 1 vertical cut in each pepper from the top to the bottom and then open it up and trim away the ribs and the seeds. Square off the ends to form a long rectangle and then cut each pepper in half. You should have 4 large rectangles. Place the pepper rectangles in the steamer and steam until tender, about 10 minutes.

Meanwhile, line a sheet pan with parchment paper. When the pepper rectangles are ready, transfer them to the prepared sheet pan, making sure they lie flat on the paper. Sprinkle them evenly with the sugar and salt, and then drizzle them with the olive oil. Scatter the sliced garlic and thyme sprigs on top. Bake the peppers, basting them several times with the oil, for 1 hour. Remove the peppers from the oven and let them cool to room temperature in the pan, about 20 minutes. Transfer the peppers to a lidded container, pour the oil remaining in the pan over the peppers, and seal the lid. The pepper confit may be stored in the refrigerator for up to 3 days.

WHIPPED HOPS

In a blender, combine the beer, lemon juice, honey, Versawhip, and xanthan gum and process until frothy. Transfer to a stand mixer fitted with the whisk attachment and whip on high speed until stiff peaks form and the mixture resembles a meringue, about 5 minutes. Use right away or store in a lidded container in the refrigerator for up to 5 days. Rewhip the mixture as needed to restore the texture.

HERE FENNEL POLLEN & TOGARASHI STAND IN FOR THE FAMILIAR FLAVORS OF CRUSHED RED PEPPER AND FENNEL SEEDS IN A MODERN TAKE ON A CLASSIC SANDWICH

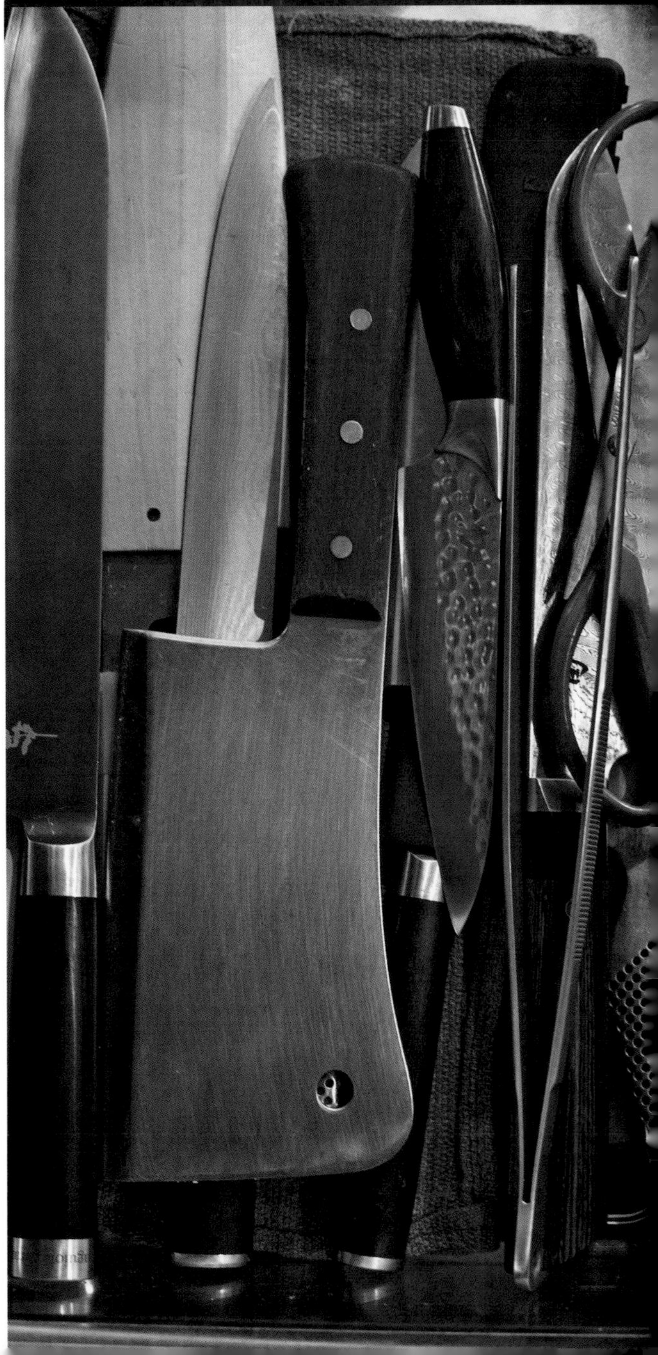

BRYAN I learned to make this vinaigrette from Dante Bocuzzi at Aureole in 2002. We combined a tarragon-infused oil and reduced carrot juice for a sweet, floral, herbal combination that we served with red snapper, pommes soufflées, and wild mushrooms. Here, the same dressing is a wonderful accent to the sweet, briny meat of lobster. The crispness of the crackers, a quality normally associated with the lobster's shell, delivers a surprising element to the finished dish.

Lobster, Forbidden Rice, Carrots, Sunchoke Purée, Carrot-Tarragon Vinaigrette

MAIN INGREDIENTS

6 live lobsters, about 1½ pounds (680 g) each
10 quarts (9600 g) plus 1 cup (225 g) water
1 cup (225 g) distilled white vinegar
2 teaspoons (12 g) fine sea salt
4½ cups (1000 g) cold unsalted butter, diced
Forbidden Rice (below)
Carrot Rounds (below)
Sunchoke Purée (below)
Carrot-Tarragon Vinaigrette (below)
Lobster Crackers (below)
Carrot fronds
Fresh tarragon leaves, finely cut crosswise into slices

Equipment

6-quart (5.7-l) pressure cooker
thermal immersion circulator
vacuum sealer and vacuum bags
high-speed blender
food dehydrator (optional)
deep fryer (optional)

Serves 6 as a main course

››

Working with 1 live lobster at a time, gently twist the tail and pull it off the body. Then, turn the lobster around and break off the 2 claws with their legs still attached. Put the tail in a 5-quart (4.7-l) heatproof container and put the claws in a separate 5-quart (4.7-l) heatproof container. Repeat with the remaining lobsters. In a large pot, combine the 10 quarts (9600 g) water and vinegar and bring to a rapid boil over high heat. When the water is boiling, carefully pour some of it over the claws and some of it over the tails, just enough to cover them completely. Top the lobster pieces in each container with a rack to ensure they are submerged completely. Let the tails remain in the water for 9 minutes and the claws for 11 minutes. Meanwhile, prepare an ice bath. As the lobster tails and claws are ready (they will turn bright red), using a large skimmer, transfer them to the ice bath and let cool completely, replenishing the ice if needed. Gently remove all of the lobster meat from the shells, keeping the pieces as large as possible. Reserve 8 of the knuckles (the meat from the front legs attached to the claws) for the lobster crackers. (The remaining 4 knuckles can be eaten as a snack.) Reserve the claw and tail meat for finishing the dish.

To serve, in a saucepan, combine the remaining 1 cup (225 g) water and the salt and bring to a simmer over medium heat. Add ¾ cup (170 g) of the butter, whisking constantly. Once it has been absorbed, whisk in another ¾ cup (170 g) of the butter. Continue to whisk in the butter in ¾-cup (170-g) additions until all of it has been absorbed and the sauce has the consistency of heavy cream. Reduce the heat to low and keep warm, stirring occasionally. Add the lobster claw and tail meat and warm over very low heat for about 8 minutes.

Bring a saucepan three-fourths full of water to a simmer over high heat. Put the Forbidden rice and any of its liquid in a small saucepan, place over medium heat, and bring to a simmer, stirring occasionally. Put the bag of carrot rounds in the pan of simmering water for 5 minutes to warm them up. Put the sunchoke purée in a small saucepan, place over medium heat, and warm, stirring occasionally, to serving temperature, 5–8 minutes.

THE FLAVORS OF TARRAGON AND CARROTS ARE WONDERFUL COMPLEMENTS TO SWEET BRINY LOBSTER MEAT AND CRUNCHY CRACKERS BRING AN UNEXPECTED TEXTURE

Using a slotted spoon, remove the lobster tails and claws from the butter sauce and drain them briefly on a paper towel–lined plate. Open the bag of carrot rounds, remove the thyme, and drain off any liquid. Put a spoonful of Forbidden rice just off center of each serving plate. Put a medium-sized spoonful of sunchoke purée in the lower left corner of the plate and a small spoonful of the purée in the upper right corner of the plate. Lay the lobster tail across the rice, running vertically from the top to the bottom of the plate. Place a few carrot rounds around the lobster tail. Arrange 1 claw slightly diagonal to the top left of the tail, and another claw at the bottom right of the tail. Drizzle the carrot-tarragon vinaigrette in small pools around the plate. Lay a lobster cracker between the tail and the claw at the bottom right of the plate. Garnish the plate with the carrot fronds and sliced tarragon.

FORBIDDEN RICE

Rinse the rice under cold running water for 2 minutes. Put the star anise, cinnamon stick, allspice, lemongrass, and ginger in the center of a 6-inch (15-cm) piece of cheesecloth, bring the corners together, and tie securely with cotton butcher's twine to make a sachet. In the pressure cooker, combine the rice, sachet, mirin, white soy, and vegetable stock. Following the manufacturer's instructions, lock the lid in place, bring up to high pressure, and cook for 36 minutes. Let the pressure dissipate naturally, then uncover. Remove and discard the sachet, and reserve both the rice and any cooking liquid. The rice and its liquid may be cooled and stored in a lidded container in the refrigerator for up to 3 days before using.

CARROT ROUNDS

Preheat the circulating water bath to 185°F (85°C).

Cut the carrots into rounds about ¼ inch (6 mm) thick. This should yield about ¼ cup (35 g). Put the carrot rounds, olive oil, thyme, and salt in a vacuum bag and vacuum seal. Cook in the circulating water bath until the carrots feel tender when gently squeezed through the bag, about 15 minutes. Meanwhile, prepare an ice bath. When the carrots are ready, transfer the bag to the ice bath and let cool completely, replenishing the ice as needed, about 15 minutes. The carrots may be stored in the bag in the refrigerator for up to 2 days before using.

SUNCHOKE PURÉE

Preheat the circulating water bath to 180°F (82°C).

Put the sunchokes, butter, and salt in a vacuum bag and vacuum seal. Cook in the circulating water bath until they feel tender when gently squeezed through the bag, about 2 hours. Just before the sunchokes are ready, prepare an ice bath. When they are done, transfer the contents of the bag to the blender and process until smooth. Strain through a fine-mesh sieve placed over a metal bowl. Set the bowl over the ice bath and let cool completely, stirring occasionally and replenishing the ice as needed, about 20 minutes. The sunchoke purée may be stored in a lidded container in the refrigerator for up to 2 days before using.

TARRAGON OIL

In the blender, combine the tarragon and oil, turn on to low speed, and then slowly increase the speed to high. Once the mixture is completely smooth, add the salt and blend briefly. Transfer the liquid to a saucepan, place over medium heat, and cook until it turns bright green, 3–5 minutes. Meanwhile, prepare an ice bath. When the mixture is ready, immediately strain it through a cheesecloth-lined fine-mesh sieve placed over a metal bowl. Set the bowl over the ice bath and let stand, stirring occasionally and replenishing the ice if needed, until completely cool, about 15 minutes. The tarragon oil may be stored in a lidded container in the refrigerator for up to 3 days before using.

CARROT-TARRAGON VINAIGRETTE

In a saucepan, combine the carrot juice, orange juice, and tarragon sprigs, place over medium-high heat, and bring to a simmer. Simmer until the liquid is reduced by half; you should have about 1½ cups (354 ml). Strain through a fine-mesh sieve placed over a bowl and let cool completely, about 30 minutes. Transfer the strained liquid to a blender, add the honey, and process until fully incorporated. Turn the blender on to low speed. Slowly increase the speed until a vortex forms in the center of the liquid. Sprinkle in xanthan gum and salt and blend for a full 5 seconds to dissolve the xanthan gum completely. Reduce the blender speed to low and slowly drizzle in the tarragon oil until fully incorporated. Strain the vinaigrette through a fine-mesh sieve. The vinaigrette may be stored in a lidded container in the refrigerator for up to 1 week before using.

LOBSTER CRACKERS

Put the lobster knuckles in a food processor and process until smooth. With the motor running, add the water and the ¾ teaspoon (4.5 g) salt. Stop the processor, add half of the tapioca starch, and then process until the starch is absorbed and the mixture is smooth. Now, with the processor running, slowly sprinkle in the remaining tapioca starch and process until it is completely absorbed and a smooth dough forms. Transfer the dough to a large vacuum bag and vacuum seal. Using a rolling pin, roll out the dough in the bag until it is spread in an even layer and reaches into all corners of the bag.

Fill a large pot three-fourths full with water and bring to a boil over high heat. Put the bag of lobster dough in the boiling water and cook until the dough is translucent, 12–15 minutes. Meanwhile, prepare an ice bath. When the dough is ready, transfer it, still in the bag, to the ice bath and let cool completely, replenishing the ice as needed, about 30 minutes.

Line a food dehydrator tray or a sheet pan with a silicone mat. Cut the bag open and lay the dough out on the mat. Place in the dehydrator set at 150°F (65°C) or the oven preheated to 175°F (80°C) until completely dry, 3–4 hours.

Pour the canola oil into a deep fryer to the fill line or into a tall-sided saucepan to a depth of 2½ inches (6 cm) and heat to 400°F (200°C).

Break the cracker into 1-inch (2.5-cm) pieces. In batches, add the pieces to the oil and fry until puffed and golden, 10–15 seconds. Using a skimmer, transfer to a paper towel-lined plate and season lightly with salt. The crackers may be stored in an airtight container at room temperature for up to 3 days.

FORBIDDEN RICE

1 cup (200 g) Forbidden rice

4 whole star anise

1 cinnamon stick

2 allspice berries

1 lemongrass stalk

1 tablespoon (5.2 g) minced, peeled fresh ginger

1⅓ cups (330 g) mirin

¼ cup (80 g) white soy sauce (see sources)

2 cups (450 g) Vegetable Stock (page 319)

CARROT ROUNDS

2 baby heirloom carrots, about 1¾ ounces (50 g) total weight, peeled

½ teaspoon (2.3 g) extra-virgin olive oil

1 fresh thyme sprig

¼ teaspoon (1.5 g) fine sea salt

SUNCHOKE PURÉE

10 sunchokes, about 13½ ounces (380 g) total weight, unpeeled

1 cup (225 g) unsalted butter

½ teaspoon (3 g) fine sea salt

TARRAGON OIL

1 cup (42.5 g) packed fresh tarragon leaves

3 cups (675 g) grape seed oil

1 teaspoon (6 g) fine sea salt

CARROT-TARRAGON VINAIGRETTE

1 cup (225 g) strained carrot juice

½ cup (113 g) fresh orange juice

23 sprigs fresh tarragon

½ tablespoon (8 g) honey

.85 gram xanthan gum (see sources)

¼ teaspoon (1.5 g) fine sea salt

1½ cups (338 g) Tarragon Oil (above)

LOBSTER CRACKERS

8 lobster knuckles

7 tablespoons (100 g) water

¾ teaspoon (4.5 g) salt, plus more to season

1½ cups plus 1 tablespoon (150 g) tapioca starch

Canola oil for deep-frying

MICHAEL Here, I took something that I have been eating all my life and turned it into something a little more whimsical. In Maryland, it is steamed crabs, corn on the cob, and Old Bay—that's it, and that's all you need for the quintessential meal. Those same components are here: you the have crunchy soft-shell crab; the corn, in the form of corn flakes, corn stock, and huitlacoche (the delicious corn fungus); and the Old Bay, not as a powder but as my version of ketchup.

Maryland Soft-Shell Crab, Glazed Roasted Corn, Huitlacoche, Old Bay Purée

MAIN INGREDIENTS

2 Maryland soft-shell crabs
Canola oil for deep-frying
1 cup (150 g) all-purpose flour
3 large eggs
1 cup (50 g) crushed corn flake cereal
Maldon sea salt
Suprêmes from 1 lime, quartered
Baby Corn (below)
Espelette pepper
Finely grated zest of 1 lime
Old Bay Purée (below)

Equipment

deep fryer (optional)
6-quart (5.7-l) pressure cooker
thermal immersion circulator
vacuum sealer and vacuum bags
8 sturdy wooden toothpicks
masticating vegetable juicer
high-speed blender
8-inch square of Styrofoam
plastic squeeze bottle

Serves 4 as a first course

DRIED CORN STOCK

4 cups (100 g) freeze-dried Russian corn or freeze-dried sweet corn (see sources)
3 quarts plus 2/3 cup (2850 g) water

BABY CORN

8 ears baby corn, husks and silk removed
4 teaspoons (20 g) unsalted butter
2 cups (450 g) plus 3 tablespoons (40 g) Dried Corn Stock (above)
1 tablespoon (18 g) fine sea salt, plus more for seasoning
1 tablespoon (6 g) freshly ground white pepper
1 pound (450 g) huitlacoche (see sources)
5 grams kappa carrageenan (see sources)
Extra-virgin olive oil

OLD BAY PURÉE

1¾ cups (400 g) red bell pepper juice (from 6–8 large peppers)
5 tablespoons (50 g) Old Bay seasoning
3 grams agar (see sources)

Using kitchen scissors, make a straight cut across the front of a crab, removing its mouth and eyes. Lift up the side edges of its shell to reveal its gills. Use a finger to separate the gills from the body of the crab, and then use the scissors to cut off the gills. Flip the crab over and remove the crab's "tail," or apron. Cut the crab in half down the middle, from the face to the apron. Repeat the trimming procedure with the second crab.

To serve, pour the oil into a deep fryer to the fill line or into a tall-sided saucepan to a depth of 2½ inches (6 cm) and heat to 350°F (180°C).

Spread the flour on a plate. Put the eggs in a shallow bowl and whip lightly with a fork. Put the crushed cereal in another shallow bowl. Dip a crab half in the flour, coating it thoroughly and then shaking off the excess. Next, dip it in the egg mixture, coating it on both sides and allowing the excess to drip off. Finally, roll the crab in the corn flakes to coat completely. Set the crab half aside on a large plate. Repeat with the remaining 3 pieces of crab. In batches, add the crabs to the oil and fry until deep golden brown and crispy, about 3 minutes. Transfer to a paper towel–lined plate and season with Maldon salt.

Scatter the lime pieces on the plates. Cut each crab half in half horizontally so each piece has 2 legs and stack the 2 pieces on the plates. Season the baby corn ears with Maldon salt, Espelette pepper, and lime zest. Garnish each plate with 2 corn ears and dots of the Old Bay and huitlacoche purées. Serve right away.

DRIED CORN STOCK

In the pressure cooker, combine the dried corn and water. Following the manufacturer's instructions, lock the lid in place, bring the pressure up to high, and cook for 45 minutes. Let the pressure dissipate naturally, then uncover. Strain the stock through a fine-mesh sieve placed over a saucepan. Place over medium-high heat and bring to a simmer. Cook until the stock is reduced by half, 1–1½ hours. You should have 2½ cups (565 g) stock. Prepare an ice bath. Pour the stock into a large metal bowl, set over the ice bath, and let cool completely, stirring occasionally and replenishing the ice as needed, about 20 minutes. The stock may be kept in a lidded container in the refrigerator for up to 5 days.

BABY CORN

Preheat the circulating water bath to 185°F (85°C).

Put the corn ears, butter, 1 cup (225 g) of the stock, 1 tablespoon (18 g) salt, and the pepper and vacuum seal. Cook in the circulating water bath until the ears feel tender when gently squeezed through the bag, about 45 minutes. Prepare an ice bath. When the corn is done, transfer the bag to the ice bath and let cool completely, replenishing the ice as needed, about 20 minutes.

Remove the cooled corn from the bag, and skewer each one through one end with a toothpick. Juice the huitlachoche in a masticating vegetable juicer and pass it through a fine-mesh sieve placed over a saucepan. Set over medium heat, bring the juice to a boil, and then strain one more time. Let the juice cool to room temperature. Measure 1 cup plus 5 teaspoons (250 g), adding a little water if needed to supplement.

In the blender, combine the strained juice and the remaining 1 cup plus 3 tablespoons (265 g) corn stock. Turn the blender on to low speed. Slowly increase the speed until a vortex forms in the center of the liquid. Sprinkle in the kappa carrageenan and continue to process on medium speed for a full 2 minutes. Transfer the mixture to a small saucepan, place over medium heat, and bring to a boil. Holding a corn ear by the toothpick, dip the ear in the hot huitlacoche mixture. Stick the skewer into the Styrofoam square so the glazed ear stands upright. Repeat with the remaining ears. Let the ears stand until the glaze has cooled and set, about 2 minutes, and then repeat the dipping process. Once the glaze has set a second time, carefully remove the corn from the skewers and season them with olive oil and salt. The glazed ears may be kept at room temperature until ready to serve, up to 1 hour, or in the refrigerator for up to 24 hours. Rewarm gently in a low oven (175°F/80°C) for 5–10 minutes, taking care not to melt the glaze.

Pour the remaining huitlacoche mixture into a shallow bowl and refrigerate, uncovered, until firmly set, about 30 minutes. Use a rubber spatula to break up the gel, transfer to the blender, and process until smooth. The huitlacoche purée may be stored in a lidded container in the refrigerator for up to 3 days. Remove it from the refrigerator about 30 minutes before serving.

OLD BAY PURÉE

Put the pepper juice in a blender and turn it on to low speed. Slowly increase the speed until a vortex forms in the center of the liquid. Sprinkle in the Old Bay and agar and process for a full 5 seconds to incorporate the ingredients fully. Transfer the juice mixture to a small saucepan, place over medium heat, and bring to a boil. Immediately pour the mixture into a heatproof bowl and place in the refrigerator, uncovered, to cool completely and firmly set, about 1 hour.

Dice the gel, transfer to a blender, and blend on low speed until a smooth purée forms. Transfer the purée to a squeeze bottle. It may be stored in the refrigerator for up to 5 days. Remove from the refrigerator 30 minutes before using.

THIS IS **MY HOMAGE**
TO MY HOME STATE
OF MARYLAND

WHERE STEAMED CRABS
CORN ON THE COB

AND OLD BAY SEASONING ARE
EVERYTHING

FRESHWATER FISH

SOCKEYE SALMON
TROUT
ARCTIC CHAR
PIKE

Freshwater lakes, rivers, and ponds abound with countless species of fish with moist, tender flesh. Whenever possible, we try to use what is fished or farmed sustainably nearby. But we also like to source special fish from more distant waters, such as arctic char from northern Canada or sockeye salmon from Alaska. We often like to smoke fish for the extraordinary flavor it produces, or transform a familiar fish into an unfamiliar guise, such as puréeing pike and shaping it into disks that even the savviest diners sometimes mistake for sea scallops.

BRYAN I discovered everything bagels in New York and they quickly became a favorite, because they are loaded with so many different flavors and textures. When I worked at Aureole, we always served smoked salmon. Because of that, I like to have different smoked foods on my menu now. Here, the texture of the delicate "bagel" crumbs pairs well with the creamy smoked salmon mousse. If you have extra crumbs, they make great "shake and bake" for meats or vegetables.

Sockeye Salmon, Flavors of Everything Bagel, Applewood Smoke, Mustard, Lemon, Chives

MAIN INGREDIENTS

6 skin-on sockeye salmon fillet portions, 2 ounces (60 g) each
2 cups (450 g) Fish Brine (page 319)
2 tablespoons (28 g) olive oil
Canola oil for frying
Smoked Sockeye Salmon Mousse (below)
Everything Bagel Crumbs (below)
Lemon Pudding (below)
Chive Pudding (below)
Pickled Mustard Seeds (page 318)
Petite red ribbon sorrel

Equipment

thermal immersion circulator
vacuum sealer and vacuum bags
high-speed blender
food mill with fine grinding disk or tamis
food dehydrator (optional)
high-speed blender

Serves 6 as a first course

››

Put the salmon portions and the fish brine in a large lock-top bag and seal the bag closed, forcing out as much air as possible. Lay the bag in a shallow baking pan and refrigerate the fish to cure for 15 minutes.

Preheat the circulating water bath to 135°F (57°C).

Remove the salmon from the brine and pat dry. Discard the brine. Put the salmon and olive oil in a vacuum bag and vacuum seal. Cook in the circulating water bath for 7 minutes.

Meanwhile, in a small saucepan, pour the canola oil into a tall-sided saucepan to a depth of 2½ inches (6 cm) and heat to 350°F (180°C). Spoon the sockeye salmon mousse into a pastry bag with a #10 tip.

Remove the bag from the water bath, open the bag, and transfer the salmon to a cutting board. Remove the skin from each salmon portion in one piece. Using a spoon, gently scrape off any flesh or bloodline still sticking to the skin. In batches, fry the skins in the hot oil until they are crispy and have curled into a tidy tube, about 2 minutes. Using a slotted spoon, transfer to a paper towel–lined plate to drain and cool completely. (If the skins do not form perfect tubes, let them cool only briefly on the towel-lined plate, then roll each still-hot skin around the handle of a wooden spoon, and let the skin cool, then slide the cooled skin off the handle.) Pipe the sockeye salmon mousse into the cooled skins, then dip both ends of each tube into the everything bagel crumbs. Place the pastry bag with the remaining salmon mousse aside.

To serve, use your fingers to gently pull the salmon portions apart into large flakes. Discard any sinew and connective tissue, keeping only the beautiful salmon flakes. Pipe an oval of the lemon pudding on each plate. Put dots of chive pudding around the oval and one dot offset. Pipe a dollop of salmon mousse in the center of the oval. Arrange the flaked salmon on the salmon mousse. Sprinkle some pickled mustard seeds over the tip of the flaked salmon. Arrange 3 red

SMOKED SOCKEYE SALMON MOUSSE

9 ounces (250 g) smoked sockeye salmon

3½ tablespoons (50 g) heavy cream

8½ ounces (250 g) cream cheese, at room temperature, diced

1 cup (240 g) crème fraîche

Zest of 1 lemon, finely grated

Fine sea salt and freshly ground black pepper

EVERYTHING BAGEL CRUMBS

2 tablespoons (20 g) julienned garlic

4½ tablespoons (30 g) red bell pepper brunoise

3 tablespoons (20 g) green bell pepper brunoise

2 tablespoons (18 g) red onion brunoise

2 tablespoons (30 g) capers

2 tablespoons (30 g) cooked applewood smoked bacon, chopped fine

2 cups (225 g) lightly toasted dried brioche crumbs

3 tablespoons (20 g) toasted white sesame seeds

3 tablespoons (10 g) toasted coriander seeds

2 tablespoons (10 g) toasted fennel seeds

1 tablespoon (7 g) black peppercorns

2 tablespoons (10 g) caraway seeds

LEMON PUDDING

6 lemons

½ cup plus 1 teaspoon (150 g) fine sea salt

½ serrano chile

3 tablespoons (10 g) toasted coriander seeds

2 whole star anise

2 green cardamom pods

1 cinnamon stick

5 fresh cilantro sprigs

1 cup (225 g) water

6 tablespoons (75 g) sugar

CHIVE PUDDING

5¼ ounces (150 g) fresh chives

3¾ tablespoons (52.5 g) water

25 grams liquid glucose (see sources)

2 tablespoons (25 g) sugar

1.5 grams agar (see sources)

ribbon sorrel leaves on the salmon flakes and sprinkle the salmon with everything bagel crumbs. Put the filled salmon skin tube on the bottom left of the plate. Serve right away.

SMOKED SOCKEYE SALMON MOUSSE

In a food processor, combine the smoked salmon and heavy cream and process until a smooth purée forms. Prepare an ice bath. To remove any sinew, pass the purée through a food mill fitted with the fine disk placed over a metal bowl, or push it through a tamis with a plastic bench scraper. Set the bowl over the ice bath.

In a stand mixer fitted with the paddle attachment, combine the cream cheese and crème fraîche and mix on medium-low speed until smooth. Switch to the whisk attachment and whip the mixture until soft peaks form. Using a rubber spatula, fold the whipped mixture into the smoked salmon mixture. Then fold in the lemon zest and season with salt and pepper.

EVERYTHING BAGEL CRUMBS

Spread out the garlic on a dehydrator tray lined with a silicone sheet. Put the tray in a food dehydrator set at 155°F (68°C) and dehydrate until completely dry, 2–3 hours. (Alternatively, you can dry the garlic on a sheet pan lined with a silicone mat in a 175°F/80°C oven.) Repeat with the red bell pepper, green bell pepper, red onion, capers, and bacon. If you have the capacity, you can put more than one item in the dehydrator at the same time, as long as they are on separate trays. Transfer each item to a separate lock-top plastic bag or other airtight container and store at room temperature for up to 1 week.

Just before using, in a food processor, combine all of the dehydrated ingredients with the brioche crumbs, sesame, coriander, and fennel seeds; peppercorns; and caraway seeds. Process until a rough, sandy mixture forms. The crumbs should be coarse enough for you to see the individual ingredients and identify their flavors when you taste them.

LEMON PUDDING

Cut the lemons in half lengthwise and remove the seeds. Put the lemons in a vacuum bag. In a food processor, combine the salt, chile, coriander seeds, star anise, cardamom pods, cinnamon, and cilantro and pulse until a uniform paste forms. Add the spice paste to the bag with the lemons and vacuum seal the bag. Put the bag in the refrigerator to cure for 5 days.

Open the bag and brush any excess spices off the lemon halves. Using a paring knife, carefully remove the lemon flesh and white pith, leaving behind only the cured lemon skins. In a saucepan, combine the lemon skins, water, and sugar, place over medium-high heat, and bring to a simmer. Cook until the skins are tender, about 45 minutes.

Transfer the contents of the pan to the blender and process until a smooth purée forms. Strain the mixture through a fine-mesh sieve placed over a metal bowl set in an ice bath and let cool completely, stirring occasionally, about 15 minutes. The lemon pudding may be stored in a lidded container in the refrigerator for up to 3 days before using.

THE CRUMBS ADD CRUNCH & FLAVOR TO EVERY BITE OF FISH AND LEFTOVERS MAKE THE BEST "SHAKE AND BAKE" IN THE WORLD FOR PORK OR CHICKEN

CHIVE PUDDING

Bring a large pot of generously salted water to a boil over high heat. Prepare an ice bath. Cut the chives in half, add to the boiling water, and blanch until bright green and tender, about 15 seconds. Using a skimmer, transfer the chives to the ice bath and let cool completely. Using the skimmer, transfer the chives to a blender, add 2 tablespoons (28 g) of the water, and process until smooth. Pass the chive purée through a fine-mesh sieve and weigh out 5¼ ounces (150 g). Discard any extra. Put the chive purée in a heatproof bowl and set aside.

In a saucepan, combine the liquid glucose, sugar, agar, and the remaining 1¾ tablespoons (24.5 g) water over medium heat and bring to a boil. Adjust the heat to maintain a strong simmer and cook, stirring often, for 5 minutes to activate the agar. Whisk the hot agar mixture into the chive purée and then pour into a shallow baking pan and refrigerate, uncovered, until cool and firmly set, about 1 hour.

Dice the gel, transfer to the blender, and process until a smooth purée forms. Strain the purée through a fine-mesh sieve placed over a bowl. The pudding may be stored in a lidded container in the refrigerator for up to 3 days.

MICHAEL This is smoked fish paired with classic condiments: pickles, vegetables, and cream cheese. Frying the trout skin gives it a texture that successfully stands in for the toast or bagel that normally accompanies the fish, plus it allows you to use every part of the fish. Don't be put off by the idea of smoking fish at home. It doesn't need to be time-consuming. Indeed, all it takes to achieve a subtle smoky flavor is a smoking gun, some wood chips, and a few minutes.

Smoked Trout, Charred Pickles, Young Radishes

MAIN INGREDIENTS

4 skin-on brook trout fillets, about 6 ounces (168 g) each

5 tablespoons (100 g) light soy sauce

7 tablespoons (100 g) water

5 tablespoons plus 1 teaspoon (75 g) mirin

2½ teaspoons (15 g) fine sea salt

2 tablespoons (25 g) sugar

Canola oil for frying

1 teaspoon (3 g) Japanese curry powder (see sources)

Pickled Cucumbers (below)

Glazed Radishes (below)

1 sheet nori, torn into pieces and finely ground in a spice grinder

Smoked Maldon salt

Goat Cream Cheese (below)

1 black radish, cut into batons

Olive oil

Tiny fresh dill sprigs

Equipment

food dehydrator (optional)

smoking gun and applewood shavings

thermal immersion circulator

vacuum sealer and vacuum bags

2 pairs long chef's tweezers

kitchen blowtorch

sewing needle

high-speed blender

Serves 8 as a first course

››

Remove the skin from each trout fillet and cut in half lengthwise. Wrap the fillets well with plastic wrap and refrigerate until ready to use. Line a food dehydrator tray or a sheet pan with a silicone mat, and lay the skins on the mat. Place in the dehydrator set at 155°F (68°C) or an oven set at 175°F (80°C) and dehydrate overnight.

Prepare an ice bath. In a small saucepan, combine the soy sauce, water, mirin, salt, and sugar, place over medium heat, and bring to a boil, stirring until the salt and sugar dissolve. Remove from the heat, pour into a metal bowl, and set over the ice bath. Let cool, stirring occasionally and replenishing the ice as needed, until the mixture is at least 39°F (4°C), about 20 minutes.

Cut each fillet lengthwise into 2 equal pieces, place in a shallow dish, and pour the cooled soy mixture over the top. Let stand for 20 minutes. Remove the fillet pieces from the soy mixture and pat dry with paper towels. Discard the soy mixture. Lay the fillet pieces flat in a large lock-top plastic bag. Slide the tube of the smoking gun into the bag and seal the top around it. Fill the chamber with applewood shavings, light the gun, and discharge the smoke into the container. Once the smoke dissipates, leave the tube in the bag, refill the chamber, light the gun, and smoke the fillet pieces again. Slide out the tube and seal the bag. Refrigerate the smoked trout for 1 hour.

Preheat the circulating water bath to 126°F (52°C).

Transfer the trout pieces to a vacuum bag (or bags, if necessary), arranging them in a single layer. Vacuum seal, making sure the fillets are lying flat and not touching one another. Cook in the circulating water bath for 6 minutes. Meanwhile, set up an ice bath. When the fish is ready, transfer the bag(s) to the ice bath and let stand until completely cool, replenishing with ice as needed, about 30 minutes. The cooled trout may be stored in the vacuum bag(s) in the refrigerator for up to 2 days.

Pour the oil into a small saucepan to a depth of 2½ inches (6 cm) and heat over medium heat until it almost starts to smoke. Using long chef's tweezers, dip

SMOKING FISH AT HOME DOESN'T NEED TO TAKE HOURS OR DAYS; WITH MY TECHNIQUE A SUBTLE SMOKY FLAVOR CAN BE ACHIEVED IN MINUTES

1 piece of the trout skin into the oil. It will puff instantly. With a second pair of chef's tweezers, pull the skin taut in the oil so it becomes a straight stick. Transfer to a paper towel–lined plate to drain, then season with some of the Japanese curry powder. Repeat with the remaining skins.

Remove the smoked trout pieces from the bag(s). Lay the trout flat on a sheet pan. Lightly run the blowtorch back and forth over the pieces until they are lightly charred. Remove the pickled cucumbers from the bag. Run the blowtorch back and forth over the cucumbers until they turn black on one side. Trim both ends of each cucumber, then cut each cucumber in half crosswise, to yield 4 uniform pieces per cucumber, or a total of 8 pieces.

For each serving, put a fillet of smoked trout in the center of a plate. Arrange the fried trout skin to the left and slightly angled away from the fish. Put the glazed radishes on and around the trout. Season the black radish batons with olive oil and crushed Maldon salt. Put a few radish batons on and around the smoked trout. Pip a squiggly line of goat cream cheese on top of the fried trout skin. Garnish the plate with a few sprigs of dill and 1 radish leaf. Serve right away.

PICKLED CUCUMBERS

Prepare a container of ice water large enough to hold the cucumbers. Using a sewing needle, poke several deep holes all over the skin of the cucumbers. Immerse the pierced cucumbers in the ice water for 1 hour. Drain the cucumbers, weigh them, and place in a bowl. Calculate 5 percent of the weight of the cucumbers and weigh out an equal amount of salt. Season the cucumbers with the salt.

In a small saucepan, combine the sugar, water, mirin, and vinegar and bring to a boil over medium-high heat, stirring to dissolve the sugar. Meanwhile, prepare an ice bath. Put the dill and garlic in a small (at least 1-pint/480-ml)

heatproof container. Pour the boiling liquid over the dill and garlic, place over the ice bath, and let completely cool, about 15 minutes. Transfer the cucumbers and brine to a vacuum bag and vacuum seal. Store in the refrigerator for at least 24 hours before serving.

GLAZED RADISHES

Remove the green tops from the radishes and reserve them. In a small saucepan, combine the radishes, water, and sugar, place over high heat, and bring to a boil. Cook until almost all of the water has reduced to a syrupy glaze coating the radishes, about 10 minutes. Remove from the heat and transfer the radishes to a small container. Pour the olive oil over the radishes and toss to coat. Let the radishes cool to room temperature, then cover the container, and refrigerate until ready to serve, up to 1 day.

GOAT CREAM CHEESE

In a saucepan, heat the goat's milk over medium heat to 180°F (82°C). Remove from the heat and add the vinegar. Using a silicone spatula, stir the milk-vinegar mixture as the curds set up until the whey becomes clear. If the whey remains milky, you can heat the mixture to 205°F (96°C). Gently pour the curdled milk mixture through a cheesecloth-lined colander placed over a bowl, then refrigerate until all of the liquid has drained off, about 1 hour.

Transfer the curds in the cheesecloth to the blender and process until smooth. With the blender on medium speed, slowly drizzle in the oils, emulsifying them into the cheese. Once the mixture is blended and smooth, season with the salt and mix well. Transfer the mixture to a pastry bag fitted with a ⅛-inch (3-mm) plain tip and set aside until ready to serve.

PICKLED CUCUMBERS

2 small Japanese cucumbers
Fine sea salt
¼ cup (50 g) sugar
3½ tablespoons (50 g) water
7 tablespoons (100 g) mirin
½ cup plus 2 tablespoons (200 g) rice vinegar
.7 ounce (20 g) fresh dill fronds
3 cloves garlic, crushed

GLAZED RADISHES

24 small white Easter Egg radishes or tiny red radishes with greens attached
1 cup (225 g) water
½ tablespoon (6.25 g) sugar
3½ tablespoons (50 g) extra-virgin olive oil

GOAT CREAM CHEESE

8 cups (2 kg) pasteurized goat's milk
½ cup (160 g) distilled white vinegar
2 tablespoons (28 g) extra-virgin olive oil
2 tablespoons (28 g) lemon-infused extra-virgin olive oil
1 teaspoon (6 g) fine sea salt

BRYAN For centuries, the Inuit have fished arctic char sustainably in the frigid waters of Canada's Nunavut Territory. But only recently have they begun to share their catch with American chefs. Now, I look forward to the several weeks each summer when this flavorful fish is available. I keep its preparation simple and seasonal. Here, I accompany the fish with my reinterpretation of succotash and a savory truffle ravigote that balances the sweetness of the corn.

Arctic Char, Corn and Fava Bean Succotash, Summer Truffle Ravigote

MAIN INGREDIENTS

2 cups (450 g) water
3/4 teaspoon (4.5 g) fine sea salt
6 skin-on arctic char fillet portions, 4 ounces (113 g) each
2 teaspoons (10 g) canola oil
2 tablespoons (28 g) unsalted butter
4 fresh tarragon sprigs
Summer Truffle Ravigote (below)
Corn and Fava Bean Succotash (below)

Equipment

6-quart (5.7-l) pressure cooker
high-speed blender

Serves 6 as a main course

SUMMER TRUFFLE RAVIGOTE

2 tablespoons (28 g) olive oil
3 shallots, minced
2 cloves garlic, finely grated or minced
3½ ounces (100 g) preserved summer black truffle, cut into small dice
5 tablespoons plus 1 teaspoon (75 g) juice from preserved summer truffle
1 tablespoon (20 g) Banyuls vinegar

CORN STOCK

6 ears corn, husks and silk removed
3 cups (675 g) water

CORN AND FAVA BEAN SUCCOTASH

Kernels from 6 ears corn reserved from Corn Stock (above)
2½ tablespoons (35 g) unsalted butter
1/4 teaspoon (1.5 g) fine sea salt
3/4 cup plus 2 tablespoons (200 g) Corn Stock (above)
8 ounces (225 g) peeled, shelled fava beans

To make a brine, in a bowl, whisk together the water and salt until the salt dissolves. Place the arctic char portions in a shallow baking dish just large enough to accommodate them in a single layer, and pour the brine over the fish. Cover and refrigerate the fish to cure for 10 minutes. Pull the arctic char from the brine, rinse under cold running water, and pat dry with paper towels.

In a sauté pan, heat the canola oil over high heat until it begins to shimmer but does not smoke. Add the fish, skin side down. After 2 minutes, reduce the heat to medium-high. Then reduce the heat to medium and cook for another 2 minutes. Flip the fish and add the butter and tarragon to the pan. When the butter begins to froth, use a wide, flat, large metal spoon to baste the fish until the butter stops frothing and begins to brown. Transfer the fish to a warmed plate and let rest in a warm spot for 5 minutes before serving.

To serve, add the truffle ravigote to the warm succotash and gently warm, stirring occasionally; do not let it boil. Put a spoonful of the ravigote-succotash mixture on each serving plate. Cut each piece of fish in half and put both pieces on top of the ravigote-succotash mixture, presenting one with the skin side up and the other with the skin side down. Serve right away.

SUMMER TRUFFLE RAVIGOTE

In a sauté pan, heat the olive oil over medium heat until it begins to shimmer. Add the shallots and garlic and cook until translucent, 3–5 minutes. Add the truffle and cook until aromatic, 1–2 minutes. Add the truffle juice and vinegar and bring to a simmer. Adjust the heat to maintain a low simmer and cook until reduced by one-third, 8–10 minutes. Remove from the heat and transfer to a bowl. Let cool naturally to room temperature. The truffle ravigote may be kept in a covered container in the refrigerator for up to 1 week.

CORN STOCK

Cut the tip off 1 ear of corn and stand it upright on a cutting board. Holding the stem, and using a chef's knife, shave the kernels from the ear, cutting from top

EVERY YEAR I LOOK FORWARD TO THE SEVERAL SHORT WEEKS IN EACH SUMMER WHEN THIS EXTREMELY FLAVORFUL COLDWATER FISH IS AVAILABLE FROM MY LOCAL FISHMONGER

to bottom and rotating the ear as you go. Repeat with the remaining 5 ears. Reserve half for the succotash and half for another use. Cut the stem off of each cob, and cut each cob into 3 equal pieces.

In the pressure cooker, combine the cob pieces and water. Following the manufacturer's instructions, lock the lid in place, bring up to high pressure, and cook for 15 minutes. Let the pressure dissipate naturally, then uncover.

Prepare an ice bath. Strain the stock through a fine-mesh sieve placed over a metal bowl. Set the bowl over the ice bath and let cool completely, stirring occasionally and replenishing the ice as needed, about 30 minutes. The stock may be stored in a lidded container in the refrigerator for up to 5 days.

CORN AND FAVA BEAN SUCCOTASH

Divide the corn kernels into 2 equal portions. Bring a large pot of generously salted water to a boil over high heat. Prepare an ice bath. Add half of the corn kernels to the boiling water and blanch for 1 minute. Using a skimmer, transfer to the ice bath. As soon as the corn is cold, drain it and set it aside.

In a saucepan, melt the butter over medium-high heat. Add the remaining corn kernels and salt and cook, stirring constantly, until the corn starts to brown slightly, about 10 minutes. Add the corn stock and bring to a simmer. Adjust the heat to maintain a low simmer and cook until the corn is completely tender, about 5 minutes. Transfer the contents of the saucepan to the blender and process until completely smooth. Strain the purée through a fine-mesh sieve placed over a saucepan, using the back of a small ladle to push the purée through. Add the blanched corn kernels and the fava beans to the purée, place over medium heat, and bring just to a simmer. Keep warm until ready to serve.

MICHAEL Mild-flavored pike is often made into a mousse, which is what I have done here. But then, in a departure from tradition, I form the mousse into disks that recall the luscious, creamy texture of scallops. This is the perfect dish for people who crave shellfish but cannot eat it because of an allergy or other reason. The sweet and sour apricot is a versatile condiment. Here, it provides that extra acid needed to brighten the neutral flavors of the fish and mushrooms.

Freshwater "Scallops," Raw and Cooked Porcini, Sweet and Sour Apricot

MAIN INGREDIENTS

8½ ounces (250 g) skinless pike fillets

¼ teaspoon (1.5 g) fine sea salt

3 grams Activa RM (see sources)

1 large egg white

3 tablespoons plus 1 teaspoon (50 g) heavy cream

4 teaspoons (20 g) canola oil

Fine sea salt

4 teaspoons (20 g) unsalted butter

2 medium porcini mushrooms

1 tablespoon (14 g) extra-virgin olive oil

1 tablespoon (5 g) chopped fresh chives

Maldon sea salt

Porcini Confit (below)

2 medium porcini mushrooms

Porcini Crackers (below)

Sweet and Sour Apricot (below)

Equipment

thermal immersion circulator

vacuum sealer and vacuum bags

Japanese-style mandoline

high-speed blender

food dehydrator (optional)

deep fryer (optional)

Serves 4 as a first course

Preheat the circulating water bath to 138°F (59°C).

Using a sharp chef's knife, mince the fish. Transfer the fish to a food processor and sprinkle the salt and Activa over the top. Turn on the food processor and slowly drizzle in the egg white. Once the egg white is fully incorporated, slowly pour in the cream. When everything is well blended and a mousselike texture has formed, remove the mixture from the food processor and divide it evenly between 2 pastry bags, each fitted with a ¾-inch (2-cm) plain tip.

Lay out a large square of plastic wrap on a work surface. Pipe the fish mousse in one bag along the bottom edge of the plastic wrap, forming a log 10 inches (25 cm) long. Roll up the plastic wrap around the mousse, being careful not to trap any air inside (air bubbles will create holes in the finished product). Twist the ends of the plastic wrap snugly to compress the mousse into a tight 10-inch (25-cm) log; it will be about 1 inch (2.5 cm) in diameter. Tie the ends with cotton butcher's twine and put the wrapped log in a vacuum bag. Repeat with the fish mousse in the second pastry bag to form a second log, and add it to the vacuum bag. Vacuum seal the bag, being sure to leave enough space between the logs so that the bag seals around each log of mousse separately.

Cook the logs of fish mousse in the circulating water bath for 20 minutes. Meanwhile, prepare an ice bath. When the mousse logs are ready, transfer the vacuum bag to the ice bath and let the fish mousse cool completely, about 10 minutes. The cooled logs may be stored in the bag in the refrigerator for up to 2 days before using.

Open the bag, remove the wrapped logs, and unwrap each log. Place the logs on a cutting board, and cut each log crosswise into 10 equal portions. The portions will resemble sea scallops; you should have 20 "scallops" total. In a sauté pan, heat the canola oil over medium-high heat until it begins to shimmer but not smoke. While the oil is heating, lightly season both cut sides of each scallop with salt. When the oil is ready, add the scallops, one cut side down, to the pan and cook until the first side is caramelized, 3–5 minutes. Add the butter

PORCINI CONFIT

2¼ cups (500 g) rendered duck fat, warm

5 medium porcini mushrooms

3 fresh thyme sprigs

3 cloves garlic, crushed

2 bay leaves

PORCINI CRACKERS

¾ cup plus 2 tablespoons (200 g) truffle juice (see sources)

8½ ounces (250 g) porcini mushrooms, diced

1¼ cups (120 g) tapioca starch

½ tablespoon (3 g) fine sea salt

Canola oil for deep-frying

SWEET AND SOUR APRICOT

2½ ounces (75 g) dried apricots

¼ cup (50 g) sugar

9 ounces (250 g) rice vinegar

2½ tablespoons (50 g) mirin

2 tablespoons (36 g) Campari

1 tablespoon (15 g) pickled ginger juice (from a jar of pickled ginger)

1 teaspoon (6 g) salt

to the pan, turn over each scallop, and when the butter begins to froth, use a wide, flat, large metal spoon to baste the scallops until the butter stops frothing and begins to brown and the scallops are warmed through. Transfer the scallops to a paper towel–lined plate and keep warm.

Using the mandoline, thinly slice the 2 porcini mushrooms, then use a knife to cut the mushroom slices into batons. Put the batons in a small bowl, add the olive oil, chives, and crushed Maldon salt, and toss to coat.

Put 3 scallops in a line down the center of each serving plate, leaving some space between each scallop. Spoon the mushroom confit between the scallops. Arrange the dressed porcini batons on top of the mushrooms and scallops. Put pieces of the porcini crackers on top of the scallops and mushrooms. Drag spoonfuls of the sweet and sour apricot on either side of the scallop arrangement. Serve right away.

PORCINI CONFIT

Put the duck fat in a heatproof bowl just large enough to hold all of the ingredients. Put the bowl over (not touching) simmering water in a small saucepan to create a double boiler. Once the duck fat melts, add the porcini mushrooms, thyme, garlic, and bay leaves to the bowl. Cover the bowl with plastic wrap and let cook over the simmering water until the mushrooms are tender, 10–15 minutes. Remove the bowl from the heat and let the mushrooms cool to room temperature in the fat, about 20 minutes.

Cut the cooked mushrooms into quarters and return them to the fat. Use immediately, or cool and store in a lidded container in the refrigerator until ready to serve, up to 3 days.

PORCINI CRACKERS

Set up a steamer on the stove top.

In a small saucepan, bring the truffle juice to a simmer over medium-high heat. Cook until reduced to about 4½ tablespoons (65 g), about 20 minutes; set aside.

In another small saucepan, combine the porcini mushrooms with water just to cover, place over medium-high heat, and bring to a steady simmer. Cook until the mushrooms are tender and almost all of the liquid has evaporated, about 15 minutes. Remove from the heat and let cool to room temperature.

Transfer the mushrooms to a food processor and pulse until finely chopped but not smooth. Add the reduced truffle juice and pulse to incorporate. Add the tapioca starch and ½ teaspoon (3 g) salt and pulse until a dough forms. Turn the dough out onto a large piece of plastic wrap. Cover with another piece of plastic wrap. Using a rolling pin, roll out the dough about ¼ inch (6 mm) thick. Place the dough, still between the sheets of plastic wrap, in the steamer and steam until translucent, about 15 minutes. Remove the dough from the steamer.

Line a food dehydrator tray or a sheet pan with a silicone mat. Remove the plastic wrap from the dough, and place the dough on the mat. Place the dough in the dehydrator set at 155°F (68°C) or an oven preheated to 175°F (80°C) until just dry to the touch, about 45 minutes. Flip the partially dehydrated dough over and continue to dehydrate until the cracker is dry but not brittle, about 45 minutes longer. It should still be flexible.

Pour the canola oil into a deep fryer to the fill line or into a tall-sided saucepan to a depth of 2½ inches (6 cm) and heat to 350°F (180°C).

Break the porcini cracker into rough 1-inch (2.5-cm) pieces. Working in batches, add the cracker pieces to the hot oil and fry until they puff up and are crisp, 1–2 minutes per batch. Using a skimmer, transfer the crackers to a paper towel–lined sheet pan and season with salt. The cooled porcini crackers may be stored in an airtight container for up to 1 day.

SWEET AND SOUR APRICOT

In a small saucepan, combine the apricots, sugar, vinegar, mirin, Campari, ginger juice, and salt and bring to a boil over medium heat. Remove from the heat, transfer the mixture to the blender, and blend on high speed until smooth, about 2 minutes. Strain the purée through a fine-mesh sieve placed over a bowl. Let the mixture cool to room temperature in the refrigerator. The mixture may be kept in a lidded container in the refrigerator for up to 3 days.

BLENDING FRESHWATER PIKE INTO A LIGHT AIRY MOUSSE AND THEN POACHING IT MIMICS THE LUSCIOUS CREAMY TEXTURE OF A SEA SCALLOP

FUNGHI

SHIITAKE
TRUFFLE
WILD MUSHROOM
MOREL

We cannot imagine life without springtime morels, winter truffles, yeasty beer, or pungent mold-ripened cheeses—all pleasures that we owe to the big fungus family. Mushrooms that we have foraged ourselves always seem to taste better than what is available at the market. They typically proliferate after a rain, and if you walk through a damp forest or meadow, you will likely spy a variety of different types poking up through the moist earth or hiding in the shadows. That search is akin to hunting for treasure, and whatever we bring home inspires us in the kitchen. Earthy, dusky morel, hedgehog, black trumpet, maitake, and shiitake are among our favorite species, all of them packed with a heady aroma and a rich savor—umami at its best.

MAIN INGREDIENTS

24 Nantucket Bay scallops

½ teaspoon (3 g) fine sea salt

2 tablespoons (28 g) *each* grape seed oil and extra-virgin olive oil

Sous Vide Bok Choy (below)

Pine Nut Foam (below)

Shiitake Velouté (below)

18 sea urchin tongues

24 sea beans

Chile Oil (below)

About 2 tablespoons (20 g) pine nuts

Equipment

iSi canister with 2 N_2O chargers (1-quart/.95-liter canister)

vacuum sealer and vacuum bags

thermal immersion circulator

Serves 6 as a first course

SOUS VIDE BOK CHOY

3 heads baby bok choy

1 tablespoon (14 g) grape seed oil

½ teaspoon (3 g) fine sea salt

PINE NUT FOAM

4 tablespoons (56 g) unsalted butter

¾ cup (120 g) pine nuts

2 cups (520 g) whole milk

½ teaspoon (3 g) fine sea salt

2 large egg yolks

SHIITAKE VELOUTÉ

½ cup (113 g) unsalted butter

13 ounces (370 g) shiitake mushrooms, stems removed and caps thinly sliced

Fine sea salt

5 cloves garlic, smashed

2 shallots, thinly sliced

2 cups (450 g) Vegetable Stock (page 319)

¾ tablespoon (14 g) sherry vinegar

CHILE OIL

1 tablespoon (9 g) blended chili powder

1 tablespoon (7 g) cayenne pepper

3 tablespoons (24 g) paprika

1 cup (225 g) grape seed oil

BRYAN The flavor combination of mushrooms and nuts, which I learned from Gerry Hayden at Aureole, has stayed with me through the years. I have used it as a building block for a number of different dishes. In this recipe, I combine earthy shiitakes, which I sauté, season, and then whip into a velvety velouté, with a rich yet airy pine nut foam—a partnership that pairs perfectly with the delicacy of both the scallops and the sea urchin.

Scallops, Uni, Shiitake, Bok Choy, Pine Nuts

Season the scallops with the salt. In a large sauté pan, heat the grape seed oil over medium-high heat until it begins to shimmer but does not smoke. Put the scallops in the pan and leave them undisturbed until they begin to brown on the underside, about 2 minutes. Using a large spoon, gently turn the scallops and cook until the bottoms are just seared, about 2 minutes. (These scallops are delicate and if sourced properly, they should not be cooked more than medium-rare.) Transfer the scallops to a large plate and set aside to rest for 1 minute.

In another sauté pan, heat the olive oil over medium-high heat until it begins to shimmer. Cut each sous vide bok choy in half lengthwise, add to the pan, and cook until browned on the cut sides, 5–8 minutes. Transfer to a paper towel–lined plate to absorb any excess oil.

In a small saucepan, bring the pine nut foam base to a bare simmer. Using a funnel, transfer the warm mixture to the iSi canister and, following the manufacturer's instructions, charge 2 times with the nitrous oxide chargers. Keep warm in a pot of simmering water until ready to serve.

In a small saucepan, bring the shiitake velouté to a simmer over medium heat.

To serve, put 1 piece of bok choy in the center of each serving plate. Spoon the shiitake velouté in a large pool on one side of the plate, allowing it to flow over part of the bok choy. Artfully arrange the scallops, dividing evenly, and 3 cold sea urchin tongues on each plate. Extrude a small cloud of pine nut foam on the other side of the plate. Garnish each plate with 4 sea beans. Drizzle the chile oil in a small pool on top of the shiitake velouté. Using a Microplane grater, grate the pine nuts into a small pile over the pool of pine nut foam on each plate. Serve right away.

SOUS VIDE BOK CHOY

Bring a large pot three-fourths full of water to a boil over high heat. Put the bok choy, grape seed oil, and salt in a vacuum bag and vacuum seal. Put the bag in the boiling water and cook until the bok choy feels tender when the bag is gently squeezed, 3–5 minutes. Meanwhile, prepare an ice bath. When the bok choy is ready, transfer the bag to the ice bath and let cool completely, about 20 minutes. The cooled bok choy may be stored in the vacuum bag in the refrigerator for up to 3 days before using.

PINE NUT FOAM

Prepare an ice bath. In a 1-quart (1-l) saucepan, melt the butter over medium-high heat. When the butter has melted and begins to froth, whisk it until the solids start to brown and give off a nutty scent, 2–3 minutes. Add the pine nuts and gently toast them in the butter, stirring constantly until golden brown, 4–6 minutes. Add the milk and salt and bring to a simmer. Adjust the heat as needed to maintain a low simmer and cook for 5 minutes to infuse the flavors. Pulse the mixture with an immersion blender, then strain it through a fine-mesh sieve into a clean saucepan; discard the solids.

In a small bowl, whisk the egg yolks until blended. Whisk in a spoonful of the hot milk mixture, then whisk in a few more spoonfuls of hot milk to warm up the yolks. Return the yolk mixture to the saucepan while whisking constantly. Set the pan over low heat and warm the mixture to 185°F (85°C). Strain the mixture through a clean fine-mesh sieve into a metal bowl set over an ice bath and let cool completely, stirring occasionally and replenishing the ice as needed, about 30 minutes. The pine nut foam base may be stored in a lidded container in the refrigerator for up to 3 days before using.

SHIITAKE VELOUTÉ

In a large sauté pan, melt the butter over high heat and cook until it begins to brown, 2–3 minutes. Add the mushrooms, season lightly with salt, and sauté until the mushrooms release all of their liquid and the liquid evaporates, about 10 minutes. When the mushrooms appear dry, add the garlic and shallots and sauté for 2 minutes. Add the stock, bring to a simmer, and simmer for 15 minutes to infuse the flavors. Transfer the mixture to a blender and process until smooth. Add the vinegar, then taste and adjust the seasoning with salt, and keep warm until ready to serve. Alternatively, cool the velouté mixture completely in an ice bath and keep in a lidded container in the refrigerator for up to 3 days.

CHILE OIL

In a small saucepan, combine the chili powder, cayenne, paprika, and grape seed oil over medium heat and cook, stirring, until the mixture is aromatic, 3–5 minutes. Remove from the heat, cover, and set aside for 1 hour to steep. Strain the chile oil through a cheesecloth-lined fine-mesh sieve into a small bowl. The cooled chile oil may be stored in a lidded container at room temperature for up to 1 week.

HERE THE PARTNERSHIP OF EARTHY SAUTÉED SHIITAKE MUSHROOMS AND RICH & AIRY PINE NUT FOAM

PAIRS PERFECTLY WITH THE DELICACY OF BOTH

SCALLOPS AND SEA URCHIN

MICHAEL These small brioches have the look and feel of the freshly baked cinnamon rolls that we drooled over as kids. As you pull them from the oven, the heady, elusive aroma of truffles permeates your kitchen. The nori butter, made from finely ground seaweed and tangy whipped goat's milk, imparts a hint of the ocean to the dish. The finished breads deliver a wonderful balance of surf and earth, ingredients from opposite ends of the pantry.

Truffle Brioche, Nori-Goat Butter

MAIN INGREDIENTS

½ cup plus 4 teaspoons (150 g) whole milk, plus 2½ tablespoons (40 g)

2 tablespoons (16.8 g) active dry yeast

1⅔ cups (250 g) all-purpose flour

2 tablespoons (25 g) sugar

1 teaspoon (6 g) fine sea salt

4 large egg yolks

¾ cup plus ½ tablespoon (175 g) unsalted butter, diced

Truffle Coulis (below)

Nonstick cooking spray

1 large egg

Nori-Goat Butter (page 319)

Makes 22 brioche

TRUFFLE COULIS

5 ounces (140 g) canned truffle peelings

5 tablespoons plus 1 teaspoon (70 g) white truffle oil

¼ teaspoon (2 g) truffle salt (see sources)

Pour the ½ cup plus 4 teaspoons (150 g) milk into a microwave-safe bowl and cook on high power in 5-second bursts until the temperature reaches 80°–90°F (27°–32°C). Rain in the yeast and let stand until the yeast is hydrated, about 5 minutes. In a stand mixer fitted with the dough hook, combine the flour, sugar, and salt. On low speed, add the milk-yeast mixture. Add the egg yolks one at a time, mixing after each addition until fully incorporated. Add the butter bit by bit, mixing until all of it is fully absorbed. Increase the speed to medium and mix until the dough pulls away from the sides of the bowl, about 10 minutes. Remove the bowl from the mixer stand, cover with plastic wrap, and leave in a warm place until the dough doubles in size, about 1 hour.

Line a sheet pan with parchment paper. Use your hands to gently deflate the dough, then divide the dough in half. On a lightly floured work surface, using a rolling pin, roll out half of the dough into a 12-inch (30-cm) square about ⅛ inch (3 mm) thick. Spread half of the truffle coulis over the dough. Roll up the dough lengthwise into a tight log, and place it, seam side down, on the prepared pan. Repeat with the remaining dough and coulis to make a second log, and add it to the pan. Refrigerate the dough logs until firm to the touch, at least 1 hour or up to 24 hours.

Lightly spray two 10-inch (25-cm) round cake pans with cooking spray. Cut each dough log crosswise into 11 equal slices. Arrange the slices, cut sides down and evenly spaced, in the prepared pans and let stand in a warm spot until the dough rises and the slices look puffy, about 1 hour.

Preheat the oven to 375°F (190°C). In a small bowl, whisk together the egg and 2½ tablespoons (40 g) milk to make an egg wash and brush over the tops of the proofed rolls. Bake until golden brown, about 25 minutes. While still warm, brush with some of the nori butter and pass the extra.

TRUFFLE COULIS

In a blender, combine the truffle peelings, oil, and salt and process until smooth. The coulis may be stored in a lidded container in the refrigerator for up to 5 days before using.

BRYAN I grew up on oatmeal. Cinnamon and brown sugar were my toppings of choice, though honey or maple syrup sometimes ended up in the bowl, too—making it almost a dessert. That childhood memory made me decide to play with savory oatmeal. I wanted to create something that truly said umami, so I looked to mushrooms, yeast, and soy. But like all highly savory ingredients, they require a few balancing flavors; here, beer and lemon perform that role.

Forest Mushrooms en Papillote, Brown Butter, Beer, Fresh Yeast, Lemon, Oatmeal

MAIN INGREDIENTS

1 cup (225 g) plus 1 tablespoon (14 g) unsalted butter

½ teaspoon (3 g) fine sea salt

1¾ ounces (50 g) fresh yeast

Finely grated zest and juice of 1 lemon

½ cup (113 g) wheat beer

1 tablespoon plus ¾ teaspoon (25 g) soy sauce

2 shallots, minced

2 ounces (56 g) maitake mushrooms

2 ounces (56 g) black trumpet mushrooms

2 ounces (56 g) hedgehog mushrooms

2¾ ounces (78 g) honeycap mushrooms

¼ teaspoon (1.5 g) fine sea salt

2 large egg whites

1 tablespoon (14 g) water

¼ teaspoon (1.5 g) fine sea salt

Savory Oatmeal (below)

Equipment

6-quart (5.7-l) pressure cooker

Serves 6 as a first course

SAVORY OATMEAL

4 ounces (113 g) shiitake mushrooms

½ cup (90 g) steel-cut oats

¼ ounce (7.5 g) kombu, shredded

1 clove garlic, finely grated

1¾ cups (455 g) whole milk

½ teaspoon (3 g) fine sea salt

1 tablespoon (20 g) soy sauce

1 tablespoon (14 g) unsalted butter

In a small saucepan, combine the 1 cup (225 g) butter and ¼ teaspoon (1.5 g) of the salt over medium heat. Cook, stirring constantly, until the butter is golden brown and aromatic, 2–3 minutes. Add the yeast while whisking constantly, and cook until the yeast is aromatic and lightly browned, 2–3 minutes. Immediately add the lemon juice and then the beer. Finish the sauce with the soy sauce and lemon zest and remove from the heat and set aside.

In a small saucepan, melt the remaining 1 tablespoon (14 g) butter over medium heat. When it begins to brown, add the shallots and sauté, letting them brown slightly in the butter. Remove the pan from the heat. Put all of the mushrooms in a bowl. Add the shallots and half of the beer-yeast sauce and stir gently with a rubber spatula to coat the mushrooms evenly. Season with the remaining ¼ teaspoon (1.5 g) salt. Set the remainig sauce aside.

Cut 3 pieces of parchment paper, each 14 by 18 inches (36 by 46 cm), to make the papillotes. Fold 1 piece in half crosswise and, using scissors, cut it so it forms a heart shape when it is unfolded. Repeat with the other 2 pieces. Lay 1 parchment heart open, and brush it lightly with some of the remaining beer-yeast sauce. Put one-third of the mushroom mixture in the center of the heart, then fold the heart in half, covering the mushroom mixture. Starting at the pointed base of the heart, fold over about 1 inch (2.5 cm) of the open edge to make a very tight narrow fold. Continue to make tight, triangular-shaped folds, almost like pleating, along the outside edge of the folded heart, making a new fold about every ¾ inch (2 cm). Run your thumb firmly over each fold to make sure that the edges are tightly sealed. Continue folding over the edges around the folded heart until you come to the rounded top of the folded heart. Twist the ends of the paper heart securely to seal them.

In a small bowl, whisk together the egg whites and water until frothy. Brush the top and outer edges of the filled packet with the egg wash, and set the packet on a sheet pan.

IN THIS SAVORY TAKE ON A **CLASSIC SWEET BREAKFAST** FROM MY CHILDHOOD I COMBINED A VARIETY OF **SAVORY INGREDIENTS** TO CREATE A DISH THAT TRULY SAID **UMAMI**

Repeat with the remaining mushroom mixture and parchment sheets to make 2 more packets, and place each packet on a sheet pan.

Put the oatmeal on to cook (see below). While it is cooking, preheat the oven to 375°F (190°C). Bake the packets until the parchment has browned and puffed from the steam of the mushrooms (this is a good indication that the mushrooms have cooked completely), 15–20 minutes.

Warm the reserved beer-yeast sauce on a saucepan over medium heat until it barely simmers. Divide the cooked oatmeal among individual serving bowls and place 1 in front of each diner. Serve the packets tableside, 1 packet for every 2 people at the table, alongside the bowls of oatmeal. Use an immersion blender to emulsify the sauce, then pour over the oatmeal, dividing evenly.

SAVORY OATMEAL

Select a metal bowl that will fit inside the pressure cooker and is large enough to hold all of the ingredients. In the bowl, combine the mushrooms, oats, kombu, garlic, milk, salt, and soy sauce. Put a metal rack on the bottom of the pressure cooker, place the filled metal bowl on top, and pour water into the pressure cooker to reach halfway up the sides of the bowl. Following the manufacturer's instructions, lock the lid in place, bring up to high pressure, and cook for 5 minutes. Let the pressure dissipate naturally, then uncover, stir in the butter, and serve right away.

MICHAEL Morels grow best in areas of the forest that have recently been exposed to fire. The idea in this recipe is to take the mushroom back to where it was found and to explore its origin in the burnt earth. Pine, forest, ash—they all tell the story of the birth of the morel and are the basis for the flavors. I wanted this dish to do two things: to reveal the tale of how we source the ingredients and also to express their true aromas, tastes, and textures.

Morel Mushroom, Asparagus, "Burnt Forest" Butter

MAIN INGREDIENTS

Canola oil for deep-frying

½ cup (20 g) dried black trumpet mushrooms, finely shredded

Fine sea salt

1 tablespoon (14 g) unsalted butter

12 large morel mushrooms

3 tablespoons plus 2 teaspoons (50 g) dry vermouth

6 tablespoons (85 g) "Burnt Forest" Butter (below)

Asparagus (below)

1 head frisée

1 tablespoon (14 g) fresh lemon juice

Asparagus-Pine Cream (below)

Mushroom Quick Bread (below)

Equipment

bincho charcoal (optional; see sources)

pineapple corer or cannoli mold

6-quart (5.7-l) pressure cooker

high-speed blender

thermal immersion circulator

vacuum sealer and vacuum bags

masticating vegetable juicer

Serves 4 as a first course

PINE NEEDLE BUTTER

1 pound (450 g) unsalted butter

2 cups (100 g) pesticide-free fresh Douglas fir needles or rosemary needles, coarsely chopped (see sources)

››

Prepare a hot fire in a charcoal grill, preferably with bincho charcoal, or preheat a gas grill to high. Pour the canola oil into a tall-sided saucepan to a depth of 2½ inches (6 cm) and heat to 325°F (165°C).

Add the black trumpet mushrooms to the hot oil and fry until crisp, 10–20 seconds. Using a skimmer, transfer the fried mushrooms to a paper towel–lined plate and season lightly with salt.

In a small saucepan, melt the butter over medium-high heat. When it begins to froth, add the morel mushrooms and sauté until they begin to release their liquid, 3–5 minutes. Add the vermouth, cover the pan, and cook for 2 minutes. Uncover and continue to cook, stirring occasionally, until the wine has evaporated and pan is dry, 8–10 minutes. Add 2 tablespoons (28 g) of the "burnt forest" butter. Add the asparagus pieces and gently shake the pan until everything is warm and well coated with the butter.

Put the frisée head on the grill and cook, turning often, until charred on all sides, 5–8 minutes. Using kitchen scissors, snip the leaves into bite-sized pieces over a large bowl. Season the greens lightly with salt and the lemon juice and toss gently with your fingers to blend. Put the asparagus-pine cream in a small saucepan and warm over medium-low heat.

For each serving, brush a log of quick bread with burnt forest butter and place it in the center of the desired serving vessel or plate. Arrange the asparagus tips and pieces and the morels around the log. Put several dollops of the asparagus-pine cream on the plate and on the asparagus pieces. Put the charred frisée on the log and the asparagus pieces, then scatter the fried black trumpet mushrooms around the ingredients on the plate. Serve right away.

PINE NEEDLE BUTTER

Preheat the circulating water bath to 149°F (65°C).

In a large sauté pan, melt the butter over medium heat and cook, stirring, until the milk solids turn golden brown and the butter begins to smell nutty. Remove

"BURNT FOREST" BUTTER

3 large leeks, halved lengthwise

1 ounce (28 g) dried black trumpet mushrooms or dried porcini mushrooms

½ teaspoon (2 g) smoked Maldon salt

Pine Needle Butter (above)

1 teaspoon (2.7 g) black cocoa powder (see sources)

ASPARAGUS

4¼ cups (955 g) water

1 pound (450 g) jumbo asparagus

Fine sea salt

ASPARAGUS-PINE CREAM

Trimmings from Asparagus (above), plus more if needed

½ cup (120 g) heavy cream

4 teaspoons (17 g) sugar

2 pesticide-free Douglas fir needles or fresh rosemary sprigs

¼ teaspoon (1.5 g) fine sea salt

4 grams low-acyl gellan gum (see sources)

MUSHROOM PURÉE

2 cups plus 3½ tablespoons (500 g) water

8 ounces (225 g) fresh shiitake mushrooms, plus 12 ounces (350 g) fresh mushroom caps

1 ounce (28 g) dried shiitake mushrooms

3 tablespoons (45 g) soy sauce

½ ounce (15 g) kombu

1 bay leaf

MUSHROOM QUICK BREAD

Nonstick cooking spray

2 cups (230 g) cake flour

1½ teaspoons (9 g) baking powder

1 teaspoon (6 g) fine sea salt

5 large eggs

¾ cup (150 g) sugar

1 cup (250 g) Mushroom Purée (above)

½ cup (113 g) Pine Needle Butter (above), melted

from the heat and let cool to room temperature, about 10 minutes. Put the brown butter and fir needles in a vacuum bag and vacuum seal. Cook in the circulating water bath for 3 hours. Remove the bag from the water bath and let the butter cool to room temperature. Store in the bag in the refrigerator until ready to use, up to 1 week. You will use ½ cup (113 g) for the quick bread; the balance will be heated for making the "burnt forest" butter.

"BURNT FOREST" BUTTER

Preheat the oven to 375°F (190°C). Line a sheet pan with parchment paper.

Place the leeks on the prepared pan and roast until black and completely dry, about 3 hours. Remove from the oven and let cool to room temperature.

Break up the burnt leeks and add to the clean blender along with the dried mushrooms and smoked salt. Process until the mixture is an ashlike powder. Transfer to a small container. In a small saucepan, melt the pine needle butter over medium heat, then strain through a fine-mesh sieve placed over a small bowl. Mix just enough of the pine needle butter (at least 6 tablespoons/90 g) with the leek-mushroom powder to create a paintlike consistency. Keep the mixture warm, and reserve the remaining pine needle butter for another use.

ASPARAGUS

In a saucepan, bring the water to a boil over high heat. Pick out the 8 largest and prettiest asparagus spears. Reserve the rest of the bunch for the asparagus-pine cream, if needed. Cut 1 asparagus spear so you have the tip plus 2½ inches (6 cm) of the stem. Set the remainder of the stalk aside for the asparagus-pine cream. Using a paring knife, and cutting ¾ inch (2 cm) below the base of the tip, lightly score the asparagus all the way around the stem. Then, using your paring knife and the line as a guide, peel the green skin away from the stem below the line. Now, measure 1 inch (2.5 cm) down from the base of the tip and cut off the peeled stem. Divide the peeled stem crosswise into 2 equal pieces, leaving you with 3 pieces total, including the tip. Repeat with the remaining 7 spears. Season the boiling water generously with salt. Prepare an ice bath. Drop the asparagus pieces into the boiling water for 45 seconds. Remove from boiling water and shock briefly in the ice bath to halt the cooking. Transfer to a paper towel–lined plate to dry. The asparagus may be stored in a lock-top bag in the refrigerator for up to 3 days before using.

ASPARAGUS-PINE CREAM

Juice the asparagus trimmings with the juicer and weigh the juice. You need 1⅓ cups (300 g); if you do not have enough, juice some asparagus spears to supplement. Set aside. In a saucepan, combine the cream and sugar over medium heat and bring to a simmer. Remove from the heat, add the fir needles, cover the pan, and let steep for 5 minutes. Uncover, remove the fir needles, add the asparagus juice, place the pan over medium-high heat, and bring to a simmer. Strain the hot cream through a fine-mesh sieve into a blender. Turn the blender on to low speed. Slowly increase the speed until a vortex forms in the center of the liquid. Sprinkle in the salt and gellan gum and blend for a full 5 seconds to incorporate thoroughly. Transfer the mixture to a clean saucepan, place over medium-high heat, and bring back to a simmer. Pour the mixture into a shallow baking dish and refrigerate, uncovered, until cool and firmly set, about 45 minutes.

Using a spoon, scrape the gelled cream into the clean blender and process until a smooth purée forms. Taste for seasoning and adjust with salt. Blend for an additional 5 seconds. The cream may be stored in a lidded container in the refrigerator for up to 3 days.

MUSHROOM PURÉE

In the pressure cooker, combine the water, the 8 ounces (225 g) fresh shiitake mushrooms, the dried shiitake mushrooms, soy sauce, kombu, and bay leaf. Following the manufacturer's instructions, lock the lid in place, bring up to high pressure, and cook for 15 minutes. Let the pressure dissipate naturally, then uncover. Strain the mushroom stock through a fine-mesh sieve placed over a bowl, discarding the solids. Return the stock to the pressure cooker, add the 12 ounces (350 g) shiitake mushroom caps, lock the lid in place, bring up to high pressure, and cook for 5 minutes. Let the pressure dissipate naturally, then uncover.

Transfer the hot mushrooms and cooking liquid to the blender. Turn the blender on to low speed and slowly increase to high speed, processing until a smooth purée forms. Strain the purée through a fine-mesh strainer placed over a bowl. Discard the solids and let the purée cool to room temperature. The purée may be stored in a lidded container in the refrigerator for up to 3 days or frozen for up to 1 month before using.

MUSHROOM QUICK BREAD

Preheat a convection oven to 350°F (180°C) or a standard oven to 375°F (190°C). Spray a 9-by-5-inch (23-by-13-cm) loaf pan with cooking spray.

In a bowl, whisk together the flour, baking powder, and salt. In a stand mixer fitted with the whisk attachment, beat together the eggs and sugar on high speed until more than doubled in volume, pale yellow, and the mixture falls in a wide ribbon that slowly dissolves on the surface when the whisk is lifted, about 5 minutes. On low speed, add the flour mixture and beat until incorporated. Using a rubber spatula, fold in the mushroom purée and then the pine needle butter. Pour the batter into the prepared pan and smooth the top with an offset spatula. Bake until a cake tester inserted into the center of the bread comes out clean, about 1 hour. Let the bread cool in the pan on a rack until just warm, then unmold onto the rack and let cool to room temperature. Put the bread into a lock-top plastic bag and refrigerate until cold, about 2 hours.

Remove the bread from the refrigerator. Using the pineapple corer or cannoli mold, and working from the top of the loaf to the bottom, punch out 4 circular logs. Set the logs aside. Reserve the rest for making stuffing or snacking.

THE IDEA HERE WAS TO TAKE THE MOREL MUSHROOM BACK TO ITS ORIGIN BY EVOKING THE RECENTLY CHARRED WOODLANDS IN WHICH IT THRIVES

GOOSEFOOT

QUINOA
SPINACH & PURSLANE
BEET
SWISS CHARD

Deep, earthy flavors and bright colors characterize some of the best-known members of the goosefoot family, all qualities that we explore–and usually intensify–when we use them in recipes. Market bins display deep red, yellow-orange, gold, striped, and white beets and bunches of Swiss chard with stems in yellow, red, white, salmon, or hot pink—vibrant colors that make the vegetables as beautiful on the plate as they are flavorful on the palate. Protein-rich quinoa, the seed of a leafy South American goosefoot cousin, also comes in an array of colors, including gold, reddish brown, and black (and, less commonly, orange, pink, and purple). But it is quinoa's nutty flavor and slightly crunchy texture, not its color, that we usually emphasize in recipes, often contrasting it with more tender members of the same family.

MICHAEL Carrots baked in salt illustrates the idea of sourcing quality ingredients and leaving them largely unadorned. The same concept applies to the greens. On one table at the farmers' market there were carrots, on another assorted greens. The idea was to bring them together on one plate as today's market special. The carrots are not even peeled, just scrubbed and baked. The warm barley milk coats like a salad dressing, while the cereal adds a nutty crunch.

Heirloom Carrots Baked in Aromatic Salt, Barley Milk and Cereal, Purslane

MAIN INGREDIENTS

4⅓ cups (650 g) all-purpose flour

1 cup plus 2½ tablespoons (300 g) kosher salt

5 large egg whites (175 g)

1⅓ cups (300 g) water

4½ tablespoons (40 g) ras el hanout powder

Canola oil or nonstick cooking spray

12 kaffir lime leaves

20 petite heirloom carrots in assorted colors, tops removed and reserved and carrots scrubbed

2 tablespoons (28 g) extra-virgin olive oil

Barley Milk (below)

2 teaspoons (10 g) cold unsalted butter

Barley Cereal (below)

12 tiny fresh purslane leaves

12 leaves ultra spinach or other hearty young spinach leaves

12 sprigs petite rainbow Swiss chard

1 tablespoon (14 g) extra-virgin olive oil

Maldon sea salt

Equipment

food dehydrator (optional)

high-speed blender

deep fryer (optional)

Serves 4 as a first course

BARLEY MILK

4½ cups (1000 g) water

¾ teaspoon (4.5 g) fine sea salt

1½ cups (250 g) pearl barley

3 tablespoons plus 1 teaspoon (50 g) grade A maple syrup

BARLEY CEREAL

Reserved barley from making Barley Milk (above)

Canola oil for deep-frying

Fine sea salt

Preheat the oven to 375°F (190°C).

In a food processor, combine the flour, salt, egg whites, water, and ras el hanout and process until a smooth dough forms.

Lightly brush the back of a sheet pan with vegetable oil or spray with cooking spray. Divide the dough in half. On a lightly floured work surface, using a rolling pin, roll out half of the dough into a rough 8-by-10-inch (20-by-25-cm) rectangle about ⅛ inch (3 mm) thick. Using a paring knife and a straight edge, trim the edges so they are even, and then transfer the dough to the center of the prepared sheet pan. Spread out 6 of the lime leaves in the center of the dough. Arrange the carrots on top of the lime leaves. Drizzle 2 tablespoons (28 g) of the olive oil over the carrots. Lay the remaining lime leaves over the carrots. Roll out the remaining dough half in the same manner. Lay the second dough rectangle over the carrots, lining up the edges with the bottom rectangle. Using your fingers, crimp all 4 sides as if you are sealing a pie or strudel. Center the carrot packet on the pan.

Bake until the crust is golden brown and firm, about 30 minutes. Remove from the oven and let stand for 5 minutes.

To serve, put 1½ cups (360 g) of the barley milk in a small saucepan and bring to a simmer over medium heat. Whisk in the butter to thicken slightly. Using a serrated knife, carefully cut through the salt crust all the way around the outline of the carrots, creating a natural lid. Lift off the lid. Remove the carrots and put them on a cutting board. Cut the carrots into thirds. Using a variety of colors, arrange the carrots standing up in each bowl. Put several clusters of the fried barley cereal into the bowls. Put the purslane, spinach, and chard in another bowl and season lightly with olive oil and crushed Maldon salt. Arrange the greens in the bowls with the carrots and fried barley cereal.

Place 1 bowl in front of each diner. Pour the hot barley milk into the bowls at the table. Reserve the extra barley milk to add to bowls as the diners desire.

FOR THIS RECIPE I LET THE FARMERS' MARKET INSPIRE ME

CHOOSING CARROTS FROM ONE TABLE AND A VARIETY OF HEARTY GOOSEFOOT GREENS

FROM ANOTHER TO CREATE AN ORIGINAL DISH

BARLEY MILK

In a small saucepan, combine the water and salt and bring to a boil over high heat. Add the barley, bring the mixture back to a boil, and then reduce the heat to simmer. Cook the barley until tender, about 25 minutes.

Transfer the barley and the cooking liquid to the blender and pulse a few times to break up the barley into coarse pieces; you do not want a smooth mixture. Strain the mixture through a clean fine-mesh sieve, pressing the solids gently with the back of a small ladle and then reserve the solids for the barley cereal. Stir in the maple syrup and season to taste with salt. The cooled milk may be stored in a lidded container in the refrigerator for up to 3 days.

BARLEY CEREAL

Line a food dehydrator tray or a sheet pan with a silicone mat, and spread the barley on the mat. Place in the dehydrator set at 155°F (68°C) or an oven preheated to 175°F (80°C) until completely dry to the touch, about 1 hour.

Pour the canola oil into a deep fryer to the fill line or into a tall-sided saucepan to a depth of 2½ inches (6 cm) and heat to 350°F (180°C). Working in batches, add the dried barley pieces to the hot oil and fry until they puff up, about 5 seconds. Using a skimmer, transfer the puffed barley to a paper towel–lined sheet pan and season lightly with salt.

BRYAN This recipe is at once the expression of an idea, the demonstration of a technique, and the exploration of a theme. Beets are harvested from the soil, so I wanted to see what would happen if I cooked them in soil to emphasize their naturally earthy taste. I added aromatic herbs for flavor, and because soil is a great insulator, the beets retained their original size and shape during cooking. For a touch of whimsy, I created some edible "soil" for the plate.

Beet Winter Garden

MAIN INGREDIENTS

1 Chioggia beet
1 red radish
2 French breakfast radishes
2 black winter radishes
4 watermelon radishes, peeled
1 tablespoon (14 g) highest-quality extra-virgin olive oil
Fine sea salt
6 bundles hydroponically grown petite upland cress
Goat Cheese Mousse (below)
Garden "Soil" (below)
Soil-Roasted Beets (below)
Hay-Smoked Baby Carrots (below)
Balsamic Fluid Gel (below)
Orange Powder (below)
Fennel pollen
Beet Meringues (below)
2 ounces (57 g) aged goat cheese

Equipment

iSi canister with 1 N_2O charger (1-quart/.95-l canister)
high-speed blender
food dehydrator
masticating vegetable juicer
acetate sheet

Serves 6 as a first course

Using a mandoline, shave the Chioggia beet into paper-thin slices. Using a 3/4-inch (2-cm) diameter ring mold, cut the beet slices into uniform rounds. Set the beet rounds aside in ice water and discard the trimmings.

Using the mandoline, thinly slice the red radish, breakfast radishes, 1 black radish, and 1 watermelon radish. Using a 1-inch (2.5-cm) round mold, cut the black and watermelon radish slices into uniform rounds. Dice the remaining black and watermelon radishes. Put the sliced and diced radishes in a bowl and toss with the olive oil and a tiny pinch of salt.

Using kitchen scissors, clip the upland cress just about where the roots stop and the stems branch off. Discard the roots. Place in a container, cover with a damp kitchen towel, and refrigerate until ready to serve.

To serve, put 3 dollops of the goat cheese mousse in the center of the plate, spacing them evenly. Sprinkle the garden "soil" down the middle of the plate. Arrange the soil-roasted beets, 2 hay-smoked carrots, and the assorted radishes between the goat cheese dollops and on top of the soil. Accent the larger beets and diced radishes with the watermelon radish rounds. Put several dots of the balsamic fluid gel into the nooks of the composition. Season the ingredients with orange powder, fennel pollen, and cress leaves. Put 2 beet meringues on top of the salad and then grate the aged goat cheese over the meringues. Serve right away.

GOAT CHEESE MOUSSE

1½ cups (340 g) heavy cream
½ cup (125 g) fresh goat cheese
½ cup (120 g) whole milk
1 teaspoon (6 g) fine sea salt
2 large egg yolks

››

Prepare an ice bath. In a small saucepan, combine the cream, cheese, milk, and salt, place over medium heat, stirring to combine, and bring to a boil. Put the egg yolks in a heatproof bowl. Whisk in a few spoonfuls of the hot cream mixture to heat the egg yolks to lukewarm. Remove the cream mixture from the heat and quickly drizzle in the warm egg yolks while whisking constantly. Strain the mixture through a fine-mesh sieve into a metal bowl. Set the bowl over the ice bath and let cool completely.

Using a funnel, transfer the cooled cream mixture to the iSi canister, filling it three-fourths full. Following the manufacturer's instructions, charge with

BEETS COME FROM THE SOIL AND TASTE A BIT LIKE SOIL

SO I WANTED TO SEE WHAT WOULD HAPPEN IF I ACTUALLY COOKED THEM IN SOIL AND AROMATIC HERBS

1 nitrous oxide cartridge. Test the consistency of the mousse before use; it should look like shaving cream. If the texture is too runny, shake the can vigorously and then refrigerate for 30 minutes before testing again.

GARDEN "SOIL"

Preheat the oven to 175°F (80°C). Line a sheet pan with parchment paper.

In a food processor, combine the all-purpose flour, 2/3 cup (85 g) of the graham flour, 1/2 cup (50 g) of the almond flour, and the sugar and pulse a few times to blend evenly. With the machine running, slowly pour in the stout, stopping occasionally to scrape down the sides of the bowl to prevent lumps, until coarse crumbles resembling streusel form. Turn the crumbles out onto the prepared sheet pan. Bake until dry and fragrant, about 3 hours. Let the mixture cool to room temperature.

In a small bowl, whisk together the remaining 2 teaspoons (20 g) graham flour, the remaining 1/2 cup (50 g) almond flour, and the salt until blended. In a sauté pan, melt the butter over medium heat. Swirl the butter as it melts and then cook until the butter solids turn golden brown and release a warm, nutty aroma, 2–3 minutes. Immediately pour the brown butter into the flour mixture in the bowl and whisk until a paste forms.

In the food processor, combine the flour paste and the baked crumble and process until the mixture has the consistency of loose potting soil, 5–10 seconds. Transfer the mixture to a lock-top bag until needed. (It may be stored at room temperature for up to 1 week.)

SOIL-ROASTED BEETS

Preheat the oven to 300°F (150°C). In a large container, combine the salt and soil and stir to blend. Put 3 1/2 cups (210 g) of the soil mixture in a large baking dish. Put all of the beets and the garlic, thyme, and rosemary on top of the soil mixture. Cover with the remaining soil mixture. Cover the dish with aluminum foil and roast in the oven until the beets are tender, about 3 hours. Pierce a larger beet with a cake tester to make sure they are done. Let the beets cool in the soil for 30 minutes, then dig them out and finish cooling them at room temperature. Discard the soil mixture, garlic, and herbs.

Rinse the beets with warm running water. Use a kitchen towel to wipe them dry and peel off the skins. Cut the beets into quarters. The beets may be stored separately in lidded containers in the refrigerator for up to 3 days.

HAY-SMOKED BABY CARROTS

Put the hay in a 3-quart (2.8-l) heavy-bottomed pot, cover with a layer of cheesecloth, and then with the lid. Place over medium heat until the hay begins to smoke and smolder. Quickly put the carrots on top of the cheesecloth and immediately re-cover the pot. Turn the heat down to low so the hay continues to smoke steadily and cook the carrots until they are just tender, about 30 minutes. Let cool to room temperature. The carrots are best served the day they are cooked but they may be stored in a lidded container in the refrigerator for up to 2 days.

BALSAMIC FLUID GEL

In a small saucepan, bring the vinegar just to a simmer over medium heat. Pour the hot vinegar into a blender. Turn on the blender to low speed, then slowly increase the speed until a vortex forms in the center of the liquid. Sprinkle in the gellan gum and continue to process until it is completely absorbed, a full 5 seconds. Pour the vinegar mixture into a shallow bowl or baking dish and let cool at room temperature until set, about 30 minutes.

Dice the gel and transfer it to a clean blender. Process for a few seconds until a smooth, fluid gel forms. The fluid gel may be stored in a lidded container in the refrigerator for up to 3 days. About 30 minutes before serving, remove the gel from the refrigerator and bring to room temperature.

ORANGE POWDER

Using a Microplane grater, remove the zest from the oranges; reserve the fruit for another use. Line a food dehydrator tray with a silicone mat or parchment paper, and spread the zest on the mat. Place in the dehydrator set at 155°F (68°C) until dry, about 3 hours. Transfer the cooled dried zest to a spice grinder and grind to a fine powder. The orange powder may be stored in a lidded container at room temperature for up to 5 days.

BEET MERINGUES

Juice the beets with the vegetable juicer. Prepare an ice bath. Put the beet juice in a small saucepan and bring to a simmer over medium heat. Immediately strain the hot beet juice through a fine-mesh sieve placed over a metal bowl. Set the bowl over the ice bath and let cool, stirring occasionally and replenishing the ice as needed, until completely cold, about 10 minutes. Measure the juice; you will need a total of 1¼ cups plus 1 tablespoon (300 g). Drink the rest of the juice, or discard.

Pour ¾ cup plus 2 tablespoons (200 g) of the beet juice into a small saucepan. Add the gelatin sheets and let soak until softened, about 5 minutes. Once the gelatin sheets are softened, place the pan over medium heat and warm the juice, stirring constantly, until the gelatin dissolves. Remove from the heat. Put the remaining 7 tablespoons (100 g) beet juice in the blender. Turn on the blender to low speed, then slowly increase the speed until a vortex forms in the center of the liquid. Sprinkle in the egg white powder and process until thoroughly combined. With the machine running, add the Methocel, sugar, and salt and then slowly pour in the beet-gelatin liquid and blend for a full 5 seconds. Transfer the mixture to a stand mixer fitted with the whisk attachment and whip on high speed until the mixture forms stiff peaks, 8–12 minutes.

Line a food dehydrator tray or a sheet pan with the acetate sheet. Transfer the mixture to a pastry bag fitted with a #12 plain tip (the hole is smaller than a dime). Pipe 3-inch (7.5-cm) logs onto the acetate-lined tray, spacing the logs 1 inch (2.5 cm) apart. Place the meringues in the dehydrator set at 140°F (60°C) or in an oven preheated to 175°F (80°C) until completely dry, at least 3 hours. Peel the meringues from the acetate sheet and store in an airtight container at room temperature until ready to serve, up to 5 days.

GARDEN "SOIL"

1⅔ cups (250 g) all-purpose flour

⅔ cup (85 g) plus 2 teaspoons (20 g) graham flour (see sources)

1 cup (100 g) almond flour

2 teaspoons (8.2 g) sugar

⅓ cup (75 g) oatmeal stout

1 teaspoon (6 g) fine sea salt

4 tablespoons (60 g) unsalted butter, diced

SOIL-ROASTED BEETS

1¼ cups (360 g) fine sea salt

9 cups (600 g) organic garden soil

7 Chioggia beets

6 small ruby beets

6 golden beets

6 white beets

2 golden rod beets

6 cloves garlic, sliced

2 fresh thyme sprigs

2 fresh rosemary sprigs

HAY-SMOKED BABY CARROTS

4 ounces (113 g) organic timothy hay or alfalfa (see sources)

6 baby red carrots, wiped dry

6 baby orange carrots, wiped dry

BALSAMIC FLUID GEL

4½ tablespoons (90 g) six-year-old balsamic vinegar

.9 gram low-acyl gellan gum (see sources)

⅛ teaspoon (.75 g) fine sea salt

ORANGE POWDER

2 oranges

BEET MERINGUES

3 large red beets

2 sheets silver-grade leaf gelatin (see sources)

5 tablespoons (25 g) egg white powder

1.4 grams Methocel F50 (see sources)

2½ teaspoons (10 g) sugar

¼ teaspoon (1.5 g) fine sea salt

BRYAN The best eggs around are produced by Will Morrow of Whitmore Farm. I was first intrigued by Will's eggs because they looked like Easter eggs straight out of the carton, and because he writes the names of the chickens on the eggs so you know who laid them. The vision of chickens wandering through grass and flowers inspired the dish. To celebrate their rich, orange-gold yolks, the eggs are cooked in toasty brown butter, which complements the nutty quinoa.

Quinoa, Farm Egg, Flowers, Hearts of Palm, Radish

MAIN INGREDIENTS

1 cup (225 g) unsalted butter

Leaves from 2 fresh thyme sprigs

6 highest-quality farm-fresh large organic eggs

2 celery ribs

1 watermelon radish, thinly sliced on a mandoline

5⅓ ounces (150 g) fresh hearts of palm

36 fresh chive blossoms (from about 2 flowering chives)

30 Johnny Jump Up flowers

30 lucky sorrel leaves

30 borage flowers

Thyme Gel (below)

Quinoa and Swiss Chard (below)

2 teaspoons (10 g) Minus 8 wine vinegar (see sources)

¼ teaspoon (.8 g) Maldon salt

Fine sea salt

2 teaspoons (10 g) extra-virgin olive oil

Equipment

thermal immersion circulator

vacuum sealer and vacuum bags

6-quart (5.7-l) pressure cooker

Serves 6 as a first course or light main course

››

In a large sauté pan, melt the butter over medium heat. Once it is completely melted, stir the butter with a silicone spatula until it begins to brown and smells like toasted nuts, 20–30 seconds. Remove from the heat and add the thyme leaves. Let cool for 10 minutes, then strain the brown butter through a fine-mesh sieve into a bowl. Discard the thyme leaves.

Preheat the circulating water bath to 145°F (63°C).

Separate the eggs, keeping the yolks whole and reserving the whites for another use. Carefully add the whole egg yolks and the brown butter to a vacuum bag and vacuum seal as gently as possible, taking care not to break the yolks. Cook in the circulating water bath for 30 minutes.

Meanwhile, peel the celery ribs and, using the peeler, cut into wide strips about ½ inch (12 mm) wide and 4 inches (10 cm) long. Store in ice water until ready to serve. Using a 1-inch (2.3 cm) round cutter, cut the radish slices into rounds. Store in ice water until ready to serve. Using a sharp knife, peel away the fibrous outer layer of the hearts of palm to expose the tender centers. Using the mandoline, slice the trimmed hearts into rounds 1⁄10 inch (2.5 mm) thick. Put the rounds in a bowl and cover with a damp kitchen towel until ready to kitchen towels until ready to serve.

To serve, using a 4-inch (10-cm) round cutter, cut the thyme gel into 6 rounds and leave on the pan. Put about 3 tablespoons of the warm quinoa and chard mixture in the center of each plate, and make a small indentation in the center. Pour the eggs and brown butter from the vacuum bag into a small bowl. Transfer about 2 tablespoons of the brown butter to another small bowl, add the vinegar, and whisk to combine. Put an egg yolk in the center of each quinoa portion, and season each yolk with a little of the Maldon salt.

Using a small offset spatula, lift the thyme gel rounds from the sheet pan and lay 1 round on top of each egg yolk to resemble an egg white. Spoon the brown butter–vinegar mixture around each plate.

Dry the celery on paper towels. Put the celery, hearts of palm, and radish rounds in a bowl and season with fine sea salt and 1 teaspoon (5 g) of the extra-virgin olive oil. In another bowl, toss the herbs and flowers with fine sea salt and the remaining extra-virgin olive oil. Arrange the mixture around the quinoa on each plate, dividing it evenly. Artfully arrange the dressed radishes, hearts of palm, and celery curls around the plate and serve right away.

THYME STOCK

In the pressure cooker, combine the water, thyme, and salt. Following the manufacturer's instructions, lock the lid in place, bring up to high pressure, and cook for 4 minutes. Let the pressure dissipate naturally, then uncover.

Prepare an ice bath. Strain the stock through a fine-mesh sieve placed over a metal bowl. Set the bowl over the bath and let cool, stirring occasionally and replenishing the ice as needed, until completely cold, about 15 minutes. The stock may be stored in a lidded container in the refrigerator for up to 3 days.

THYME GEL

Put the gelatin sheet in a small bowl of ice water and let soak until softened, about 5 minutes. In a small saucepan, combine the thyme stock, glucose, and agar, place over medium-high heat, and bring to a boil. Reduce the heat to maintain a low boil and boil for a full 5 minutes. Remove from the heat. Lift out the gelatin sheet, squeeze out the excess water, and add to the stock mixture along with the thyme leaves. Stir to dissolve the gelatin, then pour the liquid into a 9-by-13 inch (23-by-33 cm) baking pan, forming a thin layer in the bottom. Refrigerate, uncovered, until set, about 30 minutes. The thyme gel will keep in the refrigerator, covered, for up to 3 days.

QUINOA AND SWISS CHARD

Rinse the quinoa well in cold water. Repeat the rinse 2 more times. Remove the hard stems from the chard and cut the stems into small dice. Cut the leaves into chiffonade (thin ribbons) and refrigerate until needed. Put the rinsed quinoa, diced stems, stock, shallot, garlic, and salt in the pressure cooker. Following the manufacturer's instructions, lock the lid in place, bring up to high pressure, and cook for 4 minutes. Let the pressure dissipate naturally, then uncover. Fold in the chard leaves and serve immediately.

THYME STOCK

4½ cups (1000 g) water

1 bunch fresh thyme

1 teaspoon (6 g) fine sea salt

THYME GEL

1 sheet silver-grade leaf gelatin (see sources)

1 cup plus 2 tablespoons (250 g) Thyme Stock (above)

2¾ teaspoons (25 g) liquid glucose

1.25 grams agar

Leaves from 10 fresh thyme sprigs

QUINOA AND SWISS CHARD

½ cup (95 g) quinoa

½ bunch rainbow chard

1 cup (225 g) Thyme Stock (above)

1 shallot, minced

1 clove garlic, finely grated on a Microplane grater

¼ teaspoon (1.5 g) fine sea salt

MICHAEL For this recipe, I was inspired by two members of the goosefoot family, beets and quinoa. I started with the beets, using their earthy flavor and striped colors as the focal point of the dish. Then, I layered on crispy quinoa cereal to form a contrast with the tender vegetable. The yogurt provides an acidic creaminess, and the chicken skin is crunchy and aromatic with curry powder. This dish could be treated like chips and dip, or like a fun-to-eat finger salad.

Young Beets, Red Quinoa, Chicken Skin, Yogurt

MAIN INGREDIENTS

28 young Chioggia beets

6 tablespoons (84 g) extra-virgin olive oil, plus more for dressing greens

1 tablespoon (18 g) fine sea salt, plus more to season

Red Quinoa Cereal (below)

Yogurt Foam (below)

Fried Chicken Skin (below)

Leaves from 8 small sprigs purslane

Maldon sea salt

Chicken Jus (below)

Equipment

food dehydrator (optional)

deep fryer (optional)

iSi canister with 2 N_2O chargers (1-quart/.95-l canister)

6-quart (5.7-l) pressure cooker

Serves 4 as a first course

Preheat the oven to 375°F (190°C).

Trim the beet stems to a length of about ½ inch (12 mm) but do not peel. Put the beets in a bowl and gently toss with 4 tablespoons (56 g) of the olive oil and the 1 tablespoon (18 g) salt. Cut four 10-inch (25-cm) squares of aluminum foil, and put 7 beets in the center of each square. Evenly divide the olive oil left in the bowl among the 4 groups of beets. Working with 1 batch at a time, fold over the aluminum foil on each side to create a pouch, crimping all of the edges to form a secure package. Put the foil packages on a sheet pan.

Roast the beets until they are tender, about 35 minutes. Remove the packages from the oven and let them stand for 10 minutes. Open the packages and, using a paring knife, carefully peel the beets, leaving the long root tips intact.

To serve, put the beets in a large bowl, sprinkle with the fried quinoa, and toss to coat evenly. Put 3 beets in the center of each plate. Place a piece of fried chicken skin in front of the beets. Extrude the yogurt foam into a small bowl. Using a small spoon, put 3 spoonfuls of the yogurt foam on and around the chicken skin and beets on each plate. Put the purslane in a small bowl and season with olive oil and crushed Maldon salt. Arrange the dressed purslane on the beets. Sprinkle a small amount of the fried quinoa on the plate around the beets. Drizzle the chicken jus around the plate and serve right away.

RED QUINOA CEREAL

2⅔ cups (600 g) water

⅓ teaspoon (2 g) fine sea salt, plus more to season

¼ cup plus 1 teaspoon (50 g) red quinoa

Canola oil

In a small saucepan, combine the water and salt over medium-high heat and bring to a boil. Add the quinoa, reduce the heat to medium, and simmer until the quinoa is slightly overcooked, about 35 minutes.

Strain the quinoa through a fine-mesh sieve and rinse under cold running water to remove any excess starch. Line a food dehydrator tray or a sheet pan with a silicone mat, and spread the quinoa on the mat. Place in the food dehydrator set at 155°F (68°C) or an oven preheated to 175°F (80°C) until completely dry, about 1 hour and 10 minutes.

››

YOGURT FOAM

9 ounces (250 g) Fage plain Greek-style yogurt

2 tablespoons plus 2 teaspoons (40 g) water

¼ teaspoon (1.5 g) fine sea salt

FRIED CHICKEN SKIN

7 ounces (200 g) chicken skin, excess fat removed

4¼ cups (955 g) water

Canola oil for deep-frying

½ teaspoon (3 g) fine sea salt

1 tablespoon (9 g) Curry Powder (page 318)

1 tablespoon (18 g) fine sea salt

CHICKEN JUS

3 tablespoons (42 g) canola oil

1 pound (450 g) chicken wings

½ yellow onion, diced

1 carrot, diced

2 ribs celery, diced

4½ cups (1000 g) Chicken Stock (page 319)

4 teaspoons (20 g) brown butter

Pour the canola oil into a deep fryer to the fill line or into a tall-sided saucepan to a depth of 2½ inches (6 cm) and heat to 375°F (190°C).

Working in batches, add the dried quinoa to the hot oil and fry until it puffs and stops crackling, about 5 seconds. Using a skimmer, transfer immediately to a paper towel–lined sheet pan and season lightly with salt. The fried quinoa can be stored in an airtight container at room temperature for up to 2 days.

YOGURT FOAM

In a blender, combine the yogurt, water, and salt and process on medium speed for 1 minute. Using a funnel, transfer the yogurt mixture to the iSi canister. Following the manufacturer's instructions, charge 2 times with the nitrous oxide chargers. Shake vigorously and refrigerate until ready to serve.

FRIED CHICKEN SKIN

In the pressure cooker, combine the chicken skin and water. Following the manufacturer's instructions, lock the lid in place, bring up to high pressure, and cook for 25 minutes. Let the pressure dissipate naturally, then uncover.

Line a food dehydrator tray or a sheet pan with a silicone mat, and spread the chicken skin evenly on the mat. Place in the dehydrator set at 155°F (68°C) or in an oven preheated to 175°F (80°C) until completely dry, about 4 hours.

Pour the canola oil into a deep fryer to the fill line or into a tall-sided saucepan to a depth of 2½ inches (6 cm) and heat to 400°F (200°C). Break up the dehydrated chicken skin into bite-sized pieces. Working in batches, add the chicken skin pieces to the hot oil and fry until puffed and crispy, about 5 seconds. Using a skimmer, immediately transfer to a paper towel–lined sheet pan and season with the curry powder and salt. The skin pieces are best served right away.

CHICKEN JUS

Set a 6-quart (5.7-l) pressure cooker over medium-high heat and add the oil. When the oil begins to shimmer, add the chicken wings and sear on both sides, 6–8 minutes total. Add the onion, carrot, and celery and sauté until caramelized, 5–8 minutes. Add the stock and then close the lid. Following the manufacturer's instructions, cook at high pressure for 45 minutes and then let the pressure dissipate naturally. Strain the contents of the pot through a fine-mesh sieve into a clean saucepan. Set the pan over medium-high heat and cook until the liquid is reduced to the consistency of maple syrup, 30–45 minutes. Remove the pan from the heat and whisk in the brown butter. Keep the chicken jus warm until ready to serve.

GOURD

KABOCHA SQUASH
BUTTERNUT SQUASH
ZUCCHINI
MELON

Every summer and fall, we look forward to feasting on this family. One reason we favor it is that it is so wildly varied, with squashes, melons, cucumbers, and pumpkins among its marquee members. In the warm months, we like to experiment with all kinds of melons, in search of new ways to show off their sweet flesh, aromatic fragrance, and pastel colors. In the cooler months, we turn to the hard-skinned squashes, such as butternut and kabocha, which take to all kinds of preparations—roasted, pickled, made into sweet preserves, cooked in a water bath, and more. Many chefs consider the zucchini bland, too prosaic for fine dining. That challenge is met here with the addition of a little fire and a sprinkle of smoked sugar.

MICHAEL Korean barbecue, which I like to eat on my days off, is the inspiration here. I started with a quick version of bok choy kimchi, and then used the juices from it to make an even quicker kimchi of kabocha squash. The third element is kabocha preserves, a sweet, sour, rich mixture that perfectly balances the crunchy saltiness of the other two ingredients. The moment I pull the hot pink prawns off the grill, I begin dipping, spreading, and crunching my way through the meal.

Spot Prawns Roasted over Hot Coals, Caramelized and Kimchi Bok Choy, Japanese Pumpkin Preserves

MAIN INGREDIENTS

30 live Santa Barbara spot prawns

Quick Bok Choy Kimchi (below)

Quick Kabocha Kimchi (below)

⅓ cup (100 g) Kabocha Squash Preserves (page 318)

7 tablespoons (100 g) pumpkin seed oil

Equipment

10 sticks bincho charcoal (optional) and small charcoal grill

vacuum sealer and vacuum bags

thermal immersion circulator (optional)

Serves 6 as a family-style main course

QUICK BOK CHOY KIMCHI

3 quarts plus ¾ cup (3000 g) bottled spring water

1 cup plus 6 tablespoons plus 1 teaspoon (400 g) fine sea salt

2 pounds (900 g) baby or ultra baby bok choy, stem ends trimmed

7 ounces (200 g) fresh ginger, peeled and thinly sliced

3½ ounces (100 g) garlic, crushed

5 tablespoons (100 g) Asian fish sauce

5 tablespoons plus 2 teaspoons (80 g) Asian sesame oil

4½ tablespoons (80 g) Korean red chile powder (see sources)

1¼ cups (400 g) rice vinegar

QUICK KABOCHA KIMCHI

½ kabocha squash, about 1 pound (450 g), peeled and seeded

½ cup (113 g) cooking liquid from Quick Bok Choy Kimchi (above)

Heat the charcoal directly over a gas burner turned on to a high flame, or ignite using a charcoal chimney starter, until it turns white. Using tongs, transfer the charcoal to the grill. Alternatively, prepare a fire in a charcoal grill with regular charcoal so the coals are white hot. Place the grill rack on the grill. When the grill rack is hot, lay the spot prawns on the rack and cook for 2 minutes on the first side. Using tongs, flip the prawns and cook on the second side until the heads swell and the juices are just starting to boil, about 2 minutes longer. Transfer the prawns to a large serving platter, arranging them attractively. Put the bok choy kimchi and the kabocha kimchi into separate serving bowls. Spoon the squash preserves into a third serving bowl, and form an indentation in the center. Pour the pumpkin seed oil into the indentation. Serve right away.

QUICK BOK CHOY KIMCHI

In a bowl, whisk together the water and salt until the salt dissolves. Add the bok choy, cover with plastic wrap, and top with a heavy plate to keep the bok choy submerged. Refrigerate for 4 hours.

Drain the bok choy, discarding the brine, but do not rinse. In a blender, combine the ginger, garlic, fish sauce, sesame oil, chile powder, and vinegar and process until completely smooth. Divide the bok choy evenly among 5 vacuum bags, add an equal amount of the marinade to each bag, and vacuum seal. Leave the bags of kimchi at room temperature in a dark spot for 24 hours.

Open the bags, transfer the bok choy to a lidded container, and reserve the marinade. The bok choy may be stored in the refrigerator for up to 2 weeks.

QUICK KABOCHA KIMCHI

Using a mandoline, slice the kabocha squash ⅛ inch (3 mm) thick. Put the slices in a bowl with the reserved kimchi marinade and toss them together to coat the squash thoroughly. Transfer everything to a vacuum bag and vacuum seal. The kabocha kimchi may be stored in the refrigerator for up to 2 weeks.

BRYAN The most intriguing element in this dish is the marriage of chestnuts and cream soda. That combination came about one fall when I was developing a new cocktail. Chestnuts were in season, so I decided to cook them in cream soda and then dry them. The result was an amazing vanilla cream soda with roasted undertones that is both savory and sweet and carries the aromas of autumn. Here, it perfectly accents the rich, meaty texture of slow-cooked squash.

Butternut Squash, Squash Consommé, Chestnuts, Brussels Sprouts, Pumpkin Seed Oil

MAIN INGREDIENTS

3 butternut squashes, about 6 pounds (2.75 kg) total weight

½ teaspoon (3 g) fine sea salt

1½ cups plus 1 tablespoon (350 g) cooking liquid reserved from Chestnut Preparations (below)

Xanthan gum (see sources)

Brussels Sprouts (below)

1 tablespoon (14 g) extra-virgin olive oil

1 tablespoon (14 g) unsalted butter

Chestnut Preparations (below)

Pumpkin seed oil

Equipment

thermal immersion circulator

masticating vegetable juicer

vacuum sealer and vacuum bags

high-speed blender

food dehydrator (optional)

Serves 6 as a first course

››

Cut the top and bottom off each butternut squash. Stand the squash upright on a cutting board and, using a sharp knife, cut downward to remove the skin in strips, rotating the squash as you go. Lay the squash on its side and cut crosswise, separating the bulb end from the neck. Cut the bulb end into quarters and remove and reserve the seeds. Cut the neck crosswise into 4 slices, each 1 inch (2.5 cm) thick. Then, using a 1-inch (2.5-cm) ring mold, punch out rounds from each slice. Reserve the trimmings for juicing. Repeat with the remaining 2 squashes. You should end up with 12 rounds total; reserve any neck pieces for juicing.

Preheat the circulating water bath to 185°F (85°C).

Juice all of the trimmings and the quartered bulb ends of the squashes. Strain the juice through a fine-mesh sieve placed over a bowl; you should have about 1½ cups plus 1 tablespoon (350 g) juice. Add the salt, then transfer the juice to a vacuum bag, add the squash rounds, and vacuum seal. Cook the squash in the circulating water bath for 1 hour.

Remove the bag from the water bath and set aside for 10 minutes. Prepare an ice bath. Transfer the squash, still in the bag, to the ice bath and let cool completely, replenishing the ice as needed, about 30 minutes.

Open the bag, remove the squash rounds, and set aside. (The squash rounds may be stored in a lidded container in the refrigerator until ready to serve, up to 3 days.) Strain the squash juice through a fine-mesh sieve placed over a saucepan. Then strain the chestnut cooking liquid through the fine-mesh sieve placed over the same pan. Put the pan over medium-high heat and bring to just below a simmer. The liquid will separate. Remove from the heat and strain through a cheesecloth-lined fine-mesh sieve. Weigh the liquid and calculate .1 percent of the weight. Weigh out the same amount of xanthan gum. Pour the strained liquid into the blender and turn the blender on to low speed. Slowly increase the speed until a vortex forms in the center of the liquid. Sprinkle in

THE MOST **EXCITING ELEMENT** OF THIS DISH IS THE **CHESTNUT** CREAM SODA WHICH IS A **SWEET-AND-SAVORY BASE** THAT CARRIES THE AROMAS OF **FALL**

the xanthan gum and blend for a full 5 seconds until completely dissolved and the liquid has thickened slightly to make a consommé. The consommé may be stored in a lidded container in the refrigerator until ready to serve, up to 3 days.

To serve, put the squash rounds in a saucepan and add 6 tablespoons (85 g) of the consommé. Place the pan over medium heat until the squash is warmed through, 5–8 minutes, then add the Brussels sprout leaves. Pour the remaining consommé into another saucepan, place over medium-low heat, and bring to a bare simmer. In a large sauté pan, heat the olive oil over medium heat until it begins to shimmer but does not smoke. Add the Brussels sprouts and cook, turning them so they caramelize evenly, until browned, 5–8 minutes. Transfer the Brussels sprouts to a warmed plate.

In another sauté pan, melt the butter over medium heat. When it begins to froth, add the chestnuts and brown them on both sides, 3–5 minutes per side. Handle them gently, or they may fall apart when you turn them. Transfer the nuts to a paper towel–lined plate. Place 2 squash rounds, slightly offset from one another, to the left of center in each serving bowl. One should stand vertically and one should stand horizontally. Artfully arrange 2 chestnuts and 8 pieces of Brussels sprouts in each serving bowl. Pour the consommé around the vegetables and then garnish with a few drops of pumpkin seed oil, the Brussels sprout leaves, and the dried chestnuts. Serve right away.

BRUSSELS SPROUTS

Remove and discard any tough or brown outer leaves from each Brussels sprout, then trim the bottom. Remove 3 pretty leaves from each sprout, and set the 36 leaves aside. Cut each Brussels sprout in half vertically so the leaves remain attached to a bit of the core, and set the sprout halves aside.

Bring a large pot of water to a boil over high heat. While the water is heating, prepare 2 ice baths. Add the leaves to the boiling water and blanch until bright green and just tender, about 30 seconds. Using a skimmer, transfer the leaves to an ice bath. Let the leaves cool briefly, then drain immediately. Add the Brussels sprout halves to the boiling water and cook until barely tender, about 3 minutes. Using the skimmer, transfer to the second ice bath to cool briefly, then drain and pat dry with paper towels. Cut each Brussels sprout half in half; you will end up with 48 quarters. The Brussels sprout leaves and the quartered Brussels sprouts may be stored in separate lidded containers in the refrigerator for up to 3 days before using.

CHESTNUT PREPARATIONS

Preheat the circulating water bath to 189°F (87.5°C).

Put the chestnuts and cream soda in a vacuum bag and vacuum seal. Cook in the circulating water bath for 45 minutes; the chestnuts should feel tender when gently squeezed through the bag. Remove the bag from the water bath and let the chestnuts cool to room temperature in the bag, about 1 hour.

Drain the chestnuts through a fine-mesh sieve placed over a bowl, reserving both the nuts and the liquid. Set the liquid aside for making the consommé. Put 12 of the chestnuts in a lidded container in the refrigerator. Put the remaining 6 chestnuts in the freezer until frozen solid, at least 2 hours.

When the 6 chestnuts are frozen, thinly slice them on a mandoline. Line a food dehydrator tray or a sheet pan with a silicone mat, and arrange the slices in a single layer on the mat. Place in the dehydrator set at 150°F (65°C) or the oven preheated to 175° (80°C) until crisp, about 2 hours. The dried chestnut slices may be stored in an airtight container at room temperature for up to 1 week.

BRUSSELS SPROUTS

12 Brussels sprouts

CHESTNUT PREPARATIONS

18 peeled chestnuts

One 12-ounce (340 g) bottle Boylan's cream soda

⅓ teaspoon (2 g) fine sea salt

MICHAEL I like the sweet nuttiness of caramelized roasted winter squash. Here, I wanted to try to achieve that same quality with summer squash, though with more subtle effect. I prefer to use the seed section of the summer squash, which most cooks throw away but is my favorite part of the vegetable. I sprinkle it lightly with smoked sugar, which seems to intensify its flavor, and then I use a blowtorch to lightly caramelize the seed section to further heighten its sweetness.

Zucchini Tenderloin, "Lambcetta," Pickled Lamb's Tongue, Green Apple Purée

MAIN INGREDIENTS

2 cups plus 4 tablespoons (300 g) fine sea salt, plus more to season

3/4 cup (150 g) sugar

4 1/2 teaspoons (30 g) pink curing salt (see sources)

2 tablespoons (12 g) chopped fresh rosemary

4 tablespoons (22 g) chopped fresh thyme

3 tablespoons (18 g) ground pastrami pepper: 1 part Tellicherry peppercorns, 1 part pink peppercorns, 1 part long pepper (see sources), 1/2 part Sichuan peppercorns

4 cloves garlic

1 tablespoon (6 g) juniper berries

3 bay leaves

2 tablespoons (14 g) fennel seeds

4 whole cloves

2 lamb bellies

Canola oil for deep-frying

Pickled Lamb's Tongues (below)

1 green apple

Extra-virgin olive oil

Maldon sea salt

Zucchini Purée (below)

Zucchini Tenderloins (below)

Smoked Sugar (below)

Green Apple Purée (below)

Olive Powder (below)

Baby mint leaves for garnish

Equipment

thermal immersion circulator

vacuum sealer and vacuum bags

deli-style meat slicer or electric knife

food dehydrator (optional)

deep-fryer (optional)

high-speed blender

kitchen blowtorch

smoking gun and applewood chips

Serves 4 as a first course

››

To make a salt cure, in a food processor, combine the salt, sugar, pink curing salt, rosemary, thyme, pastrami pepper, garlic, juniper berries, bay leaves, fennel seeds, and cloves. Pulse until all of the ingredients are uniformly ground and incorporated. Line an 8-by-13-inch (20-by-33-cm) sheet pan with parchment paper. Spread half of the salt cure mixture on the sheet pan. Put the lamb bellies on top of the cure, leaving 2 inches (5 cm) of space between them. Cover the bellies with the remaining cure, mounding it around them so that they are completely covered. Loosely cover the pan with plastic wrap and refrigerate the bellies to cure for 12 hours.

Preheat the circulating water bath to 136.4°F (58°C).

Rinse the curing mixture from the lamb bellies under cold running water. Pat the bellies dry with paper towels. Lay 1 belly on a large sheet of plastic wrap, and roll it up in the sheet so that it forms a log. Tie both ends of the plastic wrap with cotton butcher's twine, cinching the ends tightly so a uniform roulade forms. Repeat with the remaining belly. Put the roulades in separate vacuum bags and vacuum seal. Cook the lamb bellies in the circulating water bath for 48 hours. Just before the bellies are ready, prepare an ice bath. Then transfer the bellies, still in the bags, to the ice bath and let cool completely, replenishing the ice as needed, about 30 minutes.

Remove the roulades from the bags and unwrap them. Roll each roulade tightly in cheesecloth, and again tie and cinch the ends with butcher's twine. Tie each roulade to the bottom shelf of the refrigerator so that air can circulate freely around them, and let dry for at least 1 week or up to 3 weeks.

The night before you plan to serve the lamb belly, using the meat slicer or the electric knife, very thinly slice 1 roulade. Lay the slices in a single layer on a food dehydrator tray or sheet pan. Place in the dehydrator set at 150°F (65°C) or the oven preheated to 175°F (80°C) until dry and crisp, at least 6 hours or

PICKLED LAMB'S TONGUES

2 pounds (900 g) lamb's tongues
1 yellow onion, diced
2 carrots, peeled and diced
4 celery ribs, diced
4 quarts plus 1 cup (3825 g) Chicken Stock (page 319)
3 cups (960 g) rice vinegar
4 whole cloves
5 allspice berries
2 whole star anise
8 cloves garlic, peeled but left whole
8 black peppercorns
3 tablespoons (40 g) light brown sugar
2 tablespoons (14 g) fennel seeds
Fine sea salt
4 tablespoons (82 g) pink curing salt (see sources)

ZUCCHINI TENDERLOINS

2 large green zucchini
7 tablespoons (100 g) extra-virgin olive oil
4 cloves garlic, peeled but left whole
Leaves from 1 bunch fresh basil
Fine sea salt

ZUCCHINI PURÉE

Zucchini flesh reserved from Zucchini Tenderloins (above)
Zucchini oil reserved from Zucchini Tenderloins (above)
4 cloves garlic reserved from Zucchini Tenderloins (above)
About ½ cup (120 g) heavy cream
Fine sea salt

SMOKED SUGAR

1 cup (200 g) sugar

GREEN APPLE PURÉE

3 green apples, peeled and diced (about 14 oz/400 g)
¼ teaspoon (1.5 g) fine sea salt
¼ teaspoon (2 g) sugar
1 tablespoon (14 g) unsalted butter

OLIVE POWDER

4 ounces (113 g) Kalamata olives
2 teaspoons (8 g) sugar

up to overnight. (Reserve the second lamb belly for another use, or to make the recipe on another night. It will keep in the refrigerator for up to 1 week or in the freezer for up to 1 month.)

To serve, preheat the oven to 350°F (180°C). Pour the canola oil into a deep fryer to the fill line or into a tall-sided saucepan to a depth of 2½ inches (6 cm) and heat to 350°F (180°C).

Working in batches, add the dried lamb belly slices to the hot oil and fry until golden and crisp, 5–10 seconds. Using a skimmer, transfer to a paper towel–lined plate and season very lightly with salt. Slice the pickled lamb's tongues lengthwise ⅛ inch (3 mm) thick, and lay the slices on a large plate. Peel the apple, then core and cut into brunoise. Sprinkle the apple over the tongue slices and season them lightly with olive oil and Maldon salt. Place a large spoonful of zucchini purée on the bottom of each serving plate and, using a rubber spatula, spread it across the plate. Cut the zucchini tenderloins into 12 sections, place them in a single layer in a baking pan, and sprinkle them with smoked sugar, forming a light, even layer over the tops. Using the blowtorch, caramelize the sugar. Once the tenderloins are crusted, season them with olive oil and a few flakes of Maldon salt. Lay 3 pieces of zucchini tenderloin on top of the zucchini purée, positioning them top, middle, and bottom. Put 5 dots of green apple purée on and around the zucchini. Put the fried lamb belly slices on the top and bottom zucchini tenderloins. Sprinkle the olive powder on the bottom slice of lamb tongue and in the voids around the zucchini tenderloins. Garnish the dish with baby mint leaves.

PICKLED LAMB'S TONGUES

Fill a large bowl with ice water, add the lamb's tongues, cover, and refrigerate for 24 hours. Change the ice water at least 2 times during the soaking period.

Remove the tongues from the ice water. In a large saucepan, combine the tongues, onion, carrots, celery, stock, vinegar, cloves, allspice, star anise, garlic, peppercorns, brown sugar, fennel seeds, salt, and pink curing salt. Place over medium-high heat, bring to a steady simmer, and simmer, uncovered, until tender and easily pierced with a paring knife, about 1½ hours. Remove from the heat, and remove the tongues from the liquid. Strain the liquid through a fine-mesh sieve into a container large enough to also hold the tongues. Discard the contents of the sieve. While the tongues are still hot, peel away the outer skin and trim away the connective tissue on the underside. Put the cleaned tongues in the strained liquid and let cool to room temperature, about 1 hour. Cover and refrigerate for up to 1 week before serving.

ZUCCHINI TENDERLOINS

Bring a large pot filled with water to a boil over high heat. Put the zucchini, oil, garlic, basil, and a small amount of salt in a vacuum bag and vacuum seal. Add the bag to the boiling water and cook until the zucchini feel tender when gently squeezed, about 15 minutes. Transfer the zucchini, still in the bag, to a plate and let stand at room temperature until cool enough to handle easily.

Remove the zucchini from the bag. Reserve the cooking liquid and the garlic for the zucchini purée. Discard the basil. Working with 1 zucchini at a time, cut off both ends to expose a cross-section view of the seeds. Using a paring knife, score the zucchini along its length, cutting through the flesh to the seed section; do not cut into the seeds. Run your knife around the outside of the squash to remove the skin and flesh, keeping the seed section, or "tenderloin," in a single whole piece. The flesh will be used for the zucchini purée, so you can cut into it however you need to as long as the seed section remains intact. Repeat with the second zucchini. Reserve the tenderloins for finishing the dish, and reserve the flesh for the purée. The tenderloins may be stored in a covered container in the refrigerator for up to 48 hours before using.

ZUCCHINI PURÉE

Thinly slice the zucchini flesh. In a sauté pan, combine the zucchini slices and the leftover oil, juices, and garlic from the zucchini tenderloins over high heat. Cook, stirring occasionally, until the liquid has evaporated and the zucchini is starting to caramelize, 8–10 minutes. Add just enough cream to the pan to cover the vegetables and cook until the zucchini has completely broken down, about 15 minutes. Transfer the contents of the pan to the blender and blend on high speed until a smooth purée forms. Season with salt. Line a colander with coffee filters, place the colander over a bowl, and pour the purée into the colander. Let the purée drain overnight in the refrigerator. The next day, scrape the creamy purée in the colander into a lidded container and refrigerate. Discard the liquid in the bowl. The purée will keep for up to 2 days.

SMOKED SUGAR

Select a container no more than ¼ inch (6 mm) deep and large enough so the sugar will form a thin layer in the bottom. Pour in the sugar, spreading it evenly, and wrap tightly with plastic wrap. Poke the tube of the smoking gun through the plastic. Fill the chamber with applewood shavings, light the gun, and discharge the smoke into the container. Once the smoke dissipates, repeat this process at least 2 times, or until the sugar takes on a smoky taste. The smoked sugar may be stored in an airtight container at room temperature indefinitely.

GREEN APPLE PURÉE

In a saucepan, combine the apples, salt, and sugar over medium heat. Cook, stirring occasionally, until the apples break down into a sauce, about 30 minutes. Transfer the contents of the pan to a blender and process until a smooth purée forms. Add the butter and process for 5 seconds until the butter is completely absorbed. Pass the purée through a fine-mesh sieve placed over a bowl and let cool to room temperature. The apple purée may be stored in a lidded container in the refrigerator for up to 1 week before using.

OLIVE POWDER

Pit the olives and rinse them under cold running water. In a food processor, combine the olives and sugar and pulse until finely ground. Line a food dehydrator tray or a sheet pan with a silicone mat. Turn the ground olive mixture out onto the mat and, using an offset spatula, spread it in a thin, even layer. Place in the dehydrator set at 155°F (68°C) or the oven preheated to 175°F (80°C) until brittle to the touch, about 2 hours.

Chop the cooled olive sheet until finely minced. The olive powder may be stored in an airtight container at room temperature for up to 1 week.

I FIND THAT ADDING SMOKED SUGAR TO THE ZUCCHINI MAKES IT TASTE SOMEHOW "SQUASHIER" AND MORE LIKE ITSELF THAN EATING IT PLAIN

BRYAN Although the foie gras is frozen in this recipe, it looks both fresh and beautiful. A lobe of foie gras is naturally dense and heavy. Freezing it and then slicing it on a mandoline transforms it into featherlight shards that melt easily on warm toast and in your mouth. The soft sweetness of the melons, the floral aroma of the vanilla brioche, and the spice and nut notes of the tonka bean oil all provide bright flavors that balance the earthy richness of the foie gras.

Hudson Valley Foie Gras, Compressed Melons, Tonka Bean Oil, Vanilla Brioche

MAIN INGREDIENTS

1 whole fresh Hudson Valley foie gras, 2 pounds (900 g)

Foie Gras Cure (page 318)

Compressed Melons (below)

Tonka Bean Oil (below)

Fine sea salt

Emerald Crystal lettuce

Vanilla Brioche (below)

Equipment

vacuum sealer and vacuum bags

thermal immersion circulator

masticating vegetable juicer

chamber vacuum machine (optional)

two 9-by-4-inch (23-by-10-cm) pullman loaf pans

Serves 8 as a first course

COMPRESSED MELONS

1 cantaloupe

1 honeydew

1 seedless watermelon

TONKA BEAN OIL

7 tablespoons (100 g) grape seed oil

2 tonka beans, chopped

VANILLA BRIOCHE

½ cup (130 g) plus 2 tablespoons (32.5 g) whole milk

¾ cup (110 g) plus 2⅔ cups (395 g) all-purpose flour

1 ounce (30 g) fresh yeast

9 large eggs

2 teaspoons (12 g) fine sea salt

¼ cup (50 g) sugar

Seeds from 1 vanilla bean

2 cups (450 g) room temperature unsalted butter, diced

Nonstick cooking spray

Rinse the foie gras under cold running water, pat it dry, and let soften at room temperature for 1½–2 hours; it should be pliable but not melting. Using a butter knife, cut away any green spots or blood spots. Gently locate the large vein that connects the two lobes and carefully remove it and any other smaller veins you may find. Weigh the cleaned foie gras. Calculate 10 percent of the weight and weigh out that amount of cure. Season the foie gras with the cure, put it in a vacuum bag, and vacuum seal. Cure in the refrigerator for 24 hours.

Preheat the circulating water bath to 117°F (47°C).

Open the bag, remove the foie gras, and rinse off the cure with running cold water. Pat dry the foie gras, put it in a new vacuum bag, and vacuum seal. Cook in the circulating water bath for 20 minutes. Meanwhile, prepare an ice bath. When the foie is ready, transfer the bag to the ice bath and shake it vigorously in the ice water to reemulsify the fat in the foie as it cools, about 5 minutes. Transfer the foie in the bag to the freezer and freeze for 24 hours until solid.

When ready to serve, using a mandoline, slice the compressed watermelon to create slices 4 by 1 inch (10 by 2.5 cm) and 1⁄16 inch (1.5 mm) thick. You will need 16 slices total. Lay 2 slices side by side and overlapping slighly along a short side, on a cutting board. Roll up the slices lengthwise into a 1-inch (2.5-cm) cylinder. Repeat to make 8 cylinders total. Cut the remaining unused watermelon into ¼-inch (6-mm) dice. Follow the instructions for the watermelon to slice, roll, and dice the cantaloupe and honeydew. Combine all of the diced melon in a bowl and toss with 1 teaspoon (5 g) of the tonka bean oil and a light sprinkle of salt.

Put the lettuce in a bowl and toss with another 1 teaspoon (5 g) of the tonka bean oil and a light sprinkle of salt. Lay 3–4 pieces of the dressed lettuce in the center of each plate. Arrange 1 cylinder of watermelon, cantaloupe, and honeydew around the lettuce. Using the mandoline, shave thin slices of the foie gras over the lettuce; it will form a loose pile in the center of the plate, cascading over the other ingredients. Arrange a few pieces of the diced melon around each plate and serve right away accompanied by the vanilla brioche.

COMPRESSED MELONS

Cut the top and bottom off the cantaloupe and stand it upright on a cutting board. Using a sharp knife, remove the rest of the rind, peeling it off in slices from the top to the bottom of the fruit. Split the cantaloupe in half vertically and remove and discard the seeds. Split each half in half vertically to yield 4 equal pieces. Cut each piece into a rectangle 5 inches (13 cm) long by 2½ inches (6 cm) wide. Save the trimmings for juice. Repeat to peel and cut the honeydew and the watermelon. Juice the scraps from each melon separately and reserve the juices in separate containers.

Put the 4 cantaloupe rectangles and the cantaloupe juice in a glass baking dish. Put the container in a chamber vacuum machine and vacuum on high. Repeat this process 9 more times. Remove it from the vacuum chamber, cover, and reserve in the refrigerator. Repeat with the honeydew and then with the watermelon. Alternatively, put each melon and its juice in a large lock-top plastic bag and freeze for at least 6 hours until solid. Let them thaw, still in the bag, in the refrigerator for at least 8 hours before serving.

TONKA BEAN OIL

In a small saucepan, combine the grape seed oil and tonka beans over medium heat. Bring to a boil, whisking continuously. Remove from the heat and let cool to room temperature. Strain through a fine-mesh sieve, discarding the solids. The oil will keep in an airtight container at room temperature for up to 2 weeks.

VANILLA BRIOCHE

In a small saucepan, warm the ½ cup (130 g) milk over medium heat to 120°F (49°C). Add ¾ cup (110 g) of the flour and the yeast and stir gently to combine. Let the mixture rest in a warm spot for 15 minutes to activate the yeast. In a stand mixer fitted with the paddle attachment, combine the 2⅔ cups (395 g) flour, 8 of the eggs, the salt, sugar, and vanilla seeds and mix on low speed until fully blended. Add the yeast mixture and combine well. On medium speed, begin adding the butter a couple of tablespoons at a time, allowing each addition to be fully absorbed before adding more.

Spray the loaf pans with cooking spray. Divide the dough in half and put half in each prepared pan, making sure the top is smooth. Cover the tops of the pans loosely with plastic wrap and let the loaves rise in a warm spot until they look puffy, about 40 minutes. Meanwhile, preheat the oven to 350°F (180°C).

In a small bowl, whisk together the remaining 2 tablespoons (32.5 g) milk and the remaining egg to make a wash. Brush the tops of the loaves with the egg wash. Bake until the loaves are golden brown and sound hollow when rapped gently with your finger, about 45 minutes. Let cool in the pans on wire racks for 15 minutes, then turn the loaves out onto the racks and let cool completely.

HERE A LOBE OF FOIE GRAS IS FROZEN AND THEN SHAVED

TURNING ITS TYPICAL DENSE HEAVY TEXTURE INTO

LIGHT SHARDS THAT EASILY MELT IN YOUR MOUTH

GRAIN

CORN RYE WHEAT

Grains—rye, wheat, corn, barley, oats—are the backbone of many of the comfort foods on both our tables. For example, in this chapter, wheat is used in the dough for goat cheese–filled ravioli; golden loaves of challah; and stout, curled cavatelli. Sometimes we like to give familiar comfort foods a new flavor, such as trading out semolina flour for rye flour in cavatelli or studding challah with bits of crisp, salty bacon. Other times, we cannot resist surprising—and, we hope, pleasing—diners with a truly innovative take on an everyday food. Light, airy buttered popcorn is everybody's favorite movie snack. Here, that old-fashioned cinema-house staple is transformed into a luscious buttery purée that subtly echoes the flavor of its inspiration.

MICHAEL Popcorn is one of my favorite snack foods. But why pair popcorn with octopus? I took the idea of the classic Spanish dish, pulpo alla gallega, which is soft-boiled potatoes and octopus seasoned with pimentón and olive oil. I replaced the potatoes with a rich, creamy popcorn purée reminiscent of buttered popcorn. I still add the pimentón and olive oil, but I also include strips of dried piquillo pepper "paper" for yet another intriguing hint of Spain.

Pulpo alla Gallega, Buttered Popcorn, Piquillo Paper

MAIN INGREDIENTS

4¼ cups (1000 g) water
¼ cup (70 g) red wine vinegar
1 yellow onion, cut into large dice
2 bay leaves
1½ teaspoons (3.5 g) black peppercorns
3 Mediterranean octopi, about 3 pounds (1.35 kg) each
Pimentón dulce
Extra-virgin olive oil
Fine sea salt
Popcorn Purée (below)
2 tablespoons (30 g) heavy cream
4 tablespoons (56 g) cold unsalted butter, diced
Piquillo Paper (below)
Micro cilantro

Equipment

6-quart (5.7-l) pressure cooker
high-speed blender
food dehydrator (optional)
hole punch

Serves 12 as a first course

POPCORN PURÉE

10 cups (100 g) popped popcorn
1½ cups plus 1 tablespoon (400 g) whole milk
7 tablespoons (100 g) heavy cream, plus more if needed
¾ teaspoon (4.5 g) fine sea salt

PIQUILLO PAPER

One 16½-ounce (470-g) can piquillo peppers
1 tablespoon (14 g) sherry vinegar
1 tablespoon (12.5 g) sugar
¼ teaspoon (1.5 g) fine sea salt
1 tablespoon (14 g) Arbequina olive oil

In the pressure cooker, combine the water, red wine vinegar, onion, bay leaves, and peppercorns and bring to a boil over medium-high heat. Add the octopi and bring back to a simmer. Following the manufacturer's instructions, lock the lid in place, bring up to high pressure, and cook for 30 minutes. Let the pressure dissipate naturally, then uncover.

Remove the octopi, reserving the liquid in the cooker. While the octopi are still hot, use your hands to carefully scrape the suction cups from the legs until each leg is clean and white. Cut the legs away from the bodies; discard the bodies. Place the legs back in the cooking liquid, and let cool in the liquid until ready to serve. The octopus legs can be stored in a lidded container in the refrigerator for up to 24 hours.

To serve, in a saucepan, combine the octopus legs and their liquid over medium heat just until steam begins to rise and the octopus legs are warmed through, about 10 minutes. Using a slotted spoon, transfer the octopus to a bowl. Season the octopus to taste with the pimentón, olive oil, and salt.

In a small saucepan, combine the popcorn purée and cream, place over medium heat, and heat until hot, stirring occasionally with a silicone spatula. Add a tablespoon or two of cream to the purée if it seems too thick. When the mixture is hot, add the butter and stir constantly until it is fully absorbed and the mixture has thickened. Season to taste with salt. Put a dollop of the purée in the center of each serving plate. Arrange a few pieces of the octopus on each dollop of purée. Garnish with the piquillo paper strips and punched-out circles, and the micro cilantro. Drizzle with olive oil and serve right away.

POPCORN PURÉE

In a large saucepan, combine the popcorn, milk, cream, and salt over medium-high heat and bring to a full boil. Remove from the heat and let the mixture cool to room temperature, about 30 minutes. Pour the mixture into

COOKING OCTOPUS IN A PRESSURE COOKER TENDERIZES THE MEAT LIKE NO COOKING METHOD I KNOW

the blender and process until smooth. Strain the purée through a fine-mesh sieve placed over a bowl. Use the purée immediately, or store in a lidded container in the refrigerator for up to 3 days.

PIQUILLO PAPER

In a blender, combine the piquillo peppers, vinegar, sugar, and salt. With the blender running, slowly add the olive oil and process until smooth.

Line a food dehydrator tray or a sheet pan with a silicone mat. Using an offset spatula, spread the purée in a thin layer on the mat. Place the purée in the dehydrator set at 150°F (65°C) or in an oven preheated to 175°F (80°C) until it is dry enough to peel it off the silicone mat in a single sheet, about 1½ hours. Peel it off of the mat, turn it over, return it to the mat, and return the sheet to the dehydrator or oven until it is dry to the touch but still very flexible, about 1½ hours longer.

Peel the dried purée off the silicone mat, place it on a cutting board, and cut into strips 4 by ½ inch (10 cm by 12 mm). Using a hole punch, cut a few randomly spaced holes into each strip, reserving the punched-out circles. The piquillo paper may be stored in an airtight container at room temperature for up to 3 days.

BRYAN I grew up eating pasta, and I see it as both a beloved comfort food and an essential course on a menu. Here, I have taken a traditional Italian pasta dish and woven in some new ideas. The dough for the cavatelli, a type of short, curled pasta, calls for rye flour in place of the usual semolina, and American country ham replaces the typical prosciutto. Broccoli rabe has a bitter edge, so I like to balance it with lemon, chiles, and Parmigiano-Reggiano cheese.

Rye Cavatelli, Parmigiano Broth, Broccoli Rabe, Country Ham

MAIN INGREDIENTS

1 cup plus 7 teaspoons (175 g) all-purpose flour, plus more if needed

1⅔ cups (175 g) dark rye flour

1⅓ cups (325 g) whole milk ricotta cheese

1 large egg

2 large egg yolks

Finely grated zest of 1 lemon

¼ teaspoon (.2 g) freshly grated nutmeg

½ teaspoon (3 g) fine sea salt

2 cups (450 g) Parmigiano-Reggiano Broth (below)

.45 gram xanthan gum (see sources)

1 cup (225 g) cold unsalted butter, diced

1 tablespoon (14 g) extra-virgin olive oil

1 clove garlic, sliced

Broccoli Rabe Stalks, Leaves, and Florets (below)

Pinch (.7 g) of Espelette pepper

10 very thin slices country ham (shaved like prosciutto)

2-ounce (56-g) wedge Parmigiano-Reggiano cheese, shaved

Equipment

vacuum sealer and vacuum bags (optional)

ridged gnocchi board or cavatelli maker

high-speed blender

Serves 12 as a first course or 6 as a main course

PARMIGIANO-REGGIANO BROTH

2¼ cups (500 g) water

8½ ounces (240 g) Parmigiano-Reggiano cheese, grated

BROCCOLI RABE STALKS, LEAVES, AND FLORETS

1 bunch broccoli rabe

In a food processor, combine the all-purpose flour, rye flour, ricotta cheese, egg, egg yolks, lemon zest, nutmeg, and salt and process just until a uniform dough forms, 1–2 minutes. Turn the dough out onto a work surface and knead until smooth and elastic. If the dough seems too sticky, add 1–2 tablespoons (10–20 g) flour, adding no more than is absolutely necessary. Put the dough in a vacuum bag and vacuum seal. Alternatively, wrap the dough tightly in plastic wrap. Let rest at room temperature for 20 minutes.

On a lightly floured work surface, using a rolling pin, roll out the dough into a square about ½ inch (12 mm) thick, trimming the edges to make them even. Cut the square into strips ½ inch (12 mm) wide, and then cut the strips crosswise into ½-inch (12-mm) squares. Using your thumb, roll each dough square across the ridged gnocchi board to form ridges. Alternatively, do not cut the strips into squares. Following the manufacturer's instructions, feed the strips through the cavatelli maker.

To serve, bring a large pot of generously salted water to a boil over medium-high heat. Put the Parmigiano-Reggiano broth in a blender. Turn on the blender to low speed, then slowly increase the speed until a vortex forms in the center of the liquid. Sprinkle in the xanthan gum and continue to process until it is completely absorbed, a full 5 seconds. Transfer the broth to a saucepan, place over medium heat, and bring to a simmer. Whisk in 4 tablespoons (56 g) of the butter until it melts. Continue whisking in the butter in 4-tablespoon (56-g) increments until all of it has been incorporated. Remove from the heat and set aside in a warm spot.

In a large sauté pan, heat the olive oil over medium heat until it begins to shimmer but not smoke. Add the garlic and cook, stirring constantly, until golden brown, about 2 minutes. Add the broccoli rabe stalks and leaves and the Espelette pepper and sauté until lightly browned and tender, 8–10 minutes.

Add the cavatelli to the boiling water and cook until al dente, about 7 minutes. While the pasta is cooking, cut the 2 slices of country ham into julienne. When

HERE I STARTED WITH A TRADITIONAL ITALIAN DISH

THEN I WOVE IN LOCAL INGREDIENTS & ADDED A FEW PERSONAL TOUCHES

FOR A RECIPE THAT'S THE BEST OF BOTH WORLDS

the pasta is ready, drain and add to the pan holding the broccoli rabe along with two-thirds of the warmed broth and the julienned ham. Using a silicone spatula, fold together gently until everything is hot and glossy. Remove from the heat and fold in the broccoli rabe florets. Divide the mixture evenly among 6 large, shallow bowls or 12 small ones. Garnish with the remaining country ham, torn into pieces, the Parmigiano shavings, and spoonfuls of the broth.

PARMIGIANO-REGGIANO BROTH

In a saucepan, bring the water to a rapid simmer over high heat. Whisk in the cheese until fully combined. Remove from the heat and let cool to room temperature, about 30 minutes. Transfer the broth to a lidded container and store in the refrigerator for at least 24 hours or up to 3 days to develop the flavor. Just before using, skim off any fat that has collected on the surface, and strain the broth through a fine-mesh sieve.

BROCCOLI RABE STALKS, LEAVES, AND FLORETS

Bring a large pot of generously salted water to a boil over high heat. Meanwhile, separate the florets, leaves, and stems of the broccoli rabe into separate piles. Remove the tough ends from the stems, and cut the stems on a slight diagonal into 1-inch (2.5-cm) pieces. Prepare an ice bath. Add the leaves and florets to the boiling water and blanch until bright green, about 5 seconds. Using a skimmer, transfer the leaves and florets to the ice bath to cool briefly, then transfer them to a kitchen towel–lined plate. Add the stem pieces to the boiling water and blanch until just tender, about 30 seconds. Using the skimmer, transfer to the ice bath to cool briefly, then drain. Transfer the stalks and leaves to a lidded container and the florets to a separate lidded container. Store in the refrigerator until ready to serve, up to 3 days.

MICHAEL I like challah, and I also like bacon. They're not usually paired together, but marrying them seemed like the right thing to do. Challah is usually braided into large loaves. Sometimes, I tie the same dough into little knots, and the bread becomes a secondary player that is simply on hand to carry the smoky, salty, rich flavor of bacon to the palate. The knots are delicious just as they are, or the braided loaves can be sliced and used for French toast.

Bacon Knot Challah

MAIN INGREDIENTS

5⅔ cups (850 g) bread flour

2 tablespoons (18 g) instant yeast

¼ cup plus 1 tablespoon (60 g) sugar

1 tablespoon (18 g) fine sea salt

2 cups (520 g) whole milk, at room temperature

14 large egg yolks (225 g), plus 1 large egg yolk for brushing

9 tablespoons (125 g) rendered bacon fat, at room temperature (from about 1 pound/450 g bacon)

5.5 ounces (150 g) raw bacon, preferably Benton's or Nueske's, plus 6 slices bacon, cooked and then finely chopped in a food processor

2 tablespoons (28 g) water

Smoked Maldon salt

Makes about 4 dozen knots

In a stand mixer fitted with the paddle attachment, combine the bread flour, yeast, sugar, and salt and mix on low speed until thoroughly combined. Switch to the dough hook. On low speed, slowly pour in the milk. As the flour begins to absorb the milk, increase the mixer speed to medium-low and knead for 10 minutes. Add the 14 egg yolks one at a time, mixing after each addition until fully incorporated. Add the bacon fat and continue to mix until fully absorbed. Add the diced raw bacon and mix until evenly distributed. Transfer the dough to a clean bowl and cover with plastic wrap. Let the dough rest and proof at room temperature until doubled in bulk, about 1½ hours.

Line 2 sheet pans with parchment paper. Turn the dough out onto a work surface. Gently punch down the dough and divide it in half. Knead each half briefly until it is soft and supple.

Portion the dough into 1-ounce (30-g) pieces. Roll each piece into a log about 6 inches (15 cm) long and then tie it into a knot. Place the knots on the parchment-lined sheet pan and brush each one lightly with water. Cover the knots lightly with plastic wrap and let them proof at room temperature until they have risen and look a bit like puffy marshmallows, about 20 minutes.

Preheat the oven to 375°F (190°C).

In a small bowl, whisk together the remaining egg and the water. Generously brush the knots with the egg wash. Sprinkle each knot with the smoked salt. Bake the knots, rotating the pans 180 degrees at the halfway point, until they are golden brown, about 6 minutes. Sprinkle with the chopped cooked bacon and let the knots cool on the sheet pans for at least 10 minutes. Serve warm.

MAIN INGREDIENTS

Goat Cheese Filling

1 cup (240 g) fresh goat cheese

½ teaspoon (3 g) fine sea salt

½ teaspoon (1 g) freshly ground white pepper

Pasta Dough

2 cups (300 g) all-purpose flour, plus more if needed

⅓ cup plus 3 tablespoons (40 g) vegetable ash (used for cheesemaking; see sources)

3 large eggs

8 large egg yolks

1 teaspoon (4.5 g) extra-virgin olive oil

½ teaspoon (2.7 g) whole milk

1½ teaspoons (9 g) fine sea salt

1 tablespoon (14 g) water

1 watermelon radish

6 cups (1350 g) plus ¼ cup (56 g) water

2 tablespoons (36 g) fine sea salt

½ cup (113 g) cold unsalted butter, diced

Parsley Root Purée (below)

10 ounces (285 g) maitake mushrooms

1 tablespoon (2 g) chopped fresh chives

Golden Sage Tea Froth (below)

Aged goat cheese for grating

Vegetable ash (used for cheesemaking; see sources)

Equipment

vacuum sealer and vacuum bags (optional)

pasta machine

6-quart (5.7-l) pressure cooker

large tamis or food mill

Serves 6 as a light main course

››

BRYAN Diane Kirsh and Wayne Cullen of Cherry Glen Farm in Boyd, Maryland, produce a soft-ripened goat's milk cheese that is both coated and layered with edible vegetable ash. The ash is what gave me the idea for this dish. We had goat cheese ravioli on the menu, and it made sense to me to add some ash from Cherry Glen to the pasta dough. The result is striking in both appearance and flavor: both the black pasta and the creamy white filling taste earthy, rich, and tart.

Goat Cheese and Ash Ravioli, Mushrooms, Parsley Root

To make the filling, in a food processor, combine the cheese, salt, and pepper and process until smooth. Transfer to a pastry bag fitted with a medium plain tip. Store in the refrigerator until you are ready to roll out the pasta.

To make the dough, in a clean food processor, combine the flour and ash and pulse several times to combine. In a small bowl, whisk together 2 of the eggs, all of the egg yolks, and the olive oil, milk, and salt. Turn on the food processor, pour in the egg mixture, and let the machine run until all of the ingredients just come together to form a smooth dough, 1–2 minutes. Turn the dough out onto a countertop or other work surface and knead several times until the dough feels smooth and elastic. If the dough seems sticky, add a tablespoon or two of flour. (The ash will stain some countertops. If your countertop stains easily, cover a large cutting board with plastic wrap and knead the dough on it.) Put the dough in a vacuum bag and vacuum seal, or wrap the dough in plastic wrap. Let rest at room temperature for 1 hour.

Line a sheet pan with parchment paper. Cut the dough in half and reserve half for another use. (The extra dough can be cut into noodles, frozen on sheet pans, and then transferred to plastic freezer bags and frozen for up to 2 weeks. Or you can double the filling and freeze the extra ravioli. They will keep for up to 14 days and should be cooked directly from the freezer.) Set the rollers on the pasta machine to the widest setting. Cut the pasta dough into 4 equal pieces. Run 1 piece of the dough through the rollers twice, taking care that it stays flat as you roll it. If the dough begins to stick, dust the rollers lightly with flour, adding no more than is absolutely necessary. Reset the rollers one width narrower and again pass the dough through the rollers twice. Repeat the process, resetting the rollers one width narrower and rolling the dough twice through each setting until you reach the second-to-last setting. After rolling the dough twice through this setting, lay the dough sheet flat on the prepared sheet pan. Repeat with the remaining 3 dough pieces, stacking each pasta sheet on top of the last one on the sheet pan. Keep the finished pasta sheets, lightly covered with plastic wrap, in the refrigerator until ready to use.

PARSLEY ROOT PURÉE

2 large parsley roots (about 10½ ounces/ 300 grams total weight), peeled and trimmed

½ cup (113 g) water

½ teaspoon (3 g) fine sea salt

GOLDEN SAGE TEA FROTH

16 golden sage leaves

2 cups (450 g) water

½ cup plus 2 tablespoons (125 g) sugar

½ teaspoon (2 g) fine sea salt

4 teaspoons (12 g) Sucro (see sources)

In a small bowl, whisk together the remaining egg and the water. Line a sheet pan with parchment paper. On a lightly floured work surface, lay out 1 pasta sheet. (You can line the surface with plastic wrap if you are worried about staining, but the pasta should be fairly dry at this point.) Using the dull side of a 2-inch (5-cm) round pastry cutter, mark 12 circles in a line across the pasta sheet, spacing them about 1 inch (2.5 cm) part. Brush the entire sheet with a thin layer of the egg wash. Using the circles as a guide, pipe about 1 tablespoon (15 g) of the goat cheese filling in the center of each circle. Cover the pasta sheet with a second pasta sheet, lining up the edges. Using the dull side of a 1½-inch (4-cm) round pastry cutter, press down around each mound of filling. Then, using a circular motion, carefully rotate the cutter around the filling to compress the filling into a uniform shape and to seal and flatten the pasta layers around it. Using a 2-inch (5-cm) round fluted pastry cutter, cut out the individual ravioli. Set the ravioli aside on the prepared sheet pan. Repeat the filling and cutting process with the remaining 2 pasta sheets and filling. You should end up with 24 ravioli (4 per serving). The ravioli must be cooked and served right away.

Using a mandoline, cut the radish into slices about ⅒ inch (2.5 mm) thick. Stack the slices and cut them lengthwise on the mandoline to yield strips ⅒ inch (2.5 mm) wide. Stack the strips on a cutting board, trim the tops and bottoms of each stack even, and then cut the strips into ⅒-inch (2.5-mm) squares. Set aside in ice water until you are ready to serve.

To serve, in a large soup pot, combine the 6 cups (1350 g) water and the 2 tablespoons (36 g) salt over high heat and bring to a boil. In a medium saucepan, bring the ¼ cup (56 g) water to a simmer over medium heat. Whisk 4 tablespoons (56 g) of the butter into the simmering water until smooth and thickened, then season to taste with salt. Keep the butter sauce warm over very low heat. (If the sauce separates while it is standing, whisk in 1 teaspoon (4.5 g) cold water to bring it back together.) In a small saucepan, bring the parsley root purée to a simmer over medium heat. In a large sauté pan, melt 2 tablespoons (28 g) of the butter over medium-high heat. When the butter begins to foam, add the mushrooms, reduce the heat to medium, and turn the mushrooms after 1 minute. Cook on the second side for 1–2 minutes and flip one more time. Cook until tender and lightly browned, 1–2 more minutes. Transfer the mushrooms to a paper towel–lined plate.

Add the ravioli to the boiling water and cook until the pasta is tender and the filling is warmed through, about 3 minutes. Using a skimmer, transfer the ravioli to a large sauté pan. Place the pan over medium heat, add the butter sauce, the remaining 2 tablespoons (28 g) butter, chopped chives, and radish dice, and swirl the pan to emulsify the butter into the water clinging to the ravioli.

Put a dollop of parsley root purée on each serving plate and spread it flat. Arrange 4 ravioli on top and around the purée. Spoon the radish dice onto the plate. Put 4 pieces of mushroom on the plate next to the ravioli. Use an immersion blender to aerate the golden sage tea froth. Spoon the froth into the voids on the plate. Sprinkle the plate with a blend of grated aged goat cheese and vegetable ash. Serve right away.

PARSLEY ROOT PURÉE

In the pressure cooker, combine the parsley root, water, and salt. Following the manufacturer's instructions, lock the lid in place, bring up to high pressure, and cook for 45 minutes. Let the pressure dissipate naturally, then uncover.

Drain the parsley root, reserving the cooking liquid. Transfer the parsley root to a blender and process until smooth, adding a tablespoon (14 g) or two of the cooking liquid if needed. Using a plastic bench scraper, push the purée through a large tamis into a bowl, or pass it through a food mill fitted with the fine disk into a bowl. Transfer the purée to a small saucepan, place over medium heat, and bring to a simmer. Use immediately, or let cool to room temperature, stirring occasionally. The purée may be stored in a lidded container in the refrigerator for up to 3 days.

GOLDEN SAGE TEA FROTH

In a small saucepan, combine the sage, water, sugar, and salt, place over medium-high heat, and bring just to a simmer. Remove from the heat, cover, and let stand for 10 minutes. Strain the liquid through a fine-mesh sieve into a tall, narrow heatproof container. Add the Sucro and, using an immersion blender, process until fully dissolved and absorbed, about 5 seconds. It will become light and frothy. Keep the container of tea froth in a pot of steaming (not simmering) water until ready to serve.

THE BLACK PASTA MADE FROM VEGETABLE ASH PAIRED WITH THE CREAMY WHITE GOAT CHEESE FILLING HAS A STRIKING APPEARANCE AND BOLD FLAVOR

LAUREL

CINNAMON
AVOCADO
SASSAFRAS
BAY LEAF

The laurel clan, made up primarily of trees and woody shrubs, counts avocados, cinnamon, bay leaves, and sassafras among its members. We prize avocados for their rich, creamy texture and subtle sweetness, and sassafras for its pleasant licorice notes. Cinnamon, an ingredient that always evokes memories of our mother's kitchen, comes in two types. We use the sweeter, stronger-flavored variety, also known as cassia, when we want a bright, spicy, dominant flavor. The second type, often labeled true cinnamon, has a softer, more complex flavor that is best suited to dishes in which the spice is cast in a supporting role. Although bay is typically used for adding depth and complexity to slow-cooked savory dishes, here it has been given the unexpected task of flavoring ice cream.

MAIN INGREDIENTS

1 whole red snapper, about 2 pounds (900 g)
2 bay leaves
½ Meyer lemon, cut into 4 pieces
3 pounds (1350 g) kosher salt
2 cups (450 g) water
Cinnamon Eggplant (below)
1 tablespoon (14 g) extra-virgin olive oil
Toasted Sesame–Cinnamon Salt (below)
Charcoal Vinaigrette (below)
Nori "Charcoal" (below)
Fried Eggplant Skins (below)
Fresh petite cinnamon basil leaves

Equipment

thermal immersion circulator
vacuum sealer and vacuum bags
deep fryer (optional)

Serves 4 as a main course

CINNAMON EGGPLANT

2 cinnamon sticks
2 Japanese eggplants
3 cups (675 g) ice water
5½ teaspoons (33 g) fine sea salt, plus more to season
3 tablespoons (60 g) soy sauce
1½ tablespoons (20 g) rice vinegar
2 tablespoons (33 g) honey

TOASTED SESAME–CINNAMON SALT

5 tablespoons (37.5 g) white sesame seeds
1¼ tablespoons (12.5 g) smoked Maldon salt
2 teaspoons (4 g) ground cinnamon

CHARCOAL VINAIGRETTE

6½ square sheets (20 g) nori
⅓ cup plus 2 teaspoons (200 g) seasoned rice vinegar
3½ tablespoons (50 g) mirin
3½ tablespoons (50 g) *each* grape seed oil and extra-virgin olive oil

FRIED EGGPLANT SKINS

Canola oil for deep-frying
Eggplant skins reserved from Cinnamon Eggplant (above)
Toasted Sesame–Cinnamon Salt (above)

MICHAEL The inspiration for this dish came from my friend Alex Talbot. He gave me the idea of adding a charred flavor to the protein in a dish—here, a simple salt-roasted fish—without charring the protein itself. Basically, he told me to burn things on purpose, and that's what I did. Some results were good; others weren't. In the end, I discovered that charring members of the laurel family worked particularly well, which is why cinnamon and bay are featured here.

Salt-Crusted Snapper, Cinnamon Eggplant, Charcoal Vinaigrette

Preheat the oven to 400°F (200°C). Stuff the cavity of the fish with the bay leaves and lemon pieces. In a bowl, stir together the kosher salt and water to form a paste. Line a sheet pan with parchment paper and put one-third of the paste in the center of the pan, forming it into the size and shape of the fish, but extending it an extra ½ inch (12 mm) larger than the fish on all sides. Lay the fish on top of the salt paste, and mold the remaining paste over and around the fish, encasing it completely. Spacing the holes evenly, poke the casing with a toothpick 10 times to allow some steam to escape. Bake for 20 minutes. Remove the pan from the oven and let the fish stand for 10 minutes.

To serve, preheat the oven to 250°F (120°C).

Put the cinnamon eggplant and its juices on a heatproof serving platter in the oven to warm it through, basting it occasionally with the juices, about 10 minutes. Using a chef's knife, cut around the perimeter of the salt crust, being careful not to pierce the fish. Lift off the top of the crust to expose the fish. Using a large spoon and fork, carefully remove the flesh in large pieces from the bones and put the fish on a large plate. Be careful to keep the fish in large pieces and make sure all bones are removed from the fish. Drizzle the fish with olive oil and season with the toasted sesame–cinnamon salt.

Place 1 eggplant piece in the center of each serving bowl and a second piece just to the left. Put a piece of fish on top of the center piece of eggplant. Spoon the charcoal vinaigrette on and around the fish and eggplant. Break up the pieces of nori "charcoal" left over from making the vinaigrette, and sprinkle little piles of it around the plate. Top the fish with pieces of seasoned fried eggplant skin. Garnish the dish with basil leaves and a sprinkle of the toasted sesame–cinnamon salt and serve right away.

CINNAMON EGGPLANT

Using kitchen shears, cut the cinnamon sticks in half lengthwise. Using a vegetable peeler, peel the eggplants and set the skin aside. Pour ½ cup (113 g) of the water into a microwave-safe bowl, place in the microwave, and cook on high power for 1 minute. Remove from the microwave, add the 5½ teaspoons (33 g) salt, and stir to dissolve. In a bowl, combine the salted water and the remaining 2½ cups (562 g) ice water and stir to blend. Add the peeled eggplants and let soak in the refrigerator for 1 hour.

Preheat a circulating water bath to 185°F (85°C). Remove the eggplants from the water and slide 1 cinnamon stick half into the sides of each eggplant, leaving just enough sticking out of the ends to be able to pull them out later. Put the eggplants in a vacuum bag with the soy sauce, vinegar, and honey and vacuum seal. Cook in the circulating water bath for 1 hour; the eggplants will feel tender when gently squeezed through the bag. Open the bag and put the eggplants and their juices in a medium bowl. Let cool to room temperature, about 20 minutes.

Remove the cinnamon sticks and slice the eggplants crosswise into 1-inch (2.5-cm) pieces. The eggplants may be stored with their juices in a lidded container in the refrigerator until ready to serve, up to 3 days.

TOASTED SESAME-CINNAMON SALT

In a dry frying pan, toast the sesame seeds, shaking frequently, until golden brown, 2–3 minutes minutes. Transfer to a plate to cool completely.

In a spice grinder, combine the toasted sesame seeds, salt, and cinnamon and grind to a fine powder. The salt may be stored in an airtight container at room temperature for up to 2 weeks.

CHARCOAL VINAIGRETTE

Preheat the oven to 400°F (200°C).

Put a metal rack on 1 sheet pan. Lay the nori sheets in a single layer, not touching, on top of the rack (if necessary, use 2 sheet pans and 2 racks). Invert another rack on top of the nori so that it is pressed flat between the racks. Place in the oven and bake until completely burnt and dry, about 1 hour. Remove from the oven, remove the top rack, and let the nori cool to room temperature, about 20 minutes. Crumble 6 nori sheets into the blender (reserve the remaining half-sheet for garnish). Add the vinegar, mirin, grape seed oil, and olive oil. Purée until smooth. Use immediately. (Any leftover vinaigrette can be kept in a lidded container in the refrigerator for up to 1 week.)

FRIED EGGPLANT SKINS

Pour the canola oil into a deep fryer to the fill line or into a tall-sided saucepan to a depth of 2½ inches (6 cm) and heat to 350°F (180°C).

Cut the eggplant skins into fine chiffonade. Working in batches, add the chiffonade to the hot oil and fry until the oil stops bubbling and the threads are crispy, 5–10 seconds. Using a skimmer, transfer to a paper towel–lined plate and season lightly with toasted sesame–cinnamon salt. The skin is best if used immediately. If necessary, it may be stored in an airtight container at room temperature for up to 4 hours.

ONE NIGHT AT BAZAAR JOSÉ DEMANDED ONLY SALT EGG WHITES AND A FISH

IT WAS AN IMPORTANT LESSON ABOUT SIMPLICITY AND USING THE BEST INGREDIENTS

BRYAN This recipe was inspired by both Asian summer rolls and California sushi rolls. I wanted to make a rice paper that had good flavor, so I made my own from seasoned jasmine rice stock. I used crabmeat here because it was fresh and delicious, but tuna, salmon, or other good-quality seafood can be substituted. The avocado purée is decadent, rich, and essential to the dish. If you don't want to aerate the soy, serve it in a dipping bowl alongside the rolls.

Peekytoe Crab Summer Roll, Avocado, Cilantro Leaf, Soy Air

MAIN INGREDIENTS

1 teaspoon (14 g) canola oil
½ shallot, minced
1 cup (130 g) Peekytoe crabmeat
1 tablespoon (10 g) Spicy Aioli (below)
⅛ teaspoon (.75 g) fine sea salt
Leaves from 1 fresh cilantro sprig
Rice Paper (below)
Avocado Purée (below)
Yuzu Vinaigrette (below)
Micro cilantro
Coriander blooms
Soy Air (below)

Equipment

plastic squeeze bottle
high-speed blender

Serves 4 as a first course

SPICY AIOLI

3 large eggs plus 4 large egg yolks
2 tablespoons (10 g) chili powder
½ teaspoon (10 g) Sriracha sauce
1 tablespoon (20 g) Mae Ploy sweet chili sauce
1⅔ teaspoons (10 g) fine sea salt
1⅔ cups (360 g) grape seed oil

RICE PAPER

12½ cups (2813 g) water
1 cup (200 g) jasmine rice
¼ cup (60 g) mirin
1½ teaspoons (10 g) rice vinegar

››

In a small sauté pan, heat the canola oil over medium heat until it begins to shimmer but not smoke. Add the shallot and sauté until tender but not browned, 3–5 minutes. Remove from the heat and let cool to room temperature. Put the crabmeat in a bowl, gently picking through it to remove any stray bits of shell or cartilage. Add the cooled shallot, spicy aioli, salt, and cilantro leaves to the bowl with the crab and mix gently. The crab mixture may be stored in a lidded container in the refrigerator for up to 2 days.

To serve, lay 1 sheet of rice paper on a cutting board with a 3½-inch (9-cm) side facing you. Form a log with the crab mixture 3½ inches (9 cm) long and ¼ inch (6 mm) thick on the rice paper, positioning it horizontally about ½ inch (12 mm) from the edge nearest you. Starting at the end nearest you, roll up the paper around the crab filling, continuing until you reach the opposite end of the paper and the roll is resting seam side down. It should look like a sushi roll. Repeat to form 8 summer rolls in all.

Pipe a line of the avocado purée across each serving plate slightly off center. Lay 2 summer rolls side by side and on a diagonal across the avocado. Pour the yuzu vinaigrette into the squeeze bottle, and squeeze 14–16 dots on the plate around the components. Garnish each plate with the micro cilantro and coriander blooms. Quickly process the soy air with an immersion blender to refresh it. Scoop the foam off the top with a spoon, and then place 1 large spoonful of the soy air next to each crab roll. Serve right away.

SPICY AIOLI

In a blender, combine the eggs, egg yolks, chili powder, Sriracha sauce, sweet chili sauce, and salt. Turn on the blender to low speed, then slowly increase the speed to medium. Drizzle in the oil in a slow, steady stream and process until emulsified. Use immediately, or transfer to a lidded container and store in the refrigerator for up to 3 days.

FOR THIS DISH I WANTED TO MAKE A RICE PAPER THAT REALLY TASTED LIKE SOMETHING SO I MADE MY OWN OUT OF JASMINE RICE STOCK

RICE PAPER

In a saucepan, combine 6 cups (1350 g) of the water, the rice, mirin, vinegar, and lemongrass, place over medium-high heat, and bring to a boil. Cover, reduce the heat to maintain a gentle simmer, and cook until all of the liquid has been absorbed by the rice, 40–45 minutes. Add the remaining 6½ cups (1463 g) water and let the rice stand at room temperature for 40 minutes.

Drain the rice. Weigh 13¼ ounces (375 g) of the rice and place in a saucepan. Add the glucose, agar, and salt, place over high heat, and bring to a simmer. Reduce the heat to maintain a low simmer and cook, whisking constantly, for 5 minutes. Remove from the heat. Have ready two 8-by-13-inch (20-by-33-cm) sheet pans on a level surface. Strain the rice mixture through a fine-mesh sieve into the pans, dividing it evenly. The liquid should form a layer about 1⁄16 inch (1.5 mm) thick. Discard the rice. Let the mixture cool until it is at room temperature and firmly set, about 1 hour. Once the rice paper is firm, cut it into eight 3½-by-5-inch (9-by-13-cm) rectangles.

AVOCADO PURÉE

Halve, pit, peel, and dice the avocados. In the blender, combine the diced avocados, spinach leaves, yuzu juice, and salt and purée until very smooth. Use a small ladle to push the purée through a fine-mesh sieve. Transfer the purée to a piping bag fitted with a #12 plain tip. Use the purée immediately.

YUZU VINAIGRETTE

Peel and chop the ginger. In a saucepan, combine the yuzu juice, orange juice, chopped ginger, lemongrass, and sugar, place over medium heat, and bring to a simmer. Cook until the liquid is reduced to by half, about 10 minutes. Remove from the heat, add the cilantro, and let cool to room temperature,

about 20 minutes. Strain the liquid through a fine-mesh sieve placed over a small bowl. Add the mustard and whisk to blend. Slowly whisk in the olive oil until emulsified. Use immediately, or store in a lidded container in the refrigerator for up to 1 week.

SOY AIR

In a tall, narrow container, combine the water, soy sauce, soy lecithin, and mirin and process with an immersion blender until a light, airy foam forms, about 20 seconds. Serve immediately.

½ lemongrass stalk

2 tablespoons (55 g) liquid glucose (see sources)

5.25 grams agar (see sources)

¼ teaspoon (1.5 g) fine sea salt

AVOCADO PURÉE

3 ripe avocados

½ cup (50 g) spinach leaves

1½ tablespoons (21 g) yuzu juice (see sources)

1 teaspoon (6 g) fine sea salt

YUZU VINAIGRETTE

6 tablespoons (85 g) yuzu juice (see sources)

6½ tablespoons (100 g) fresh orange juice

1½ ounces (40 g) fresh ginger

2 lemongrass stalks, chopped

1 teaspoon (4 g) sugar

¼ bunch (14 g) fresh cilantro

¼ teaspoon (2 g) Dijon mustard

2 cups (450 g) olive oil

SOY AIR

⅔ cup plus 2 teaspoons (150 g) water

5 tablespoons (100 g) soy sauce

½ teaspoon (2.5 g) soy lecithin (see sources)

1 tablespoon (15 g) mirin

MICHAEL This dish showcases a trio of ingredients from the laurel family: sassafras, which is used to flavor root beer; cinnamon; and bay leaf. The laurel "molasses," which is both the sauce and the cooking medium for the venison, unites the flavors of the dish and balances out the gaminess of the meat. The butternut bark and the sprout leaves evoke something you might find in a deer's natural habitat. And it turns out that deer like to eat sassafras, which brings the recipe full circle.

Venison, Root Beer Molasses, Butternut Bark, Charred Sprout Leaves

MAIN INGREDIENTS

2 pounds (900 g) Axis venison loin
Laurel Molasses (below)
Fine sea salt
Butternut Hooks (below)
Butternut Bark (below)
Charred Sprout Leaves (below)

Equipment

thermal immersion circulator
vacuum sealer and vacuum bags
food dehydrator (optional)
masticating vegetable juicer
high-speed blender
deep fryer (optional)

Serves 4 as a light main course

LAUREL MOLASSES

3⅓ cups (750 g) highest-quality root beer
2½ sticks (10 g) cinnamon
2 bay leaves
2 tablespoons (28 g) fresh lemon juice
¼ cup plus 1 teaspoon (119.2 g) liquid glucose (see sources)

BUTTERNUT HOOKS

2 large butternut squash, about 2 pounds (900 g) each
2 tablespoons (28 g) extra-virgin olive oil
1 tablespoon (18 g) fine sea salt
1 stick cinnamon

BUTTERNUT BARK

Squash flesh reserved from making the butternut hooks
40 grams tapioca maltodextrin (see sources)
2 tablespoons (40 g) confectioners' sugar
3 grams low-acyl gellan gum (see sources)
Canola oil for deep-frying
Fine sea salt

CHARRED SPROUT LEAVES

6 Brussels sprouts
4 teaspoons (20 g) unsalted butter
1 stick cinnamon
Fine sea salt

Preheat the circulating water bath to 133°F (56°F).

Trim the venison. Divide the laurel molasses in half and set one half aside. Brush the venison with some of the second half of the molasses and season generously with salt. Put the coated venison and the rest of the second half of molasses in a vacuum bag and vacuum seal. Cook in the circulating water bath for 1 hour. Remove the bag from the bath and let rest for 5 minutes.

To serve, remove the venison from the bag and cut it crosswise into 16 equal portions. Arrange 2 portions in the center of each plate, leaving some space between them. Put a spoonful of the laurel molasses to the left of the venison. Set a squash hook on top of the venison, connecting the two pieces. Put the charred sprout leaves on top of and around the venison. Arrange the butternut bark on top of the venison, so that meat is almost completely buried beneath the leaves and bark. Serve right away.

LAUREL MOLASSES

In a bowl, combine the root beer, cinnamon, bay leaves, lemon juice, and glucose and mix well. Pour the liquid into a shallow plastic container if using the food dehydrator or a shallow heatproof glass container if using the oven. Place the container in the dehydrator set at 155°F (68°C) or in the oven preheated to 175°F (80°C) until the liquid becomes a thick, viscous syrup similar in consistency to molasses, about 12 hours. Strain the molasses through a fine-mesh sieve placed over a ceramic container. Cover and set aside at room temperature until needed. Any leftover laurel molasses may be stored in a lidded container at room temperature for up to 1 week.

BUTTERNUT HOOKS

Preheat the circulating water bath to 185°F (85°C).

Using a serrated knife, and working with 1 squash at a time, cut off both the top and bottom of the squash. Stand it upright on the cutting board and, using the knife, pare away the skin, cutting long slices from the top to the bottom. Split

BOTH THE COOKING MEDIUM AND THE SAUCE FOR THE DISH

THE LAUREL MOLASSES UNITES THE FLAVORS AS WELL AS BALANCES THE GAMINESS OF THE MEAT

the squash in half lengthwise and scoop out and discard the seeds. Cut off the bottom 2 inches (5 cm) of the curved squash base from both halves. Reserve the top halves of both squashes; you will only need the two 2-inch (5-cm) base pieces for the hooks. Cut the base pieces crosswise into 8 equal pieces each; you will end up with 16 pieces that resemble hooks. Put the hook-shaped pieces, olive oil, salt, and cinnamon stick in a vacuum bag and vacuum seal. Cook in the circulating water bath for 30 minutes. Meanwhile, prepare an ice bath. When the squash is ready, transfer the bag to the ice bath and let cool completely, replenishing the ice as needed, about 20 minutes. Preheat the broiler. Line a sheet pan with parchment paper. Remove the squash hooks from the bag. Lay out the hooks on the prepared sheet pan and broil, watching closely, until the squash has caramelized on top, 3–5 minutes. Use immediately.

BUTTERNUT BARK

Dice the reserved squash and juice it with the vegetable juicer; it should yield about 2½ cups (550 g) of juice. In a saucepan, bring the juice to a boil over medium-high heat and cook until reduced by one-third, 30–45 minutes. Strain the juice through a fine-mesh sieve, and measure out 1⅓ cups (300 g). Use the remainder for another purpose. Transfer the juice to the blender and let cool to room temperature, about 20 minutes. Turn on the blender to low speed, then slowly increase the speed until a vortex forms in the center. Sprinkle in the maltodextrin, confectioners' sugar, and gellan gum and continue to process until all of the powders are completely absorbed, a full 15 seconds. Transfer the mixture to a saucepan, place over medium heat, and bring to a boil. Remove from the heat, pour into a heatproof bowl, and let cool, uncovered, in the refrigerator until firmly set, about 1 hour.

Using an offset spatula, dice the squash gel in the bowl, transfer to the clean blender, and process until smooth. Line 2 dehydrator trays or sheet pans with silicone mats. Using the offset spatula, spread the purée on the mats in a smooth, thin layer. Place the purée in the dehydrator set at 155°F (68°C) or an oven preheated to 175°F (80°C) until completely dry and brittle, about 8 hours.

Pour the canola oil into a deep fryer to the fill line or into tall-sided saucepan to a depth of 2½ inches (6 cm) and heat to 350°F (175°C). Using your hands, break the dried squash into pieces resembling tree bark. In batches, add the pieces to the oil and fry until crisp and dry, about 5 seconds. Using a skimmer, transfer to a paper towel–lined sheet pan and season lightly with salt.

CHARRED SPROUT LEAVES

Bring a saucepan filled with generously salted water to a boil over high heat. Prepare an ice bath. Trim the stem end of the Brussels sprouts ¼ inch (6 mm) from the bottom and pull off the whole leaves from each sprout. Add the leaves to the boiling water and blanch until they turn bright green, about 10 seconds. Using a skimmer, transfer them to the ice bath. Let cool briefly, then drain and pat dry with paper towels. In a small sauté pan, melt the butter over medium heat. When it starts to bubble, add the dry sprout leaves and the cinnamon stick and season with salt. Sauté until the butter begins to brown and the leaves are cooked but still have some bite, about 2 minutes. Transfer the leaves to a paper towel–lined plate. Discard the cinnamon stick. Use right away.

Stronghold
Los Angeles

MAIN INGREDIENTS

Unsalted butter and all-purpose flour for preparing pans

Topping

- 1/2 cup (75 g) all-purpose flour
- 1/2 cup (50 g) almond flour
- 1/4 cup (107 g) firmly packed light brown sugar
- 1/8 teaspoon (.15 g) freshly grated nutmeg
- 1/2 teaspoon (1 g) ground cinnamon
- 1/4 teaspoon (1.5 g) fine sea salt
- 1/8 teaspoon (.25 g) cayenne pepper
- 4 tablespoons (56 g) unsalted butter, at room temperature, diced

Cake

- 2 1/2 cups (375 g) all-purpose flour
- 2 teaspoons (12 g) baking powder
- 1/2 teaspoon (2.5 g) baking soda
- 5 teaspoons (10 g) ground cinnamon
- 1/2 teaspoon (3 g) fine sea salt
- 1/8 teaspoon (.25 g) cayenne pepper
- 3 large eggs
- 1/4 cup (55 g) buttermilk
- 3/4 cup (170 g) unsalted butter, at room temperature
- 1 1/2 cups (300 g) granulated sugar
- 1 cup (200 g) crème fraîche

Bay Leaf Ice Cream (below)

Equipment

- two 5 1/2-by-3-inch (14-by-7.5-cm) loaf pans
- thermal immersion circulator
- vacuum sealer and vacuum bags
- ice-cream maker

Serves 10 as a family-style dessert

BAY LEAF ICE CREAM

- 2 3/4 cups (715 g) whole milk
- 3/4 cup (180 g) heavy cream
- 3/4 cup (150 g) granulated sugar
- 3 large egg yolks
- 1 teaspoon (6 g) fine sea salt
- 8 fresh bay leaves, cut into julienne
- 1 allspice berry, cracked
- 6 grams ice cream stabilizer (see sources)

BRYAN Mom always had freshly baked coffee cake in the house on Saturday mornings. That cinnamon-laced memory inspired this cake, which we also bake at the restaurant for guests to take home for their breakfast the next morning. The idea for the bay leaf ice cream emerged as we were exploring the family structure for this book. Cinnamon and bay leaves are in the same botanical family and are wonderful together. So, I thought, why not serve breakfast for dessert?

Cinnamon Coffee Cake, Bay Leaf Ice Cream

Preheat the oven to 325°F (165°C). Butter the loaf pans and dust with flour, tapping out the excess. Line the bottom and long sides of each pan with a rectangle of parchment paper cut to fit precisely with a slight overhang at the top of the sides.

To make the coffee cake topping, in a food processor, combine the all-purpose flour, almond flour, brown sugar, nutmeg, cinnamon, salt, and cayenne and pulse to blend. Scatter the butter over the top and pulse until the mixture has the texture of wet sand. Transfer the topping mixture to a bowl, cover, and refrigerate until ready to use.

To make the cake, in a bowl, sift together the flour, baking powder, baking soda, 1 teaspoon (2 g) of the cinnamon, the salt, and the cayenne pepper. In another bowl, whisk together the eggs and buttermilk.

In a stand mixer fitted with the paddle attachment, combine the butter and sugar and mix on medium-low speed until light and fluffy, about 3 minutes. Add the buttermilk and egg to the butter mixture. Mix on low speed until fully combined. Stop the machine, add all of the flour mixture, and mix on medium-low speed until a smooth batter forms. Using a rubber spatula, fold in the crème fraîche just until blended.

Put about one-third of the batter into a bowl, add the remaining 4 teaspoons (8 g) cinnamon, and stir until smooth. Gently fold the cinnamon batter into the remaining batter to create a swirl effect.

Divide the cake batter evenly between the prepared cake pans. Set each cake pan on a sheet pan. Divide the crumb topping evenly between the cakes, scattering it evenly over the tops and gently pressing it into the batter. Bake the cakes, rotating the sheet pans 180 degrees after 30 minutes, until a cake tester inserted in the center of each cake comes out with only a few crumbs clinging to it, 40–45 minutes.

MOM ALWAYS HAD
FRESHLY BAKED
COFFEE CAKE
AROUND THE HOUSE
ESPECIALLY ON SATURDAY MORNINGS
AND THAT CINNAMON-LACED
MEMORY
INSPIRED THIS DISH

Let the cakes cool in the pans for 30 minutes. Then, run an offset spatula or butter knife around the inside edge of each pan to loosen the cake sides and gently invert, lifting off the pans. Slice and serve warm, with the bay leaf ice cream on the side.

BAY LEAF ICE CREAM

Preheat the circulating water bath to 180°F (82°C).

In a large bowl, whisk together the milk, cream, sugar, egg yolks, salt, bay leaves, allspice, and ice cream stabilizer. Transfer to a vacuum bag and vacuum seal. Cook in the circulating water bath for 30 minutes.

Meanwhile, prepare an ice bath. When the milk-cream mixture is ready, remove the bag from the water bath and shake it rapidly for 30 seconds. Place the bag in the ice bath and let cool, replenishing the ice as needed, until completely cold to the touch, about 30 minutes. Open the bag and pour the mixture through a fine-mesh sieve into a bowl. Cover and refrigerate for at least 4 hours or up to 24 hours.

Transfer the chilled mixture to the ice-cream maker and freeze according to the manufacturer's instructions. Transfer to a freezer container and freeze for at least 2 hours or up to 2 weeks.

LEGUME

FAVA BEAN
CRANBERRY BEAN
GREEN PEA
CHICKPEA

We always have some kind of legume in our kitchens. Thick pods bulging with delicate English peas in early spring give way to spongy fava shells filled with slender, slightly musky beans. Fat sugar snaps, flat, crisp snow peas, chickpeas with their little pointed tails, colorful cranberry beans, long, skinny green beans—we like them all. We use them fresh off the vine in spring and summer and shelled and dried in late fall and winter. Their flavors and textures are varied and versatile, making them good candidates for nearly any technique or cooking method: sautéing, simmering, braising, roasting, frying, puréeing—even grinding into flour. But perhaps the best way to eat most legumes is straight from the garden, promptly shucked and then lightly cooked with a hint of sweet butter and salt.

MICHAEL Franc, a pastry chef at the Ritz-Carlton in Naples, Florida, was brilliant at putting flavors together. He would steal our peeled fava beans, spread sweet butter on grilled toast, dot the toast with the purloined beans, and sprinkle coarse salt on top. The combination was amazing. Years later, recalling Franc's inspired marriage of ingredients, I set about making fava bean butter with the creamy consistency of dairy butter. I have paired it here with other legume specimens.

Veal Breast, Fava Bean Butter, Coffee-Cardamom Soil, Beans and Sprouts

MAIN INGREDIENTS

3 *each* grapefruits, lemons, limes, and oranges

2.5 gallons (11,365 g) water

5⅓ cups (1136 g) firmly packed light brown sugar

2½ cups (360 g) table salt

8 ounces (225 g) fresh ginger, peeled and thinly sliced

½ cup (28 g) coriander seeds

¼ cup (26 g) whole cloves

¼ cup (28 g) black peppercorns

¼ cup (30 g) allspice berries

¼ cup (32 g) yellow mustard seeds

15 fresh thyme sprigs

10 teaspoons (68 g) pink curing salt (see sources)

1 boneless veal breast, 1½ pounds (680 g)

¼ cup (56 g) extra-virgin olive oil, plus more for drizzling

Maldon sea salt

Fava Bean Butter (below)

Veal Jus (below)

Peas, Beans, and Sprouts (below)

Coffee-Cardamom "Soil" (below)

4 slices grilled country bread

12 fava bean flowers

Equipment

thermal immersion circulator

vacuum sealer and vacuum bags

deep fryer (optional)

6-quart (5.7 l) pressure cooker

high-speed blender

Serves 4 as a first course

››

To make a brine, using a Microplane grater, zest and then juice all of the citrus fruits. Add the zest to the juice and reserve. In a large pot, combine the water, brown sugar, table salt, ginger, coriander seeds, cloves, black peppercorns, allspice, mustard seeds, thyme, and pink salt and bring to a boil over high heat, stirring to dissolve the sugar. Meanwhile, prepare an ice bath. When the brine is at a boil, remove from the heat, add the citrus juice and zest mixture, and transfer to a large metal bowl. Set the bowl over the ice bath and let cool until the brine is ice-cold, stirring occasionally and replenishing the ice as needed, about 45 minutes.

Put the veal breast in a deep bowl or baking dish. Pour the cold brine over the breast and top with a heavy plate, if necessary, to keep the meat fully submerged. Cover and refrigerate for 12 hours.

Preheat the circulating water bath to 158°F (70°C).

Remove the veal breast from the brine and pat dry. Put the breast and ¼ cup (56 g) olive oil in a vacuum bag and vacuum seal. Cook in the circulating water bath for 12 hours. Transfer the veal, still in the bag, to a sheet pan and place a second sheet pan on top. Put about 10 pounds (4.5 kg) of kitchen items, such as canned goods or bags of flour, on top of the second pan and refrigerate the veal breast for 8–12 hours.

When ready to serve, remove the veal breast from the bag and cut into slices 1⁄16 inch (1.5 mm) thick and 6 inches (15 cm) long. Liberally drizzle the veal breast slices with olive oil and season with Maldon salt. Put a spoonful of fava bean butter on each plate. Drape the veal breast slices down the middle of each plate, dividing evenly. Drizzle the veal breast with the veal jus and top with the peas, beans, and sprouts mixture. Put a few small spoonfuls of the coffee-cardmom "soil" in the empty spots on each plate. Spread the grilled bread with the fava bean butter and divide among the plates. Top each piece with a fava bean and 3 fava bean flowers. Serve right away.

MY GOAL FOR THIS RECIPE WAS TO CAPTURE THE ESSENCE OF **FAVA BEANS** WITH A **CREAMY CONSISTENCY** AND I ENDED UP WITH SOMETHING **ETHEREAL** THAT COULD EVEN STAND IN AS **VEGAN "BUTTER"**

FAVA BEAN BUTTER

22 ounces (600 g) fava beans in the pod

1⅓ cups (300 g) Arbequina extra-virgin olive oil

30 grams glycerine powder (see sources)

½ teaspoon (3 g) fine sea salt

VEAL JUS

Canola oil for deep-frying

2 pounds (900 g) veal shanks, cut into 1-inch (2.5-cm) pieces (ask the butcher to do this)

8½ cups (1900 g) Chicken Stock (page 319)

½ yellow onion, diced

1 carrot, diced

2 celery ribs, diced

4 teaspoons (20 g) unsalted butter

Fine sea salt

Banyuls vinegar

FAVA BEAN BUTTER

Shell the fava beans and discard the pods. You should have about 10½ ounces (300 g) beans. Bring a saucepan filled with water to a boil over medium heat. Prepare an ice bath. Add the fava beans to the boiling water and blanch for 3 minutes. Using a skimmer, transfer the beans to the ice bath. When the beans are cool, drain and peel them and put them in the blender.

Line a shallow baking dish with plastic wrap. In a small saucepan, heat the olive oil to 140°F (60°C). Add the glycerine powder and salt and stir well to combine. Pour the oil-glycerine mixture over the fava beans in the blender and process until completely smooth. Transfer the purée to the prepared baking dish, cover loosely with plastic wrap, and freeze overnight or up to 16 hours.

Remove the frozen fava mixture from the freezer and transfer it to a cutting board. Chop it up, return it to the blender, and process one more time to make sure the purée is completely smooth. Transfer to a lidded container and refrigerate until ready to serve. It will keep for up to 3 days. When ready to serve, put the fava bean butter in a stand mixer fitted with the whisk attachment and whip on high speed until light. It should have the consistency of whipped butter. Serve immediately.

VEAL JUS

Pour the canola oil into a deep fryer to the fill line or into a tall-sided saucepan to a depth of 2½ inches (6 cm) and heat to 350°F (180°C). Set a metal rack over a sheet pan.

Rinse the veal shanks under cold running water and pat them completely dry with paper towels. Add the shanks to the hot oil and fry until they are a dark golden brown, 5–8 minutes. Using tongs, transfer the shanks to the rack on the sheet pan and let drain for 2–3 minutes.

In the pressure cooker, combine the veal shanks, stock, onion, carrot, and celery. Following the manufacturer's instructions, lock the lid in place, bring the pressure up to high, and cook for 45 minutes. Let the pressure dissipate naturally, then uncover.

Strain the sauce though a fine-mesh sieve placed over a saucepan. Discard the solids. Place the pan over medium-high heat, bring to a simmer, and adjust the heat to maintain a low simmer. Cook until reduced to a syrupy consistency reminiscent of cold maple syrup, about 45 minutes. Add the butter to the simmering sauce and stir until completely absorbed, then season to taste with the salt and vinegar and use immediately. Alternatively, once the sauce is reduced to a syrupy consistency, pour it into a metal bowl, place the bowl over an ice bath, and let cool completely, about 30 minutes. Transfer to a lidded container and store in the refrigerator for up to 5 days. Just before serving, return the sauce to a simmer and add the butter, salt, and vinegar as directed.

PEAS, BEANS, AND SPROUTS

Bring a saucepan filled with generously salted water to a boil over high heat. Meanwhile, prepare an ice bath. Julienne the snow peas and snap peas lengthwise. Put them in a small bowl and season with ½ teaspoon (2.25 g) of the olive oil and with salt to taste. Cut the fava beans into small batons. Add the English peas to the boiling water and blanch for about 10 seconds. Using a small sieve, transfer them immediately to the ice bath, leaving them in the sieve as they cool. Drain the peas well, pat dry with paper towels, and transfer them to a bowl. Add the fava beans, bean sprouts, carrots, turnips, radishes, borage flowers, and the remaining ½ teaspoon (2.25 g) olive oil, and sea salt to taste and toss to mix. Serve right away.

COFFEE-CARDAMOM "SOIL"

Preheat the oven to 325°F (165°F). Line a sheet pan with a silicone mat.

In a bowl, whisk together the sugar, almond flour, all-purpose flour, coffee, salt, cocoa powder, and cardamom until well blended. Add the melted butter and mix with a rubber spatula to incorporate. It will have the texture of wet sand. Spread the mixture in a thin, even layer on the prepared sheet pan.

Bake until aromatic and dry to the touch, about 15 minutes. Remove from the oven and let cool to room temperature on the pan. Sift the soil through a fine-mesh sieve placed over an airtight container. The "soil" may be stored at room temperature for up to 1 week.

PEAS, BEANS, AND SPROUTS

8 snow peas

8 sugar snap peas

1 teaspoon (4.5 g) extra-virgin olive oil

Fine sea salt

12 shelled fava beans, blanched and peeled

28 English pea pods, shelled

20 bean sprouts

4 baby carrots

4 baby turnips

4 baby radishes

8 borage flowers

COFFEE-CARDAMOM "SOIL"

¾ cup (150 g) sugar

1⅔ cups (155 g) almond flour

⅔ cup (100 g) all-purpose flour

7 tablespoons plus 2 teaspoons (35 g) ground coffee

1 teaspoon (6 g) fine sea salt

6 tablespoons (50 g) black cocoa powder (see sources)

5 teaspoons (15 g) ground cardamom

7 tablespoons (100 g) unsalted butter, melted

MAIN INGREDIENTS

3 pounds (1.36 kg) pork belly
¼ cup plus 2 tablespoons (50 g) kosher salt
2 tablespoons (27 g) light brown sugar
2¾ teaspoons (18.7 g) pink curing salt (see sources)
5 tablespoons plus 2 teaspoons (40 g) black peppercorns
14 long peppers (see sources)
2 tablespoons plus 2 teaspoons (10 g) juniper berries
1 whole nutmeg
5 fresh bay leaves, cut into fine chiffonade
3 cloves garlic
Leaves from 6 fresh thyme sprigs
7 tablespoons (100 g) water
25 grams Activa GS (see sources)
Reserved oil from Soffrito (below)
Whole Beans (below)
Cranberry Bean Purée (below)
Soffrito (below)
Candied Citrus Zest (below)
Stewed Mustard Seeds (below)
Pork Sauce (below)
Petite red mustard greens

Equipment

vacuum sealer and vacuum bags
thermal immersion circulator
high-speed blender
6-quart (5.7-l) pressure cooker

Serves 6 as a main course

WHOLE BEANS

4 cloves garlic
4 fresh flat-leaf parsley sprigs
2 tablespoons (14 g) black peppercorns
2 fresh bay leaves
1 cup (210 g) *each* dried cranberry beans and scarlet runner beans, soaked overnight in cold water
8 cups (1800 g) Vegetable Stock (page 319)
5 teaspoons (30 g) fine sea salt
1 *each* yellow onion and carrot, diced
2 celery ribs, diced
4 tablespoons (56 g) canola oil

»

BRYAN Two key influences inspired this dish. In culinary school, I tasted cassoulet for the first time, and I was seduced by the combination of beans, bacon, and duck confit. The second was my favorite restaurant dish when I was a young cook: I found Tom Colicchio's pork belly with mostarda at Gramercy Tavern revelatory—and I still feel that way about it. Here, I have teamed up Colicchio's pork belly and mustard with the beans and cured meat of a traditional cassoulet.

Pork Belly, Cranberry Bean Variations, Citrus, Mustard

To clean the pork belly, remove the skin and about ¼ inch (6 mm) of the fat layer underneath. The cleaned belly should weigh about 2½ pounds (1125 g). To make a salt cure, in a food processor, combine the kosher salt, brown sugar, pink salt, peppercorns, long peppers, juniper berries, nutmeg, bay leaves, garlic, and thyme and process until finely ground. Coat the pork belly evenly with the cure, and wrap the belly securely in plastic wrap. Refrigerate the belly for 10 days, turning the belly over each morning and evening.

In a bowl, combine the water and the Activa GS. Using a handheld mixer, beat on high speed until soft peaks form, 5–8 minutes. Set aside to allow the foam to subside. Rinse the curing mixture from the pork belly under cold running water. Dry well with paper towels. Cut open the belly lengthwise, slicing through the middle and leaving the last inch (2.5 cm) of the end still attached. Lay the pork belly flat on the cutting board so that it forms a large rectangle with the short sides at the top and bottom. Lay a large sheet of plastic wrap on the work surface. Evenly brush the pork belly on both sides with the Activa GS mixture. Starting at the bottom of the rectangle, roll the belly up into a tight log. Transfer the log to the sheet of plastic wrap, and roll it up tightly in the sheet. Twist the ends of the plastic wrap in opposite directions to compress the log and ensure uniform pressure on all parts of the pork belly, then tie securely with cotton butcher's twine. Put in a vacuum bag and vacuum seal. Refrigerate for 8 hours.

Preheat the circulating water bath to 180°F (82°C).

Cook the pork in the circulating water bath for 16 hours. Remove the pork belly from the water bath and set it aside to cool to room temperature, about 1 hour. Prepare an ice bath. Transfer the pork, still in the bag, to the ice bath and let cool completely, replenishing the ice as needed, about 30 minutes. Refrigerate until ready to serve, up to 5 days.

To serve, unwrap the pork belly and cut it crosswise into 6 even portions. Each portion will weigh about 5 ounces (140 g). In a large sauté pan, warm reserved oil over low heat until it begins to shimmer. Add the pork belly to the pan and

cook, turning once, until seared on the top and bottom and heated through, 3–4 minutes per side.

Meanwhile, in a saucepan, bring the cranberry beans and their liquid to a simmer over medium heat. In another saucepan, bring the runner beans and their liquid to a simmer over medium heat. In a small saucepan, heat the cranberry bean purée over medium heat, stirring occasionally, just until it begins to steam. In another small saucepan, combine the soffrito, candied citrus zest, stewed mustard seeds, and pork sauce over medium heat and bring to a bare simmer, stirring to combine all of the ingredients into a sauce. Remove from the heat.

Put a spoonful of cranberry bean purée in the center of the plate. Cut each portion of pork in half and place 1 piece on top of the purée. Stand the other pork piece on its side slightly above and to the left of the first piece. Add a couple spoonfuls of drained cranberry beans and runner beans around the plate. Coat the standing pork piece with a spoonful of sauce and put a little sauce just below the other pork piece. Garnish with petite red mustard leaves and serve.

WHOLE BEANS

Divide the garlic, parsley, peppercorns, and bay leaf in the center of two 6-inch (15-cm) squares of cheesecloth, bring the corners together, and tie securely with cotton butcher's twine to make 2 sachets. In a saucepan, combine 1 sachet, the cranberry beans, and half each of the stock, salt, onion, carrot, celery, and canola oil over medium-high heat. In a second saucepan, combine the second sachet, the runner beans, and the remaining stock, salt, onion, carrot, celery, and oil over medium-high heat. Bring the liquid in both pans to a simmer, adjust the heat to maintain a very slow simmer, cover, and cook until the beans are tender, about 2½ hours.

Remove from the heat and let the beans cool naturally, uncovered, in the pans, about 45 minutes. The cooled beans may be stored separately in their liquid in lidded containers in the refrigerator for up to 5 days before using.

CRANBERRY BEAN PURÉE

Put the garlic, parsley, peppercorns, and bay leaf in the center of a 6-inch (15-cm) square of cheesecloth, bring the corner together, and tie with cotton butcher's twine to make a sachet. In a large saucepan, combine the sachet, cranberry beans, stock, celery, onion, carrot, and canola oil over medium-high heat. Bring to a simmer, adjust the heat to maintain a very slow simmer, cover, and cook until the beans are tender, about 2½ hours.

Remove from the heat, add the salt, and let the beans cool naturally, uncovered, in the pan, stirring occasionally, about 1 hour. Transfer the beans and their cooking liquid to the blender and process until a smooth purée forms. The purée may be stored in a lidded container in the refrigerator for up to 3 days.

SOFFRITO

In a shallow saucepan, combine the red onion, fennel, parsnip, and olive oil over low heat. Allow the mixture to caramelize slowly, stirring occasionally, for about 2 hours. Remove from the heat and let cool to room temperature.

Drain the mixture through a fine-mesh sieve placed over a bowl, and reserve both the soffrito and the oil. The soffrito may be stored in a lidded container in the refrigerator for up to 3 days before using. Store the oil in a separate container in the refrigerator to use for searing the pork belly.

CANDIED CITRUS ZEST

Cut a thin slice off the top and bottom of the grapefruit. Using a vegetable peeler, remove the zest from the grapefruit. Lay the pieces of zest, colored side down, on a cutting board, and use a knife to trim away all the remaining white pith. Repeat with the lemon and orange. Cut the zests into brunoise, keeping each type separate. Put each zest in a separate small saucepan, cover with cold water, and bring to a boil. Drain the zests and repeat the blanching process 2 more times.

Combine the 3 types of zest in a saucepan, add the water and sugar, and cook slowly over low heat until the zest is translucent, tender, and almost dry, 30–45 minutes. Remove from the heat and let cool to room temperature. The candied zest may be stored in a lidded container in the refrigerator for up to 2 weeks before using.

STEWED MUSTARD SEEDS

In a small saucepan, combine the honey, mustard seeds, sherry, sugar, salt, and water over low heat. Cook until the liquid has reduced to a glaze that barely moistens the mustard seeds, about 45 minutes. Remove from the heat and let cool to room temperature, about 30 minutes. The stewed mustard seeds may be stored in a lidded container in the refrigerator for up to 1 month.

PORK SAUCE

In a large sauté pan, heat the olive oil over medium-high heat until it begins to shimmer but does not smoke. Add the onion and parsnip and caramelize slowly for about 15 minutes. Once the vegetables are evenly browned, add the tomato paste and rosemary and cook, stirring constantly, for 10 minutes; take care that the mixture does not burn. Add the wine and cook until it reduces and glazes the vegetables, about 10 minutes. Transfer the contents of the pan to the pressure cooker and add the ham hock and water. Following the manufacturer's instructions, lock the lid in place, bring the pressure up to high, and cook for 1 hour. Let the pressure dissipate naturally, then uncover.

Strain the sauce through a fine-mesh sieve placed over a clean saucepan and, using a small ladle, skim any fat off the top. Place over medium-high heat and simmer slowly until the sauce reduces to a syrupy consistency, 15–20 minutes. Use immediately, or transfer to a metal bowl, set over an ice bath, and let cool completely, stirring occasionally and replenishing the ice as needed, about 30 minutes. The cooled sauce may be stored in a lidded container in the refrigerator for up to 1 week before using.

CRANBERRY BEAN PURÉE

2 cloves garlic
2 fresh flat-leaf parsley sprigs
1 tablespoon (17 g) black peppercorns
1 fresh bay leaf
2 cups (420 g) dried cranberry beans, soaked overnight in cold water
2 quarts (1800 g) Vegetable Stock (page 319)
½ celery rib, diced
¼ yellow onion, diced
¼ carrot, peeled and diced
2 tablespoons (28 g) canola oil
1 tablespoon (18 g) fine sea salt

SOFFRITO

¼ cup (35 g) red onion brunoise
¼ cup (35 g) fennel brunoise
¼ cup (30 g) parsnip brunoise
1 cup (225 g) extra-virgin olive oil

CANDIED CITRUS ZEST

1 Ruby Red grapefruit
1 lemon
1 orange
2 cups (450 g) water
½ cup (100 g) sugar

STEWED MUSTARD SEEDS

2 tablespoons (32.5 g) honey
2 tablespoons (16 g) yellow mustard seeds
2 teaspoons (10 g) dry sherry
2 teaspoons (8 g) sugar
1 teaspoon (6 g) fine sea salt
1 cup (225 g) water

PORK SAUCE

2 tablespoons (28 g) olive oil
¾ cup (100 g) diced yellow onion
1 parsnip, peeled and diced
1 tablespoon plus 1 teaspoon (32 g) tomato paste
Leaves from 1 fresh rosemary sprig
½ cup (120 g) dry red wine
1 pound (450 g) roasted ham hock
4 cups (900 g) water

MAIN INGREDIENTS

Pea Purée (below)

Carrot Spheres (below)

1 teaspoon (5 g) extra-virgin olive oil

Fine sea salt

½ teaspoon (1.5 g) freshly cracked black peppercorns

24 pea tendrils

Carrot Slices (below)

¼ teaspoon (.38 g) fennel pollen or toasted ground fennel seed

Equipment

high-speed blender

vacuum sealer and vacuum bags

Serves 6 as a first course

PEA PURÉE

2 pounds (900) English peas in the pod

2 cups (450 g) water

1 teaspoon (6 g) fine sea salt

.5 gram xanthan gum (see sources)

CARROT PURÉE

2 carrots, about 5¼ ounces (150 g) total weight, diced

⅔ cup (150 g) carrot juice

¼ teaspoon (1.5 g) fine sea salt

CARROT SPHERES

1 cup (275 g) Carrot Purée (above)

1 teaspoon (3 g) calcium gluconate (see sources)

4½ cups (1000 g) water

5 grams alginate (see sources)

¼ cup (56 g) carrot juice

CARROT SLICES

1 yellow carrot

1 maroon carrot

BRYAN In the film *Forrest Gump,* Forrest says: "Me and Jenny were like peas and carrots again." Well, me and my wife, Jennifer, are like peas and carrots, too. That sentiment is why I decided to make a dish that not only is fun but also showcases how well these two garden staples go together. The pea purée is smooth and silky, and the carrot spheres are timed-release explosions of flavor. A few pea tendrils and carrot shavings complete the dish.

Peas and Carrots

To serve, put 3 large spoonfuls of pea purée in each shallow serving bowl. Drain the carrot spheres and season each one with olive oil, salt, and pepper. Put 1 carrot sphere on top of each spoonful of pea purée. Dress the pea tendrils and carrot slices lightly with salt and olive oil and arrange on the plate. Sprinkle the fennel pollen over the dish. Serve right away.

PEA PURÉE

Shell the peas, setting the pods aside; you should end up with about 2 cups (320 g) shelled peas. Bring a saucepan of generously salted water to a boil over high heat. Prepare an ice bath. Line a sheet pan with parchment paper. Add the shelled peas to the boiling water and cook until tender, 2–3 minutes. Drain and immediately transfer to the ice bath until cold. Drain the peas, pat them dry, and lay them in a single layer on the prepared pan. Put the pan with the peas in the freezer until the peas are frozen solid, about 3 hours.

To make a stock, in a saucepan, combine the pea pods and water over medium heat and bring to a boil. Reduce the heat to maintain a simmer and cook for 30 minutes to extract the maximum pea flavor. Meanwhile, prepare an ice bath. When the stock is ready, strain it through a fine-mesh sieve placed over a metal bowl. Set the bowl over the ice bath and let cool completely, stirring occasionally and replenishing the ice as needed, about 30 minutes.

In the blender, combine the peas and 1 cup (225 g) of the pea stock and process until a smooth purée forms. You will need to stop the blender and stir the mixture a bit every now and again to keep the mixture moving through the blades. With the blender running, add the salt and xanthan gum and process for a full 5 seconds to incorporate fully. The pea purée may be stored in a lidded container in the refrigerator for up to 2 days before using. Any leftover pea stock can be used for other dishes or discarded.

CARROT PURÉE

Bring a large saucepan three-fourths full of water to a boil over high heat. Put the diced carrot, carrot juice, and salt in a vacuum bag and vacuum seal. Add the

INSPIRED BY A LINE
IN A MOVIE
THIS DISH IS NOT ONLY
FUN TO EAT
BUT ALSO CAPTURES THE
ESSENCE
OF THE RAW INGREDIENTS
IN A NEW AND EXCITING WAY

bag to the boiling water and cook until the carrots feel completely tender and mushy when the bag is pressed gently, about 30 minutes. Open the bag, transfer the contents to the clean blender, and process on high speed until completely smooth. Pass the purée through a fine-mesh strainer. Use immediately, or transfer to a metal bowl, set over an ice bath until cool, then store in a lidded container in the refrigerator for up to 3 days.

CARROT SPHERES

In the clean blender, combine the carrot purée and calcium gluconate and process on low speed until fully combined. Transfer the mixture to a lidded container and refrigerate overnight. Put 2 cups (450 g) of the water in the blender and turn it on to low speed. Slowly increase the speed until a vortex forms in the center of the liquid. Sprinkle in the alginate and process for a full 5 seconds until the alginate is fully dissolved. Transfer the mixture to a 9-by-5-inch (23-by-13-cm) loaf pan, add the remaining 2½ cups (550 g) water, and stir to blend. Fill a large bowl with cold water. Using a ½-teaspoon measure, drop spoonfuls of the carrot purée into the alignate bath. Let stand until a delicate skin forms on the outside of each sphere, about 1 minute. Then, using a slotted spoon, gently remove the spheres from the bath, dip them in the cold water to rinse, and transfer them to a lidded container; you will need 18 spheres total. When all of the spheres are in the container, add the carrot juice, cover, and refrigerate. They will keep for up to 2 days.

CARROT SLICES

Using a mandoline on the narrowest setting, cut both carrots into paper-thin slices. Pick out 6 beautiful slices of each color carrot, and store them in ice water until you are ready to serve or for up to 1 hour. The remaining slices can be used for a salad the next day.

MICHAEL This dish draws on both the French and the Lebanese kitchen, where lamb, chickpeas, and tomatoes often find themselves on the same plate. Here, the chickpeas turn up in the form of flour for making panisses, small, crisp, savory French cakes. The idea for the sauce comes from a Lebanese chef I once cooked with, who marinated lamb overnight in a purée of raw onion and tomato. The addition of the coconut brings out the sweet fruitiness of the tomato.

Lamb Shoulder, Smoked Panisses, Tomato-Coconut Jus

MAIN INGREDIENTS

17½ ounces (500 g) overripe tomatoes

½ sweet onion, chopped

¾ teaspoon (4.5 g) fine sea salt

1 Jameson Farm lamb shoulder, 5–7 pounds (2.2–3.2 kg)

5 tablespoons plus 1 teaspoon (75 g) extra-virgin olive oil

Canola oil for deep-frying

Tomato-Coconut Jus (below)

Spring Onions (below)

Smoked Panisses (below)

Onion sprouts

Equipment

vacuum sealer and vacuum bags

thermal immersion circulator

bincho charcoal (optional; see sources)

deep fryer (optional)

vegetable grill tray

high-speed blender

6-quart (5.7-l) pressure cooker

smoking gun and applewood shavings

deli-style meat slicer or electric knife

food dehydrator (optional)

Serves 8 as a main course

››

In a food processor, process the tomatoes, onion, and salt until a paste forms. Coat the lamb shoulder all over with the paste, then put the lamb and any remaining paste in a vacuum bag and vacuum seal. Refrigerate for 12 hours.

Preheat the circulating water bath to 132°F (56°C).

Remove the lamb from the bag and wipe off any excess paste. Put the lamb and olive oil in a clean vacuum bag and vacuum seal. Cook in the circulating water bath for 48 hours. Remove the bag from the water bath and place on a sheet pan. Let cool at room temperature for 15 minutes. Prepare an ice bath. Transfer the lamb, still in the bag, to the ice bath and let cool completely, replenishing the ice as needed, about 45 minutes. The cooled lamb may be stored in the bag in the refrigerator for up to 3 days.

To serve, preheat the circulating water bath to 132°F (56°C). Put the bag with the lamb in the circulating water bath for 30 minutes.

Heat the charcoal directly over a gas burner turned on to a high flame, or use a charcoal chimney starter until it turns white. Using long-handled tongs, transfer the hot charcoal to a grill. Alternatively, prepare a fire in a charcoal grill with regular charcoal so the coals are white hot. Place the grill rack on the grill and let it heat up.

Pour the oil into a deep fryer to the fill line or into a tall-sided saucepan to a depth of 2½ inches (6 cm) and heat to 350°F (180°C).

In a small saucepan, bring the tomato-coconut jus to a simmer over medium heat. Remove the lamb from the bag and cut it into 8 equal portions, each about 5 ounces (140 g). Place the lamb portions on the grill rack and grill, turning once, until they are lightly grill marked on both sides and have taken on a light smoky flavor, 2–3 minutes on each side. Transfer to a plate and keep warm. Place a vegetable grill tray on the grill rack, add the spring onion slices to the tray, and grill, turning once, until lightly grill marked and warm, 1–2 minutes total. Transfer to a plate and keep warm.

TOMATO-COCONUT JUS

4½ pounds (2 kg) overripe tomatoes

Canola oil for deep-frying

2 pounds (900 g) lamb shanks

1 cup (250 g) unsweetened coconut milk

4 teaspoons (20 g) cold unsalted butter

1 tablespoon (11.5 g) nigella seeds

SMOKED PANISSES

4¼ cups (955 g) Chicken Stock (page 319)

1 tablespoon (18 g) fine sea salt

3 cups (300 g) chickpea flour

4 teaspoons (20 g) Arbequina extra-virgin olive oil

SPRING ONIONS

12 spring onions

8 teaspoons (40 g) extra-virgin olive oil

50 grams maltodextrin (see sources)

7 tablespoons (100 g) water

Add 12 smoked panisses to the hot oil and fry until golden brown and crisp, 2–3 minutes. Using a skimmer, transfer to a paper towel–lined plate to drain. Put 1 lamb portion on each serving plate. Put 1 spring onion half next to the lamb piece, and place 3 panisses on the spring onion half. Garnish with the spring onion rings and onion sprouts. Glaze the lamb with the tomato-coconut jus. Serve right away.

TOMATO-COCONUT JUS

Line a colander with cheesecloth and place the colander over a container large enough to hold 7–8 cups (1.75–2 l) liquid. Quarter the tomatoes, put them in the blender, and blend until a smooth purée forms. Transfer the purée to a saucepan, place over medium-high heat, and bring to a boil. Simmer the mixture until it begins to separate, about 30 seconds, then pour it into the cheesecloth-lined colander. Transfer the colander setup to the refrigerator and let stand, undisturbed, until all of the clear liquid has dripped through the cheesecloth into the bowl below, 6–8 hours. You should have about 6½ cups (1463 g) tomato liquid.

Pour the canola oil into a deep fryer to the fill line or into a tall-sided saucepan to a depth of 2½ inches (6 cm) and heat to 350°F (180°C). Set a metal rack over a sheet pan.

Rinse the lamb shanks under cold running water and pat them completely dry with paper towels. Add the shanks to the hot oil and fry until they are dark golden brown, 10–15 minutes. Using tongs, transfer the shanks to the rack on the sheet pan and let drain briefly. In the pressure cooker, combine the tomato liquid, coconut milk, and lamb shanks. Following the manufacturer's instructions, lock the lid in place, bring up to high pressure, and cook for 45 minutes. Let the pressure dissipate naturally, then uncover.

Remove and discard the shanks, then strain the contents of the pressure cooker though a fine-mesh sieve placed over a saucepan. Discard the solids. Place the pan over medium-high heat, bring to a boil, and cook until reduced by half, about 30 minutes. Whisk in the cold butter and the nigella seeds and remove from the heat. Keep warm until ready to serve.

SMOKED PANISSES

In a saucepan, bring the stock to a simmer over medium-high heat. Add the salt. Whisk in the chickpea flour, reduce the heat to low, and cook, stirring occasionally, until the mixture becomes very thick and resembles polenta, about 20 minutes. Remove from the heat, transfer to a food processor, add the olive oil, and process until a smooth purée forms.

Line a sheet pan with parchment paper. Spoon the warm chickpea flour mixture into a pastry bag fitted with a ½-inch (12-mm) plain tip and pipe straight logs onto the prepared pan. Let the logs stand until they are cool and have firmed up, about 30 minutes. Cut the logs into 1½-inch (4-cm) pieces. Transfer them to a deep container and cover the top tightly with plastic wrap. Poke the tube of the smoking gun through the plastic. Fill the chamber with applewood shavings, light the gun, and discharge the smoke into the container. Once the smoke dissipates, leave the tube in the container, refill the chamber, light the gun, and smoke the pieces again. Repeat one more time. Leave covered until all of the smoke has dissipated. Use immediately, or store in an airtight container in the refrigerator for up to 3 days.

SPRING ONIONS

Trim off the root ends from 8 of the onions. Trim the tops, leaving 3 inches (7.5 cm) intact from where the bulb begins. Cut the onions in half lengthwise, put them in a vacuum bag with the olive oil, and vacuum seal. Place the bag in a microwave oven and cook on high power for 2 minutes. Take the bag out of the microwave and let it deflate completely (this prevents the bag from exploding when it is returned to the microwave). Repeat the cycle twice. At this point, the onions should be fully cooked and tender. Transfer the onions, still in the bag, to an ice bath and let cool completely, about 30 minutes. The onions may be stored in the refrigerator until ready to serve, up to 3 days.

Trim off the root end of the remaining 4 onions. Use the green top to hold the onion in place as you slice the onion. Using the meat slicer or the electric knife, slice the bulbs to expose all of the rings.

In the blender, combine the maltodextrin and water and process for a full 15 seconds to dissolve the maltodextrin completely. Put the onion slices in a microwave-safe bowl, and pour the maltodextrin mixture over them. Mix gently to coat the onion rings evenly, then cook in the microwave on high power for 30 seconds.

Line a food dehydrator tray or sheet pan with a silicone mat (you may need 2 trays or pans). Carefully lay the onion rings in a single layer on the mat. Place in the dehydrator set at 155°F (68°C) or the oven preheated to 175°F (80°C) until dry and crisp, about 5 hours. The onion rings may be stored in an airtight container at room temperature for up to 5 days before serving.

IN THIS FRENCH- AND LEBANESE-INSPIRED DISH THE CHICKPEAS TURN UP IN THE FORM OF FLOUR FOR MAKING THE SMALL CRISP SAVORY CAKES KNOWN AS PANISSES

LILY

CIPPOLINI ONION ASPARAGUS GREEN GARLIC

The family name evokes a garden full of beautiful flowers, rather than a kitchen full of ingredients. But, in fact, many members of this clan are edible and delicious, including some of the flowers. And while you may not be ready to toss your daylilies into a salad (although you could), you can eat plenty of their kin, such as onions, garlic, asparagus, leeks, and chives. Many family members are crisp and juicy when raw, yet sweet, soft, and aromatic when cooked, making them particularly versatile. Sometimes their use is driven by the season, such as asparagus and green garlic in spring. Other times we welcome the challenge of trying to use a single family member, such as the onion, in as many different ways as possible in a dish.

BRYAN The technique in this recipe uniformly cooks the entire sweetbread for a beautiful presentation. It is something that chefs struggled with for years before the introduction of Activa, an enzyme that allows cooks to bind proteins together. The rest of the dish gives me the chance to show off my passion for exploring different ways to use the same ingredient to arrive at a variety of textures and flavors. Here, that ingredient is the lily family's highly versatile onion.

Sweetbreads, Green Apple–Onion Soubise, Onion Consommé, Onion Rounds, Braised Cippolini Onions

MAIN INGREDIENTS

25½ ounces (720 g) sweetbreads
1 carrot, peeled and sliced ¼ inch (6 mm) thick
2 celery ribs, sliced ¼ inch (6 mm) thick
1 yellow onion, julienned
3 cloves garlic, peeled but left whole
1 tablespoon (3 g) fresh thyme leaves
1 tablespoon (7 g) black peppercorns
4½ cups (1000 g) water
2 tablespoons plus 2¼ teaspoons (50 g) fine sea salt, plus more to season
Activa RM (see sources)
Wondra flour or other instant flour
1 tablespoon (14 g) extra-virgin olive oil
Onion Consommé (below)
Soubise (below)
Braised Cippolini Onions (below)
Apple Julienne (below)
Micro chives
Cippolini Onion Rounds (below)
Chive Oil (below)
Espelette pepper
Maldon sea salt

Equipment

vacuum sealer and vacuum bags
masticating vegetable juicer
high-speed blender
6-quart (5.7-l) pressure cooker
thermal immersion circulator
food dehydrator (optional)

Serves 6 as a first course

››

In a large pot, combine the sweetbreads, carrot, celery, onion, garlic, thyme, peppercorns, water, and salt and bring to a low simmer over medium-high heat. Adjust the heat to maintain a low simmer and cook for 10 minutes. Meanwhile, prepare an ice bath. When the sweetbreads are ready, using a skimmer, transfer them to the ice bath and discard the cooking liquid. When the sweetbreads are completely cool, after about 15 minutes, drain them, pat them dry, and gently peel the outside membrane. Weigh the sweetbreads and calculate 1 percent of the weight. Weigh out that amount of Activa RM. Break up the sweetbreads into large nuggets, each 2–3 inches (5–7.5 cm) long, and put them in a bowl. Sprinkle the Activa over the sweetbread nuggets and mix thoroughly with a rubber spatula.

Transfer about one-fifth of the sweetbreads to a food processor and process until a smooth purée forms. Return the puréed sweetbreads to the bowl with the sweetbread chunks and mix well. Transfer to a vacuum bag and vacuum seal. Put the bag in a sheet pan and place a second sheet pan on top. Place about 10 pounds (4.5 kg) of kitchen items, such as canned goods or bags of flour, on top of the second pan and refrigerate for 12 hours.

To serve, remove the sweetbreads from the bag and cut them into planks 1 inch (2.5 cm) wide. Dredge the planks lightly in the flour. In a large sauté pan, heat the olive oil over medium-high heat until it begins to shimmer but does not smoke. Add the sweetbread planks and cook, turning once, until evenly browned on both sides, about 3 minutes per side. Transfer the sweetbreads to a paper towel–lined plate, season lightly with fine sea salt, and keep warm.

In a saucepan, bring the onion consommé to a simmer over medium heat. In a small saucepan, bring the soubise to a bare simmer over medium heat, being careful that it does not scorch. Open the bag of cippolini onions and transfer the onions to a work surface and pat dry; discard the contents remaining in the bag. Add the onions to the consommé to heat through.

THE BEAUTIFUL PRESENTATION OF THIS DISH IS ONLY POSSIBLE THANKS TO THE DISCOVERY OF THE ENZYME ACTIVA WHICH ALLOWS CHEFS TO BIND PROTEINS TOGETHER

Slice the sweetbread planks crosswise ¼ inch (6 cm) thick and divide the slices into 6 equal portions. Gently mix together the julienned apple and chives. Arrange a small stack of apple julienne to the left of center in each serving bowl. Lay out 1 portion of the sweetbreads, slightly overlapping the slices in a vertical line directly to the right of the apple stack. To the right of the sweetbreads, put a spoonful of soubise. Put a cippoline onion at the top of the bowl and another at the bottom of the bowl. Pour the consommé around all of the elements. Add a large drop of chive oil to the consommé. Garnish the sweetbreads with the dehydrated cippolini onion rounds. Season the top of the sweetbreads with Espelette pepper and Maldon salt and serve right away.

ONION CONSOMMÉ

In a large saucepan, combine the onions and garlic, place over medium-high heat, and cook, stirring constantly, until caramelized, 10–15 minutes. Add the thyme and cook until it becomes aromatic, about 2 minutes. Add the sherry and stir to scrape up the browned bits on the pan bottom. Add the onion juice, soy sauce, and Worcestershire sauce, bring the mixture to a low simmer, and cook for 30 minutes. Add the water, bring the mixture back up to a simmer, and cook for 15 minutes more. Strain the mixture through a fine-mesh sieve placed over a saucepan. You should have about 6 cups (1350 g).

Place the pan over medium-high heat, whisk in the agar, and bring to a boil. Adjust the heat to maintain a simmer and cook for 5 minutes. Pour the mixture into a large, shallow baking dish and set aside at room temperature until cooled and firmly set, about 1 hour. Scrape the gel into a bowl and use a whisk to break it up into small pieces. Transfer the broken gel to a large square of cheesecloth, bring the corners together, and tie securely with cotton butcher's twine to form a purselike bag. Put the bag in a large conical sieve placed over another container to catch the liquid that passes through the cheesecloth, place the setup in the refrigerator, and let drain for at least 4 hours.

Discard the solids in the cheesecloth, transfer the liquid to the blender, and turn it on to low speed. Slowly increase the speed until a vortex forms in the center of the liquid. Sprinkle the xanthan gum and salt into the vortex and process for a full 5 seconds to dissolve completely. The consommé may be stored in a lidded container in the refrigerator for up to 3 days before using.

SOUBISE

In the pressure cooker, combine the onion, apples, mirin, vinegar, rice, and salt. Following the manufacturer's instructions, lock the lid in place, bring up the pressure to high, and cook for 10 minutes. Let the pressure dissipate naturally, then uncover.

Prepare an ice bath. Transfer the contents of the pressure cooker to the clean blender and process until a smooth purée forms. Pour the purée into a metal bowl, set the bowl over the ice bath, and let cool completely, stirring occasionally and replenishing the ice as needed, about 20 minutes. Transfer to a lidded container and refrigerate until ready to serve or for up to 3 days.

BRAISED CIPPOLINI ONIONS

Preheat the circulating water bath to 194°F (90°C).

In a small bowl, toss the onions with the salt. Transfer the onions to a vacuum bag, add the olive oil and thyme, and vacuum seal. Cook in the circulating water bath until they feel tender when the bag is pressed gently, about 1 hour. Just before the onions are ready, prepare an ice bath. When they are ready, transfer the bag to the ice bath and let cool completely, replenishing the ice as needed, about 20 minutes. The onions may be stored in the bag in the refrigerator for up to 3 days before using.

APPLE JULIENNE

Peel and core the apple, then cut into julienne ¼ inch (6 mm) wide and 1 inch (2.5 cm) long. In a bowl, mix together the water and citric acid and add the julienned apple. It will keep for up to 10 minutes.

CIPPOLINI ONION ROUNDS

On a mandoline, slice the onion paper-thin. Separate the slices into individual rings. Line a food dehydrator tray or a sheet pan with a silicone mat. Lay out the nicest, larger rings on the mat, discarding any small pieces or broken circles. Using a fine-mesh sieve or a sugar duster, sprinkle the confectioners' sugar evenly over the slices. Put the onion slices in the dehydrator set at 155°F (68°C) or the oven preheated to 175°F (80°C) until dry and crisp, about 2 hours. The dehydrated onions may be stored in an airtight container at room temperature for up to 1 week.

CHIVE OIL

Line a conical sieve with cheesecloth and place over a metal bowl. Prepare an ice bath. Put the chives in the blender. In a small saucepan, heat the grape seed oil to 120°F (49°C). Immediately pour the oil over the chives and blend until a smooth purée forms. Let the purée drain, undisturbed, until all of the oil is extracted into the bowl, replenishing the ice as needed, about 1 hour. Discard the cheesecloth without pressing it in any way. Store the chive oil in a lidded container in the refrigerator until ready to serve, up to 2 days.

ONION CONSOMMÉ

3 large red onions, julienned
5 cloves garlic, thinly sliced on a mandoline
Leaves from 10 fresh thyme sprigs, chopped
½ cup (120 g) dry sherry
Juice from 7 large yellow onions (juiced in a masticating vegetable juicer)
2 tablespoons (40 g) soy sauce
1 tablespoon (10 g) Worcestershire sauce
4 cups (900 g) water
3.5 grams agar (see sources)
.53 gram xanthan gum (see sources)
½ teaspoon (3 g) fine sea salt

SOUBISE

½ large yellow onion, diced
2 Granny Smith apples, peeled, cored, and diced
½ cup (120 g) mirin
1 cup (320 g) rice vinegar
¼ cup (50 g) jasmine rice
¾ teaspoon (4.5 g) fine sea salt

BRAISED CIPPOLINI ONIONS

12 small cippolini onions, trimmed and peeled
⅛ teaspoon (.75 g) fine sea salt
3 tablespoons (42 g) extra-virgin olive oil
2 fresh thyme sprigs

APPLE JULIENNE

1 Granny Smith apple
1 cup (225 g) water
2.25 grams citric acid (see sources)

CIPPOLINI ONION ROUNDS

1 cippolini onion, trimmed and peeled
1 tablespoon (7 g) confectioners' sugar

CHIVE OIL

24 fresh chives, cut into 1-inch (2.5-cm) pieces
½ cup grape seed oil

MICHAEL A classic roast beef sandwich with shaved raw onions set this idea in motion. I have used shaved beef tongue in place of the roast beef and paired it with onion in various forms. The deep-fried "funions" give the dish a delicious crunch, the pickled onions provide sweetness and acidity, and the nigella seeds add an onion note that is slightly bitter and sharp. The mustard ice cream came about because I like both mustard and mayonnaise on my roast beef sandwich.

Beef Tongue Cold Cuts, Mustard Ice Cream, Pickled Onions, "Funions," Onion Slices

MAIN INGREDIENTS

2½ quarts (2250 g) water

1¼ cups plus 2 tablespoons (293 g) firmly packed light brown sugar

½ cup (144 g) fine sea salt

½ cup (55 g) thinly sliced fresh ginger

¼ cup (14 g) coriander seeds

2 tablespoons (10 g) whole cloves

2 tablespoons (14 g) black peppercorns

2 tablespoons (7.5 g) allspice berries

2 tablespoons (16 g) yellow mustard seeds

1 teaspoon (6.8 g) pink curing salt (see sources)

3 limes

2 oranges

½ grapefruit

½ lemon

¼ bunch fresh thyme

1 beef tongue

Arbequina extra-virgin olive oil

Fine sea salt

Pickled Onions (below)

Mustard Ice Cream (below)

"Funions" (below)

1 tablespoon nigella seeds

2 green onions, green tops only, thinly sliced

Equipment

thermal immersion circulator

vacuum sealer and vacuum bags

ice cream maker

food dehydrator (optional)

deep fryer (optional)

Serves 6 as a first course

››

To make a brine, in a large pot, combine the water, brown sugar, sea salt, ginger, coriander, cloves, peppercorns, allspice, mustard seeds, and pink salt and bring to a boil over high heat. Meanwhile, cut the limes and oranges in half horizontally. Squeeze the juice from each citrus half into a heatproof 3-gallon (12-l) container. Drop the spent citrus halves into the container and add the thyme. Once the liquid comes to a boil, pour it over the citrus and thyme. Put the liquid, uncovered, in the refrigerator until completely cool, about 2 hours. Strain the liquid through a fine-mesh sieve into a large bowl. Measure out 2 cups (450 g) of the brine and refrigerate in a lidded container. Put the remaining brine in a bowl, add the tongue, cover, and refrigerate for 24 hours.

Preheat the circulating water bath to 158°F (70°C).

Drain the tongue and discard the brine it was soaked in. Put the tongue and the reserved 2 cups (450 g) brine in a vacuum bag and vacuum seal. Cook in the circulating water bath for 24 hours.

Remove the bag from the bath, then remove the tongue from the bag and reserve the brine. While the tongue is still hot, peel away the outer skin and trim away the connective tissue on the underside. Let the tongue cool completely to room temperature, about 45 minutes. Put the cooled tongue and the reserved brine in a new vacuum bag and vacuum seal. The tongue may be stored in the refrigerator for up to 5 days before serving.

To serve, trim both ends of the tongue to square them, and then cut the tongue lengthwise into thin slices as if you are slicing ham for a sandwich. Arrange 4 or 5 slices on each serving plate. Drizzle the meat with olive oil and season lightly with sea salt. Place 5 pieces of pickled onion on the tongue. Using 2 demitasse spoons, put a few small, irregular dollops of mustard ice cream on top of the tongue slices. Place a few "funions" on top of 1 of the spoonfuls of ice cream. Sprinkle a few nigella seeds and sliced green onions over the top and serve.

PONDERING HOW TO
USE ONIONS
A POPULAR MEMBER OF THE
LILY FAMILY
MADE ME THINK OF A
FAVORITE CHILDHOOD
SNACK FOOD
WHICH I'VE RECREATED HERE

PICKLED ONIONS

6 red pearl onions
¼ teaspoon (1.5 g) fine sea salt
6 tablespoons plus 2 teaspoons (100 g) mirin
5 tablespoons (100 g) red wine vinegar
¼ cup (50 g) sugar

MUSTARD ICE CREAM

1 large egg
1 large egg yolk
6 tablespoons plus 2 teaspoons (100 g) heavy cream
2¼ cups (585 g) whole milk
¼ cup plus 2 tablespoons (75 g) sugar
¾ cup plus 2 tablespoons (50 g) dry milk powder
½ cup plus 1 teaspoon (75 g) glucose powder (see sources)
2 tablespoons (30 g) Trimoline (see sources) or light corn syrup
½ teaspoon (3 g) mustard powder
5½ tablespoons (100 g) Dijon mustard
¼ teaspoon (1.5 g) fine sea salt

PICKLED ONIONS

Peel the pearl onions, split them in half vertically, remove the cores at the base, and separate the layers into petals. Put the onion petals on a plate and sprinkle them with the salt. Let the petals sit for 1 hour. Meanwhile, in a small bowl, stir together the mirin, vinegar, and sugar until the sugar dissolves. Pat dry the onion petals and add them to the vinegar mixture. Put the petals and vinegar mixture in a vacuum bag and vacuum seal. Refrigerate the pickled onions for at least 24 hours to develop the flavor before using. They will keep for several days.

MUSTARD ICE CREAM

Prepare an ice bath. In a small bowl, whisk together the egg, egg yolk, and cream until blended. In a saucepan, combine the milk, 2 tablespoons (25 g) of the sugar, and the milk powder over medium-high heat. When the temperature reaches 95°F (35°C), add the remaining ¼ cup (50 g) sugar, the glucose powder, Trimoline, and mustard and stir well to combine. Slowly drizzle the egg mixture into the hot milk mixture while stirring continuously. Cook over medium heat, stirring constantly, until the mixture reaches 180°F (82°C). Remove from heat and strain through a fine-mesh sieve placed over a metal bowl. Set the bowl over the ice bath and let cool completely, stirring occasionally and replenishing the ice as needed, about 25 minutes. Transfer the cooled mixture to a lidded container and refrigerate for at least 12 hours or up to 48 hours to develop the flavors.

Transfer the chilled mixture to the ice-cream maker and freeze according to the manufacturer's instructions. Transfer to a freezer container and freeze for at least 2 hours to firm up before serving. It will keep for 2 weeks.

"FUNIONS"

In a bowl, whisk together the granulated onion and tapioca starch. Add the water and, using a rubber spatula, stir until a dough forms. Lay a large sheet

of plastic wrap on a work surface and turn out the dough onto the center of the sheet. Gently press the dough into a rectangle in the center of the sheet, with room to roll it out on all sides. Cover with a second large sheet of plastic wrap. Using a rolling pin, roll out the dough until it is thin enough to see your hand through the dough if you slide it under the bottom sheet of plastic wrap.Prepare a large steamer, place the plastic-wrapped dough flat on the steamer tray, and steam for 12 minutes. Remove the dough from the steamer and let cool to room temperature, 30–45 minutes. (If necessary to fit your steamer, you can cut the dough into smaller pieces and rewrap them in plastic wrap.) Alternatively, bring a large pot of water to a boil over high heat. Put the dough in a vacuum bag and vacuum seal, add to the boiling water, and boil for 12 minutes. Remove the bag from the pot, remove the onion dough from the bag, and let cool as directed for the steamed dough.

Line a food dehydrator tray or a sheet pan with a silicone mat. Unwrap the dough and place it on the mat. Place in the dehydrator set at 150°F (65°C) or the oven preheated to 175°F (80°C) until dry but still pliable, about 45 minutes. Using a 1-inch (2.5-cm) round cutter and a ½-inch (12-mm) round cutter, cut out small rings of dough. Return the rings to the silicone mat, then return to the dehydrator or oven until completely dry and brittle to the touch, about 25 minutes longer.

Pour the canola oil into a deep fryer to the fill line or into a tall-sided saucepan to a depth of 2½ inches (6 cm) and heat to 375°F (190°C).

Add the rings to the hot oil and fry until they have expanded and are light and puffy, 2–3 minutes. Using a skimmer, transfer the rings to a paper towel–lined sheet pan and season with the salt. The rings may be stored in an airtight container at room temperature for up to a day.

"FUNIONS"

¼ cup plus 1 tablespoon (35 g) granulated onion

½ cup (50 g) tapioca starch

¼ cup (56 g) water

Canola oil for deep-frying

⅛ teaspoon (.75 g) fine sea salt

MAIN INGREDIENTS

24 green asparagus, about 1¼ pounds (565 g)

4 ounces (113 g) prosciutto ends

3 black peppercorns

2 cloves garlic

½ cup (57 g) spring garlic trimmings from Grilled Garlic Stalks (below)

3 cups plus 2 tablespoons (700 g) water

¾ teaspoon (4.5 g) fine sea salt

1½ grams Sucro (see sources)

1 teaspoon (4.5 g) fresh lemon juice

1 tablespoon (14 g) extra-virgin olive oil

24 petite sorrel blooms

12 petite sorrel sprigs

Grilled Garlic Stalks (below)

Spring Garlic Roots (below)

1 garlic top reserved from Spring Garlic Roots (below), cut into ¼-inch (6-mm) dice

Equipment

6-quart (5.7-l) pressure cooker

Misto oil pump (optional)

deep fryer (optional)

Serves 6 as a first course

SPRING GARLIC ROOTS

12 spring garlic stalks with roots attached

Canola oil for deep-frying

Fine sea salt

GRILLED GARLIC STALKS

12 spring garlic shoots reserved from Spring Garlic Roots (above)

¼ teaspoon (1.5 g) fine sea salt

½ teaspoon (2 g) canola oil

BRYAN When I was at Charlie Palmer Steak in Washington, D.C., guests would sometimes ask for asparagus in the dead of winter. There, I was taught to honor such requests, even if it meant serving Chilean asparagus in January. At Volt, it's another story. I celebrate asparagus when it's in season, and when it's not, I suggest something that is. This dish is quite simple, because if you buy its elements in spring when they are at their best, their flavors will pop with little help from you.

Asparagus, Spring Garlic, Sorrel Leaves and Blooms, Prosciutto

Cut off the fibrous bottoms of the asparagus stalks and reserve them. Using a horizontal vegetable peeler, run it down the stalk of 1 asparagus, from the top of the tip to the bottom of the spear, to cut a long ribbon. Repeat to get as many whole pieces as possible, then cut 5 more asparagus the same way. Put the prettiest ribbons in a small covered bowl in the refrigerator.

To make a stock, select a metal bowl that will fit inside the pressure cooker and is large enough to hold all of the ingredients. Put the asparagus trimmings and stalk bottoms in the bowl and add the prosciutto ends, peppercorns, garlic cloves, and spring garlic trimmings. Add the water to the bowl; it should just cover the ingredients. Put a rack on the bottom of the pressure cooker, place the bowl on top, and pour water into the pressure cooker to reach halfway up the sides of the bowl. Add ½ teaspoon (3 g) of the salt. Following the manufacturer's instructions, lock the lid in place, bring the pressure up to high, and cook for 12 minutes. Let the pressure dissipate naturally, then uncover. Remove the bowl from the pressure cooker, and strain the contents through a fine-mesh sieve. You should have about 2 cups (450 g). Reserve half for cooking the asparagus and the other half for making the stock.

Put half of the asparagus-prosciutto stock in a sauté pan, place over medium-high heat, and bring to a simmer. Adjust the heat to maintain a low simmer, add the asparagus spears, and cook until tender, about 8 minutes. Meanwhile, put the remaining stock in a small saucepan, place over medium-high heat, and bring to a simmer. Sprinkle in the Sucro and, using an immersion blender, emulsify to form a sauce. Keep warm.

When the asparagus is ready, remove the spears from the stock and pat dry. In the Misto pump, combine the lemon juice, olive oil, and remaining ¼ teaspoon (1.5 g) salt and shake well. Put the sorrel blooms, sorrel sprigs, and asparagus ribbons in 3 separate bowls and dress them with a few sprays from the pump. Alternatively, in a bowl, whisk together the olive oil, lemon juice, and salt and use a teaspoon or so to dress each garnish. Put 3 asparagus spears on each serving plate in offset angles. Put one grilled garlic stalk over the asparagus.

IF YOU GET ALL THE INGREDIENTS FOR THIS DISH IN THE SPRING WHEN THEY ARE FRESH AND BEAUTIFUL THE FLAVORS WILL POP WITH LITTLE EXTRA ADORNMENT

Put a few pieces of the reserved asparagus ribbons on the plate. Arrange a small pile of fried garlic roots on the left hand side of the plate and garnish them with the sorrel leaves and blooms. Sprinkle the reserved diced garlic stalks over the asparagus. Using the immersion blender, froth the warm sauce. Put several spoonfuls of the sauce in the empty spaces on the plate and serve right away.

SPRING GARLIC ROOTS

Cut the roots off of each piece of garlic; reserve the green stalks for the grilled garlic stalks (below). Wash the roots very well under cool water. Put them in the pressure cooker and add water to a depth of 2 inches (5 cm). Following the manufacturer's instructions, lock the lid in place, and cook at high pressure for 15 minutes. Let the pressure dissipate naturally, then uncover. Remove the roots from the pressure cooker, pat dry with paper towels, and spread on a sheet pan. Let cool to room temperature, about 30 minutes.

Pour the canola oil into a deep fryer to the fill line or into a tall-sided saucepan to a depth of 2½ inches (6 cm) and heat to 350°F (175°C.)

Add the roots to the hot oil and fry until crisp and golden brown, 10–15 seconds. Using a skimmer, transfer to a paper towel–lined sheet pan and season lightly with salt. Serve right away.

GRILLED GARLIC STALKS

Prepare a fire in a charcoal grill until the coals are white hot, or preheat a gas grill to medium-high.

Season the garlic stalks with canola oil and salt, and grill, turning often, until the outer layer of the garlic starts to caramelize, about 5 minutes. Transfer to a paper towel–lined plate. Cut 6 of the stalks into dice. Use right away.

MICHAEL Here, the mild flavor of frog legs allows springtime's green garlic, the star of this recipe, to shine. The almond imparts a pleasant nuttiness to the dish, and the parsley-garlic financier, a delicate crouton, echoes the flavors of the soup. The milk skins are a bit of a surprise. We think of milk as being fluid, so the crispy, nutty skins, which are a stand-in for the fried garlic that traditionally accompanies this soup, are the opposite of what diners expect.

Green Garlic Milk Soup, Almonds, Green Financier, Fried Milk, Frog Leg Confit, Almond Praline

Place a saucepan over medium heat. When the pan is hot, add the olive oil and reduce the heat to low. Put the onion and garlic in the pan and cook, stirring occasionally, until tender and translucent but not browned, about 10 minutes. Add the green garlic and cook for 5 minutes. Add the parsley leaves, milk, water, sugar, and salt, raise the heat to medium-high, and bring just to a simmer. Carefully transfer the hot mixture to the blender. Turn the blender on to low speed, then slowly increase the speed to purée the mixture (this can be done in batches if you have a small blender).

Prepare an ice bath. Strain the purée through a fine-mesh sieve placed over a large, shallow metal bowl. Set the bowl over the ice bath and let cool until ice-cold, stirring constantly to retain the bright green color and replenishing the ice as needed, about 15 minutes. The soup may be stored in a lidded container in the refrigerator for up to 5 days before serving.

To serve, in a saucepan, bring the soup to a simmer over medium heat. While the soup is heating, put the duck fat into a small sauté pan and turn the heat on to low. When the fat is warm, add the frog leg confit and heat gently until warmed through. The key is to warm the leg meat slowly so it stays moist and tender. Divide the frog leg confit into 8 equal portions.

Spoon 3 dots of the Marcona almond praline around the inside of each bowl. Tear 2 parsley-garlic financiers in half and put the 4 pieces in a bowl. Repeat with the remaining financiers. Add a portion of frog leg confit to each bowl. Arrange the frog legs into 4 piles in each bowl, putting 1 pile of frog legs on top of each piece of financier. Garnish 2 of the frog leg piles with a fried milk skin. Put 3 garlic flowers in each bowl and drizzle the legs with the extra-virgin olive oil.

When the soup is hot, using an immersion blender, blend until light and frothy. Spoon the soup into the bowl around the garnishes and serve right away.

MAIN INGREDIENTS

½ cup (113 g) olive oil or oil reserved from frying Marcona almonds (below)

1 sweet onion, thinly sliced

6 cloves garlic, thinly sliced

9 ounces (250 g) green garlic or garlic chives, finely sliced

Leaves from 1 bunch fresh flat-leaf parsley

3 cups plus 2 tablespoons (800 g) whole milk

¾ cup plus 2 tablespoons plus 1 teaspoon (200 g) water

1 tablespoon (12.5 g) sugar

1½ teaspoons (9 g) fine sea salt

2 tablespoons (28 g) duck fat reserved from Frog Leg Confit (below)

Frog Leg Confit (below)

Marcona Almond Praline (below)

Parsley-Garlic Financiers (below)

Fried Milk Skins (below)

24 garlic flowers

1 tablespoon (14 g) extra-virgin olive oil

Equipment

high-speed blender

thermal immersion circulator

vacuum sealer and vacuum bags

24-cup miniature muffin tin

food dehydrator (optional)

Serves 8 as a first course

››

FROG LEG CONFIT

2 teaspoons (12 g) coarse sea salt

Finely grated zest of 2 limes

12 frog legs

¼ teaspoon (1 g) Espelette pepper

½ cup (113 g) rendered duck fat

MARCONA ALMOND PRALINE

1 cup (140 g) unsalted roasted Marcona almonds

1 cup (225 g) extra-virgin olive oil

½ teaspoon (3 g) fine sea salt

PARSLEY-GARLIC PURÉE

2 cups (450 g) water

1 clove garlic, thinly sliced

1 bunch fresh flat-leaf parsley, coarsely chopped

2 tablespoons plus 2 teaspoons (37.5 g) extra-virgin olive oil

PARSLEY-GARLIC FINANCIERS

Nonstick cooking spray

2½ (92.5 g) large egg whites (for the ½ egg white, whisk 1 white and divide in half)

¾ cup (75 g) almond flour

⅓ cup (50 g) all-purpose flour

¾ cup (84 g) confectioners' sugar

¾ teaspoon (4.5 g) baking powder

⅓ teaspoon (2 g) fine sea salt

2¾ ounces (75 g) Parsley-Garlic Purée (above), at room temperature

4 tablespoons plus 2 teaspoons (65 g) unsalted butter, at room temperature

FRIED MILK SKINS

¾ cup (60 g) nonfat dry milk powder

1 cup (260 g) whole milk

2 cups (450 g) canola oil

Fine sea salt

FROG LEG CONFIT

Preheat the circulating water bath to 149°F (65°C).

In a bowl, stir together the salt and lime zest. Put the frog legs into the salt mixture and stir to coat them evenly. Cover the bowl with plastic wrap and refrigerate for 30 minutes. Wipe off any residual lime salt from the frog legs and pat them dry with paper towels. Sprinkle the legs evenly with the Espelette pepper. Put the frog legs and duck fat into a vacuum bag and vacuum seal. Cook in the circulating water bath for 1 hour.

Remove the bag from the bath and set aside for 10 minutes. Cut open the bag and remove the frog legs. Pour the duck fat into a bowl, cover, and refrigerate until serving. Using your fingers, remove the individual leg muscle pieces from the leg bones. Put the leg meat into a bowl and cover with plastic wrap. Refrigerate until ready to serve or for up to 2 days.

MARCONA ALMOND PRALINE

In a small saucepan, combine the almonds and oil over medium-low heat and cook, stirring occasionally, until the almonds are deep brown but are not burned, 5–8 minutes. Pour into a fine-mesh sieve placed over a bowl, reserving both the oil and the almonds. Transfer the almonds to a blender, add the salt, and turn on the blender to medium speed. Add a few spoonfuls of the reserved oil as needed for the almonds to blend easily and process until the mixture is completely smooth and is the consistency of almond butter. The almond mixture may be stored in a lidded container for up to 1 week before using. Let the remaining almond oil cool, then cover the oil and reserve for making the soup.

PARSLEY-GARLIC PURÉE

In a saucepan, bring the water to a boil over high heat. While the water is heating, prepare an ice bath. Add the garlic and parsley to the boiling water and cook until the parsley is deep green and the garlic is tender, about 2 minutes. Remove from the heat and pour into a colander placed over a heatproof bowl, reserving both the parsley and garlic and the cooking liquid. Transfer the hot parsley and garlic to the blender and turn it on to medium speed. Add a few spoonfuls of the reserved cooking liquid to help the mixture blend easily. Increase the speed to high and process until a smooth purée forms. With the blender running, slowly pour in the olive oil and process until emulsified.

Pour the purée into a metal bowl, set the bowl over the ice bath, and let cool until ice-cold, stirring from time to time so the purée retains its vibrant green color and replenishing the ice as needed, about 20 minutes. The purée may be stored in a lidded container in the refrigerator for up to 3 days before using.

PARSLEY-GARLIC FINANCIERS

Preheat the oven to 400°F (200°C). Spray the wells of the miniature muffin tin with nonstick cooking spray.

In a stand mixer fitted with the whisk attachment, whip the egg whites on medium-high speed until stiff peaks form, about 5 minutes. In a separate bowl, whisk together the almond flour, all-purpose flour, confectioners' sugar, baking powder, and salt. Using a rubber spatula, fold the flour mixture into the egg whites. Then add the parsley-garlic purée and fold until almost completely incorporated. Finally, add the butter and continue to fold until fully blended.

Spoon the batter into a pastry bag fitted with a large, plain tip. Pipe the batter into the prepared muffin molds, filling the cups two-thirds full. Put the muffin tin on a sheet pan, place in the oven, and bake until the cakes have risen and are firm to the touch in the center, about 10 minutes. Remove from the oven and immediately turn the cakes out onto a rack. Let cool completely. They may be stored in an airtight container at room temperature for up to 2 days.

FRIED MILK SKINS

In a bowl, whisk together the milk powder and the whole milk until the powder dissolves. Line a food dehydrator tray or a sheet pan with a silicone mat, and pour the milk mixture onto the mat, using an offset spatula to spread it evenly in a thin layer. Place in the dehydrator set at 155°F (68°C) or the oven preheated to 175°F (80°C) until completely dry, about 4 hours. If dehydrating in the oven, watch closely to avoid browning.

In a tall-sided saucepan, heat the canola oil to 350°F (180°F). Gently peel the milk skin from the silicone mat. It will break into pieces. Add the pieces to the hot oil and fry until golden brown, 2–3 seconds. Using a skimmer, transfer to a paper towel–lined sheet pan and season lightly with salt. Serve right away.

WE THINK OF MILK AS FLUID SO THE CRISPY NUTTY MILK SKINS THAT I HAVE CREATED FOR THIS DISH ARE THE OPPOSITE OF WHAT YOU MIGHT EXPECT

MAMMAL

VENISON
BEEF
PORK

We do our best to make sure that the mammals we eat—pigs, cows, deer, sheep—live well, are slaughtered humanely, and are treated with respect once they are in our kitchens. That means that we source them with care and then strive to use every part of the animal. We find satisfaction in pushing ourselves to put every "ingredient" to use, especially unusual ones. For example, using a pig's head to make head cheese, a time-consuming and technique-demanding preparation, utilizes part of the animal that is often discarded, but yields a beautiful and delicious dish. We also like to explore new ways to use conventional members of this family in unconventional ways, such as marrying a venison loin and granola or reinventing a Chinese restaurant staple, beef with broccoli.

BRYAN I am a hunter. When I get up in the morning to go hunting, my breakfast of choice is always the same: coffee and granola. When I return home, I typically drink a bottle of cream soda. So whenever I think about preparing venison, coffee, granola, and cream soda automatically come to mind. Here, the coffee is used to make an oil and a crumblike topping, a disk of granola rests just above the venison, and the cream soda flavors the potatoes.

Venison, Creamsicle Potatoes, Cranberry Granola, Coffee

MAIN INGREDIENTS

3 pounds (1.36 kg) venison strip loin
2¼ teaspoons (13.5 g) fine sea salt
1½ teaspoons (3.5 g) black peppercorns
4 juniper berries
Finely grated zest of 1 orange
4 cloves garlic, smashed
4 fresh thyme sprigs
¼ cup (56 g) extra-virgin olive oil
2½ teaspoons (3 g) freshly ground black pepper
Cranberry Granola (below)
¼ cup (56 g) grape seed oil
4 tablespoons (56 g) unsalted butter
Venison Sauce (below)
Coffee Oil (below)
Creamsicle Potato Purée (below)
Coffee "Soil" (below)
Leaves from 2 fresh thyme sprigs

Equipment

thermal immersion circulator
vacuum sealer and vacuum bags
deep fryer (optional)
6-quart (5.7-l) pressure cooker

Serves 6 as a main course

››

Preheat the circulating water bath to 137°F (58.5°C).

Trim the silver skin and any sinew or gristle from the loin. In a mortar, combine 1½ teaspoons (9 g) of the salt, the peppercorns, juniper berries, and orange zest and grind with a pestle into an aromatic rub. Season the venison evenly with the mixture, rubbing it onto the meat.

Put the seasoned venison, garlic, 1 sprig of the thyme, and the olive oil in a vacuum bag and vacuum seal. Cook the venison in the circulating water bath for 55 minutes. Remove the bag from the water, then remove the venison from the bag and pat it dry with paper towels. Discard the contents of the bag.

Preheat the oven to 250°F (120°C).

Put a 2-inch (5-cm) ring mold on a sheet pan, press the cranberry granola into it, and lift away the ring. Repeat to make a total of 6 granola rounds. Place in the oven to warm through, about 20 minutes.

Reseason the venison with the remaining ¾ teaspoon (4.5 g) salt, and 1 teaspoon (2 g) of the ground pepper. In a sauté pan, heat the grape seed oil over medium-high heat until it begins to shimmer but does not smoke. Add the venison and cook, turning once, until well seared on both sides, 3–4 minutes on each side. Add the butter and the remaining 3 thyme sprigs and, using a wide, flat, large metal spoon, baste the venison with the fat and herbs to flavor the meat and encourage browning, 2–3 minutes. Transfer the venison to a rack set over a sheet pan and let rest for 5 minutes. Put the venison sauce in a small saucepan set over medium heat and bring it to a simmer. Brush the venison with the sauce, and then roll in the coffee soil until covered. Slice the venison crosswise into 6 equal medallions.

Place a granola ring on the top third of each serving plate. If desired, turn the ring on its side on the serving plate. Place a medallion of venison just below the granola and spoon the venison sauce over the left side of the meat. Using a demitasse spoon, put a few drops of the coffee oil on the sauce where it runs onto the plate. Place 2 spoonfuls of Creamsicle potato purée below the meat,

ON VENISON HUNTING DAYS WHEN I LEAVE THE HOUSE EARLY

MY BREAKFAST OF CHOICE IS COFFEE & GRANOLA

AND I INCORPORATED THOSE FLAVORS INTO THIS DISH

CRANBERRY GRANOLA

Canola oil

¾ sweet potato, about 3½ ounces (100 g), peeled and thinly shaved on a mandoline

1 teaspoon (6 g) fine sea salt, plus more to season

½ celery root, about 3½ ounces (100 g), peeled and thinly shaved on a mandoline

½ cup (100 g) long-grain white rice

½ cup (50 g) old-fashioned rolled oats

¼ cup (35 g) pine nuts, toasted and roughly chopped

3 tablespoons (82.5 g) liquid glucose (see sources)

2½ tablespoons (40 g) honey

½ cup (50 g) fresh cranberries

VENISON SAUCE

3 pounds (1.36 kg) venison bones

4 cups (900 g) Chicken Stock (page 319)

1 bay leaf

4 teaspoons (13.3 g) soy sauce

11 juniper berries

1 cup (110 g) dried cranberries

Finely grated zest of 1 orange

¾ ounce (20 g) Volt blend coffee beans (see sources)

slightly offset from each other. Sprinkle the coffee "soil" and fresh thyme leaves along the right side of the plate. Serve right away.

CRANBERRY GRANOLA

Pour the canola oil into a deep fryer to the fill line or into a tall-sided saucepan to a depth of 2½ inches (6 cm) and heat to 350°F (180°C).

Working in batches, add the sweet potato shavings to the hot oil and fry until crisp and golden brown, about 30 seconds. Using a skimmer, transfer to a paper towel–lined plate to drain and season lightly with salt. Fry, drain, and season the celery root shavings the same way. Raise the oil temperature to 400°F (200°C), add the rice to the oil, and fry until it puffs up, 20–30 seconds. Using the skimmer, transfer the puffed rice to a paper towel–lined plate to drain and season lightly with salt.

Lightly grease a sheet pan with canola oil. In a large bowl, combine the fried sweet potato, celery root, and rice; the oats; and the pine nuts. In a microwave-safe bowl, combine the glucose, honey, cranberries, and the 1 teaspoon (6 g) salt. Cook on high power for 1 minute. Immediately pour the hot honey mixture over the dry ingredients in the bowl and mix until well blended. Spread the granola out on the prepared sheet pan and let cool to room temperature before using. The cooled granola may be stored in a lock-top bag at room temperature for up to 1 week before using.

VENISON SAUCE

Preheat the oven to 400°F (200°C). Line a sheet pan with parchment paper. Put the venison bones on the prepared pan and roast until golden brown, about 30 minutes. Let them cool to room temperature on the sheet pan.

In the pressure cooker, combine the stock, roasted bones, bay leaf, soy sauce, juniper berries, and dried cranberries. Following the manufacturer's instructions, lock the lid in place, bring up to high pressure, and cook for 1 hour. Let the pressure dissipate naturally.

Uncover the pressure cooker and add the orange zest and coffee beans. Replace the lid and let stand for 15 minutes to infuse the flavors. Strain the sauce through a fine-mesh sieve placed over a saucepan. Bring to a simmer over medium-low heat and cook until reduced by half, 30–45 minutes. Use immediately, or transfer to a metal bowl set over an ice bath and let cool completely, stirring occasionally and replenishing the ice as needed, for about 20 minutes. The cooled sauce may be stored in a lidded container in the refrigerator for up to 3 days.

COFFEE OIL

In a small saucepan, combine the ground coffee and grape seed oil over low heat. Whisking constantly, warm the mixture until it reaches 158°F (70°C), then remove the pan from heat, cover, and let the mixture steep for 1 hour to develop the flavors. Strain the oil through a coffee filter into a bowl and set aside at room temperature until serving. The coffee oil may be stored in a lidded container at room temperature for up to 1 week.

COFFEE "SOIL"

Preheat the oven to 350°F (180°C). Line a sheet pan with a silicone mat.

In a bowl, combine the butter, almond flour, coffee, vanilla seeds, brown sugar, and salt. Using your hands, mix well until a smooth mixture forms that is reminiscent of streusel. Spread the mixture on the prepared pan. Bake for 8 minutes. Rotate the pan 180 degrees and continue to bake until the crumbs are dry and fragrant, about 8 minutes more. Let cool to room temperature on the sheet pan before using. The "soil" may be stored in a lock-top bag at room temperature for up to 3 days.

CREAMSICLE POTATO PURÉE

In a saucepan, combine the potatoes, cream, vanilla seeds, and salt, place over medium-low heat, and bring to a simmer. Cook until completely tender when pierced with a skewer, about 1 hour.

Using a slotted spoon, transfer the potatoes and a few tablespoons of the cooking liquid to a food processor and process until smooth. Take care not to overprocess. Using a ladle, push the purée through a fine-mesh sieve placed over a heatproof container. Keep warm until ready to serve.

COFFEE OIL

7 tablespoons (50 g) Volt blend ground coffee (see sources)

¾ cup (150 g) grape seed oil

COFFEE "SOIL"

5 tablespoons plus 1 teaspoon (75 g) unsalted butter, at room temperature

2⅔ cups (250 g) almond flour

7 tablespoons (50 g) Volt blend ground coffee (see sources)

Seeds scraped from 1 vanilla bean

3 tablespoons (40 g) firmly packed light brown sugar

1 teaspoon (6 g) fine sea salt

CREAMSICLE POTATO PURÉE

2 pounds (900 g) White Creamsicle potatoes, peeled and cut into large dice

4 cups (960 g) heavy cream

Seeds scraped from 1 vanilla bean

1½ teaspoons (9 g) fine sea salt

MICHAEL This dish came about for two reasons: I hated broccoli as a child, and I wanted to reinvent Asian-style beef with broccoli. When I was younger, broccoli always seemed to be army green and mushy. Here, I've changed the color, texture, and appearance of the vegetable that haunted me in my youth. Garam masala, a heady mix of Indian spices that you can blend to your own taste, flavors not only the beef but also the accompanying sauce.

Beef with Cream of Dehydrated Broccoli, Horseradish "Styrofoam," Caramelized Soy

MAIN INGREDIENTS

4 boneless beef short ribs (about 3½ pounds/1.6 kg)

Fine sea salt

¼ cup (56 g) canola oil, plus more for deep-frying

1 tablespoon (6.5 g) Garam Masala (page 318)

¼ cup plus 1 tablespoon (70 g) extra-virgin olive oil, plus more for dressing

Dried Broccoli (below)

Broccoli Purée (below)

3 tablespoons (42 g) cold unsalted butter

Horseradish "Styrofoam" (below)

Spicy Soy-Caramel Sauce (below)

1 bunch broccoli flowers

Maldon sea salt

Equipment

thermal immersion circulator

vacuum sealer and vacuum bags

deep fryer (optional)

food dehydrator (optional)

masticating vegetable juicer

high-speed blender

Serves 4 as a main course

Preheat the circulating water bath to 149°F (65°C).

Trim the short ribs, removing all of the silver skin. Season the ribs generously with salt. In a large sauté pan, heat the ¼ cup (56 g) canola oil over medium-high heat until it begins to shimmer but does not smoke. Add the short ribs and cook, turning once, until nicely seared on both sides, 5–8 minutes on each side. Transfer to a plate and let cool to room temperature, about 20 minutes.

Sprinkle the short ribs with the garam masala. Put the short ribs and the ¼ cup (56 g) olive oil in a vacuum bag and vacuum seal. Cook the short ribs in the circulating water bath for 36 hours. Remove the bag from the water bath and let cool at room temperature for 20 minutes. Store the short ribs in the bag in the refrigerator until ready to serve or for up to 3 days.

To serve, preheat the circulating water bath to 140°F (60°C). Reheat the short ribs, still in the bag, in the circulating water bath for 30 minutes.

Pour the canola into a deep fryer to the fill line or into a small, tall-sided saucepan to a depth of 2½ inches (6 cm) and heat to 400°F (200°C).

Using a small, fine-mesh sieve to dip them in and out of the oil, carefully fry the dried broccoli. They will pop and burst open like popcorn. Transfer the fried broccoli to a paper towel–lined plate to drain and season lightly with salt.

In a small saucepan, heat the broccoli purée over medium heat, stirring constantly with a small whisk. Whisk in 1 tablespoon (14 g) of the butter until absorbed. Place a large sauté pan over medium-high heat. Remove the short ribs from the bag and pat dry. When the pan is hot, add the remaining 1 tablespoon (14 g) olive oil and sear the short ribs on both sides. Add the remaining 2 tablespoons (28 g) butter to the pan and use a wide, flat, large metal spoon to baste the short ribs with the melting butter until it melts completely and begins to brown. Transfer the meat to a plate and let stand for 5 minutes.

››

DRIED BROCCOLI

3 crowns broccoli

Fine sea salt

BROCCOLI PURÉE

3 large crowns broccoli, about 2 pounds (900 g) total weight

3 tablespoons plus 1 teaspoon (50 g) heavy cream

¼ cup (56 g) extra-virgin olive oil

.5 gram xanthan gum (see sources)

¼ teaspoon (1.5 g) fine sea salt

HORSERADISH "STYROFOAM"

2¼ cups (500 g) water

2½ teaspoons (10 g) sugar

½ cup plus 5 teaspoons (150 g) prepared horseradish

¼ teaspoon (1.5 g) fine sea salt

5 tablespoons (25 g) egg white powder

.4 gram xanthan gum (see sources)

SPICY SOY-CARAMEL SAUCE

½ cup plus 1 tablespoon (112.5 g) sugar

¼ cup plus 1 teaspoon (60 g) water

1 tablespoon (14 g) fresh lemon juice

1½ tablespoons (30 g) light corn syrup

¼ cup (80 g) soy sauce

1 tablespoon (6.5 g) Garam Masala (page 318)

1 tablespoon (14 g) sherry vinegar

Using a sharp knife, cut small, irregular pieces of the horseradish "Styrofoam." Move the seared short ribs to a cutting board, brush them with the spicy soy-caramel sauce, and then let them rest for a minute or two. Cut the short ribs into 1-inch (2.5-cm) slices. Put a piece of short rib in the center of the plate. Put small spoonfuls of the broccoli purée at the top and bottom of the plate close to the short rib. Put a few pieces of the fried broccoli on the short rib and one on the top spoonful of broccoli purée. Put a piece of horseradish Styrofoam on the top of the plate and another on the bottom. Put the broccoli flowers in a bowl and season with crushed Maldon salt and olive oil. Put several dressed broccoli flower clusters on and around the short ribs. Put 3 small spoonfuls of the spicy soy-caramel sauce on the plate and serve right away.

DRIED BROCCOLI

Bring a saucepan filled with generously salted water to a boil over high heat. Meanwhile, cut very small florets, about the size of a nickel, from the broccoli crown, saving the stems for another use. Prepare an ice bath. Add the florets to the boiling water and blanch until bright green and tender, about 1½ minutes. Using a skimmer, transfer to the ice bath and let stand until cool. Drain the blanched florets and pat dry with paper towels.

Arrange the florets on a food dehydrator tray, taking care that they do not touch one another. Place in the dehydrator set at 150°F (65°C) until completely dry and firm, about 3 hours. Alternatively, you can dry the florets on a sheet pan lined with parchment paper in a 175°F (80°C) oven. The cooled dried broccoli may be stored in an airtight container at room temperature for up to 2 days before using.

BROCCOLI PURÉE

Using a sharp knife, carefully shave only the tips of the florets from the broccoli crowns, yielding a pile of finely shaved buds. Set aside. Using the vegetable juicer, juice the broccoli crowns and stems. Measure ½ cup plus 3 tablespoons (150 g) juice; reserve the remainder for another use or discard.

In a small saucepan, combine the juice and cream over medium-high heat and bring to a boil. In a small sauté pan, heat the olive oil over medium-high heat until it begins to shimmer but does not smoke. Add the finely shaved broccoli and sauté until it turns bright green, about 1 minute. Immediately pour the boiling juice mixture over the broccoli and let simmer for 30 seconds. Carefully transfer the mixture to the blender and turn it on low speed. Slowly increase the speed until a vortex forms in the center of the mixture. Sprinkle in the xanthan gum and salt, increase the speed to high, and process until smooth, about 30 seconds. Prepare an ice bath. Strain the purée through a fine-mesh sieve placed over a metal bowl. Set the bowl over the ice bath and let cool completely, stirring occasionally and replenishing the ice as needed, about 20 minutes. The broccoli purée may stored in a lidded container in the refrigerator until ready to serve or for up to 3 days.

HORSERADISH "STYROFOAM"

In a saucepan, combine the water, sugar, and horseradish, place over medium-high heat, and bring to a simmer. Reduce the heat so the mixture simmers slowly and cook for 45 minutes to infuse the liquid with flavor.

THIS PREPARATION ALLOWED ME TO CHANGE THE TEXTURE AND COLOR OF A VEGETABLE THAT HAUNTED MY YOUTH TO CREATE A MODERN AND INTRIGUING VERSION OF A CLASSIC BEEF DISH

Strain the hot liquid through a fine-mesh sieve placed over a clean saucepan. Place over high heat, bring to a boil, adjust the heat to maintain a low simmer, and cook, stirring occasionally, until reduced by half, about 25 minutes. Add the salt and stir to dissolve. Remove from the heat and let cool to room temperature, about 30 minutes.

Transfer the cooled mixture to the clean blender. Add the egg white powder and xanthan gum and process until the ingredients are fully incorporated and the mixture is frothy, about 15 seconds. Transfer the mixture to a stand mixer fitted with the whisk attachment. On high speed, whip until meringuelike soft peaks form, about 10 minutes.

Line a food dehydrator tray or a sheet pan with a silicone mat. Using an offset spatula, spread the meringue on the mat, forming a layer ½ inch (12 mm) thick. Place in the dehydrator set at 150°F (65°C) or in the oven preheated to 175°F (80°C) until light and crisp, about 2 hours. Peel the horseradish Styrofoam off the mat and store in an airtight container at room temperature until ready to serve, up to 3 days.

SPICY SOY-CARAMEL SAUCE

In a saucepan, combine the sugar, water, and lemon juice, place over medium-high heat, and bring to a boil. Add the corn syrup and continue to cook, swirling the pan occasionally if needed to prevent uneven cooking, until the mixture turns a deep amber, 5–8 minutes. Remove from the heat and add the soy sauce. Return to low heat and cook, stirring with a heatproof spatula, to dissolve any hardened caramel, until the mixture reaches 230°F (110°C). Remove from the heat and let the mixture cool to room temperature, about 30 minutes. Stir in the garam masala and vinegar. The sauce may be stored in a lidded container in the refrigerator until ready to serve or for up to 1 week.

MAIN INGREDIENTS

3 gallons (11 kg) plus 10 cups (2268 g) water
3 cups (780 g) kosher salt
4½ cups (960 g) firmly packed light brown sugar
8¼ teaspoons (57 g) pink curing salt (see sources)
1 whole head garlic plus 5 cloves
1 orange, sliced into rounds and visible seeds removed
2 lemons, sliced into rounds and visible seeds removed
2 limes, sliced into rounds and visible seeds removed
1 green apple, quartered
½ cup (20 g) juniper berries
3 tablespoons (10.5 g) coriander seeds
2 tablespoons (12 g) green cardamom pods
5 tablespoons (35 g) plus 4 teaspoons (10.5 g) black peppercorns
3 fresh sage sprigs
2 fresh cilantro sprigs
1 pig's head from a 180- to 200-pound (80 to 90-kg) pig
2 *each* yellow onions and carrots
4 celery ribs
2 fresh rosemary sprigs
3 fresh thyme sprigs
1¾ cups (504 g) fine sea salt
1 shallot, minced
1 teaspoon (5 g) Dijon mustard
½ teaspoon (1.25 g) Espelette pepper
4 teaspoons (26.6 g) Banyuls vinegar
10 grams Activa RM (see sources)
Canola oil for deep-frying
½ cup (75 g) all-purpose flour
2 eggs
1 cup (113 g) fine panko bread crumbs
Sunchoke Relish (below)
Green Garlic Aioli (below)
Pickling Spice Vinaigrette (below)
Petite mustard greens

Equipment

vacuum sealer and vacuum bags
deep fryer (optional)
deli-style meat slicer (optional)
high-speed blender

Serves 8 as a first course

››

BRYAN I decided to learn how to make head cheese because I believe it is important to utilize every part of an animal. First, of course, I had to learn how to cook a pig's head, but once I did, I knew that I wanted to find a beautiful way to present it. Here, I serve the head cheese two ways: in thin slices and in deep-fried cubes. The pleasantly tart sunchoke relish and pickling spice vinaigrette temper the richness of the dish. A bold sauce made from fresh green garlic is the perfect accent.

Head Cheese, Sunchoke Relish, Green Garlic Aioli

To make a brine for the pigs head, in a large pot, combine the 3 gallons (11 kg) water, the kosher salt, brown sugar, pink salt, whole garlic head, orange, lemons, limes, apple, juniper berries, coriander, cardamom, 5 tablespoons (35 g) peppercorns, sage, and cilantro. Place the pot over medium-high heat, bring the liquid to a boil, and remove from the heat. Let the brine cool completely, about 3 hours.

Rinse the pig's head and put it in a 5-gallon (20-l) bucket. Pour the cooled brine over the pig's head. It should be completely submerged. Cover the bucket and refrigerate the pig's head for 10 days.

Alternatively, put the pig's head in a clean, heavy-duty plastic trash bag. Put a thick layer of ice in the bottom of a large (40–50 quart/38–47 l) chest-type cooler with a drain, and put the bag holding the pig's head on top of the ice. Carefully pour the cooled brine over the pig's head in the bag and then close the bag. Tie the bag securely. If there is room, add more ice on top of the bag. As the ice melts, make sure the water is draining out of the cooler, and replenish the cooler with fresh ice as needed to keep the pig's head and the brine very cold for 10 days.

Remove the pig's head from the brine and discard the brine. In a large pot, combine the pig's head, onions, carrots, celery, rosemary, thyme, sea salt, and the remaining 10 cups (2268 g) water, 5 garlic cloves, and 4 teaspoons (10.5 g) peppercorns. Place over medium-high heat and bring to a boil. Reduce the heat to keep the liquid at a simmer and cook the pig's head until the meat is falling off the bones, 4–5 hours.

Remove the pot from the heat and let the pig's head cool to room temperature in the cooking liquid, 1–2 hours.

Using your clean fingers, thoroughly pick all the meat and tender skin from all over the pig's head, keeping the meat chunks together as much as possible, and put the meat into a medium bowl. You should end up with about 4 cups (900 g) meat total.

SUNCHOKE RELISH

7¼ ounces (200 g) sunchokes
4¾ ounces (135 g) green bell peppers
4¼ ounces (120 g) yellow onion
2½ cups (563 g) water
1 tablespoon (18 g) fine sea salt
1 tablespoon (8 g) yellow mustard seeds
2 teaspoons (6 g) celery seeds
¼ cup (80 g) cider vinegar
½ cup (160 g) distilled white vinegar
¼ cup (50 g) granulated sugar
3 tablespoons (28 g) all-purpose flour
½ teaspoon (1 g) ground turmeric

GREEN GARLIC AIOLI

1 large egg
Juice of 1 lemon (20 g)
1 teaspoon (6 g) fine sea salt
7 tablespoons (100 g) garlic oil
7 tablespoons (100 g) parsley oil

PICKLING SPICE VINAIGRETTE

¼ cup (56 g) extra-virgin olive oil
1 teaspoon (2.2 g) Pickling Spice (page 318)
⅛ teaspoon (.75 g) plus ¼ teaspoon (1.5 g) fine sea salt
1 shallot, minced
¼ cup (80 g) cider vinegar
1 teaspoon (6.5 g) honey

In a small saucepan, combine the shallot, mustard, Espelette pepper, and vinegar, place over medium heat, and bring to a simmer. Simmer until almost all of the liquid has evaporated and the shallots are just glazed with the sauce, 5–8 minutes. Add the reduced mixture to the meat in the bowl and fold together. Sprinkle on the Activa RM and mix gently but thoroughly, preferably with your hands. Put the meat mixture into a vacuum bag, shape it into an 8½-by-4-inch (22-by-10-cm) rectangle about 1½ inches (4 cm) thick, and vacuum seal. Put the bag on a sheet pan, place a second sheet pan on top, and add a few plates to weight it down. Refrigerate overnight.

To serve, pour the canola oil into a deep fryer to the fill line or into a tall-sided saucepan to a depth of 2½ inches (6 cm) and heat to 350°F (180°C).

Remove the molded meat from the bag. Using the meat slicer or a sharp knife, and cutting lengthwise, cut 4 slices, each about ⅛ inch (3 mm) thick, from the molded meat. Cut each slice in half lengthwise for a total of 8 servings. Cut the remaining molded meat into ¾-inch (2-cm) cubes. You will need 3 cubes for each serving, or a total of 24 cubes.

Put the flour in a small bowl. In a second small bowl, whisk the eggs until blended. Put the bread crumbs in a third small bowl. Dip the meat cubes in the flour and shake to remove the excess. Then, dip the floured cubes in the beaten egg, letting the excess drip back into the bowl. Finally, roll the cubes in the bowl of bread crumbs, coating them well on all sides. Place the coated cubes on a large plate.

Working in batches, add the coated meat cubes to the hot oil and fry until golden brown and crisp, 1–2 minutes. Using a skimmer, transfer to a paper towel–lined plate to drain briefly.

Place 1 slice of meat vertically on the center of each serving plate. Put a narrow line of sunchoke relish along the left border of the meat. Put 4 small dots of green garlic aioli on top of the sliced meat. Place 1 fried meat cube next to each dot. Spoon the pickling spice vinaigrette around the plate. Garnish with petite mustard greens and serve right away.

SUNCHOKE RELISH

Peel and finely dice the sunchokes. Stem, seed, and finely dice the bell peppers. Peel and finely dice the onion.

In a small lidded container, combine the sunchokes, peppers, onion, 2 cups (450 g) of the water, and the salt and mix well. Refrigerate for 24 hours to firm the vegetables.

Drain the relish mixture in a fine-mesh sieve and discard the liquid. In a small saucepan, combine the relish mixture, mustard seeds, celery seeds, the remaining ½ cup (113 g) water, the cider vinegar, and the white vinegar and bring to a simmer over medium heat. Cook for 4 minutes, then add the sugar and stir to dissolve. Reduce the heat to maintain a low simmer and cook for 3 minutes. Whisk in the flour and turmeric and continue to simmer until the mixture thickens, about 12 minutes more. Transfer the relish to a small container and let cool completely. Use immediately, or store in a lidded container in the refrigerator for up to 5 days.

GREEN GARLIC AIOLI

Separate the egg, discarding the egg white or saving it for another use. In the blender, combine the lemon juice, egg yolk, and salt and turn on the blender to low speed. Once the mixture begins to emulsify, slowly drizzle in the garlic oil and parsley oil. Once the mixture has emulsified into a thick aioli, transfer it to a lidded container. The green garlic aioli may be stored in the refrigerator for up to 3 days before serving.

PICKLING SPICE VINAIGRETTE

In the clean blender, combine the olive oil, pickling spice, and ⅛ teaspoon (.75 g) salt and process on high speed for 1 minute. Let the oil stand for 5 minutes so the spices can settle. Carefully pour the oil into a small container, leaving the spices in the blender. Discard the spices.

Measure ¼ cup (56 g) of the pickling spice oil, pour into a small saucepan, and place over medium heat. Reserve the remaining oil for another use. When the oil begins to shimmer but does not smoke, add the shallot and sauté until translucent, 3–5 minutes. Remove from the heat and let cool to room temperature, about 10 minutes. Transfer the oil mixture to a small bowl and whisk in the vinegar and honey. Season with the remaining ¼ teaspoon (1.5 g) salt. Use immediately.

THE FIRST TIME I WAS INTRODUCED TO **OFFAL** WAS IN THE KITCHEN OF MY GRANDMOTHER RUTH

AND THAT EXPERIENCE TAUGHT ME TO BE **CURIOUS** IN THE KITCHEN

MICHAEL The depth of flavor of the pork broth is the true measure of all great bowls of ramen. I particularly like the richness and stickiness of the broth in this recipe, which calls for both pork belly and pig's feet and is prepared in a pressure cooker to concentrate its taste. For the ramen, instead of wheat noodles, I use giant squid, which I roll up, freeze, and then thinly slice. The squid noodles are sweet and slightly springy, just like the best ramen noodles.

Pork Belly, Big Squid Ramen

MAIN INGREDIENTS

⅓ cup plus 4 teaspoons (95 g) canola oil, plus 3½ tablespoons (50 g) for reheating the pork, plus more for deep-frying

1 pound (450 g) pork belly

1 pound (450 g) chicken necks

1 pound (450 g) pig's feet

1 cup (320 g) usukuchi soy sauce (see sources)

2 yellow onions, 1 thinly sliced and 1 julienned

3 ounces (84 g) fresh ginger, peeled and sliced

2 ounces (56 g) kombu

8½ cups (1913 g) plus 3⅓ cups (750 g) water

6 giant squid or cuttlefish

1 shallot, minced

2 cloves garlic, smashed and minced

5¼ ounces (150 g) spinach

4 teaspoons (72 g) squid ink (includes the saved ink)

⅓ cup (96 g) rice vinegar

8 quail eggs

Fine sea salt

Micro chives

Equipment

6-quart (5.7-l) pressure cooker

liquid nitrogen (optional)

small Styrofoam cooler (optional)

high-speed blender

food dehydrator (optional)

thermal immersion circulator

deep fryer (optional)

Serves 6 as a first course

In the pressure cooker, heat the ⅓ cup (75 g) of the canola oil over high heat until it begins to shimmer but does not smoke. Add the pork belly, skin side down, and cook until the skin is golden brown, 5–8 minutes. Flip the pork belly over and add the chicken necks, pig's feet, ⅔ cup (213 g) of the usukuchi soy sauce, sliced onion, 2 ounces (56 g) of the ginger, the kombu, and 8½ cups (1913 g) of the water. Following the manufacturer's instructions, lock the lid in place, bring up to high pressure, and cook for 1 hour. Let the pressure dissipate naturally, then uncover. Carefully transfer the pork belly to a shallow baking dish to cool. Strain the cooking liquid through a fine-mesh sieve placed over a lidded container and let cool. Discard the remaining solids. Store the broth in the refrigerator until serving time.

Lay 1 squid on a cutting board. Remove the tentacles and set aside. Remove the innards from the body tube and discard. Set the ink sac aside. Rinse the tube thoroughly. Carefully pop out the long piece of cartilage on the inside of the tube. Peel the skin off the tube. Rinse the tube again until it is white and clean. Repeat with the remaining 5 squid. Lay 1 tube out on the cutting board and slice it open from top to bottom. Turn it on its side with the point to the left, and then roll it up into a log. Wrap it tightly in plastic wrap, twisting the ends of the wrap to compact the squid and create a uniform shape. Repeat with 3 more tubes. Place the wrapped tubes in the freezer for at least 4 hours.

Chop the remaining 2 squid tubes into tiny pieces and place in the Styrofoam cooler. Pour the liquid nitrogen over the squid pieces and stir gently to freeze completely. Put the frozen squid pieces in the blender and process to a fine powder. Line a food dehydrator tray or a sheet pan with a silicone mat, and pour the powder onto the mat in an even layer about ¼ inch (6 mm) thick. Dehydrate the squid powder in the dehydrator set at 155°F (68°C) or the oven preheated to 175°F (80°C) until it forms a completely dry sheet, about 4 hours. Once the squid sheet is completely dry, break it into 8 roughly equal pieces. The dried squid may be stored in an airtight container at room temperature for up to 1 week.

Alternatively, wrap the remaining 2 squid tubes tightly in plastic wrap and freeze them solid as you did the other 4 tubes. Using a wide rasp grater, finely grate

THE PRESENCE OF A **DEEP & RICH PORK BROTH** IS THE TRUE MEASURE OF ALL THE **GREAT BOWLS OF RAMEN** THAT I HAVE EATEN AND I'VE TRIED TO RECREATE THAT **POWERFUL FLAVOR HERE**

the 2 frozen tubes over the silicone-lined tray, forming an even layer ¼ inch (6 mm) thick, and then dehydrate, break, and store as directed above.

Remove the 4 squid rolls from the freezer, and remove and discard the plastic wrap. Using a sharp mandoline, thinly slice the squid rolls to yield pinwheels. Transfer the slices to a baking dish and refrigerate until thawed.

In a large sauté pan, heat the 4 teaspoons (20 g) canola oil over medium-high heat. Add the shallot and garlic and sauté until translucent but not browned, 2–3 minutes. Add the spinach and sauté just until it wilts and is tender, 2–3 minutes. Transfer to a heatproof colander set over a bowl. When cool enough to handle, squeeze out as much of the water as possible from the spinach. Transfer the spinach to a large piece of plastic wrap, roll up into a tight cylinder about 2 inches (5 cm) long, and twist the ends of the wrap to compact the spinach and create a uniform shape. Refrigerate until ready to serve.

In a saucepan, combine the remaining 3⅓ cups (750 g) water, the reserved squid tentacles, the remaining 1 ounce (28 g) ginger, the julienned onion, the squid ink, and the remaining ⅓ cup (107 g) usukuchi soy sauce, place over medium-high heat, and bring to a slow simmer. Cook for 20 minutes. Remove from the heat, drain the liquid through a fine-mesh sieve placed over a clean saucepan, and place over medium-high heat. Bring to a simmer and cook until reduced to 1⅓ cups (300 g), 30–45 minutes. Meanwhile, prepare an ice bath. Remove the reduced liquid from the heat, stir in the vinegar, and transfer to a metal bowl. Set over the ice bath and let cool completely, stirring occasionally and replenishing the ice as needed, about 15 minutes.

Preheat the circulating water bath to 167°F (75°C).

Cook 8 quail eggs (this allows for breakage) in their shells in the circulating water bath for 5 minutes. Meanwhile, prepare an ice bath. When the eggs are ready, carefully transfer them to the ice bath and let cool completely, replenishing the

ice as needed, about 15 minutes. Remove the eggs from the ice bath. Using a small egg cutter or small sharp scissors, cut off the top of 1 egg and pour the contents of the shell into your palm, brushing off any loose cooked egg whites. Slip the egg into the cooled tentacle broth. Repeat with the remaining eggs. Let them marinate for at least 4 hours before serving.

To serve, pour the canola oil into the deep fryer to the fill line or into a tall-sided saucepan to a depth of 2½ inches (6 cm) and heat to 375°F (190°C). Put the broth from cooking the pork belly in a large saucepan and bring to a simmer over medium-high heat; keep at a low simmer.

In a large sauté pan, heat the 3½ tablespoons (50 g) canola oil over high heat until it begins to shimmer. Add the pork belly, turn down the heat to medium, and cook, turning once, until warmed through, 2–3 minutes on each side. Transfer the pork belly to a cutting board and cut crosswise into pieces about ⅛ inch (3 mm) thick. Cut the wrapped spinach roll into 4 equal rounds, each about ½ inch (12 mm) thick, and remove the plastic wrap. Put the spinach slices into a small baking dish. Pour ¼ cup (56 g) of the hot pork broth over them to bring them up to room temperature. Put 1 spinach round into each serving bowl. Arrange 3 pork belly slices on the bottom of the bowl. Using a slotted spoon, remove the quail eggs from the tentacle broth one at a time and place next to the spinach. Divide the thawed squid pinwheels into 6 equal portions. Using a small wire skimmer, plunge each portion in the hot broth for 5 seconds and immediately transfer to a bowl, arranging the "noodles" over the pork. Add the dehydrated squid pieces to the hot oil and fry until crisp and puffed, about 5 seconds. Using a skimmer, transfer the squid pieces to a paper towel–lined plate to drain briefly, season lightly with salt, and place 2 fried squid pieces in each bowl. Pour 7 tablespoons (100 g) of the simmering pork broth into each bowl, garnish each bowl with micro chives and serve right away.

MINT

BASIL
LAVENDER
PEPPERMINT
SPEARMINT

Sometimes pungent, sometimes sweet, and always loaded with volatile oils, the fragrant members of the rambling mint family put a surprisingly big bouquet of flavors into our hands. And that suits us just fine. Indeed, we never tire of trying to weave the family's myriad tastes into new dishes, happily tinkering as we match cool, bracing mint, earthy sage, seductively floral lavender, woodsy rosemary, or anisey basil with a pantryful of sweet or savory ingredients. Many members of the family come in several different varieties, too. For example, if we have settled on working with mint, we can choose from peppermint, spearmint, apple mint, chocolate mint, pineapple mint, orange mint, and more, each of which will take us in a slightly different direction in the kitchen.

MAIN INGREDIENTS

Pasta Filling

2 tablespoons (28 g) canola oil

1 leek, white part only, halved and cut crosswise into 1-inch (2.5-cm) pieces

1 white onion, diced

2 celery ribs, diced

5 cloves garlic, peeled but left whole

5 fresh flat-leaf parsley sprigs

¾ cup plus 2 tablespoons (200 g) dry white wine

4¼ cups (955 g) Chicken Stock (page 319)

8½ ounces (250 g) basil-fed snails (see sources)

2 teaspoons (12 g) fine sea salt

2 sheets silver-grade leaf gelatin (see sources)

2¼ cups (500 g) water

3½ ounces (100 g) fresh flat-leaf parsley leaves

¾ ounce (25 g) fresh basil leaves

7 tablespoons (100 g) unsalted butter

Pasta Dough

1⅔ cups (250 g) all-purpose flour, plus more for rolling

1 teaspoon (6 g) fine sea salt

7 large egg yolks

7 tablespoons (115 g) whole milk

2 teaspoons (10 g) extra-virgin olive oil

Fine sea salt

Pine Nut Praline (below)

Garlic Chips (below)

Assorted fresh petite basil leaves

Basil flowers

Finely grated Parmigiano-Reggiano cheese

2 tablespoons (28 g) extra-virgin olive oil

Equipment

6-quart (5.7-l) pressure cooker

24 miniature hemisphere molds (each 1½–1¾ inch/3.75–4.4 cm in diameter)

high-speed blender

vacuum sealer and vacuum bags

pasta machine

Serves 4 as a first course or 8 as a midcourse

››

MICHAEL I sometimes like to cook things that don't appeal to me because I enjoy the challenge of turning them into something I like. For example, I have never cared for snails, though I have always liked the garlic-and-parsley-flavored butter that they traditionally swim in. This recipe is all about that buttery bath. I added more basil because of the basil-fed snails, and I cook them in a pressure cooker in a broth that makes them taste so good that even I like them.

Basil Snail Agnolotti, Pine Nut Praline, Basil Leaves and Flowers

To make the filling, in the pressure cooker, heat the canola oil over medium heat until it begins to shimmer but does not smoke. Add the leek, onion, celery, and 3 cloves of the garlic. Cook, stirring occasionally, until the vegetables are tender but have not browned, 5–8 minutes. Add the parsley sprigs and cook for 30 seconds. Add the wine and stir well to loosen and dissolve any caramelized bits on the pot bottom. Bring the wine to a boil and cook until reduced by half, 5–7 minutes. Add the stock, snails, and 1 teaspoon (6 g) of the salt. Following the manufacturer's instructions, lock the lid in place, bring up to high pressure, and cook for 20 minutes. Let the pressure dissipate naturally, then uncover and let the snails cool completely in the cooking liquid.

Remove the snails from the stock and discard the stock. Put 1 snail in each hemisphere mold. (Any extra snails can be saved for another use.)

Put the gelatin sheets in a small bowl of ice water and let soak until softened, about 5 minutes. In a small saucepan, combine the water and the remaining 1 teaspoon (6 g) salt over medium-high heat and bring to a boil. Cut the remaining 2 garlic cloves in half lengthwise, drop them into the boiling water, and cook for 20 seconds. Add the parsley and basil leaves and cook until the leaves are a vibrant green, 10–15 seconds. Remove from the heat, drain, and transfer the herbs and garlic to the blender. Retrieve the gelatin sheets, squeeze out the excess water, add the sheets to the blender, and process on medium speed until smooth. With the blender running, add the butter 2 tablespoons at a time. Once the butter has been emulsified into the mixture, turn off the blender and pour the mixture over the snail in each mold, filling the mold to the rim. Put the molds in the refrigerator until the parsley mixture is cool and set, about 1 hour.

To make the dough, in a food processor, combine the flour and salt and pulse a few times to combine. In a small bowl, whisk 6 of the egg yolks until blended. With the food processor running, drizzle in the beaten egg yolks followed by 3 tablespoons (50 g) of the milk and the olive oil and let the machine run until

PINE NUT PRALINE

¾ cup (105 g) pine nuts

7 tablespoons (100 g) grape seed oil

½ teaspoon (3 g) fine sea salt

GARLIC CHIPS

3 cloves garlic

1 cup (260 g) whole milk

Canola oil for frying

Fine sea salt

a smooth dough forms. Turn the dough out onto a sheet of parchment paper, form it into a ball, and knead a few times. Put the dough in a vacuum bag and vacuum seal. Let rest for 5 minutes.

Set the rollers on the pasta machine to the widest setting. Divide the dough in half. Wrap 1 half in plastic wrap and set it aside while you work with the other half. Run the dough through the rollers twice, taking care that it stays flat as you roll it. If the dough begins to stick, dust the rollers lightly with flour, adding no more than is absolutely necessary. Reset the rollers one width narrower and again pass the dough through the rollers twice. Repeat the process, resetting the rollers one width narrower and rolling the dough twice through each setting until you reach the second-to-last setting. After rolling the dough twice through this setting, lay the dough sheet flat on a lightly floured work surface. Using a knife, cut the sheet into strips 3½ inches (9 cm) wide.

In a small bowl, whisk together the remaining egg yolk and the remaining 4 tablespoons (65 g) milk to make an egg wash. Lay out 1 pasta strip with a long edge facing you. Starting ½ inch (12 mm) in from the top edge, position individual pieces of the parsley-snail filling in a line along the strip, spacing them ¾ inch (2 cm) apart. Brush the bottom ½ inch (12 mm) of the opposite long edge with the egg wash. Pull the pasta edge nearest you up over the tops of the snail mounds, and press the top and bottom edges of the long sides together, forming a ½-inch (12-mm) border. Use a finger to gently press the dough around each side of each mound of filling to seal. Use a sharp knife to trim each agnolotti, leaving ¼ inch (6 mm) of sealed dough around each side of the filling to form individual agnolotti. Repeat with the remaining strips of dough until all of the filling is used.

To serve, bring a large pot three-fourths full of generously salted water to a boil over high heat. Add the agnolotti to the boiling water and cook until the

AS A CHEF I ENJOY THE **CHALLENGE** OF TAKING THINGS THAT DON'T **NECESSARILY** APPEAL TO ME IN THEIR **RAW STATE** & TURNING THEM INTO SOMETHING DELICIOUS

filling is warmed through and the pasta is tender, about 1½ minutes. Using a slotted spoon, transfer the agnolotti to a bowl, drizzle with olive oil, and season with salt. Put 3 agnolotti on each plate, dollop the pine nut praline on and around the agnolotti, and garnish each plate with the garlic chips, and basil leaves and flowers. Garnish each plate with a small amount of olive oil and Parmigiano-Reggiano cheese and serve right away.

PINE NUT PRALINE

In a small saucepan, combine the pine nuts and grape seed oil and cook, stirring continuously, until the nuts turn an even, deep golden brown, 5–8 minutes. Drain the nuts through a fine-mesh sieve, reserving both the nuts and the oil. Transfer the nuts to a blender, add 2½ tablespoons (35 g) of the oil and the salt, and process until smooth. Transfer to a small bowl and let stand at room temperature until ready to serve.

GARLIC CHIPS

Cut off the stem end of each garlic clove and then split them in half vertically. Use the tip of a small paring knife to remove the germ from the center of each clove and discard. Using a mandoline, cut the cloves into thin slices. In a small saucepan, combine the garlic slices and milk and set it over medium heat. Bring the milk to a simmer, remove from the heat, and strain the garlic, discarding the milk. Pour canola oil into a small, high-sided saucepan to a depth of 2½ inches (6 cm) and heat to 350°F (180°C). In batches, fry the garlic chips in the hot oil until they are golden brown. Use a small metal sieve to transfer them to a paper towel–lined plate and season lightly with salt. Use right away, or cool and store in an airtight container at room temperature for up to 3 days.

BRYAN For Christmas, I used to buy my wife, Jennifer, gifts of bath salts, lotions, or oils. Recalling the aromas of coconut and lavender in the shop and the memory of making Jennifer happy were the spark for this recipe. I wanted the dish to be completely white, so I transformed purple lavender flowers into a white powder. The simple presentation allows the diner to focus on the aromas—aromas so intense that you feel you have tasted the dish before you take your first bite.

Coconut, Lavender, Vanilla

MAIN INGREDIENTS

Coconut Pudding (below)
Coconut Domes (below)
Lavender Powder (below)
Lavender Oil (below)
Coconut Sorbet (below)
Vacherins (below)
Vanilla Syrup (below)

Equipment

plastic squeeze bottle
high-speed blender
ice-cream maker
liquid nitrogen (optional)
small Styrofoam cooler (optional)

Serves 8 as a dessert

Put the coconut pudding in the squeeze bottle. For each serving, put 1 large drop of coconut pudding in the center of a plate. Put 1 coconut dome, hollow side up (so it forms a small bowl), in the center of the pudding. Put a squeeze of coconut pudding in the dome. Top the squeeze of pudding with a spoonful of lavender powder, and then squeeze a bit more coconut pudding on top of the powder. Put a large quenelle of coconut sorbet on top of the upside-down coconut dome. Arrange 1 vacherin on each end of the quenelle. Put several drops of vanilla syrup around the perimeter of the plate and serve right away.

COCONUT PUDDING

1 cup plus 3 tablespoons (300 g) unsweetened coconut milk
½ cup (100 g) sugar
5 tablespoons plus 2 teaspoons (156 g) liquid glucose (see sources)
½ lemongrass stalk, bruised
3 grams agar (see sources)
½ teaspoon (3 g) fine sea salt

In a saucepan, combine the coconut milk, sugar, glucose, lemongrass, agar, and salt and stir well. Place over medium-high heat, bring to a boil, and cook for 5 minutes. Remove from the heat and strain through a fine-mesh sieve placed over a shallow baking dish. Discard the solids and let the mixture cool to room temperature, about 20 minutes. Refrigerate the mixture, uncovered, until firmly set into a gel, about 30 minutes.

Dice the gel, transfer to a blender, and blend until a smooth purée forms. Strain the purée through a fine-mesh sieve placed over a bowl. The pudding may be stored in a lidded container in the refrigerator for up to 3 days.

COCONUT DOMES

1½ cups plus 2 teaspoons (390 g) unsweetened coconut milk
2 tablespoons plus 1 teaspoon (17 g) confectioners' sugar
⅛ teaspoon (.75 g) fine sea salt
3 grams xanthan gum (see sources)

In the blender, combine the coconut milk, sugar, and salt and turn on to low speed. Slowly increase the speed until a vortex forms in the center of the liquid. Sprinkle in the xanthan gum and blend for a full 5 seconds to incorporate fully. Strain the liquid through a fine-mesh sieve placed over a small, shallow bowl.

Bring a small saucepan filled with water to a simmer over medium heat and keep at a simmer. Pour the liquid nitrogen into the Styrofoam cooler; it should be about 3 inches (7.5 cm) deep. Have ready a glass baking dish in the freezer. Dip the base of a 2-ounce (60-ml) ladle in the nitrogen for 5 seconds. Remove the ladle from the nitrogen and hold it over the pot of steaming water for 2 seconds. Dip the base of the ladle in the coconut mixture to create a hollow dome shape.

››

LAVENDER POWDER

24 grams tapioca maltodextrin (see sources)

1/8 teaspoon (.75 g) fine sea salt

5 tablespoons plus 2 teaspoons (80 g) lavender oil (below)

LAVENDER OIL

7 tablespoons (100 g) light olive oil

3 tablespoons (6 g) pesticide-free dried lavender flowers

COCONUT SORBET

1¾ cups plus 1½ tablespoons (475 g) unsweetened coconut milk

2/3 cup plus 1 tablespoon (200 g) Sorbet Base (page 319)

1 teaspoon (6 g) fine sea salt

VACHERINS

4 large egg whites

Seeds from ½ vanilla bean

1/8 teaspoon (.5 g) fine sea salt

1¾ cups plus 1 teaspoon (170 g) confectioners' sugar

VANILLA SYRUP

½ cup plus 1 teaspoon (100 g) sugar

1/3 cup plus 1 teaspoon (75 g) water

1 vanilla bean

Immediately dip the ladle back into the nitrogen and count for 9 seconds. Using the tip of a small spoon, gently pry the coconut dome off the ladle and put it in the shallow baking dish in the freezer. Repeat the process until you have 8 domes total in the freezer. The domes may be covered or put into an airtight container and stored in the freezer for up to 1 week.

Alternatively, have ready a nonstick standard muffin tin with at least 8 cups. Blow up 8 small balloons, making each one 2 inches (5 cm) in diameter. One at a time, dip each balloon halfway into the coconut mixture and then put it in a muffin cup. When all of the balloons are dipped, put the muffin tin in the freezer for at least 1 hour or up to 12 hours. Pull the muffin tin from the freezer, dip each balloon halfway in the coconut mixture again, return the balloons to the cups, and return the tin to the freezer. Repeat one more time. Deflate the balloons and remove them from the coconut domes. Keep the domes in an airtight container in the freezer for up to 1 week.

LAVENDER POWDER

Put the tapioca maltodextrin and salt in a food processor. With the processor running, slowly pour in half of the lavender oil, then stop and scrape down the sides of the processor to ensure everything is combined. Turn on the machine and slowly add the remaining lavender oil. Continue to process until all of the oil has been absorbed. The lavender powder may be stored in an airtight container at room temperature for up to 5 days before using.

LAVENDER OIL

In a small saucepan, combine the olive oil and lavender over low heat. Bring to a bare simmer and cook gently for 15 minutes to extract the flavor. Remove from the heat and strain through a fine-mesh sieve placed over a bowl. Discard the lavender and let the oil cool to room temperature, about 30 minutes. The finished oil may be stored in a lidded container at room temperature for up to 2 weeks before using.

COCONUT SORBET

In a bowl, whisk together the coconut milk, sorbet base, and salt until well blended. Transfer to a lidded container and store in the refrigerator for at least 24 hours to allow the flavors to develop.

Transfer the chilled mixture to the ice-cream maker and freeze according to the manufacturer's instructions. Transfer to a freezer container and freeze for at least 2 hours before serving. The sorbet will keep for up to 2 weeks.

VACHERINS

Preheat the oven to 175°F (80°C). Line a sheet pan with a silicone mat.

In a stand mixer fitted with the whisk attachment, combine the egg whites, vanilla seeds, and salt and beat the mixture on high speed until soft peaks form, 5–8 minutes. Using a fine-mesh sieve, sprinkle the confectioners' sugar over the egg white mixture. Then, using a rubber spatula, fold in the sugar until fully combined.

THE SIMPLE ALL-WHITE PRESENTATION HERE ALLOWS YOU TO FOCUS ON INTENSE AROMAS CREATING A POWERFUL IMPRESSION BEFORE YOU EVEN TAKE A BITE

Spoon the whipped egg whites into a pastry bag fitted with a ½-inch (1.25-cm) plain tip. Pipe the mixture into 3-inch (7.5 cm) logs onto the prepared pan, spacing them 1½ inches (4 cm) apart. Bake the logs until completely dry, about 2 hours. Remove from the oven and let cool on the pan on a rack to room temperature. The vacherins may be stored in an airtight container for up to 3 days before using.

VANILLA SYRUP

In a small saucepan, combine the sugar and water. Split the vanilla bean lengthwise, scrape the seeds into the pan, and then add the pods. Place over medium heat and bring to a simmer, stirring to dissolve the sugar. Remove from the heat and let cool to room temperature. The syrup may be stored with the vanilla pod in a lidded container in the refrigerator for up to 2 weeks.

MICHAEL The inspiration for this dish was my desire to explore the different flavors of mint. I chose a traditional dessert, the s'more, and re-created it in a way that transports the diner to its origins, a campfire in the forest. I assembled the components as if in a campfire-like setting, but instead of being surrounded by the aroma of a pine forest, you breathe in the heady, refreshing fragrance of mint—a perfect counterbalance to the sweetness, char, and richness of the dish.

Peppermint S'mores, Menthol Marshmallows, Graham Cracker Ice Cream, Burnt Twigs

MAIN INGREDIENTS

6 tablespoons (100 g) whole milk
7 tablespoons (100 g) water
6½ tablespoons (90 g) unsalted butter
¾ teaspoon (.5 g) fine sea salt
1 teaspoon (4 g) sugar
⅔ cup (100 g) all-purpose flour
3½ tablespoons (35 g) mesquite flour
¼ teaspoon (1.5 g) baking powder
2 large eggs
Menthol Marshmallows (below)
Graham Cracker Crumbs (below)
Graham Cracker Ice Cream (below)
Peppermint leaves

Equipment

kitchen blowtorch
high-speed blender
ice cream maker
1 flexible water-bottle-stick ice tray
small paint sprayer (optional)

Serves 4 as a dessert

Preheat the oven to 350°F (180°C).

In a saucepan, combine the milk, water, butter, salt, and sugar and bring to a simmer over medium-high heat. In a bowl, whisk together the all-purpose flour, mesquite flour, and baking powder until well blended. Add the flour mixture to the liquid and stir well with a wooden spoon. Continue to cook, stirring vigorously and constantly, until the mixture starts to pull away from the sides of the pan and forms a ball of dough, 3–5 minutes. Transfer the dough to a stand mixer fitted with the paddle attachment. On low speed, add the eggs one at a time, mixing well after each addition until fully incorporated.

Line a sheet pan with parchment paper. Transfer the dough to a pastry bag fitted with an ⅛-inch (3-mm) plain tip. Pipe the dough into 6-inch (15-cm) logs onto the prepared pan. Add a few small, irregular offshoot lines, no more than 1 inch (2.5 cm) long, on both sides of each log to resemble small "branches." Pipe out a total of 16 logs (to allow for breakage), spacing them about 2 inches (5 cm) apart. Bake for 3½ minutes, then rotate the pan 180 degrees and continue to bake until golden brown and dry to the touch, about 3½ minutes longer. Let cool on the pan on a rack to room temperature. Store in an airtight container at room temperature and serve within a few hours of baking.

To serve, using the blowtorch, lightly char the branches and marshmallows. Put some graham cracker crumbs in a vertical line down the center of each plate. Lay 1 ice cream stick on the crumbs. Stack 2 branches on top of one another in the same direction on each plate and place 3 marshmallows on and around the logs. Garnish with the mint leaves.

MENTHOL MARSHMALLOWS

2 cups (400 g) sugar
¼ teaspoon (1.5 g) fine sea salt
⅔ cup (150 g) water
3 tablespoons plus 1 teaspoon (92 g) liquid glucose (see sources)
19 sheets silver-grade leaf gelatin (see sources)
5 large egg whites
.02 ounce (.5 g) menthol crystal (see sources), ground to a powder in a spice grinder
¼ cup (28 g) cornstarch
¼ cup (28 g) confectioners' sugar, plus more for dusting cut marshmallows

In a saucepan, combine the sugar, salt, water, and glucose over medium-high heat and heat to 248°F (120°C). Meanwhile, put the gelatin sheets in a large bowl of ice water and let soak until softened, about 5 minutes. In a stand mixer

››

GRAHAM CRACKER CRUMBS

¼ cup (50 g) granulated sugar

3 tablespoons plus 2 teaspoons (50 g) dark brown sugar

1⅓ cups (200 g) all-purpose flour

½ cup plus 3½ tablespoons (100 g) whole-wheat flour

2 tablespoons (12 g) ground cinnamon

⅔ cup (150 g) cold unsalted butter, cubed

2 tablespoons plus 1 teaspoon (50 g) blackstrap molasses

3 tablespoons (50 g) honey

2 teaspoons (8 g) pure vanilla extract

GRAHAM CRACKER ICE CREAM

1½ cups minus 1 tablespoon (375 g) whole milk

½ cup (120 g) heavy cream

½ cup (100 g) sugar

¼ cup (35 g) glucose powder (see sources)

½ cup (40 g) dry milk powder

4 grams ice-cream stabilizer (see sources)

3 large egg yolks

½ cup plus 1 teaspoon (75 g) Graham Cracker Crumbs (above)

7 ounces (200 g) 62 to 65 percent cacao bittersweet chocolate

7 ounces (200 g) cocoa butter

fitted with the whisk attachment, whip the egg whites on the second-lowest speed until they become foamy. When the sugar mixture reaches 248°F (120°C), increase the mixer speed by 1 setting. Continue to cook the sugar until it reaches 284°F (140°C) and remove from the heat. Retrieve the gelatin sheets from the ice water, squeeze out the excess water, and add the sheets to the sugar mixture. Stir with a silicone spatula to melt the gelatin. Reduce the mixer speed to its lowest setting and slowly drizzle in the hot sugar mixture. When all of the sugar mixture has been incorporated, add the menthol, turn the mixer up to medium-high speed, and continue to whip until the mixture becomes very thick and cools to lukewarm, 12–15 minutes.

Line an 8-by-13-inch (20-by-33-cm) sheet pan with parchment paper. In a small bowl, stir together the cornstarch and confectioners' sugar, transfer to a small fine-mesh sieve, and dust half of it in a thin even layer in the parchment-lined pan. Pour the marshmallow mixture into the pan and, using an offset spatula, spread it in an even layer about ½ inch (12 mm) thick. Sift the remaining cornstarch-sugar mixture evenly over the top of the marshmallow mixture. Let stand, uncovered, at room temperature for at least 4 hours or up to 12 hours.

Turn the marshmallow sheet out onto a cutting board. Using a large chef's knife, cut it into ½-inch (12-mm) squares. Dust your knife and any cut edges with more cornstarch–confectioners' sugar mixture to prevent sticking. The marshmallows may be stored in an airtight container for up to 1 week.

GRAHAM CRACKER CRUMBS

Preheat the oven to 325°F (165°C).

Line a sheet pan with parchment paper. In a food processor, combine the granulated sugar, brown sugar, all-purpose flour, whole-wheat flour, and cinnamon. Process for 5 seconds until well blended. Scatter the butter over the top and process until the mixture begins to look like dry sand, about 20 seconds. Stop the machine, add the molasses, honey, and vanilla extract, turn the processor back on, and process until a dough forms. Turn the dough out onto the prepared pan. Using your fingertips, break the dough up into small pieces and sprinkle it evenly over the sheet pan, as if making streusel.

Bake for 8 minutes. Stir the mixture with a fork, rotate the pan 180 degrees, and continue to bake until dry to the touch and lightly browned, about 7 minutes longer. Remove the pan from the oven and let the crumbs cool to room temperature, about 30 minutes. Divide the crumbs in half, and use half for the ice cream base and the other half for serving. (The crumbs may be stored in an airtight container at room temperature for up to 1 week.)

GRAHAM CRACKER ICE CREAM

In a small saucepan, combine the milk, cream, and ¼ cup (50 g) of the sugar over medium heat and bring to a simmer. Meanwhile, in a bowl, whisk together the remaining ¼ cup (50 g) sugar, the glucose powder, milk powder, and the stabilizer. In another bowl, whisk the egg yolks until blended. When the milk mixture begins to simmer, rain in the sugar mixture and stir to blend. Continue to heat the mixture until it reaches 183°F (84°C), then whisk in 3–4 spoonfuls of the hot milk mixture into the egg yolks to warm them slightly. Add another

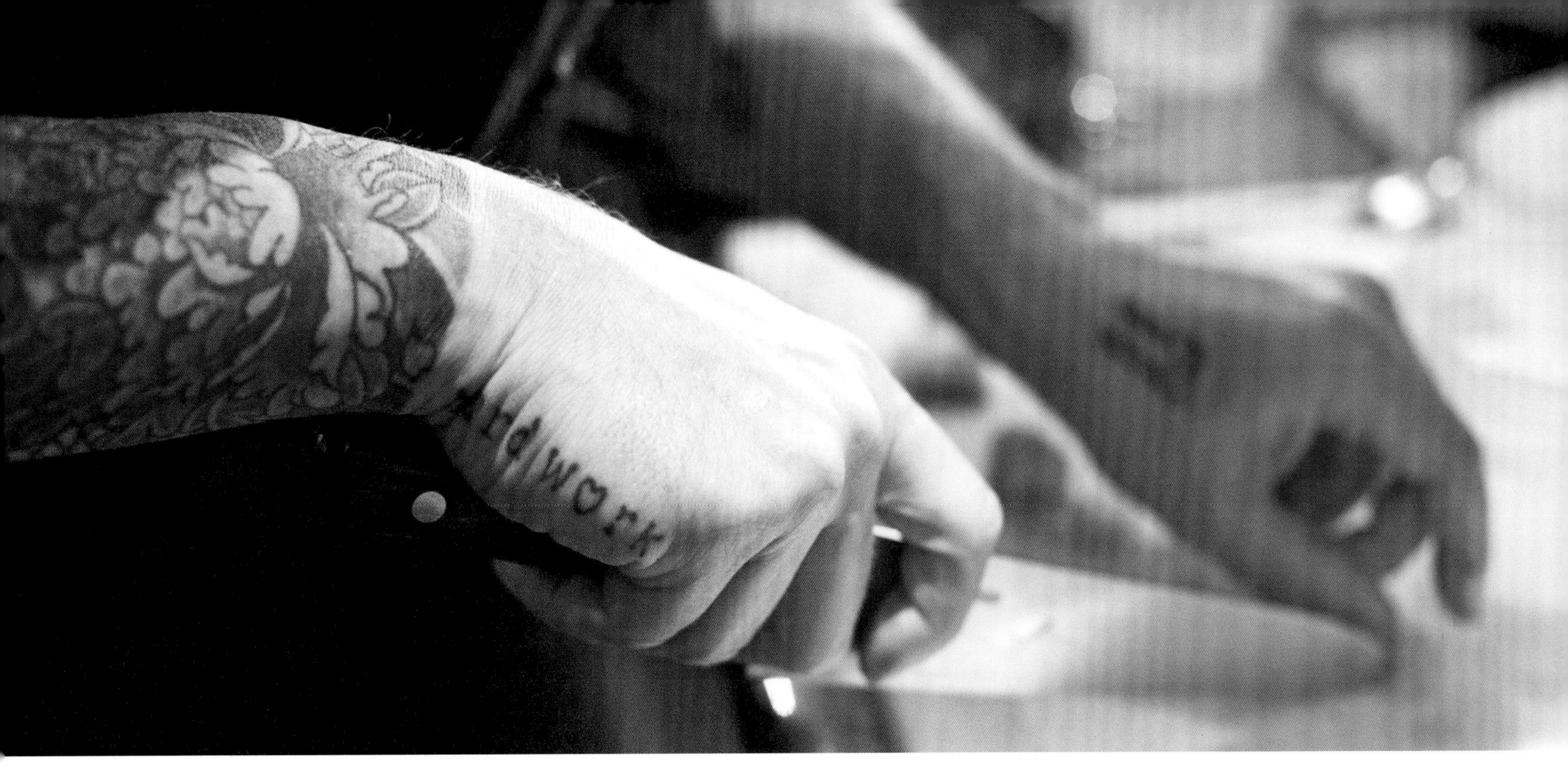

3–4 spoonfuls of the hot milk mixture to the eggs while whisking constantly. Then slowly whisk the warmed egg yolk mixture into the hot milk mixture until well blended. Cook, stirring constantly, until the mixture reaches 179°F (82°C) and the custard coats the back of a spoon. Transfer the mixture to the blender, add the graham cracker crumbs, and process until smooth. Pour into a lidded container and refrigerate for at least 4 hours.

Transfer the chilled mixture to the ice-cream maker and freeze according to the manufacturer's instructions. Spread the freshly churned ice cream in the water-bottle-stick ice tray, cover loosely with plastic wrap, and freeze until firm, about 3 hours. Any extras may be stored in a covered container in the freezer for up to 2 weeks.

Line a sheet pan with parchment paper. Pop the frozen ice-cream sticks out of the ice tray onto the prepared pan. Return them to the freezer until you are ready to coat them.

In a heatproof bowl, combine the chocolate and cocoa butter and place over (not touching) simmering water in a saucepan. Heat until melted, then remove from the heat and stir to blend well. Load the chocolate mixture into the paint sprayer, then spray the ice-cream sticks, coating them evenly on all sides with a fine layer of chocolate. Immediately return the ice cream sticks to the freezer to set the chocolate. Alternatively, lay the sticks on a rack set on a sheet pan and spoon the chocolate mixture over them to coat lightly and evenly, then return to the freezer to set the chocolate. The coated sticks may be stored in a covered container in the freezer for up to 3 days before serving.

BRYAN I like to see how many ways I can represent a single flavor or a combination of flavors in a dish. I also like dishes in which each bite is not only different but also intriguing, so that it leaves you wanting just a little bit more. I applied those ideas to the chocolate variations and mint preparations here, creating a variety of different textures and several unique forms of both ingredients that promise to keep you interested in the dish to the final bite.

Textures of Chocolate: Milk Chocolate Gelato, Raw Organic Cocoa, Chocolate Caramel

MAIN INGREDIENTS

Mint White Chocolate Ganache (below)
Chocolate Powder (below)
Chocolate Tuile (below)
Chocolate Caramel (below)
Milk Chocolate Gelato (below)
2 tablespoons (30 g) coarsely chopped cocoa nibs

Equipment

acetate sheet
kitchen blowtorch
ice-cream maker

Serves at least 8 as a dessert

To serve, cut the ganache into long rectangles, each about 6 by 1 inch (15 by 2.5 cm). You will need 8 total. Put 1 ganache slice in each bowl, bending and twisting it so it forms a rough S curve. Put a spoonful of the chocolate powder to the left of the ganache. Put 2 pieces of the chocolate tuile on the ganache, positioning them so they extend beyond the end of the S curve. Put 1 spoonful of the chocolate caramel at the top of the bowl and a second spoonful at the bottom of the bowl. Put a scoop of gelato on top of the chocolate powder, sprinkle the gelato with the cocoa nibs, and serve right away.

MINT WHITE CHOCOLATE GANACHE

Nonstick cooking spray
1½ cups (360 g) heavy cream
100 (5 g) fresh spearmint leaves
1½ sheets silver-grade leaf gelatin (see sources)
4 cups (450 g) white chocolate chunks
¼ cup (56 g) water
½ cup (100 g) sorbitol (see sources)
4 grams agar (see sources)
½ teaspoon (2.3 g) liquid glucose (see sources)
½ teaspoon (3 g) fine sea salt

Line a sheet pan with the acetate sheet. Spray the acetate with the cooking spray, then wipe lightly with a paper towel.

In a saucepan, bring the cream to a simmer over medium heat. Add the mint leaves, stir briefly, cover, and let stand until completely cool, about 1 hour. Transfer to a lidded container and refrigerate for 12 hours.

Put the gelatin sheets in a small bowl of ice water and let soak until softened, about 5 minutes. Strain the cream through a fine-mesh sieve placed over a bowl and discard the mint. Put the white chocolate in a large heatproof bowl. When the gelatin is ready, retrieve the sheets from the ice water, squeeze out the excess water, and add to the bowl with the chocolate. In a saucepan, combine the water, sorbitol, and agar over medium-high heat, bring to a boil, and boil for 5 minutes, then remove from the heat. Meanwhile, in another saucepan, combine the glucose, salt, and the strained cream and bring to a simmer over medium heat. Add the hot cream mixture to the sorbitol-agar mixture and stir well. Pour the combined hot mixtures over the white chocolate and gelatin. Whisk until all of the chocolate has melted and the mixture has a uniform, glossy appearance.

»

I LIKE DISHES THAT **ENGAGE YOU**

AND WHERE EVERY BITE IS SO DIFFERENT AND **INTRIGUING**

THAT IT LEAVES YOU WANTING JUST A LITTLE BIT MORE

Strain the chocolate mixture through a fine-mesh sieve held over the prepared sheet pan. Tap the pan gently on the countertop to eliminate air bubbles in the ganache and to help spread it evenly in the pan. Use the blowtorch to remove any bubbles on the surface. Allow the mixture to cool to room temperature, about 30 minutes, and then cover and refrigerate until serving time. It will keep for up to 3 days.

MINT CHOCOLATE OIL

In a small saucepan, combine the mint leaves and grape seed oil and bring to a simmer over medium heat. Remove from heat, cover, and let the oil steep for 1 hour. Strain through a fine-mesh sieve placed over a microwave-safe bowl and discard the mint. Add the chocolate to the bowl, put the bowl in a microwave, and cook on high power for 30 seconds. Stir the mixture, then return to the microwave and cook on high for 20 seconds more. Whisk until the chocolate is melted and the mixture is smooth, then let cool to room temperature. Use immediately to make the chocolate powder.

CHOCOLATE POWDER

Put the maltodextrin and salt in a food processor. With the machine running, slowly pour in half of the mint chocolate oil, then stop and scrape down the sides of the processor to ensure everything is combined. Turn on the machine and slowly add the remaining mint chocolate oil. Continue to process until all of the oil has been absorbed. The chocolate powder may be stored in an airtight container at room temperature for up to 5 days before using.

CHOCOLATE TUILE

Prepare an ice bath. In a saucepan, combine the sugar, pectin, butter, glucose, salt, and water over medium heat and bring to a boil. Remove from the heat. Whisk in the cocoa powder until smooth. Strain the mixture through a fine-mesh sieve placed over a metal bowl. Set the bowl over the ice bath and let cool completely, replenishing the ice as needed, about 30 minutes.

Preheat the oven to 350°F (180°C). Line a sheet pan with a silicone mat.

Pour the batter onto the silicone mat and, using an offset spatula, spread it in a thin, even layer. Bake until crisp, about 12 minutes. Let cool completely on the pan on a rack, then break into large pieces. The tuile pieces may be stored in an airtight container in a cool, dry place for up to 3 days before using.

CHOCOLATE CARAMEL

In a saucepan, combine the sugar and water over medium-high heat and cook, without stirring, until the mixture is a dark amber caramel, 10–15 minutes. Watch closely and reduce the heat slightly if it threatens to burn. Meanwhile, combine the cream and salt in a microwave-safe bowl, place in a microwave, and cook on high power for 1 minute. Once the sugar is a dark caramel, remove the pan from the heat and add the butter and then the cream mixture. Return to low heat and stir to melt any caramel that has solidified. Finally, add the chocolate and stir until the chocolate is melted and the sauce is completely smooth. Use right away, or let cool, transfer to a lidded container, and refrigerate. It will keep for up to 1 week. Reheat gently before using.

MILK CHOCOLATE GELATO

In a large saucepan, combine the milk, cream, menthol crystal, sugar, ice-cream stabilizer, and salt over medium-high heat and bring to a boil. Put the chopped milk chocolate in a large, heatproof bowl. Pour the hot milk mixture over the chopped chocolate and whisk until the chocolate is melted and the mixture is smooth.

Prepare an ice bath. In a bowl, whisk the egg yolks until incorporated. Gradually whisk some of the melted chocolate mixture into the yolks until they are lukewarm, then add the chocolate-yolk mixture to the chocolate mixture and whisk to blend. Transfer the mixture to a large saucepan, place over medium heat, and heat, stirring occasionally, until it reaches 180°F (82°C). Strain the mixture through a fine-mesh sieve placed over a metal bowl. Set the bowl over the ice bath and let cool completely, stirring occasionally and replenishing the ice as needed, about 30 minutes. Cover the bowl and refrigerate the chocolate mixture for at least 4 hours.

Transfer the chilled mixture to the ice cream maker and freeze according to the manufacturer's instructions. Transfer to a freezer container and freeze for at least 2 hours to firm up before serving. The gelato will keep for 2 weeks.

MINT CHOCOLATE OIL

½ cup (2.5 g) firmly packed fresh mint leaves

½ cup (113 g) grape seed oil

4½ ounces (128 g) 71 percent cacao bittersweet chocolate

CHOCOLATE POWDER

60 grams tapioca maltodextrin (see sources)

¼ teaspoon (1.5 g) fine sea salt

½ cup (130 g) Mint Chocolate Oil (above), warmed to 85°F (30°C)

CHOCOLATE TUILE

1½ cups (300 g) sugar

½ teaspoon (5 g) apple pectin powder

7 tablespoons (100 g) unsalted butter

¼ cup (110 g) liquid glucose (see sources)

¼ teaspoon (1.5 g) fine sea salt

⅔ cup (150 g) water

1 cup minus 1 tablespoon (120 g) black cocoa powder (see sources)

CHOCOLATE CARAMEL

1¼ cups plus 1½ tablespoons (270 g) sugar

2¾ tablespoons (38 g) water

½ cup plus 4 teaspoons (140 g) heavy cream

1 teaspoon (6 g) fine sea salt

3 tablespoons (42 g) unsalted butter, at room temperature, diced

1½ ounces (45 g) 62 percent bittersweet chocolate, chopped

MILK CHOCOLATE GELATO

3 cups (780 g) whole milk

1 cup (240 g) heavy cream

1-inch piece (.4 g) menthol crystal (see sources)

1 cup (200 g) sugar

5 grams ice-cream stabilizer (see sources)

½ teaspoon (3 g) fine sea salt

8 ounces (225 g) milk chocolate, chopped

9 large egg yolks

MOLLUSK

MUSSEL
OYSTER
GEODUCK
LITTLENECK
CLAM

The mollusk family is wide ranging, including everything from mussels, clams, and oysters, all of which you will find in this chapter, to octopi, snails, scallops, and squid. Several family members are farmed sustainably, which encourages us to seek interesting, innovative ways to use them. Most have sweet meat, too, which means they must be handled carefully in the kitchen. Here, we use a variety of cooking methods to preserve and showcase that sweetness. For example, geoduck clam is gently cooked in a water bath for twelve hours, while oysters are treated to smoke-infused low heat for just fifteen minutes. In another recipe, the sweet, briny taste of mussels is slowly extracted to create a glaze, which bathes a new batch of quickly sautéed mussels for an intense flavor.

MICHAEL I like the flavor of mussel sauce more than mussels themselves, so the first step here was to cook a batch of mussels in the sauce to enrich it. Then, I used the sauce to glaze a fresh batch of mussels. Next, I had to decide how to serve the mollusks. I created fennel-flavored "sand" to replace the bread typically dipped into the sauce, and I fashioned shells from a potato-based dough as a riff on the French fries of a classic moules frites.

Mussels Glazed in a Broth of Themselves, Shells, "Sand," Fennel

MAIN INGREDIENTS

1 pound (450 g) Prince Edward Island mussels, preferably small ones, plus 16 extra mussels

½ cup plus 6 tablespoons plus 1 teaspoon (175 g) canola oil

1 head garlic, cloves peeled and smashed

1 yellow onion, diced

1 fennel bulb, diced

1 tablespoon (7 g) fennel seeds

Pinch of saffron threads

½ cup plus 1 teaspoon (100 g) Pernod

8½ cups (1913 g) water

1 tablespoon (14 g) cold unsalted butter

Baby Fennel (below)

Fennel "Sand" (below)

Mussel Shells (below)

12 fresh fennel fronds

12 fresh fennel flowers

Equipment

vacuum sealer and vacuum bags

food mill fitted with the medium grinding disk

food dehydrator (optional)

deep fryer (optional)

Serves 4 as a first course

››

Rinse and debeard all of the mussels. In a wide saucepan, heat ½ cup (113 g) of the canola oil over high heat until it begins to shimmer but does not smoke. Add the 1 pound (450 g) mussels and cook, stirring occasionally, until the mussels open and begin to release their juice, 8–10 minutes. Add the garlic, onion, fennel, and fennel seeds and sauté until the vegetables are translucent, 5–8 minutes. Add the saffron, then pour in the Pernod and stir to scrape up the browned bits on the pan bottom. Cook until the liquid is reduced to a glaze, 3–5 minutes. Add the water and simmer for 20 minutes to infuse the flavors.

Remove the pan from the heat and scoop out the mussels. Strain the sauce through a fine-mesh sieve placed over a clean saucepan. Remove the mussels from their shells, discard the mussels, and rinse the shells. Select 16 nice-looking shell halves and set aside to use as molds later. Place the pan over high heat and cook the sauce until it is reduced by half, 20–30 minutes. Meanwhile, prepare an ice bath. When the sauce is ready, pour it into a metal bowl, set the bowl over the ice bath, and let cool completely, stirring occasionally and replenishing the ice as needed, about 30 minutes.

To serve, in a large sauté pan, heat the remaining canola oil over high heat until it begins to smoke. Add the remaining 16 mussels, cover the pan, reduce the heat to medium-high, and cook for 2 minutes. Uncover and check to see if the mussels have opened. If not, re-cover, cook for another minute, and check again. Once the shells have opened, add the sauce to the pan and bring to a simmer. Remove the pan from the heat and, using a large slotted spoon, transfer the mussels to a bowl. Whisk the butter into the sauce until it melts and the sauce is slightly thickened.

Remove the cooked baby fennel from the vacuum bags, and split each bulb in half lengthwise. Take each mussel out of its shell and discard the shells. Return the cooked mussels to the pan with the sauce and add the split fennel and turn gently to coat well with the sauce.

I ENJOY THE FLAVOR OF MUSSEL SAUCE MORE THAN THE TASTE OF THE MUSSELS THEMSELVES

SO THE FIRST STEP HERE WAS TO COOK A BATCH OF THE MOLLUSKS

IN THE SAUCE TO ENRICH IT

Put 2 tablespoons (22 g) of the fennel "sand" on each serving plate. Arrange the mussel shells on the "sand," and place 1 mussel meat in each shell. Spoon some sauce in and around each shell. Place the glazed split fennel around the mussels. Garnish with the fennel fronds and flowers.

BABY FENNEL

Cut off the tops of the baby fennel and then trim the bulbs so that from base to the end of the stems, the bulbs are 2½ inches (6 cm) long. In a small bowl, combine the baby fennel and grape seed oil and season to taste with the fennel pollen, sugar, and salt. Transfer to a vacuum bag and vacuum seal. Put the bag in a microwave oven and cook on high power until the bag expands and fills with steam, 1–2 minutes. Transfer the bag to a plate and let cool at room temperature until the bag completely deflates. Repeat the steaming process at least 2 times, until the fennel is completely tender. Be careful not to overheat or the bag could explode. Let the fennel cool to room temperature and then refrigerate in the bag until ready to use, up to 3 days.

FENNEL "SAND"

Preheat the oven to 325°F (165°C). Line a sheet pan with a silicone mat.

In a bowl, combine the almond flour, all-purpose flour, sugar, fennel, sea salt, and garlic powder and stir to blend. Add the butter and stir to mix. Spread the mixture in a thin, even layer on the prepared pan. Bake the mixture until it looks dry, about 15 minutes. Remove from the oven and let cool completely.

Sift the mixture through a fine-mesh sieve into an airtight container. Store at room temperature until ready to serve, up to 3 days.

MUSSEL SHELLS

Put the potatoes in a saucepan, add water to cover, place over high heat, and bring to a boil. Boil until tender, 45–60 minutes. Meanwhile, line a sheet pan with parchment paper. When the potatoes are ready, drain well. While they are still hot, pass them through the food mill fitted with the medium disk, then spread them on the prepared pan in a thin layer. Let cool to room temperature, about 15 minutes.

In a small bowl, whisk together the water and squid ink. Once the potatoes are cool, weigh 10 ounces (285 g) and place in a bowl (reserve any remaining potato for another use). Add the flour and butter to the potatoes and mix with your hands until a sandy texture forms. Add the squid ink mixture and the 1¼ teaspoons (7.5 g) salt and mix well.

On a lightly floured work surface, using a rolling pin, roll out the potato "dough" about ⅛ inch (3 mm) thick. Using an oval cutter slightly larger than the diameter of the mussel shells, cut the dough into 16 ovals. Lightly grease the outside of each shell with a few drops of canola oil. Press a dough oval onto each shell, flip the shell over onto a flat surface, and cut away the excess dough around the perimeter with a paring knife. Arrange the dough-lined shells, dough side up, on a food dehydrator tray or a sheet pan. Place in the food dehydrator set at 150°F (65°C) or in the oven preheated to 175°F (80°C) until the dough shells are completely dry to the touch, about 2 hours. The potato shells may be stored in an airtight container at room temperature for up to 2 days before frying.

Pour the canola oil into a deep fryer to the fill line or into a tall-sided saucepan to a depth of 2½ inches (6 cm) and heat to 325°F (165°C). One at a time, add the potato shells to the hot oil and fry until crisp, 10–20 seconds. Using a skimmer, transfer the fried shells to a paper towel–lined plate to drain. (The mussel shells should pop off during frying. If necessary, use a pairing knife to pry them free.) Season with salt and serve right away.

BABY FENNEL

4 baby fennel bulbs, each about 3 inches (7.5 cm) long

3½ tablespoons (50 g) grape seed oil

Fennel pollen

Sugar

Fine sea salt

FENNEL "SAND"

¾ cup plus 2 teaspoons (75 g) almond flour

⅓ cup (50 g) all-purpose flour

6 tablespoons (75 g) sugar

2 tablespoons (18 g) ground fennel

½ teaspoon (3 g) fine sea salt

1 tablespoon (6.75 g) garlic powder

3½ tablespoons (50 g) unsalted butter, melted

MUSSEL SHELLS

2 Idaho potatoes

4 tablespoons plus 1 teaspoon (60 g) water

½ teaspoon (9 g) squid ink

1½ cups (225 g) all-purpose flour, plus more for rolling

4 tablespoons plus 1 teaspoon (60 g) unsalted butter

1¼ teaspoons (7.5 g) fine sea salt, plus more to season

16 mussel shells, reserved from mussel sauce

Canola oil for oiling shells and for deep-frying

MAIN INGREDIENTS

5 ounces (140 g) timothy hay (preferably organic; see sources)

24 Olde Salt Rappahannock River Virginia oysters, or the freshest local oysters you can find, rinsed

Pickling Spice Oil (page 318)

Apple and Cucumber (below)

Cucumber-Apple Air (below)

Pickling Spice (page 318)

Equipment

2 round Staub cocottes, each 8⅞ quarts (8.3 l) or other similar-size Dutch ovens, preferably enameled cast iron

⅜-inch (9-mm) parisienne scoop or melon baller

masticating vegetable juicer

vacuum sealer and vacuum bags

Serves 6 as a first course

APPLE AND CUCUMBER

1 English cucumber, peeled

Fine sea salt

7 Granny Smith apples

1.25 grams citric acid (see sources)

CUCUMBER-APPLE AIR

3½ tablespoons (50 g) apple juice

3½ tablespoons (50 g) cucumber juice

3 tablespoons (30 g) mirin

1 gram Sucro (see sources)

BRYAN This dish came about by chance. We were making hay-smoked carrots, and when they were done, we decided to throw other things in the pot. Because Maryland has amazing oysters, we reached for them first. They were incredible, though slightly overcooked. We immediately knew we were on to something, so the next step was to get the timing right. After that, all we needed was a garnish. Here, I have used apple and cucumber, but nearly any seasonal garnish will do.

Hay-Smoked Oysters

Turn on your kitchen ventilation. Line the bottom of each cocotte with half of the hay, cover with the lid, and place over low heat. After 5 minutes have elapsed, uncover the pots; the hay should be gently smoking. Put 12 oysters on top of the hay in each pot and re-cover. Let the oysters cook in the smoke for 15 minutes. Turn off the heat and let the oysters stand in the covered pots for an additional 5 minutes. Remove the oysters from the pots and gently twist off and discard the top shells. Slide an oyster knife under each oyster to cut it away from the shell. Be careful not to lose any of the liquid. You can either serve the oysters family-style in the cocottes or arrange 4 oysters on each plate. Add ¼ teaspoon of the pickling spice oil to each oyster, then arrange 3 apple balls and 3 cucumber balls on top of each. Spoon some cucumber-apple air on top of each oyster, garnish with a tiny pinch of pickling spice, and serve right away.

APPLE AND CUCUMBER

Using the parisienne scoop, cut 72 cucumber balls. Using the juicer, juice the remaining cucumber flesh; you should have 9–10 tablespoons (126–130 g) juice. Season the juice with a tiny pinch of salt. Put the cucumber balls and juice in a vacuum bag, vacuum seal, and refrigerate until serving.

Peel 5 of the apples. Remove the cores from 4 of the apples, then juice the apples with the vegetable juicer. Strain the apple juice through a fine-mesh sieve into a bowl, and skim off any foam or residue on the surface. Measure 9 tablespoons (126 g) of the juice, and place in a bowl. Add the citric acid and a tiny pinch of salt and stir to dissolve. Using the parisienne scoop, cut 72 round balls from the remaining 2 apples. Put the apple juice and apple balls in a vacuum bag and vacuum seal. Store in the refrigerator until ready to serve.

CUCUMBER-APPLE AIR

In a bowl, whisk together the apple juice, cucumber juice, mirin, and Sucro until well blended. Transfer the mixture to a tall, narrow container and, using an immersion blender, process until aerated and a light layer of bubbles forms on top, 15–20 seconds. The cucumber-apple air may be kept in a covered container in the refrigerator for up to 2 days; re-aerate before using.

STAUB

MICHAEL This ode to the ocean came about one day when everyone in the kitchen was talking about sea life. The sea "sponge" is dusted with nori powder, the tender sous-vide-cooked clam explodes with marine flavor, the sea urchin curd is creamy and rich, and the sea beans provide a light salty accent that ties everything together. Geoduck clams are brilliant served raw, but when cooked at a low temperature for a long time, they recall the luscious texture of crabmeat.

Sea Clam, Sea "Sponge," Sea Urchin Curd, Sea Grass, Lime Vinaigrette, Garlic Croutons

MAIN INGREDIENTS

Fine sea salt
1 geoduck clam
¼ cup (56 g) extra-virgin olive oil
Sea Urchin Curd (below)
Lime Vinaigrette (below)
Smoked Maldon salt
Sea "Sponge" (below)
4 square sheets nori, ground to a fine powder
Garlic Croutons (below)
Sea beans (see sources)

Equipment

thermal immersion circulator
vacuum sealer and vacuum bags
plastic squeeze bottle

Serves 6 as a first course

Preheat the circulating water bath to 158°F (70°C).

Bring a large pot filled with water to a boil over medium-high heat. Add a generous amount of fine sea salt to the water; it should taste like the sea. While the water is heating, rinse the clam well. Run a knife along the inside edge of the shell to cut the adductor muscle (it will be slightly open to begin with). Open the shell completely, and slide the knife underneath the clam to separate the meat from the shell. Discard the shell. Lay the clam on a cutting board. Separate and discard the gills and stomach. You should have the clam's siphon and the C-shaped body remaining.

Add the siphon and the body to the boiling water and blanch for 30 seconds, then remove them from the water. While the body is still hot, use your fingers to remove the outer skin. Using a chef's knife, split the entire thing lengthwise down the middle. Rinse the interior of the siphon thoroughly. Put both clam pieces in a vacuum bag with the olive oil and vacuum seal. (If they will not fit in 1 bag, use 2 bags and divide the olive oil between them.) Cook the clam pieces in the circulating water bath for 12 hours.

Remove the bag(s) from the water bath and set aside for 20 minutes. Prepare an ice bath and add the bag(s) to the bath. Let the clam pieces cool completely in the ice bath, replenishing the ice as needed, about 1 hour. They may be stored in the bag(s) in the refrigerator for up to 3 days before serving.

To serve, spoon the sea urchin curd into a pastry bag fitted with a ¼-inch (6-mm) plain tip. Pipe the a dollop of the sea urchin curd about the size of a nickel off center on each plate. Remove the geoduck from its bag(s). Cut the body and the siphon on the diagonal into slices ¼ inch (6 mm) thick. Dress the geoduck with the lime vinaigrette. Lay a few slices on each serving plate and season with the smoked salt. Cut the sea "sponge" into 2-by-¾-inch (5-by-1.9-cm) rectangles. Coat each sponge with the nori powder. Place 1 piece of sea sponge on each plate. Arrange a couple of croutons in between the components on each plate.

››

SEA URCHIN CURD

3 tablespoons (50 g) whole milk

3 tablespoons plus 1 teaspoon (50 g) mirin

4 tablespoons (50 g) pickled ginger juice (from a jar of pickled ginger)

2 teaspoons (10 g) cornstarch

1 teaspoon (4 g) sugar

2 sheets silver-grade leaf gelatin (see sources)

1 large egg

2 large egg yolks

34 tongues sea urchin (about 4 ounces/110 g)

2 tablespoons (28 g) unsalted butter

¼ teaspoon (1.5 g) fine sea salt

LIME VINAIGRETTE

1 lime

2 teaspoons (10 g) Arbequina olive oil

Maldon salt

SEA "SPONGE"

2⅔ cups (600 g) Dashi (page 72)

12 sheets silver-grade leaf gelatin (see sources)

2½ teaspoons (15 g) fine sea salt

GARLIC CROUTONS

3 slices soft white sandwich bread (pullman loaf), each ⅛ inch (3 mm) thick

1 tablespoon (14 g) olive oil

2 cloves garlic, crushed

Garnish the geoduck with a few sea beans and some of the lime segments from the vinaigrette. Serve right away.

SEA URCHIN CURD

In a small saucepan, combine the milk, mirin, ginger juice, cornstarch, and sugar, place over medium heat, and bring to a simmer. Meanwhile, put the gelatin sheets in a small bowl of ice water and let soak until softened, about 5 minutes. In a bowl, whisk together the egg, egg yolks, and sea urchin until smooth. When the milk mixture is at a simmer, remove from the heat and slowly pour in the egg mixture while whisking continuously. Once the mixtures are fully incorporated, return the pan to medium-low heat and cook, stirring continuously, until it reaches 170°F (77°C). Remove from the heat. Retrieve the gelatin sheets from the ice water, squeeze out the excess water, add to the milk mixture, and stir to dissolve completely. Whisk in the butter and salt. Pour into a shallow heatproof container and refrigerate, uncovered, until the mixture has a puddinglike texture, about 1½ hours. The finished curd may be covered and stored in the refrigerator for up to 3 days.

LIME VINAIGRETTE

Use a Microplane to zest half of the lime into a small bowl. Cut the lime in half and add the juice from 1 lime half to the bowl with the zest. Cut the other lime half into segments and add them to the vinaigrette. Whisk in the olive oil and Maldon salt to taste. Use right away.

SEA "SPONGE"

Pour 1¼ cups (280 g) of the dashi into a small shallow pitcher or measuring cup and place in the freezer until very cold, about 1 hour; do not allow to freeze. Put the gelatin sheets in a small bowl of ice water and let soak until softened, about 5 minutes. Pour the remaining 1¼ cups plus 3 tablespoons (320 g) dashi in a saucepan, place over medium heat, and bring to a simmer. Remove from the heat. Retrieve the gelatin sheets from the ice water, squeeze out the excess water, and add to the dashi along with the salt. Stir until the gelatin and salt dissolve. Transfer the mixture to a stand mixer fitted with the whisk attachment, and turn the mixer on low speed. Slowly increase the speed to high and beat until stiff peaks form, about 10 minutes.

With the mixer still running on high speed, add the chilled dashi and beat until incorporated. Immediately transfer to an 8-inch (20-cm) square glass baking dish and refrigerate, uncovered, until set, about 2 hours. Once the gelatin has set, cover the dish. It will keep in the refrigerator for up to 3 days before using.

GARLIC CROUTONS

Freeze the bread until solid, about 3 hours.

Cut the bread into brunoise. Put the olive oil and garlic in a medium sauté pan and set it over medium heat. Let the garlic cook, stirring occasionally, until it just begins to brown and become fragrant, 2–3 minutes. Add the bread cubes and cook, stirring, until the cubes are coated with the oil and golden brown. Transfer the bread cubes to a paper towel–lined sheet pan and season lightly with salt. The croutons are best used right away, but you may store them in an airtight container at room temperature for up to 2 days.

TCB

BRYAN Like many contemporary chefs, I like to take apart a classic dish and then reconstruct it in an unfamiliar way that captures the essence of the original. Too many chowders suffer from overcooked clams or a base that overwhelms all of the other ingredients. Here, I created clam noodles as a way of extracting and highlighting the briny, juicy flavor of perfectly cooked clams. This dramatic transformation of the clams' texture guarantees that they will be at center stage in the dish.

Constructed Then Deconstructed Clam Chowder

MAIN INGREDIENTS

2 ounces (56 g) Newsom's or other high-quality hickory-smoked slab bacon, cut into lardons

2 tablespoons (28 g) canola oil

1 leek, white part only, sliced

1 celery root, peeled and diced

1 parsnip, peeled and diced

½ cup (120 g) dry white wine

1 large Yukon gold potato, peeled and diced

2 teaspoons (12 g) fine sea salt

2 cups (520 g) whole milk

1 cup (240 g) heavy cream

1 bay leaf

1 fresh thyme sprig

Finely grated zest of ½ lemon

2 dashes (1 g) of Tabasco Sauce

Clams and Clam Liquor (below)

Clam Liquor Noodles (below)

Carrot Purée (below)

Celery Root Purée (below)

Rutabaga Purée (below)

Turnip Purée (below)

Dehydrated Bacon (below)

Parsley Powder (below)

Equipment

iSi canister with 2 N_2O chargers (1-quart/.95-l canister)

thermal immersion circulator

vacuum sealer and vaccum bags

Spaghetti Kit from John Koerner & Company or plastic food syringe and plastic tubing, about 42 inches (107 cm) long

high-speed blender

acetate sheet

food dehydrator (optional)

Serves 6 as a first course

To make the soup base, in a large saucepan, cook the bacon over medium heat, stirring occasionally, until the fat has rendered and the bacon is golden brown, 10–15 minutes. Using a slotted spoon, transfer the bacon to a paper-towel lined plate to drain and cool. Add the canola oil to the bacon fat left in the pan, place over medium heat, and heat until the fat begins to shimmer but does not smoke. Add the leek, celery root, and parsnip and cook, stirring constantly, until the vegetables are tender but not brown, 5–8 minutes. Add the wine and stir to scrape up the browned bits on the pan bottom. Add the potato, salt, milk, cream, bay leaf, and thyme and bring to a simmer. Reduce the heat to low and simmer, uncovered, for 1 hour to blend the flavors.

Remove the pan from the heat, and remove and discard the bay leaf and thyme. Stir in the lemon zest and Tabasco. Prepare an ice bath. Working in batches if necessary, transfer the soup base to a blender and process until smooth. Strain the soup base through a fine-mesh sieve placed over a metal bowl. Set the bowl over the ice bath and let cool completely, stirring occasionally and replenishing the ice as needed, about 30 minutes. The soup base can be stored in a covered container in the refrigerator for up to 3 days.

To serve, in a saucepan, heat the soup base over medium-high heat to a simmer. Using a funnel, transfer the soup base to the iSi canister. Following the manufacturer's instructions, charge 2 times with the nitrous oxide chargers. (At this point, the charged canister can be held in a pot of barely simmering water until ready to serve.)

In a saucepan, combine the clams and clam liquor and the clam liquor noodles, place over over low heat, and bring to a bare simmer. Cut the carrot, celery root, rutabaga, and turnip purées into ¼-inch (6-mm) dice and set aside in separate bowls, discarding any oddly shaped pieces.

Add 4 clams to each wide, shallow bowl. Add 1 long noodle to each bowl. Scatter 1 teaspoon of each type of diced vegetable purée around the clams. Extrude a large dollop of soup base from the canister, positioning it slightly to one side of the bowl. Garnish with the dehydrated bacon and parsley powder.

››

CLAMS AND CLAM LIQUOR

2 dozen littleneck clams

4½ cups (1000 g) water

2 tablespoons plus 2 teaspoons (50 g) fine sea salt

½ cup (113 g) dry white wine

½ cup (113 g) water

1 shallot

2 cloves garlic

1 fresh thyme sprig

Finely grated zest of 1 lemon

CLAM LIQUOR NOODLES

1½ cups (350 g) infused Clam Liquor (above)

4.7 grams agar (see sources)

CARROT PURÉE

1 large (200 g) carrot, peeled and diced

¾ cup (169 g) carrot juice

2 teaspoons (12 g) fine sea salt

3 grams agar (see sources)

CELERY ROOT PURÉE

½ celery root, 7 ounces (200 g), peeled and diced

¾ cup (169 g) Vegetable Stock (page 319)

2 teaspoons (12 g) fine sea salt

2 grams agar (see sources)

RUTABAGA PURÉE

½ large rutabaga, about 7 ounces (200 g), peeled and diced

¾ cup (169 g) Vegetable Stock (page 319)

2 teaspoons (12 g) fine sea salt

2 grams agar (see sources)

TURNIP PURÉE

1 large turnip, about 7 ounces (200 g)

¾ cup (169 g) Vegetable Stock (page 319)

2 teaspoons (12 g) fine sea salt

2 grams agar (see sources)

››

CLAMS AND CLAM LIQUOR

Rinse the clams. In a large bowl, mix together the water and salt, stirring to dissolve the salt completely. Add the clams to the bowl and let soak in the refrigerator for 4–6 hours to purge any sand and impurities.

Preheat the circulating water bath to 118.4°F (48°C).

Drain the clams and discard the water. Shuck the clams and place the clam meats and the clam liquor in a bowl. Discard the shells. Transfer the clams and their liquor to a vacuum bag and vacuum seal. Cook in the circulating water bath for 30 minutes. Just before the clams are ready, prepare an ice bath. Then, when the clams are done, transfer the bag to the ice bath and let cool completely, replenishing the ice as needed, about 20 minutes.

Remove the clams from the bag, reserving the clam liquor. Trim away the outer flaps and the firm foot muscle, leaving only the meaty center portion of each clam. Reserve the trimmings. Put the clams in a lidded container with just enough of the clam liquor to cover them. In a saucepan, combine the trimmings, the remaining liquor, the wine, water, shallot, and garlic, place over medium high, and bring just to a simmer. Remove from the heat and add the thyme and lemon zest. Cover the pan and let the mixture stand for 20 minutes to infuse the flavors. Prepare an ice bath. Strain the infused clam liquor through a fine-mesh sieve into a metal bowl. Set the bowl over the ice bath and let cool completely, replenishing the ice as needed, about 20 minutes. Transfer to a lidded container and refrigerate until serving.

CLAM LIQUOR NOODLES

Prepare a large ice bath. In a saucepan, combine the infused clam liquor and agar, place over medium-high heat, and bring to a boil. Reduce the heat to maintain a slow boil and cook, whisking constantly, for 5 minutes. Remove the pan from the heat.

Fill the syringe with some of the clam liquor and release it into the plastic tubing. When the tubing is full, immerse it in the ice bath and let stand until completely cool, about 5 minutes. Use the empty syringe to blow air into the tubing to push out the finished noodle into an individual cup. Repeat 5 times to make a total of 6 noodles.

CARROT PURÉE

Put the carrot, carrot juice, and salt in a vacuum bag and vacuum seal. Bring a large saucepan filled with water to a boil over high heat. Add the bag to the water and boil until the carrots are completely tender when pressed through the bag, about 45 minutes. Transfer the contents of the bag to the blender and process until completely smooth.

Weigh 10½ ounces (300 g) of the purée and return it to the blender; save the rest for another use. Turn the blender on to low speed. Slowly increase the speed until a vortex forms in the center of the liquid. Sprinkle in the agar and blend for a full 5 seconds to hydrate the agar. Transfer to a saucepan, place over medium-high heat, and bring to a boil. Reduce the heat to a simmer and cook for 5 minutes. Immediately pour the purée into an 8-inch (20-cm) square baking pan and let cool to room temperature, about 30 minutes. Cover the pan and refrigerate until firmly set, about 2 hours. The purée may be stored in the refrigerator for up to 3 days before using.

CELERY ROOT PURÉE

Put the celery root, stock, and salt in a vacuum bag and vacuum seal. Bring a large saucepan filled with water to a boil over high heat. Add the bag to the water and boil until the celery root is completely tender when pressed through the bag, about 45 minutes. Transfer the contents of the bag to the clean blender and process until completely smooth.

Weigh 10½ ounces (300 g) of the purée and return it to the blender; save the rest for another use. Turn the blender on to low speed. Slowly increase the speed until a vortex forms in the center of the liquid. Sprinkle in the agar and blend for a full 5 seconds to hydrate the agar. Transfer to a saucepan, place over medium-high heat, and bring to a boil. Reduce the heat to a simmer and cook for 5 minutes. Immediately pour the purée into an 8-inch (20-cm) square baking pan and let cool to room temperature, about 30 minutes. Cover the pan and refrigerate until firmly set, 2 hours. The purée may be stored in the refrigerator for up to 3 days before using.

RUTABAGA PURÉE

Put the rutabaga, stock, and salt in a vacuum bag and vacuum seal. Bring a large saucepan filled with water to a boil over high heat. Add the bag to the water and boil until the rutabaga is completely tender when pressed through the bag, about 45 minutes. Transfer the contents of the bag to the clean blender and process until completely smooth.

Weigh 10½ ounces (300 g) of the purée and return it to the blender; save the rest for another use. Turn the blender on to low speed. Slowly increase the speed until a vortex forms in the center of the liquid. Sprinkle in the agar and blend for a full 5 seconds to hydrate the agar. Transfer to a saucepan, place over medium-high heat, and bring to a boil. Reduce the heat to a simmer and cook for 5 minutes. Immediately pour the purée into an 8-inch (20-cm) square baking pan and let cool to room temperature, about 30 minutes. Cover the pan and refrigerate until firmly set, 2 hours. The purée may be stored in the refrigerator for up to 3 days before using.

TURNIP PURÉE

Put the turnip, stock, and salt in a vacuum bag and vacuum seal. Bring a large saucepan filled with water to a boil over high heat. Add the bag of to the water and boil until the turnip is completely tender when pressed through the bag, about 45 minutes. Transfer the contents of the bag to the clean blender and process until completely smooth.

Weigh 10½ ounces (300 g) of the purée and return it to the blender; save the rest for another use. Turn the blender on to low speed. Slowly increase the speed until a vortex forms in the center of the liquid. Sprinkle in the agar and blend for a full 5 seconds to hydrate the agar. Transfer to a saucepan, place over medium-high heat, and bring to a boil. Reduce the heat to a simmer and cook

LIKE MANY CONTEMPORARY CHEFS I LIKE TO TAKE APART A CLASSIC DISH AND THEN RECONSTRUCT IT IN AN UNFAMILIAR WAY THAT CAPTURES THE ESSENCE OF THE ORIGINAL

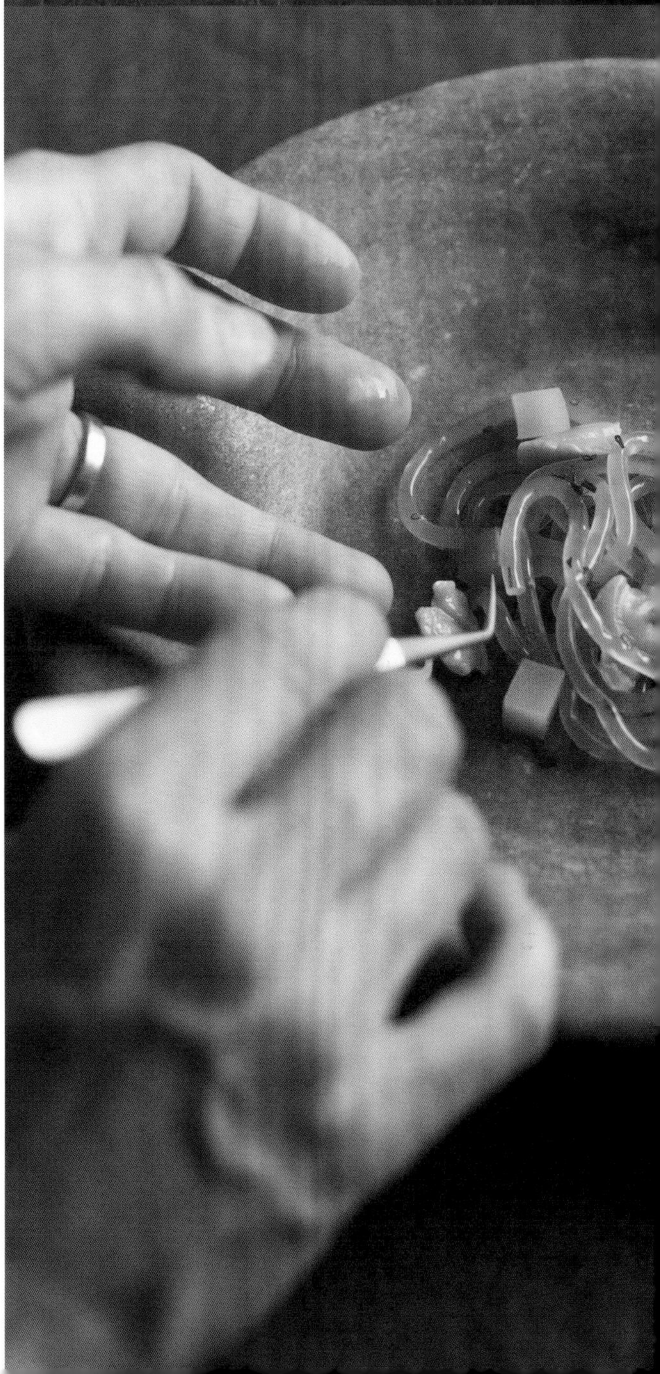

for 5 minutes. Immediately pour the purée into an 8-inch (20-cm) square baking pan and let cool to room temperature, about 30 minutes. Cover the pan and refrigerate until firmly set, 2 hours. The purée may be stored in the refrigerator for up to 3 days before using.

DEHYDRATED BACON

Freeze the bacon overnight. Line a food dehydrator tray or a sheet pan with the acetate sheet. Using a Microplane grater, shave the frozen bacon evenly over the acetate. Place in the dehydrator set at 150°F (65°C) or the oven preheated to 175°F (80°C) until completely dry, about 1½ hours. Transfer the cooled bacon to an airtight container lined with a paper towel and set aside at room temperature. The bacon is best used the same day, but it may be stored in the airtight container at room temperature for up to 3 days.

PARSLEY POWDER

Bring a saucepan filled with water to a boil over high heat. Prepare an ice bath. Add the parsley to the boiling water and blanch for 10 seconds. Using a skimmer, immediately transfer the parsley to the ice bath. Lay a few paper towels on a work surface. Arrange the leaves on the towels in a shallow layer. Top with another layer of paper towels, then gently roll up the parsley in the towels and wring out any excess water.

Line a food dehydrator tray or a sheet pan with a silicone mat, and arrange the parsley leaves in a single layer on the mat. Place in the food dehydrator set at 150°F (65°C) or the oven preheated to 175°F (80°C) until completely dry, about 4 hours. Transfer the cooled dehydrated parsley to a mortar, and grind with a pestle to a fine powder. The parsley powder may be stored in an airtight container at room temperature for up to 1 month.

DEHYDRATED BACON

2½ ounces (70 g) Newsom's or other high-quality hickory-smoked slab bacon

PARSLEY POWDER

Leaves from 1 bunch fresh flat-leaf parsley

MUSTARD

CAULIFLOWER
KOHLRABI
MUSTARD GREENS
MUSTARD SEED

We like working with the robust flavors of the mustard family. Some of its members—cauliflower, kohlrabi, mustard greens—are included here, while others—bok choy, Brussels sprouts, cabbage, turnips, kale, rutabaga, and more—crop up in recipes in other chapters. All of them contain healthful sulfur-rich phytochemicals, which give them a similar aromatic profile. More important, the members of this family, even the most sharply flavored ones, tend to soften and sweeten when treated to a little heat and a little fat. Pairing this family with a protein is often a balancing act: here, earthy cauliflower complements delicately flavored sturgeon, while two particularly assertive members, kohlrabi and mustard greens, hold their own against the big flavors of a beef strip loin.

BRYAN Sturgeon has a dense, meaty texture and a layer of fat covering the flesh that crisps when roasted or slowly renders when cooked under vacuum. Here, I wanted to come up with a subtle way to prepare it that would pair well with cauliflower and truffle. I brine the sturgeon briefly and then cooked it sous vide, which produces gently cooked fillets that complement the sweet, earthy flavor of the cauliflower and allows each element to shine.

Sturgeon with Cauliflower, Truffle, German Butterball Potatoes

MAIN INGREDIENTS

6 skinless white sturgeon fillet portions, 4 ounces (113 g) each (see sources)

4½ cups (1000 g) plus 2 tablespoons (28 g) water

2 tablespoons plus 2¼ teaspoons (50 g) fine sea salt, plus more to season

2 fresh thyme sprigs

5 black peppercorns

½ bay leaf

½ clove garlic, smashed

¼ cup (56 g) extra-virgin olive oil

2 tablespoons (28 g) cold unsalted butter, diced

Cauliflower Florets (below)

Cauliflower Purée (below)

Potato Balls (below)

Truffle Gel (below)

Truffle Sauce (below)

24 thin slices fresh or preserved black truffle

Pommes Soufflées (below)

Finely grated purple cauliflower

Zhatar spice blend

Equipment

thermal immersion circulator

vacuum sealer and vacuum bags

high-speed blender

⅜-inch (9-mm) parisienne scoop or melon baller

food dehydrator (optional)

Serves 6 as a main course

››

Lay the fish flat in a baking dish, cover, and refrigerate. To make a brine, in a saucepan, combine the 4½ cups (1000 g) water, the 2 tablespoons plus 2¼ teaspoons (50 g) salt, the thyme, peppercorns, bay leaf, and garlic. Place over high heat and bring to a simmer. Meanwhile, prepare an ice bath. When the brine begins to simmer, remove from the heat and strain through a fine-mesh sieve placed over a metal bowl. Set the bowl over the ice bath and let cool completely, stirring occasionally and replenishing the ice as needed, about 30 minutes.

Preheat the circulating water bath to 135°F (57°C).

Pour the cooled brine over the fish. Cover the dish and refrigerate for 10 minutes. Remove the fish from the brine and pat dry with paper towels. Put the fish and olive oil in a vacuum bag and vacuum seal. Cook in the circulating water bath for 12 minutes.

To serve, in a saucepan, bring the remaining 2 tablespoons (28 g) water to a simmer over medium heat. Add the butter and stir constantly until the mixture has thickened and is opaque. Add all of the cauliflower florets and stir to coat them with the butter sauce. Season to taste with salt. Reduce the heat to medium-low and cook, stirring occasionally, until the cauliflower is warmed through, about 5 minutes. If the butter sauce begins to break, add a splash of water and stir briskly to bring it back together. Remove the sturgeon fillets from the bag and put them on a plate, gently removing any coagulated proteins on the outside of the fillets. Place a large spoonful of the cauliflower purée on each serving plate. Put another, smaller spoonful a few inches away and slightly to the left. Lay 1 sturgeon fillet next to the large spoonful of purée. Arrange 2 potato balls and a few cauliflower florets around the fish. Scatter the diced truffle gel around the purée. Spoon the truffle sauce over the fish. Place 4 truffle slices on top of the fish and potatoes. Garnish the plates with 2 pommes soufflée. Sprinkle the grated purple cauliflower on the plate. Season the cauliflower florets with the zhatar and serve right away.

CAULIFLOWER FLORETS

4 cups (900 g) water

1 tablespoon (18 g) fine sea salt

16 white cauliflower florets

16 yellow cauliflower florets

16 purple cauliflower florets

CAULIFLOWER PURÉE

1 cup (120 g) diced cauliflower florets

1 cup (240 g) heavy cream

.5 gram xanthan gum (see sources)

Fine sea salt and freshly ground black pepper

POTATO BALLS

24 Yukon gold potatoes

¼ cup (56 g) Clarified Butter (page 319)

4 tablespoons (56 g) unsalted butter

¼ cup (56 g) Vegetable Stock (page 319)

TRUFFLE PURÉE

1 tablespoon (14 g) canola oil

1 shallot, minced

1 cup (200 g) diced small fresh or preserved black truffles

1 cup (255 g) Vegetable Stock (page 319)

TRUFFLE GEL

¾ cup (200 g) Truffle Purée (above)

2 grams low-acyl gellan gum (see sources)

TRUFFLE SAUCE

½ cup (113 g) Chicken Stock (page 319)

1 fresh thyme sprig

¼ bay leaf

6 black peppercorns, toasted

¼ cup (50 g) minced fresh or preserved black truffle

2 shallots, minced

¼ cup (80 g) Banyuls vinegar

POMMES SOUFFLÉES

1 large Yukon gold potato

Canola oil for deep-frying

Fine sea salt

CAULIFLOWER FLORETS

In a large saucepan, combine the water and salt and bring to a boil over high heat. Meanwhile, clean the cauliflower florets and keep each type separate. Prepare an ice bath. Add the white cauliflower to the boiling water and cook just until tender, 2–3 minutes. Using a skimmer, transfer the cauliflower to the ice bath until cold, then remove from the ice bath and pat dry. Repeat with yellow and purple florets, cooking them separately, cooling them in the ice bath, and patting them dry. The cooked florets may be stored in a lidded container in the refrigerator for up to 3 days before using.

CAULIFLOWER PURÉE

In a saucepan, combine the cauliflower and cream, place over medium-high heat, and bring to a simmer. Reduce the heat to maintain a low simmer and cook the cauliflower until it is tender when pierced with the tip of a small knife, about 10 minutes. Remove from the heat and transfer to the blender. Turn the blender on to low speed. Slowly increase the speed until a vortex forms in the center of the liquid. Sprinkle in the xanthan gum, increase the speed to medium-high, and process until completely smooth. Strain the mixture through a fine-mesh sieve into a clean saucepan and season to taste with salt and pepper and keep warm until serving time. Or, strain the cauliflower purée into a metal bowl, set over an ice bath, and let cool completely, then transfer to a lidded container and refrigerate for up to 2 days before using.

POTATO BALLS

Preheat the circulating water bath to 190°F (89°C).

Peel the potatoes. Then, using the parisienne scoop, cut out 24 balls. Put the potato balls and clarified butter in a vacuum bag and vacuum seal. Cook in the circulating water bath until tender when gently squeezed through the bag, about 20 minutes. Meanwhile, prepare an ice bath. When the potato balls are ready, use immediately or transfer the bag to the ice bath and let cool completely, replenishing the ice as needed, about 15 minutes. The potatoes may be stored in the bag in the refrigerator for up to 3 days before using.

TRUFFLE PURÉE

In a small sauté pan, heat the canola oil over medium heat until it begins to shimmer but does not smoke. Add the shallot, reduce the heat to medium-low, and cook, stirring occasionally, until just tender but not browned, 3–5 minutes. Add the truffle and cook, stirring occasionally, for 5 minutes. Add the stock, increase the heat to medium-high, and bring to a simmer. Pour the mixture into the clean blender and process until smooth. Strain the purée through a fine-mesh sieve placed over a bowl. Measure ¾ cup (200 g) of the purée and set it aside for the truffle gel (below). Reserve the remaining purée for another use. It may be stored in a lidded jar in the refrigerator for up to 1 week.

TRUFFLE GEL

Put the truffle purée into the clean blender and turn the blender on to low speed. Slowly increase the speed until a vortex forms in the center of the liquid. Sprinkle in the gellan gum and blend until fully dispersed, about 5 seconds. Quickly pour the mixture into an 8-inch (20-cm) square baking dish and let stand until cool and firmly set, about 1 hour.

Cut the gel into ¼-inch (6-mm) cubes. Transfer the cubes to a lidded container and store in the refrigerator until serving or for up to 3 days.

TRUFFLE SAUCE

In a small saucepan, bring the stock to a simmer over medium heat. Remove from the heat, add the thyme, bay leaf, and peppercorns, cover the pan, and let steep for 30 minutes. Meanwhile, in a small saucepan, combine the truffle, shallots, and vinegar, place over medium heat, and bring to a simmer. Cook until reduced by one-third, 10–15 minutes. Remove from the heat.

When the stock mixture is ready, strain through a fine-mesh sieve placed over a clean saucepan. Add the vinegar-truffle reduction to taste and keep warm until serving. Or, pour into a metal bowl, set over an ice bath, and let cool completely, then transfer to a lidded container and refrigerate until serving or for up to 3 days.

POMMES SOUFFLÉES

Peel the potato. Using a mandoline, cut into slices 1⁄10 inch (2.5 mm) thick. Using a 1½-inch (4-cm) round cutter, punch out circles in the potato slices. Discard the trimmings.

Pour the canola oil into 2 tall-sided saucepans to a depth of 4 inches (10 cm). Place the pans over medium-high heat and heat the oil in one pan to 300°F (150°C) and the other pan to 375°F (190°C). Add the potato circles to the oil heated to 300°F (150°C) and stir constantly with a skimmer until small blisters form on the surface of the circles, about 2 minutes. Immediately transfer the potatoes to the 375°F (190°C) oil and cook until the circles expand and puff up, 30–60 seconds. Using the skimmer, transfer the potato circles to a paper towel–lined plate to drain briefly. Season lightly with salt and serve right away.

THE GENTLY COOKED FISH IS A WONDERFUL COMPLEMENT TO THE SWEET EARTHY FLAVOR OF THE CAULIFLOWER IN A DISH THAT LETS EACH ELEMENT SHINE

MICHAEL I don't really have a story for this dish. It is like art: it goes together because I feel it does. I wanted all of the basic tastes on one plate: bitter, sweet, sour, salty, umami. I dust the sweetbreads with cocoa powder, sear them, and then coat them with brown butter to add something comforting to what can be, to some, an intimidating ingredient. The chocolate brioche, the sweet-and-sour lemon jam, and the cauliflower scramble all play supporting roles in the production.

Cocoa-Dusted Veal Heartbreads, Scrambled Cauliflower, Lemon Jam, Chocolate Brioche

MAIN INGREDIENTS

9 ounces (250 g) veal sweetbreads (heart section)

4½ cups (1000 g) whole milk

9 cups (2025 g) plus 7 tablespoons (100 g) water

7 tablespoons (100 g) Champagne vinegar

Fine sea salt

5½ tablespoons (78 g) unsalted butter, plus 2 tablespoons (28 g) cold butter, diced

7½ teaspoons (20 g) black cocoa powder (see sources)

2 tablespoons (28 g) canola oil

Maldon sea salt

Cauliflower Purée (below)

Lemon Jam (below)

Chocolate Brioche (below)

Crispy Cauliflower (below)

Equipment

thermal immersion circulator

vacuum sealer and vacuum bags

high-speed blender

deli-style meat slicer or electric knife

food dehydrator (optional)

24 paper baking molds (3-inch/7.5 cm molds)

Serves 4 as a first course

››

Combine the sweetbreads and milk in a lidded container and refrigerate overnight to draw the blood out of the sweetbreads.

The next day, in a large saucepan, combine the 9 cups (2025 g) water and the vinegar. Rinse the sweetbreads under cold running water, then add them to the vinegar-water mixture. Place over medium heat and bring to a boil. Using a skimmer, immediately transfer the sweetbreads to a plate and let them cool to room temperature, about 20 minutes.

Preheat the circulating water bath to 185°F (85°C).

Gently peel any excess membrane from the sweetbreads and season lightly with salt. Put the sweetbreads and 3½ tablespoons (50 g) of the butter in a vacuum bag and vacuum seal. Cook in the circulating water bath for 15 minutes. Transfer the sweetbreads, still in the bag, to a sheet pan. Place a second sheet pan on top and add about 5 pounds (2.4 kg) of weights, such as canned goods, spacing them to apply uniform pressure to the sweetbreads. Refrigerate for 3 hours to cool and flatten the sweetbreads. After 3 hours, the weights can be removed and the sweetbreads, still in the bag, may be refrigerated for up to 2 days before serving.

To serve, remove the sweetbreads from the bag and put them on a large plate. Using a small sieve, dust them on both sides with the cocoa powder. In a large sauté pan, heat the canola oil over medium-high heat until it begins to shimmer but not smoke. Add the sweetbreads to the pan and cook until golden brown on one side, 2–3 minutes. Flip the sweetbreads and add 2 tablespoons (28 g) butter to the pan. When the butter begins to froth, use a wide, flat, large metal spoon to rapidly baste the sweetbreads with the butter mixture until all the foam subsides. Once the second side is golden brown, after 2–3 minutes, flip the sweetbreads again and baste a few more times with the butter mixture. Transfer the sweetbreads to a large paper towel–lined plate. Season with the Maldon salt and keep warm.

CAULIFLOWER PURÉE

7 ounces (200 g) cauliflower reserved from Crispy Cauliflower (below)

1 cup (240 g) heavy cream

½ teaspoon (3 g) fine sea salt

3.6 grams Methocel SG A7C (see sources)

LEMON JAM

3 large lemons

5 tablespoons (100 g) Simple Syrup (page 319)

7 tablespoons (100 g) lemon oil

CHOCOLATE BRIOCHE

¾ cup plus 1 teaspoon (200 g) plus 4 tablespoons plus 2 teaspoons (76 g) whole milk

2 tablespoons (16.8 g) active dry yeast

2⅔ cups (400 g) all-purpose flour

2 tablespoons (25 g) sugar

1 teaspoon (6 g) fine sea salt

4 large egg yolks plus 2 whole eggs

5½ ounces (150 g) unsalted butter

2 tablespoons (15 g) black cocoa powder (see sources)

CRISPY CAULIFLOWER

1 head cauliflower

In a small saucepan, bring the remaining 7 tablespoons (100 g) water to a simmer over medium-high heat. Add the cauliflower purée, adjust the heat to maintain a low simmer, cover, and let the cauliflower warm up and begin to take on a firm texture, without stirring, for about 5 minutes. When the cauliflower is fully set, pour out three-fourths of the water and stir in the remaining 2 tablespoons (28 g) diced cold butter. Using a silicone spatula, gently break up the cauliflower mixture until it looks like white scrambled eggs. Keep warm.

Put 2 pieces of the sweetbreads in the center of each plate. Put 3 dots of the lemon jam around the sweetbreads. Put several spoonfuls of the scrambled cauliflower around the sweetbreads. Put 2 pieces of the chocolate brioche and some of the crispy cauliflower around the sweetbreads. Spoon the foamy hot butter from roasting the sweetbreads over the top of the sweetbreads and around the plate. Serve right away.

CAULIFLOWER PURÉE

Slice the cauliflower thin. In a saucepan, combine the cauliflower, cream, and salt over medium heat and bring to a gentle simmer. Cook until the cauliflower is tender, about 10 minutes. Meanwhile, prepare an ice bath. Transfer the hot cauliflower-cream mixture to the blender and process on high speed until completely smooth. Reduce the blender speed to medium-low and process until a vortex forms in the center of the liquid. Sprinkle in the Methocel and increase the speed to disperse the Methocel completely, a full 10 seconds. Pour the cauliflower mixture into a metal bowl and set the bowl over the ice bath. Let cool until ice cold to ensure proper hydration, stirring occasionally and replenishing the ice as needed, about 30 minutes. The purée may be stored in a lidded container in the refrigerator for up to 3 days before using.

LEMON JAM

Using a fork, puncture 12 holes through the skin and the pith of each lemon, spacing the holes evenly. Put the lemons in a small saucepan, add water to cover, and bring just to a boil over medium-high heat. Remove from the heat, drain the lemons, and repeat 2 more times with fresh cold water. Quarter the lemons and remove all of the seeds.

Put the lemons in a microwave-safe bowl, cover the bowl with plastic wrap, and cook on high power for 2 minutes. Let the lemons stand for 1 minute, and then cook on high power for another 2 minutes. Let the lemons stand again for 1 minute, then cook on high for 2 minutes more, for a total cooking time of 6 minutes. Immediately remove the plastic wrap from the bowl and transfer the lemon quarters to the clean blender. Add the simple syrup and lemon oil and process until smooth. Prepare an ice bath. Strain the mixture through a fine-mesh sieve into a metal bowl. Set the bowl over the ice bath and let cool completely, replenishing the ice as needed, about 20 minutes. The jam may be stored in a lidded container in the refrigerator for up to 2 weeks before serving.

CHOCOLATE BRIOCHE

Lightly butter a medium bowl and set aside. Put the ¾ cup plus 1 teaspoon (200 g) milk in a small bowl and heat in the microwave on high power in 10-second intervals until it reaches 80–90°F (26–32°C). Stir in the yeast and let it stand until the yeast is hydrated, about 2 minutes. Meanwhile, put the flour, sugar, and salt in the bowl of a stand mixer fitted with the dough hook. Turn the mixer on low speed and add the milk-yeast mixture. Add the 4 egg yolks, one at a time, making sure that each yolk is fully absorbed before adding the next. Dice the butter and add it bit by bit, until it is fully absorbed into the dough. Mix the dough on medium speed until the dough pulls away from the sides of the bowl, about 10 minutes. Transfer the dough to the buttered bowl, cover with plastic wrap, and leave in a warm place until it doubles in size, about 1 hour.

Use your hands to gently deflate the brioche dough and divide it into 2 equal-size balls. Use a rolling pin to roll one ball of dough into a 12-inch (30-cm) square that is about ⅛ inch (3 mm) thick. Sift half of the cocoa powder evenly over the dough. Roll up the dough into a tight log, resembling a jelly roll, and place it, seam side down, on a parchment-lined sheet pan. Repeat to roll and fill the second ball of dough. Refrigerate the dough logs until they become firm to the touch, about 1 hour.

Remove the dough from the refrigerator and cut each log crosswise into 12 even slices. Drop 1 slice into each of the 24 prepared paper baking molds. Lay the molds out on a sheet pan and let stand in a warm spot until they look puffy, about 1 hour.

Preheat the oven to 375°F (190°C).

Mix together the 2 eggs and 4 tablespoons plus 2 teaspoons milk to make an egg wash. Brush the egg wash over the tops of the dough and bake in the oven until golden brown, about 15 minutes. Let them cool on the sheet pan and set aside at room temperature until ready to serve.

CRISPY CAULIFLOWER

Line a food dehydrator tray or a sheet pan with a silicone mat. Remove 3 large florets from the cauliflower head and reserve the remainder for the cauliflower purée. Using a mandoline, carefully shave each floret into thin slices, preserving the natural shape of the floret with each slice. Lay the slices in a single layer on the prepared tray or pan. Place in the dehydrator set at 150°F (65°C) or in the oven preheated to 175°F (80°C) until dry and crisp, about 6 hours. The cooled crispy slices may be stored in an airtight container at room temperature for up to 3 days before using.

I APPROACHED THIS DISH LIKE
AN ARTIST
WITH THE GOAL
OF HAVING
BITTER, SWEET
SALTY, SOUR
AND UMAMI
ALL ON ONE PLATE

BRYAN Beef, cheese, beer, and mustard are a classic ingredient combination. Here, the purée of beer, Cheddar, and kohlrabi brings an underutilized vegetable to the forefront. Mustard is often paired with beef and cheese to cut their respective richness. In this recipe, I have reversed that approach: the role of the beef and cheese is to bring out the flavor of the mustard. If you're feeling daring, you can thin any leftover kohlrabi purée and serve it as a soup.

Beef, Mustard, Kohlrabi

MAIN INGREDIENTS

5 pounds (2.25 kg) boneless beef strip loin, untrimmed

1 tablespoon (8.4 g) active dry yeast

2 yellow onions, diced

2 tablespoons (16 g) yellow mustard seeds

2½ cups (560 g) plus 3½ tablespoons (50 g) water

1 celery rib, diced

1 large carrot, diced

½ ounce (15 g) kombu

¼ cup (56 g) Worcestershire sauce

¼ cup (56 g) dry red wine

½ teaspoon (6.6 g) red wine vinegar

.25 gram xanthan gum (see sources)

3 bunches mustard greens

¼ teaspoon (1.5 g) fine sea salt, plus more to season

5 tablespoons (70 g) beef fat reserved from cooking the beef

3 baby kohlrabi, unpeeled and sliced into rounds ½ inch (12 mm) thick

Kohlrabi Purée (below)

3 cloves garlic, thinly shaved on a mandoline

2 shallots, minced

1 tablespoon Pickled Mustard Seeds (page 318)

Micro mustard greens

Equipment

meat grinder (optional)

6-quart (5.7-l) pressure cooker

high-speed blender

thermal immersion circulator

vacuum sealer and vacuum bags

Serves 6 as a main course

Trim the fat, sinew, and silver skin from the strip loin and reserve all of the trimmings. Cut the loin in half lengthwise, and then cut 6 square-shaped steak portions (3 per half), each weighing about 5 ounces (140 g).

In the meat grinder, grind the fat, sinew, silver skin, and other trimmings, or finely chop in a food processor. In a saucepan, combine the ground mixture, yeast, 1 diced onion, mustard seeds, and ½ cup (110 g) of the water, place over medium heat, and cook until the water evaporates and the fat renders completely, 1–2 hours. Continue to cook, stirring occasionally, until the fat is caramelized and resembles pork cracklings, about 20 minutes. Remove from the heat and strain the mixture through a fine-mesh sieve placed over a heatproof container, reserving both the fat and the solids. The cooled fat may be stored in a lidded container in the refrigerator for up to 2 weeks.

In the pressure cooker, combine the solids from rendering the fat, the celery, carrot, the remaining diced onion, the kombu, the remaining 2 cups plus 3½ tablespoons (500 g) water, the Worcestershire sauce, and the red wine. Following the manufacturer's instructions, lock the lid in place, bring up to high pressure, and cook for 45 minutes. Let the pressure dissipate naturally, then uncover the pot.

Strain the mixture through a fine-mesh sieve placed over a clean saucepan; discard the solids. Cook the liquid over medium-high heat until reduced to 1 cup (250 g) total. Transfer the reduced liquid to the blender, add the vinegar, and turn the blender on to low speed. Slowly increase the speed until a vortex forms in the center of the liquid. Sprinkle in the xanthan gum and blend for a full 5 seconds to dissolve the xanthan gum completely and form a sauce. The sauce may be cooled and stored in a lidded container in the refrigerator for up to 5 days before using.

Bring a large pot of generously salted water to a boil over high heat. Prepare an ice bath.

Cut off and discard the stems from the mustard greens. Add the greens to the boiling water and cook until just tender, about 1 minute. Using a skimmer, transfer the greens to the ice bath to cool briefly, then drain the cooled greens, pat them

››

THE FAMILIAR COMBINATION OF

BEEF BEER AND

CHEDDAR CHEESE

HELPS BRING KOHLRABI AN UNDERUTILIZED VEGETABLE

TO THE **FOREFRONT**

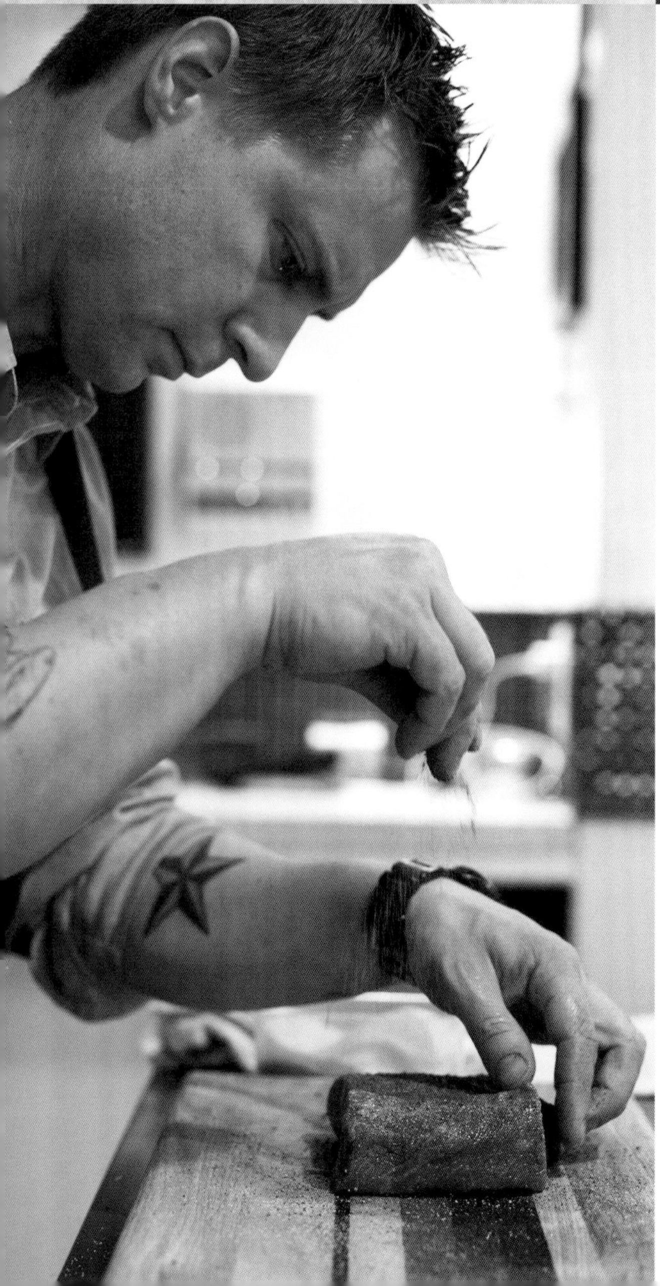

dry, and chop fine. The greens may be stored in a lidded container in the refrigerator for up to 2 days before using.

To serve, preheat the circulating water bath to 125.6°F (52°C).

Season the 6 beef strip loin steaks generously with salt. Put the steaks and 2 tablespoons (28 g) of the rendered beef fat in a vacuum bag and vacuum seal. Cook in the circulating water bath for 1 hour. Put the baby kohlrabi and the ¼ teaspoon (1.5 g) salt in a vacuum bag and vacuum seal. Bring a large pot filled with water to a boil over high heat. Put the beef sauce in a small saucepan, place over medium heat, and bring just to a simmer. Keep warm. In a small saucepan, bring the kohlrabi purée to a bare simmer over low heat. Keep warm. Place a large sauté pan over medium-high heat. When the pan is hot, open the bag of steaks, pat them dry, and add them to the pan. Quickly sear them on the tops and bottoms to form a caramelized crust, 2–3 minutes on each side. Transfer to a warmed plate to rest.

Set another large sauté pan over medium-high heat and add the remaining 3 tablespoons (42 g) rendered beef fat. When the fat melts and begins to shimmer, add the garlic, shallots, and mustard seeds and sauté until fragrant and slightly caramelized, 1–2 minutes. Add the blanched, chopped mustard greens and cook, folding everything together into a uniform ragout, until heated through, 2–3 minutes longer.

Remove the baby kohlrabi slices from the bag, and line the center of each serving plate with 6 slices. Form a line of mustard greens along the center of the plate on top of the kohlrabi. Slice each piece of beef into 2 parts, one twice as large as the other. Leave the smaller piece as a large chunk. Cut the larger piece into 4 slices. Arrange the 4 slices, slightly overlapping, on the mustard greens. Stand the large chunk of beef up on the plate to the left

of the meat slices. Put a spoonful of the kohlrabi purée to the right of the sliced meat. Put the sauce on the large chunk of meat, and garnish the kohlrabi purée and the chunk of meat with the micro mustard greens. Serve right away.

KOHLRABI PURÉE

To make a Cheddar stock, in a saucepan, combine the ale and cheese, place over medium heat, and bring to a simmer, whisking constantly. Remove from heat and let stand for 20 minutes. Line a fine-mesh sieve with cheesecloth and place over a metal bowl. Prepare an ice bath. When the stock is ready, strain it through the sieve into the bowl. Set the bowl over the ice bath and let the purée cool completely, stirring occasionally and replenishing the ice as needed, about 15 minutes.

Preheat the circulating water bath to 194°F (90°C). Measure 1 cup (225 g) of the Cheddar stock. Put the kohlrabi and the stock in a vacuum bag and vacuum seal. Cook in the circulating water bath until tender when gently squeezed through the bag, about 2 hours.

Prepare an ice bath. Transfer the kohlrabi to a blender and process on high speed until smooth. Add some of the cooking liquid, if needed, to help form a smooth purée. Adjust the blender speed so that a vortex forms in the center of the purée, then sprinkle in the xanthan gum and blend for a full 5 seconds until completely absorbed. Pass the purée through a fine-mesh sieve placed over a metal bowl. Set the bowl over the ice bath and let cool completely, stirring occasionally and replenishing the ice as needed, about 15 minutes. The purée may be stored in a lidded container in the refrigerator for up to 3 days before using.

KOHLRABI PURÉE

1½ cups (340 g) light ale

5 ounces (140 g) Cheddar cheese, shredded

2 large kohlrabi, about 10 ounces (280 g) total weight, peeled and chopped

.52 gram xanthan gum (see sources)

MICHAEL This dish was inspired by the pleasant discovery that seaweed and mustard marry well. I always have dashi on hand, which plays a major role here. To intensify the ocean flavor of the abalone, I put kombu in the vacuum bag along with it and then I cook the abalone sous vide for 24 hours to tenderize it. When I realized that seaweed and mustard were so harmonious, I started adding mustard to the bag, as well, and used the resulting juices as a sauce.

Grilled Monterey Bay Abalone, Mustard Seaweed, Mustard Dashi

MAIN INGREDIENTS

2 live Monterey Bay abalone in the shell (see sources)
½ ounce (15 g) kombu
1 tablespoon (18 g) Dijon mustard
Extra-virgin olive oil
Maldon sea salt
Wakame Pasta (below)
2 tablespoons (28 g) Seaweed Butter (page 280)
Mustard Dashi (below)
12 small branches sea beans (see sources)
12 small branches saltwort (see sources)

Equipment

thermal immersion circulator
vacuum sealer and vacuum bags
pasta machine

Serves 4 as a first course

WAKAME PASTA

1⅔ cups (250 g) all-purpose flour, plus more for rolling
1 teaspoon (6 g) fine sea salt
¾ ounce (20 g) dried wakame seaweed, ground to a powder in a spice grinder
6 large egg yolks
3 tablespoons (50 g) Dijon mustard
½ teaspoon (9 g) squid ink
5 tablespoons (80 g) whole milk
2 teaspoons (10 g) extra-virgin olive oil

MUSTARD DASHI

7 tablespoons (100 g) Dashi (page 72)
7 tablespoons (100 g) reserved abalone liquid
1 tablespoon (18 g) Dijon mustard
2 tablespoons (28 g) Seaweed Butter, diced (page 280)

Preheat the circulating water bath to 149°F (65°C).

Rinse away any sand or dirt from the abalone shells. Brush the kombu with the mustard. Put the live abalones in their shells in a vacuum bag, press the kombu up against the flesh at the shell's opening, and vacuum seal. Cook in the circulating water bath for 24 hours. Just before the abalones are ready, prepare an ice bath. Transfer the abalones, still in the bag, to the ice bath and let cool completely, replenishing the ice as needed, about 30 minutes.

Cut open the bags, strain the cooking liquid through a fine-mesh sieve into a clean container, and set aside. Slip a spoon or short, dull butter knife into the thin, flat front side of an abalone shell, and slide it under the abalone and toward the back of the shell. Press and pop the abalone loose from the shell until it is held in place only by its viscera. Pull the back of the abalone muscle toward you gently so that you do not split any of the organs. It should easily separate on its own and only require cutting with a small, sharp knife at the back to free it from the shell. Remove and discard the viscera. Wash the muscle under running cold water and scrub off the black membrane. Find the radula, the part that looks pinched together. Cut it out in a V-shaped section with a sharp knife. Discard the radula. Repeat with the second abalone.

Preheat the circulating water bath to 145°F (63°C). Bring a saucepan filled with salted water to a boil over high heat.

To serve, put the abalones in a vacuum bag, vacuum seal, and heat in the circulating water bath for 10 minutes. Open the bag, drizzle the abalone with olive oil, and season with Maldon salt. Cut each abalone in half lengthwise, then cut each half on the diagonal into thin slices; you will need a total of 16 slices. Keep warm. Add the wakame pasta to the boiling water and cook until just tender, about 1½ minutes. Using a skimmer, lift out the pasta squares, letting the excess water drip off, and put them in a sauté pan along with the seaweed butter. Turn on the heat to low and toss the pasta gently to coat it evenly with the butter. Add several spoonfuls of the mustard dashi and toss to coat evenly. Arrange 2 pasta squares in the center of each plate. Put 4 slices

THIS DISH WAS INSPIRED BY THE PLEASANT DISCOVERY THAT SEAWEED AND MUSTARD MARRY WELL AND TOGETHER MAKE A FASCINATING SAUCE FOR SEAFOOD

of abalone on and around the pasta squares. Use an immersion blender to froth the mustard dashi and add 1–2 spoonfuls to each plate. Put the sea beans and saltwort into another bowl and season with olive oil and crushed Maldon salt. Put 3 each pieces of the sea beans and saltwort on the pasta sheets and abalone. Serve right away.

WAKAME PASTA

In a food processor, combine the flour, salt, and wakame. Turn on the processor and slowly add the egg yolks through the feed tube. Allow the machine to run for a full 5 seconds to mix the ingredients, then add the mustard, squid ink, milk, and olive oil and continue to process until a dough forms, 5–10 seconds. Turn the dough out onto a sheet of parchment paper and form into a ball. Put the dough in a vacuum bag and vacuum seal on high power. Let the dough rest for 5 minutes. Set the roller on the pasta machine to the widest setting. Remove the dough from the bag and dust with flour. Run the dough through the rollers twice, taking care that it stays flat. If it sticks a little, dust the rollers lightly with flour. Reset the rollers one width narrower and again pass the dough through the rollers twice. Repeat the process, resetting the rollers one width narrower and rolling the dough twice through each setting, until you reach the narrowest setting. Add as little flour as possible to prevent sticking. Lay the dough flat on a cutting board, and cut into eight 4-inch (10-cm) squares. Line a sheet pan with parchment paper, and transfer the pasta squares to the pan. Cover with plastic wrap until ready to cook.

MUSTARD DASHI

Put the dashi, abalone liquid, and mustard in a saucepan over medium heat and whisk to blend. When it comes to a simmer, add the seaweed butter and stir until the butter is absorbed. Remove from the heat and use immediately.

NIGHTSHADE

TOMATO
BELL PEPPER
POTATO
EGGPLANT

The nightshade family is said to have its dark side, with tobacco, belladonna, and that favorite of black-magic practitioners, mandrake root, among its members. But it also includes such kitchen staples as potatoes, tomatoes, sweet and hot peppers, and eggplants. This is a family whose members play exceptionally well together, and we enjoy the challenge of mixing and matching them to explore new flavors and textures within the same recipe. In Lamb Caponata, for example, eggplant and peppers are puréed separately to form the layers of a terrine, and are also finely diced and then sautéed together in an updated version of caponata. Or, in a reinvented gazpacho, tomatoes and peppers are combined and then frozen in small drops that recall the classic chilled Spanish soup in an entirely new way.

MAIN INGREDIENTS

1 tablespoon (14 g) canola oil

1 red bell pepper, roasted, seeded, peeled, and diced

½ red onion, thinly sliced

4 cloves garlic, thinly sliced

2 tablespoons (40 g) red wine vinegar

1¾ teaspoons (10.5 g) fine sea salt

1 teaspoon (1.2 g) coriander seeds

1 teaspoon (2 g) cumin seeds

Leaves from 6 fresh basil sprigs, plus 6 sprigs

Leaves from 8 fresh cilantro sprigs, plus 2 bunches

1 large cucumber, peeled and diced, plus 2 large seedless cucumbers, 17 ounces (475 g) total weight, peeled, halved, and errant seeds discarded

One 28-ounce (780-g) can whole San Marzano tomatoes

.33 gram plus .4 gram xanthan gum (see sources)

1 fennel bulb, 11½ ounces (325 g)

1 cup (225 g) Vegetable Stock (page 319)

1¾ cups (300 g) water

½ cup (100 g) sugar

¼ cup (110 g) liquid glucose (see sources)

1.5 grams agar (see sources)

1 cup (20 g) spinach

½ cup (113 g) extra-virgin olive oil

Shrimp Confit (below)

Coriander blooms

Fresh opal basil leaves

Equipment

high-speed blender

vacuum sealer and vacuum bags (optional)

6-quart (5.7-l) pressure cooker

4 plastic squeeze bottles

liquid nitrogen (optional)

small Styrofoam cooler (optional)

thermal immersion circulator

Serves 4 as a first course

››

BRYAN I became the coolest person in the world when I figured out how to use liquid nitrogen to make "dipping dots" for my wife. Now her favorite ice cream, they are the starting point for this new version of a Spanish classic. I took the idea of gazpacho and froze the main elements—here, tomato and bell pepper, fennel, cucumber—separately. Then, when I combined them in serving bowls, they came together to create the familiar flavor of gazpacho.

Gazpacho, Shrimp Confit

In a saucepan, heat the canola oil over high heat until it begins to shimmer but does not smoke. Add the bell pepper, onion, and garlic and sauté until the vegetables caramelize and are golden brown and fragrant, 5–8 minutes. Add 1 tablespoon (20 g) of the vinegar and stir to scrape up any caramelized bits from the pan bottom. Add the salt, remove from the heat, and set aside.

In a small sauté pan, toast the coriander and cumin seeds over medium heat, shaking the pan occasionally to prevent scorching, until aromatic, 2–3 minutes. Add the toasted seeds, basil leaves, cilantro leaves, diced cucumber, tomatoes, and the remaining 1 tablespoon (20 g) vinegar to the vegetables and stir well. Working in batches, transfer the mixture to a blender and process until smooth. Set the tomato purée aside. Rinse the blender.

Add the 2 seeded cucumbers to the blender and process until a smooth purée forms. Weigh 11½ ounces (325 g) of the purée. Discard the remainder. Return the purée to the blender and turn it on low speed. Slowly increase the speed until a vortex forms in the center of the liquid. Sprinkle in ⅜ teaspoon (2.25 g) of the salt and the .33 gram xanthan gum and process for a full 3 seconds to dissolve completely. Strain the cucumber purée through a fine-mesh sieve, then store in a lidded container in the refrigerator overnight to allow the air bubbles to dissipate. Alternatively, transfer the purée to a vacuum bag and vacuum seal to remove the bubbles, then use the purée right away.

In the pressure cooker, combine the fennel, stock, and ⅜ teaspoon (2.25 g) of the salt. Following the manufacturer's instructions, lock the lid in place, bring up to high pressure, and cook for 10 minutes. Let the pressure dissipate naturally, then uncover the pot.

Prepare an ice bath. Transfer the contents of the pressure cooker to the blender and process until a smooth purée forms. Strain the purée through a fine-mesh sieve, using a small ladle to push it through. Weigh 14 ounces (400 g) of the purée. Discard the remainder. Return the purée to the blender and turn the blender on to low speed. Slowly increase the speed until a vortex forms in the center of the liquid. Sprinkle in the .4 gram xanthan gum and process for a full 3 seconds to dissolve completely. Transfer the purée to a metal bowl, set the bowl over

Thermo
SCIENTIFIC

the ice bath, and cool let completely, stirring occasionally and replenishing the ice as needed, about 15 minutes. Store the fennel purée in a lidded container in the refrigerator overnight to allow the air bubbles to dissipate. Alternatively, transfer the purée to a vacuum bag and vacuum seal to remove the bubbles, then use the purée right away.

Line a sheet pan with plastic wrap. In a small saucepan, combine the water, sugar, glucose, the remaining 1/4 teaspoon (1.5 g) salt, and the agar and bring to a boil over high heat. Reduce the heat to maintain a low boil and cook for 5 minutes. Put the 2 cilantro bunches, 6 basil sprigs, and spinach in the clean blender and pour the hot liquid over the top. Process on high speed until the mixture is smooth. Quickly pass the mixture through a fine-mesh sieve held over the prepared sheet pan. Quickly put the sheet pan in the freezer and allow the mixture to set but not freeze, about 20 minutes. Rinse the blender, transfer the set herb mixture to the blender, and process until smooth. Pour the herb mixture into a squeeze bottle and set aside.

To serve, pour the liquid nitrogen into the Styrofoam cooler, filling it half full. Transfer the tomato purée to a squeeze bottle and drop small dots of the mixture into the liquid nitrogen bath. They will freeze in 5–10 seconds. Once all of the dots are set, carefully pour the contents of the cooler into a fine-mesh sieve placed over a stainless-steel container large enough to hold all of the nitrogen. Transfer the tomato dots from the sieve to a lidded container and place in the freezer immediately. Return the nitrogen to the Styrofoam cooler, and repeat the process with the cucumber, fennel, and herb purées, keeping them in separate containers in the freezer and replenishing the nitrogen in the cooler as it evaporates. Finally, drizzle the olive oil into the nitrogen bath and collect the filaments that form with a skimmer. Put them in a covered container in the freezer.

Alternatively, you can put the tomato, cucumber, and fennel purées in separate, shallow dishes in the freezer for a minimum of 3 hours, stirring each of them every 30 minutes or so to make them into separate granitas. Leave the herb purée in its squeeze bottle in the refrigerator and use to garnish the finished granitas in the bowl. Pour the olive oil into a freezerproof container and freeze alongside the granitas. It will become more viscous, but won't form filaments.

Divide the vegetable dots evenly among 4 chilled bowls. Place 4 shrimp on top of the dots in each bowl. Scatter the olive oil filaments on top of the shrimp. Slip the coriander blooms and opal basil into the nooks between the dots for garnish and serve right away.

SHRIMP CONFIT

Preheat the circulating water bath to 131°F (55°C).

In a bowl, combine the shrimp, lime zest, cilantro, basil, olive oil, and salt and mix well to coat the shrimp evenly. Transfer the mixture to a vacuum bag and vacuum seal. Cook in the circulating water bath for 20 minutes. Meanwhile, prepare an ice bath. When the shrimp are ready, transfer them, still in the bag, to the ice bath and let cool completely, replenishing the ice as needed, about 20 minutes. Refrigerate until ready to serve.

SHRIMP CONFIT

16 Marvesta Farm shrimp (21–25 count)
Finely grated zest of 1 lime
6 fresh cilantro sprigs
4 fresh basil leaves
1/4 cup (56 g) extra-virgin olive oil
1/2 teaspoon (3 g) fine sea salt

MICHAEL This dish is inspired by Joël Robuchon's classic recipe for mashed potatoes, in which the butter outweighs the taste of the potato. I serve these potatoes as a side dish with fish—as a little extra something that, while not necessary, contributes deliciously to the experience. They combine the aroma of the sea with the richness of the earth. And while I especially like flavoring butter with seaweed, nearly any flavored butter makes a better mashed potato.

Seaweed Mashed Potatoes

MAIN INGREDIENTS

5 cups (2000 g) water

1 sheet (15 g) kombu

¾ ounce (20 g) shaved bonito flakes

3 Idaho potatoes, peeled and cut into large dice

½ cup plus 2 tablespoons (150 g) heavy cream

2 tablespoons (30 g) cold Seaweed Butter (below), diced, plus frozen Seaweed Butter for shaving

½ teaspoon (3 g) fine sea salt

One 2-inch block bonito

Equipment

food mill fitted with the fine grinding disk

high-speed blender

Serves 6 as a side dish

SEAWEED BUTTER

1½ ounces (45 g) dried mixed seaweed, preferably equal amounts arame, wakame, nori, dulse, kombu

1 pound (450 g) salted butter, diced

In a saucepan, combine the water and kombu over medium-high heat and bring to a simmer. Adjust the heat to maintain a low simmer and cook for 20 minutes. Remove the pan from the heat and add the bonito flakes. Cover the pot and let stand for 10 minutes.

Strain the liquid through a fine-mesh sieve placed over a clean saucepan and discard the contents of the sieve. Add the potatoes, place the pan over medium-high heat, and bring to a boil. Reduce the heat to medium-low, cover, and simmer until the potatoes are tender when pierced with the tip of a paring knife, about 40 minutes.

Just before the potatoes are ready, in a small saucepan, bring the cream to a simmer over medium heat.

Drain the potatoes, discarding the liquid. Pass the potatoes through a food mill fitted with the fine grinding disk into a small saucepan. Add the cream and whisk well to incorporate. Place over low heat and stir until the mixture is smooth. Whisk the 2 tablespoons seaweed butter into the potato-cream mixture until well blended and add the salt. This can be served family-style in a large serving bowl, or as a side dish in individual bowls. At this point, transfer the potatoes to the desired serving vessel. Using a mandoline, finely shave several pieces of the frozen seaweed butter and place a few pieces on top of the potatoes. Using a Microplane grater, grate a little of the bonito over the top. Serve right away.

SEAWEED BUTTER

Put the seaweed in the blender and process on high speed until broken into fine pieces, 30–45 seconds. Transfer the seaweed to a large bowl and rinse under cold running water until fully hydrated, about 10 minutes. Drain the seaweed, return it to the blender, add the butter, and process until fully blended. Divide the butter in half and transfer each half to a large sheet of plastic wrap. Roll the butter up in the plastic wrap pieces, forming two thick logs; refrigerate one half and freeze the other. It will keep for up to 2 weeks.

MAIN INGREDIENTS

2 bone-in lamb saddles, 12–14 pounds (5.4–6.4 kg) total weight

2¼ teaspoons (13.5 g) fine sea salt

2½ teaspoons (5 g) freshly ground black pepper

4 cloves garlic, smashed

4 fresh marjoram sprigs

4 fresh thyme sprigs

4 tablespoons (56 g) extra-virgin olive oil

Vegetable Terrine (below)

¼ cup (56 g) grape seed oil

4 tablespoons (56 g) unsalted butter

Lamb Sauce (below)

Baby Fennel (below)

Caponata (below)

Basil Pudding (below)

Caper Powder (below)

Equipment

thermal immersion circulator

vacuum sealer and vacuum bags

6-quart (5.7-l) pressure cooker

tamis or food mill fitted with the fine grinding disk

high-speed blender

masticating vegetable juicer

food dehydrator (optional)

Serves 8 as a main course

LAMB SAUCE

Bones and flanks reserved from lamb saddles (above)

4 cups (900 g) Chicken Stock (page 319)

1 bay leaf

5¼ ounces (150 g) piquillo peppers

1 teaspoon (8 g) harissa

6 cloves garlic

1 fresh rosemary sprig

2 fresh thyme sprigs

4 ounces (113 g) fresh basil leaves

››

BRYAN This dish is all about how beautifully three members of the nightshade family—eggplants, tomatoes, peppers—go together. I have paired a traditional caponata with a modern terrine version to show how to present a vegetable dish in two very different ways on the same plate. Both harmonize with the lamb, which is seasoned with bright herbs that help tie all the elements together. If preparing the modern caponata seems too daunting, try only the traditional version.

Lamb Caponata

Cut the tenderloins off the lamb saddles, then remove the loins, leaving their fat caps attached. Trim the lamb well. Reserve the bones for the sauce (below). Cut the flanks off the outside of each loin and reserve to fortify the sauce. Carefully trim the fat caps on the loins so they are ⅛ inch (3 mm) thick.

Preheat the circulating water bath to 137°F (58.5°C). Preheat the oven to 250°F (120°C).

Season the lamb with 1½ teaspoons (9 g) of the salt and 1½ teaspoons (3 g) of the pepper. Put 2 garlic cloves, 1 marjoram sprig, 1 thyme sprig, 2 tablespoons (28 g) of the olive oil, and the lamb loins in a large vacuum bag and vacuum seal. Put the tenderloins, the remaining 2 garlic cloves, 1 each of the marjoram and thyme sprigs, and the remaining 2 tablespoons (28 g) oil in another bag and vacuum seal. Cook the lamb loins in the circulating water bath for 55 minutes, adding the tenderloins for the last 30 minutes. Remove the bags from the water and let the meat rest in the bags at room temperature for 10 minutes.

Line a sheet pan with parchment paper. Slice the vegetable terrine into 8 slices about ½ inch (12 mm) thick and lay the slices in a single layer on the prepared pan. Place in the oven until warmed through, about 10 minutes.

To serve, remove the lamb loins and tenderloins from the bags and dry well. Season the lamb with the remaining ¾ teaspoon (4.5 g) salt and 1 teaspoon (2 g) pepper. Place a rack on a sheet pan. In a large sauté pan, heat the grape seed oil over medium-high heat until it begins to shimmer but does not smoke. Add the lamb loins and tenderloins and cook, turning once, until evenly browned on both sides, 3–4 minutes per side. Add the butter, the remaining 2 marjoram sprigs, and the remaining 2 thyme sprigs and, using a large, flat metal spoon, baste the lamb with the fat and aromatics until it is golden brown and the butter stops frothing, 2–3 minutes. Transfer the lamb to the rack on the sheet pan and let rest for 5 minutes. Cut the lamb loins crosswise into 16 equal medallions. Do the same with the tenderloins. Put 2 lamb loin medallions in the center of each plate, with the piece on the left skin side up and the piece on the right positioned horizontally beside it so you can see the pink center. Lay 2 tenderloin medallions to the right of the loin pieces, with the pink centers facing up. Spoon a little sauce

VEGETABLE TERRINE

1 globe eggplant

1 cup (225 g) water

¾ teaspoon (4.5 g) fine sea salt

7.5 grams agar (see sources)

1 large fennel bulb

1¾ pounds (780 g) red bell peppers, seeded, stemmed, and juiced

1 piquillo pepper, seeded

BABY FENNEL

8 baby fennel bulbs, trimmed

4 cloves garlic, smashed

½ cup (113 g) extra-virgin olive oil

1 teaspoon (6 g) fine sea salt

CAPONATA

2 tablespoons (28 g) extra-virgin olive oil

1 large eggplant, peeled and cut into brunoise

3 red bell peppers, roasted, peeled, and cut into brunoise

⅓ cup (45 g) red onion brunoise

⅓ cup (35 g) celery brunoise

2 tablespoons (17 g) finely chopped garlic

⅓ cup (75 g) peeled, seeded, and finely diced tomato

1 tablespoon (10 g) chopped capers

1 tablespoon (10 g) chopped Kalamata olives

1 teaspoon (6 g) fine sea salt

BASIL PUDDING

2¼ cups (500 g) water

1 cup (200 g) sugar

5 grams agar (see sources)

¼ cup plus 1½ tablespoons (150 g) liquid glucose (see sources)

1 teaspoon (6 g) fine sea salt

8 ounces (225 g) fresh basil sprigs

CAPER POWDER

2 tablespoons (15 g) capers

between the loin pieces and over the edges of the tenderloin, taking care that you can still see the pink centers. Put a slice of vegetable terrine below the horizontal loin piece. Put 3 pieces of baby fennel on the plate. Put a spoonful of caponata above the top piece of lamb and a large dot of basil pudding to the right of it. Sprinkle caper powder in the empty space at the top right of the plate. Serve right away.

LAMB SAUCE

Preheat the oven to 400°F (200°C).

Arrange the lamb bones and flanks on a large sheet pan and roast until golden brown, about 30 minutes. Let them cool on the pan to room temperature. In the pressure cooker, combine the roasted lamb bones and flanks, the stock, bay leaf, piquillo peppers, harissa, garlic, rosemary, and thyme. Following the manufacturer's instructions, lock the lid in place, bring the pressure up to high, and cook for 1 hour. Let the pressure dissipate naturally, then uncover, add the basil, re-cover, and let the ingredients steep for 15 minutes. Strain the contents of the cooker through a fine-mesh sieve into a saucepan, then place over medium-high heat and bring to a bare simmer. Reduce the heat to medium-low and cook until the liquid is reduced to a syrupy consistency, 1½–2 hours.

Prepare an ice bath. Pour the reduced liquid into a metal bowl, set over the ice bath, and let cool completely, stirring occasionally and replenishing the ice as needed, about 20 minutes. The cooled lamb sauce may be stored in a lidded container in the refrigerator for up to 1 week before using.

VEGETABLE TERRINE

Select a metal bowl that will fit inside the pressure cooker and is large enough to hold the eggplant. Put a rack on the bottom of the cooker, place the bowl with the eggplant on top, and pour ½ cup (113 g) of the water into the cooker. Following the manufacturer's instructions, lock the lid in place, bring the pressure up to high, and cook for 4 minutes. Let the pressure dissipate naturally, then uncover. Prepare an ice bath. Remove the eggplant from the pressure cooker, peel it, and pass the flesh through the tamis placed over a metal bowl. Set the bowl over the ice bath and let cool until ice-cold, stirring occasionally and replenishing the ice as needed, about 30 minutes. Weigh 8½ ounces (250 g) of the cold eggplant purée, transfer it to a small saucepan, add ¼ teaspoon (1.5 g) of the salt and 2.5 grams of the agar, and place over medium-high heat. Bring the purée to a boil while whisking constantly, then boil for 5 minutes. Remove from the heat and pour into an 8-inch (20-cm) square glass baking dish, forming a thin, even layer. Let cool, uncovered, in the refrigerator until firmly set, about 1 hour.

Following the instructions above for the eggplant, cook the fennel in the pressure cooker with the remaining ½ cup (113 g) water. Cut up the fennel, transfer it to the clean blender, and process until a smooth purée forms. Pour the purée into a fine-mesh sieve placed over a metal bowl and cool in an ice bath as directed above for the eggplant. Weigh 8½ ounces (250 g) of the cold fennel purée. Following the instructions above for the eggplant, boil the fennel purée with another ¼ teaspoon (1.5 g) of the salt and 2.5 grams of the agar and let cool in the refrigerator in another square glass baking dish.

Weigh 3¼ ounces (90 g) of the pepper juice. Transfer the juice to the clean blender, add the piquillo pepper, and process until smooth. Pour the liquid into a fine-mesh sieve placed over a metal bowl and cool in an ice bath as directed for the eggplant. Weigh 8½ ounces (250 g) of the cold pepper purée. Following the instructions above for the eggplant, boil the pepper purée with the remaining ¼ teaspoon (1.5 g) salt and 2.5 grams agar, and let cool in the refrigerator in a third square glass baking dish.

Transfer the eggplant gel from its baking dish to a cutting board and cut it in half. Repeat with the fennel and red pepper gels. Stack the gels in alternating layers on a large piece of plastic wrap, wrap the stack tightly, and store in the refrigerator until serving. The terrine will keep for up to 2 days.

BABY FENNEL

Bring a large saucepan three-fourths full of water to a boil over high heat. Put the baby fennel, garlic, olive oil, and salt in a vacuum bag and vacuum seal. Add the bag to the boiling water and cook until the bulbs feel tender when gently squeezed through the bag, about 14 minutes. Meanwhile, prepare an ice bath. When the fennel is ready, transfer it, still in the bag, to the ice bath and let cool completely, replenishing the ice as needed, about 30 minutes. The fennel may be stored in the bag in the refrigerator for up to 3 days before using.

CAPONATA

In a saucepan, heat the olive oil over medium-high heat until it begins to shimmer. Add the eggplant and sauté until tender and browned, about 5 minutes. Add the peppers and cook, stirring, until softened, about 3 minutes. Add the onion and celery and sauté until tender and translucent, about 5 minutes. Add the garlic and sauté until softened and aromatic, about 3 minutes. Add the tomato, capers, olives, and salt and bring to a simmer, stirring constantly. Simmer until most of the juices have evaporated and the mixture is thick, about 10 minutes. Remove from the heat and let cool to room temperature. The caponata may be stored in a lidded container in the refrigerator for up to 3 days.

BASIL PUDDING

Prepare an ice bath. In a saucepan, combine the water, sugar, agar, glucose, and salt over high heat. Bring to a boil, reduce the heat to maintain a low boil, and cook for 5 minutes. Remove from the heat. Put the basil in the clean blender, pour the hot liquid over it, and process until a smooth purée forms. Strain the purée through a fine-mesh sieve placed over a metal bowl. Set the bowl over the ice bath and let cool undisturbed, replenishing the ice as needed, until the mixture is firm, about 15 minutes. Rinse the blender, then using a spoon, scoop the basil gel into it. Process until a smooth purée forms. The basil pudding may be stored in a lidded container in the refrigerator for up to 3 days.

CAPER POWDER

Spread the capers on a food dehydrator tray or a sheet pan. Place in the dehydrator set at 129°F (54°C) or an oven set to 175°F (80°C) until completely dry, about 18 hours. Grind the cooled capers in a spice grinder to a fine powder. It may be stored in an airtight container at room temperature for up to 1 month.

THIS DISH IS ALL ABOUT HOW THE COMBINATIONS OF INGREDIENTS FROM THE SAME FAMILY

HERE EGGPLANT PEPPERS & TOMATO

OFTEN GO TOGETHER REALLY WELL

MICHAEL The tomato can be naturally sweet enough to be used in desserts. Here, this star of the nightshade family is presented in a variety of different preparations, some of which are also wonderful on their own. For example, the pâte de fruit can be eaten by itself as a candy, or you can top the granola with a spoonful of yogurt for a delicious breakfast. You can also use the sorbet, the pâte de fruit, and the basil seeds in other savory dishes.

Tomato Granola, Sorbet, Caramel, Pâte de Fruit, Almond Milk Gelée, Basil Seeds and Flowers

MAIN INGREDIENTS

3½ tablespoons (50 g) grape seed oil

1¾ cups (250 g) unsalted roasted Marcona almonds, plus more for grating

2 cups plus 1 tablespoon (500 g) heavy cream

2 cups (520 g) whole milk

¼ cup (50 g) sugar

1½ sheets silver-grade leaf gelatin (see sources)

1 large, ripe tomato

Tomato Granola (below)

Tomato Pâte de Fruit (below)

Maldon sea salt

Extra-virgin olive oil

Basil Seeds (below)

Tomato Sorbet (below)

Tomato-Caramel Sauce (below)

Petite basil leaves and blooms

Equipment

large conical sieve

high-speed blender

refractometer

ice-cream maker

Serves 4 as a first course

››

In a saucepan, heat the grape seed oil over medium-high heat until it begins to shimmer but does not smoke. Add the Marcona almonds and cook, stirring, until they are golden brown on both sides, 5–8 minutes. Add the cream, milk, and sugar and simmer until the almonds are tender, about 15 minutes. Remove from the heat, transfer to a blender, and process until the almonds are broken up and the liquid is almost smooth. Line the large conical sieve with a double layer of cheesecloth and set over a pitcher. Pour the almond liquid into the sieve, place the setup in the refrigerator, and let drain, undisturbed, overnight.

Put the gelatin sheets in a small bowl of ice water and let soak until softened, about 5 minutes. Weigh 17½ ounces (500 g) of the strained almond milk. Reserve the remainder for another use. Put 3½ ounces (100 g) of the almond milk in a heatproof bowl. Retrieve the gelatin sheets, squeeze out the excess water, and add the sheets to the bowl. Set the bowl over (not touching) simmering water in a saucepan and heat, stirring occasionally, until the gelatin melts, 3–5 minutes. Remove from the heat, transfer to the blender, add the remaining 14 ounces (400 g) almond milk, and process until smooth. Divide the liquid evenly among 4 shallow soup bowls. Refrigerate the bowls until the almond mixture sets, about 2 hours. Cover each bowl with plastic wrap and keep in the refrigerator until ready to serve, up to 2 days.

To serve, cut the top and bottom off the tomato and stand it upright on a cutting board. Using a sharp knife, cut downward to remove the outer layer of flesh in 4 equal segments. Using a spoon, scoop out the exposed seeds in each segment, trying to keep each segment as intact as possible. Put a spoonful of the tomato granola at the top and bottom of each serving bowl. Cut the tomato pâte de fruit into 8 strips, each about 4 inches (10 cm) long and ¼ inch (6 mm) thick. Roll up each strip halfway into a tight spiral that opens up at the outer perimeter. Put 1 rolled strip at the top of each bowl, standing it upright, and 1 strip on its side on the opposite side of the bowl. Cut each tomato seed segment in half crosswise. Season the segments with Maldon salt and a

HERE THE NATURALLY SWEET TOMATO THE STAR OF THE NIGHTSHADE FAMILY

IS PRESENTED IN A VARIETY OF DIFFERENT PREPARATIONS

WHICH ARE ALSO WONDERFUL ON THEIR OWN

light drizzle of extra-virgin olive oil. Put 1 tomato seed segment in the top and bottom of each bowl to the right of the granola. Using a Microplane grater, grate the Marcona almonds into a small pile at the left perimeter of each bowl. Put a spoonful of basil seeds lightly coated with their syrup in the center of each bowl. Put a quenelle of tomato sorbet on top and slightly to the right of the seeds. Season the sorbet with a little extra-virgin olive oil and Maldon salt. Drizzle the tomato-caramel sauce and a little more extra-virgin olive oil around the perimeter of the bowl, garnish the plates with petite basil leaves and blooms, and serve right away.

TOMATO GRANOLA

Preheat the oven to 200°F (95°C).

Line a sheet pan with a silicone mat. In a small saucepan, combine the water, Malto, maple syrup, and tomato paste over medium heat and stir to blend well. Bring to a simmer and then remove from the heat. Add the butter and argan oil and stir to combine. Put the oats and almonds in a bowl and pour the hot syrup mixture over them. Stir well to coat the ingredients fully with the syrup. Turn the mixture out onto the prepared pan, spread in an even layer, and bake until dry and crunchy, 4–5 hours. Remove from the oven and let cool on the pan to room temperature, about 45 minutes. Sprinkle with the tomato powder and salt, mix to blend, and transfer to an airtight container. The granola may be stored at room temperature for up to 2 weeks.

TOMATO PÂTE DE FRUIT

Coat a 13-by-18-inch (33-by-46-cm) sheet pan with cooking spray and then line the bottom with parchment paper. Coat the parchment with cooking spray. Have the prepared sheet pan, a fine-mesh sieve, and a medium-sized ladle ready to go on your work surface.

Put the tomatoes in the clean blender and process until a smooth purée forms. Transfer to a saucepan, place over medium-high heat, and bring to a full boil. In a small bowl, stir together 3⁄4 cup (150 g) of the sugar and the pectin. Whisk the pectin mixture into the boiling tomato purée. Once it dissolves, stop whisking and switch to a wooden spoon. In another bowl, stir together the remaining 3⁄4 cup (150 g) sugar, the glucose powder, and the citric acid. Add this mixture to the boiling tomato purée in 3 equal additions, maintaining a boil and stirring constantly to prevent scorching on the pan bottom. If the sugar clumps, break it up against the side of the pan with the wooden spoon. Cook the tomato mixture, stirring continuously, until it reaches 221°F (105°C). Immediately pour the mixture through the fine-mesh sieve directly onto the prepared sheet pan, pushing it through with the ladle to strain it as quickly as possible. Let it stand, undisturbed, at room temperature to cool completely, about 1½ hours. Cover the cooled pâte de fruit with plastic wrap. It may be stored in the refrigerator for up to 5 days before using.

BASIL SEEDS

In a small bowl, combine the basil seeds with water to cover and let soak at room temperature for 1 hour. Drain the seeds and transfer to a lidded storage container. In the clean blender, combine the basil leaves and simple syrup and process until smooth. Strain the syrup through a fine-mesh sieve placed over the container of basil seeds. Cover the container and let the seeds stand for 1 hour before using.

TOMATO SORBET

Chop the tomatoes and season lightly with celery salt and a few drops of Tabasco sauce. Put the tomatoes in the clean blender, add the bell pepper, and process until a smooth purée forms. Transfer the purée to a saucepan, place over medium-high heat, and bring to a boil. Meanwhile, rinse the blender and prepare an ice bath. When the purée begins to boil, transfer it to the blender, add the olive oil, and process until smooth. Pour the tomato mixture into a metal bowl, and set the bowl over the ice bath. Stir the sorbet base into the tomato mixture a little at a time until tomato mixture measures between 28 and 30 Brix on the refractometer. Cover and refrigerate for at least 4 hours.

Transfer the chilled mixture to the ice-cream maker and freeze according to the manufacturer's instructions. Transfer to a freezer container and freeze for at least 2 hours to firm up before serving. It will keep for 2 weeks.

TOMATO WATER

Dice the tomatoes and put them in a food processor with the salt. Purée until smooth. Transfer the purée to a large fine-mesh sieve lined with a double layer of cheesecloth set over a large bowl. Let the purée drain, undisturbed, in the refrigerator for 12 hours. Use as soon as possible.

TOMATO-CARAMEL SAUCE

In a small saucepan, combine the sugar, tomato water, lemon juice, and corn syrup over medium heat and cook, stirring, until it reaches 230°F (110°C), about 20 minutes. Remove from the heat and add the hot water. Return the pan to low heat and stir to melt any sugar that has solidified. Once the caramel is smooth, whisk in the tomato powder and then remove from the heat and let cool to room temperature. The cooled sauce may be stored in a lidded container in the refrigerator for up to 3 days. Bring back to room temperature before serving.

TOMATO GRANOLA

7 tablespoons (100 g) water
25 grams Malto (see sources)
6 tablespoons plus 2 teaspoons (100 g) grade A maple syrup
½ cup (120 g) tomato paste
7 tablespoons (100 g) unsalted butter
3½ tablespoons (50 g) argan oil (see sources)
1½ cups (150 g) old-fashioned rolled oats
1 cup (100 g) sliced almonds
1 tablespoon (7 g) tomato powder (see sources)
1 tablespoon (18 g) fine sea salt

TOMATO PÂTE DE FRUIT

Nonstick cooking spray
3 pounds (1360 g) very ripe Ugly or other heirloom tomatoes, diced
1½ cups (300 g) sugar
1.4 ounces (40 g) apple pectin
2 cups plus 4 teaspoons (300 g) glucose powder (see sources)
2 teaspoons (10 g) citric acid

BASIL SEEDS

4 teaspoons (12 g) basil seeds
5 or 6 fresh basil leaves
1 cup (320 g) Simple Syrup (page 319)

TOMATO SORBET

17½ ounces (500 g) ripe tomatoes
Celery salt
Tabasco Sauce
1 red bell pepper, seeded and diced
7 tablespoons (100 g) extra-virgin olive oil
Sorbet Base (page 319) as needed

TOMATO WATER

5 pounds (2.3 kg) ripe tomatoes
2 teaspoons (12 g) fine sea salt

TOMATO-CARAMEL SAUCE

2⅓ cups (470 g) sugar
1 cup (225 g) tomato water (above)
Juice of ½ lemon
6 tablespoons (117 g) light corn syrup
1½ cups (350 g) hot water
1 tablespoon (7 g) tomato powder (see sources)

PARSLEY

PARSNIP
PARSLEY ROOT
CELERY ROOT
CARROT

When we were growing up, parsley was that curly sprig that sat on plates at every midlevel chain restaurant. But as chefs, we have come to know the far more interesting parsley family, which embraces not only its namesake herb but also dozens of other herbs and vegetables, including parsley root, carrot, parsnip, and celery root. This is another family of ingredients where we like to take one member and use it in a variety of different guises in a single recipe. For example, Composition of Parsnips showcases the subtly sweet, ivory-colored root in more than a half dozen different ways, including transforming its skin into an intriguing "bark," while carrots are used not only in a reinvented carrot cake, but also as the glazed garnish and flavoring for the sorbet that accompanies it.

BRYAN This recipe was an exercise in seeing how many forms and shapes I could produce from a bunch of parsnips: hot, cold, crispy, raw, roasted, braised, round, oblique, julienne. The base for the dish is the parsnip bark, which I developed when I was on *Top Chef.* To make it, I roast the parsnips, peel them, brush the skins with caramel, dehydrate the skins, and then finally deep-fry them. The roasted flesh is cooked again with butter and parsnip stock.

Composition of Parsnips

MAIN INGREDIENTS

6 parsnips, about 2 pounds (900 g) total weight

8 tablespoons (113 g) unsalted butter

½ teaspoon (3 g) fine sea salt

2 tablespoons (28 g) Parsnip Stock (below)

Bourbon Caramel Parsnip Bark (below)

Parsnip Obliques (below)

Parsnip Salad (below)

Equipment

thermal immersion circulator

vacuum sealer and vacuum bags

high-speed blender

6-quart (5.7-l) pressure cooker

food dehydrator (optional)

deep fryer (optional)

Serves 4 as a first course

››

Preheat a convection oven to 300°F (150°C). Alternatively, preheat a standard oven to 325°F (160°C).

Line a sheet pan with parchment paper. Put 3 of the parsnips on the prepared pan and roast until tender, about 1 hour. Remove from the oven and while still hot, peel the parsnips, aiming to remove the peels in large pieces. Set the peels aside for the bourbon-caramel parsnip bark.

Preheat the circulating water bath to 185°F (85°C).

Put the roasted parsnip flesh, 4 tablespoons (56 g) of the butter, and ¼ teaspoon (1.5 g) of the salt in a vacuum bag and vacuum seal. Cook in the circulating water bath for 45 minutes. Remove the bag from the water bath, and leave the bath set at 185°F (85°C).

Prepare an ice bath. Transfer the cooked parsnip flesh to the clean blender and process until a smooth purée forms. Pour the purée into a metal bowl, set the bowl over the ice bath, and let cool completely, stirring occasionally and replenishing the ice as needed, about 20 minutes. The purée may be stored in a lidded container in the refrigerator for up to 2 days before using.

Peel the 3 remaining parsnips. Cut off the tip of each parsnip about 5 inches (13 cm) from the end. Set the tips aside for the parsnip obliques and the parsnip julienne. Cut the rest of the parsnips into pieces about ½ inch (12 mm) thick. Using a 1-inch (2.5-cm) round cutter, punch out perfect rounds from the pieces. Save the trimmings for the parsnip stock. You will need 12 rounds total. Put the parsnip rounds, the remaining 4 tablespoons (56 g) butter, and the remaining ¼ teaspoon (1.5 g) salt in a vacuum bag and vacuum seal. Cook in the circulating water bath until just tender when gently squeezed through the bag, about 1 hour.

Remove the bag from the water bath and let the parsnips cool in the bag at room temperature for 10 minutes. Prepare an ice bath. Transfer the bag to the ice bath and let cool completely, about 20 minutes. The parsnip rounds may be stored in the bag in the refrigerator for up to 24 hours before using.

To serve, place a large sauté pan over medium-high heat. When the pan is hot, add the parsnip rounds and all of the butter from the bag and cook, turning once,

THIS WAS AN EXERCISE IN SEEING HOW MANY THINGS I COULD MAKE FROM A BUNCH OF PARSNIPS HERE HOT, COLD CRISP ROASTED BRAISED ROUND, OBLIQUE JULIENNE

PARSNIP OBLIQUES

2 parsnip tips, each 5 inches (13 cm) long, reserved from forming parsnip rounds (above)

½ cup (113 g) plus 2 tablespoons (28 g) cold Parsnip Stock (below)

2 tablespoons (28 g) cold unsalted butter

Leaves from 1 fresh rosemary sprig

PARSNIP STOCK

Parsnip trimmings reserved from forming parsnip rounds and parsnip obliques (above)

2 cups (450 g) water

½ teaspoon (3 g) fine sea salt, plus more for seasoning

until browned on both sides and warmed through, 2–3 minutes per side. Add the parsnip stock to the pan to deglaze and emulsify the parsnip butter. Put the parsnip purée in a small saucepan over medium heat and heat through.

Put a piece of bourbon-caramel parsnip bark on each plate. Place a spoonful of parsnip purée in the center of each piece of bark. Briefly transfer the parsnip rounds to a paper towel–lined plate to remove excess sauce and then arrange the parsnip rounds and obliques around the purée. Put a small cluster of parsnip salad on top of the rounds and obliques. Drizzle the reserved bourbon-caramel on the parsnip rounds and on the plate, if desired.

PARSNIP OBLIQUES

Cut the parsnip tips in half lengthwise, then cut each half into ½-inch (12-mm) obliques. Reserve the trimmings for the parsnip stock (below). Put the parsnip obliques in a lidded container in the refrigerator until just before serving. Meanwhile, make the stock (below).

In a saucepan, combine the parsnip obliques and the ½ cup (113 g) stock and bring to a boil over high heat. Cook until the stock evaporates, 8–10 minutes. Add the butter and rosemary leaves and continue to cook for 1–2 minutes until the butter stops foaming and the rosemary is fragrant and crisp. Add the remaining 2 tablespoons (28 g) cold parsnip stock and stir well to emulsify the sauce. Immediately remove from the heat and set aside until serving.

PARSNIP STOCK

In the pressure cooker, combine the parsnip trimmings, water, and salt. Following the manufacturer's instructions, lock the lid in place, bring the pressure up to high, and cook for 5 minutes. Let the pressure dissipate naturally, then uncover.

Prepare an ice bath. Strain the stock through a fine-mesh sieve placed over a metal bowl. Set the bowl over the ice bath and let cool completely, stirring occasionally and replenishing the ice as needed, about 20 minutes. Use right away. (Any leftover cooled stock may be stored in a lidded container in the refrigerator for up to 3 days.)

BOURBON-CARAMEL PARSNIP BARK

Put the sugar in a small saucepan and place over low heat. Once the sugar begins to caramelize, after 3–5 minutes, stir it slowly with a silicone spatula and continue to cook until it turns a dark amber, 5–8 minutes. Immediately remove the pan from the heat and add the stock. Once the stock stops sputtering, return the pan to low heat and stir to melt any sugar that has solidified. Stir in the bourbon and salt and remove from the heat.

Line a food dehydrator tray or sheet pan with a silicone mat. Lay the parsnip peels, with the outer part of the peel down, on the mat. Generously brush the top of the peels with the caramel mixture. Reserve any remaining caramel. Place the peels in the dehydrator set at 140°F (60°) or the oven preheated to 175°F (80°C) until they are dry and are easily broken between your fingers, 2–3 hours. Add vinegar to the remaining caramel and set aside until serving.

Pour the canola oil into a deep fryer to the fill line or into a tall-sided saucepan to a depth of 2½ inches (6 cm) and heat to 350°F (180°C).

Working in batches, add the dried peels to the hot oil and fry until they darken, turn crisp, and resemble tree bark, about 5 seconds. Using a skimmer, transfer to a paper towel–lined plate and season lightly with salt. The bark is best served within 1 hour of frying.

PARSNIP SALAD

Using a mandoline, cut the parsnip tip into julienne. Put the parsnip julienne in a bowl of ice water and refrigerate until serving time, up to 15 minutes.

Drain the parsnip julienne and pat dry. In a bowl, whisk together the salt, lemon juice, and olive oil. Add the parsnip fronds and parsnip julienne and toss lightly to coat evenly. Use right away.

BOURBON-CARAMEL PARSNIP BARK

½ cup (100 g) sugar

2 tablespoons (28 g) Parsnip Stock (above)

2 tablespoons (28 g) bourbon

⅛ teaspoon (.75 g) fine sea salt

Reserved parsnip peels from roasted parsnips (above)

2 tablespoons (28 g) red wine vinegar

Canola oil for deep-frying

PARSNIP SALAD

1 parsnip tip, 5 inches (13 cm) long, reserved from forming parsnip rounds (above)

⅛ teaspoon (.75 g) fine sea salt

Juice of ¼ lemon

1 teaspoon (5 g) extra-virgin olive oil

Torn parsnip fronds

MICHAEL From the beginning, I knew I wanted to keep the parsley root white here, but I wasn't sure how to season it. I had eaten a delicious anchovy-dressed sunchoke salad on a trip to Seattle, which inspired the anchovy crackers. From there, I came up with the idea of a Caesar salad, with the egg yolk sauce, the black garlic purée, and the romaine. The anchovy olive oil left over from making the crackers was a stroke of luck: I used it to season the parsley root.

Parsley Root Caesar Salad

MAIN INGREDIENTS

12 small parsley roots, about 1½ pounds (680 g) total weight

3½ tablespoons (50 g) anchovy oil reserved from Anchovy Crackers (below)

½ teaspoon (3 g) fine sea salt

Anchovy Crackers (below)

Black Garlic Purée (below)

Egg Yolk Sauce (below)

Petite romaine lettuce leaves

Maldon sea salt

Equipment

thermal immersion circulator

vacuum sealer and vacuum bags

food dehydrator (optional)

deep fryer (optional)

high-speed blender

Serves 6 as a first course

ANCHOVY CRACKERS

¾ cup plus 1 tablespoon (150 g) potato starch

7 tablespoons (100 g) water

One 2-ounce (60-g) can olive oil–packed anchovy fillets

Canola oil for deep-frying

BLACK GARLIC PURÉE

7 ounces (200 g) black garlic (see sources), peeled but left whole

Water as needed

Fine sea salt

EGG YOLK SAUCE

5 large eggs

2 tablespoons (28 g) extra-virgin olive oil

⅛ teaspoon (.75 g) fine sea salt

Preheat the circulating water bath to 185°F (85°C).

Peel the parsley roots, put them in a vacuum bag, add the anchovy oil and salt, and vacuum seal. Cook the roots in the circulating water bath until they feel just tender when gently squeezed through the bag, about 2 hours.

Remove the parsley roots from the bag. Pour the oil from the bag into a bowl and reserve for the salad.

Put an anchovy cracker in the top center of each plate. Put 2 pieces of parsley root on each cracker. Put 1 dot of black garlic purée on the cracker and a larger dot on the plate below the cracker. Pipe a squiggly line of egg yolk sauce over the parsley root, connecting to the black garlic purée on the plate. Put the petite lettuce leaves in a bowl and season with 1 teaspoon (5 g) of the reserved oil and a small amount of crushed Maldon salt. Arrange the leaves on top of the parsley root and serve right away.

ANCHOVY CRACKERS

In a food processor, combine the potato starch and water and process until smooth. Drain the anchovies, reserving the oil. Roughly chop the anchovies and add them to the food processor. Pulse the machine 3 or 4 times until the ingredients are incorporated, being careful not to purée the anchovies too much. You want a rough paste. Turn the mixture out onto a large sheet of plastic wrap, and cover with another large sheet of plastic wrap. Using a rolling pin, roll out the mixture 1⁄16 inch (1.5 mm) thick.

Prepare a large steamer, place the plastic-wrapped dough flat on the steamer tray, and steam for 15 minutes. Remove the dough from the steamer and let cool to room temperature. Line a food dehydrator tray or a sheet pan with a silicone mat. Unwrap the dough and place it on the mat. Place in the dehydrator set at 155°F (68°C) or the oven preheated to 175°F (80°C) until dry but still pliable, about 1 hour. Cut the dough into pieces 10 inches (25 cm) long and ½ inch (12 mm) wide. Return the dough pieces to the dehydrator or oven until completely dry, about 1 hour longer.

ON A TRIP TO SEATTLE I ATE A DELICIOUS ANCHOVY-DRESSED SUNCHOKE SALAD WHICH INSPIRED THE IDEA OF A CAESAR SALAD MADE FROM ROOT VEGETABLES

Pour the canola oil into a deep fryer to the fill line or into a tall-sided saucepan to a depth of 2½ inches (6 cm) and heat to 375°F (190°C).

Working in batches, add the crackers to the hot oil and fry until they puff up and are crisp, 5–10 seconds. Using a metal skimmer, transfer to a paper towel–lined sheet pan to drain and cool. The crackers may be stored in an airtight container at room temperature for up to 2 days.

BLACK GARLIC PURÉE

In the blender, process the garlic with just enough water to form a smooth purée. Season to taste with salt. The purée may be stored in a lidded container in the refrigerator for up to 5 days.

EGG YOLK SAUCE

Preheat the circulating water bath to 153°F (67°C).

Separate the eggs and reserve the egg whites for another use. Push the egg yolks through a fine-mesh sieve placed over a bowl. Pour the egg yolks into a vacuum bag and vacuum seal. Cook the egg yolks in the circulating water bath for 45 minutes.

Let the yolks cool naturally in the bag at room temperature for about 20 minutes. Transfer the yolks to the clean blender, add the olive oil and salt, and process until smooth. Transfer the egg sauce to a pastry bag fitted with an ⅛-inch (3-mm) plain tip and use right away.

MAIN INGREDIENTS

¾ cup plus 2 tablespoons (200 g) Celery Root Stock (below)

2 sheets silver-grade leaf gelatin (see sources)

5 tablespoons plus 2 teaspoons (30 g) egg white powder

2½ teaspoons (10 g) sugar

1.5 grams Methocel F50 (see sources)

Seeds from ½ vanilla bean

Foie Gras Mousse (below)

Pear Butter (below)

10–12 petite parsley stems

Equipment

high-speed blender

food dehydrator (optional)

⅜-inch (9-mm) parisienne scoop or melon baller

6-quart (5.7-l) pressure cooker

vacuum sealer and vacuum bags

thermal immersion circulator

tamis or food mill fitted with the fine grinding disk

Serves 10–12 as hors d'oeuvres

CELERY ROOT STOCK

1 pound (450 g) celery root

3 cups (675 g) water

¾ teaspoon (4.5 g) fine sea salt

FOIE GRAS MOUSSE

1 pound (450 g) B grade foie gras or foie gras pieces (see sources)

4 cups (1040 g) whole milk

Foie Gras Cure (page 318)

¼ cup (56 g) sweet Riesling

PEAR BUTTER

2 Anjou pears, peeled, cored, and diced

½ cup (113 g) pear juice

¼ cup (50 g) sugar

1 small cinnamon stick

1½ whole star anise

BRYAN The idea for these came to me one day while I was watching Michael make a light, crispy element for a dish. I decided I wanted to create something similar and settled on using the French macaron as my model. My first test was beet macarons with foie gras. But I soon discovered that the technique is easily applied to different flavors, and now I make several seasonal versions. Celery root macarons with foie gras and pear butter are among my favorites.

Celery Root Macarons, Foie Gras, Spiced Pear Butter

Put half of the stock in a small saucepan, add the gelatin sheets, and let soak until softened, about 5 minutes. Place the pan over medium-high heat and bring just to a simmer, stirring occasionally. When the gelatin has melted, remove from the heat. Pour the other half of the stock into the blender and turn the blender on to low speed. Slowly increase the speed until a vortex forms in the center of the liquid. Sprinkle in the egg white powder, sugar, Methocel, and vanilla seeds and process for a full 5 seconds to incorporate the Methocel fully. Increase the speed to medium-high, pour in the gelatin mixture, and process for a full 5 seconds to combine fully. Transfer the liquid to a stand mixer fitted with the whisk attachment and whip on medium-high speed until stiff peaks form, about 8 minutes.

Spoon the whipped celery root mixture into a pastry bag fitted with a ⅜-inch (9-mm) plain tip. Line a food dehydrator tray or a sheet pan with a silicone mat. Pipe dollops of the whipped mixture the size of large marshmallows onto the silicone mat. You should have about 36 dollops. Place in the dehydrator set at 118°F (48°C) or in the oven preheated to 175° (80°C) until completely dry, 6–8 hours. The cooled macarons may be stored in lock-top plastic bags at room temperature for up to 3 days.

To serve, using a parisienne scoop or melon baller, hollow out the center of each macaron. Put the foie gras mousse in a pastry bag fitted with a small plain tip and fill the hollow in each macaron three-fourths full with the mousse. Put the pear butter in another pastry bag fitted with a small plain tip and pipe a small amount of the pear butter on top of the mousse. Using a butter knife or a small offset spatula, smooth the pear butter. Flip the macarons over onto a serving platter, so that the unbroken macaron top is presented to the diner. Pipe a dot of the pear butter on top of each macaron, top with a parsley stem, and serve right away.

CELERY ROOT STOCK

In the pressure cooker, combine the celery root, water, and salt. Following the manufacturer's instructions, lock the lid in place, bring the pressure up to high, and cook for 5 minutes. Let the pressure dissipate naturally, then uncover. Prepare an ice bath. Strain the liquid through a fine-mesh sieve placed over a metal bowl. Set the bowl over the ice bath and let cool completely, stirring occasionally and replenishing the ice as needed, about 20 minutes. The stock may be stored in a lidded container in the refrigerator for up to 5 days before using.

FOIE GRAS MOUSSE

Put the foie gras and milk in a large lock-top plastic bag set in a bowl and seal the bag, pressing out as much air as possible. Let stand in the refrigerator for at least for 12 hours or up to 24 hours.

Remove the foie gras from the milk and discard the milk. Rinse the foie gras under cold running water, pat it dry, and let stand at room temperature for 1½–2 hours. During that time, it should become pliable, but not be melting. Then, using a butter knife, cut away any green spots or blood spots from the foie gras. Locate the large vein that connects the two lobes and carefully remove it and any other small veins you may find. Weigh the cleaned foie gras. Calculate 1.5 percent of the weight and weigh out that amount of foie gras cure. Season the foie gras on all sides with the cure. Put the seasoned foie gras and the Riesling in a vacuum bag and vacuum seal. Refrigerate for 6 hours.

Preheat the circulating water bath to 147°F (64°C).

Cook the foie gras in the circulating water bath for 20 minutes. Meanwhile, prepare an ice bath. When the foie gras is ready, transfer the bag to the ice bath and let cool completely, replenishing the ice as needed, about 2 hours.

Use a plastic bench scraper to push the foie gras through the tamis placed over a bowl, or pass the foie gras through a food mill. Transfer the foie gras to a food processor and process until completely smooth. The mousse may be vacuum sealed or put into a lock-top plastic bag and stored in the refrigerator for up to 3 days before using.

PEAR BUTTER

In a small saucepan, combine the pears, pear juice, sugar, cinnamon stick, and star anise over very low heat and cook, stirring occasionally, until the pears break down into a sauce, 2–3 hours. Remove and discard the cinnamon stick and star anise. Prepare an ice bath. Transfer the pear mixture to the clean blender and process until smooth. Pour the purée into a metal bowl, set the bowl over the ice bath, and let cool completely, stirring occasionally, about 15 minutes. The pear butter may be stored in a lidded container in the refrigerator for up to 2 weeks.

THE IDEA FOR THESE CAME TO ME WHILE I WAS WATCHING MICHAEL MAKE A LIGHT CRISPY ELEMENT FOR A DISH AND I WANTED TO CREATE SOMETHING SIMILAR

MICHAEL I wanted this cake to have a deep carrot flavor, and carrot juice concentrate proved the key. I knew that I had to juice only very sweet carrots, because they had to bring their natural sugar to the recipe, as well. This means you will have to keep tasting the carrots until you discover a good batch. The frozen cream cheese frosting, an intriguing riff on the classic, dissolves without leaving a sugary film on the tongue, allowing the carrot to remain the star of this dish.

Carrot Cake, Yuzu Curd, Cream Cheese Frosting, Dried Ginger Beer

MAIN INGREDIENTS

1⅓ cups (300 g) Carrot Juice Concentrate (below)

5 tablespoons plus 2 teaspoons (30 g) egg white powder

8 large egg yolks

¾ cup plus 1 tablespoon (120 g) all-purpose flour

7 tablespoons (100 g) unsalted butter, melted

1¾ teaspoons (10.5 g) fine sea salt

1 teaspoon (2 g) ground cinnamon

1 teaspoon (1 g) freshly grated nutmeg

Nonstick cooking spray

Yuzu Curd (below)

Glazed Petite Carrots (below)

Pecan Crumble (below)

Carrot Sorbet (below)

Cream Cheese Frosting (below)

Dried Ginger Beer (below)

Equipment

iSi canister with 3 N_2O chargers (1-quart/.95-l canister)

eight 1-cup (240 ml) paper coffee cups

masticating vegetable juicer

thermal immersion circulator

vacuum sealer and vacuum bags

high-speed blender

refractometer

ice-cream maker

liquid nitrogen (optional)

small Styrofoam cooler (optional)

food dehydrator (optional)

Serves 8 as a dessert

To make the cake batter, in a food processor, combine the carrot juice concentrate, egg white powder, egg yolks, flour, butter, salt, cinnamon, and nutmeg and process until smooth.

To serve, using a funnel, transfer the batter to the iSi canister and, following the manufacturer's instructions, charge 3 times with the nitrous oxide chargers. Shake vigorously. Using a paring knife, poke 4 holes in a paper coffee cup, 1 hole on the bottom and 3 holes evenly spaced around the sides of the cup. Spray the inside of the cup with nonstick cooking spray. Repeat with the remaining 3 paper cups.

Extrude the batter into 1 prepared cup, filling it half full. Place in a microwave and cook on high for about 45 seconds. The batter will expand and look like a sponge. Every microwave is different, so the timing may vary. Remove the cup from the microwave, invert it onto a plate, and leave it upside down for 1 minute so the cake will steam in the cup and finish cooking. Tap the cup gently on the counter top to loosen the cake and remove it from the cup. Repeat to make 7 more carrot cakes.

Using a 2½-inch (6-cm) ring mold, cut 8 rounds from the yuzu curd and lay 1 round of curd on each serving plate. Insert 5 glazed petite carrots upright in each curd round. Using kitchen scissors, cut the carrot cakes into bite-sized pieces and place a few pieces between the carrots. Arrange little piles of the pecan crumble around the cake pieces. Place a quenelle of carrot sorbet on the curd off to one side. Put a couple spoonfuls of cream cheese frosting over the cake pieces. Break the dried ginger beer into pieces and place 2 or 3 pieces over the top of each plate. Serve right away.

CARROT JUICE CONCENTRATE

2¼ pounds (1 kg) Nantes carrots

1¼ cups (250 g) sugar

Juice the carrots using the vegetable juicer. In a saucepan, combine the carrot juice and sugar over medium-high heat and bring to a simmer. Adjust the heat to maintain a gentle simmer and cook until slightly thickened, about 10 minutes. Meanwhile, prepare an ice bath. Transfer the juice to a metal bowl, set over the

››

YUZU CURD

4 sheets silver-grade leaf gelatin (see sources)

½ cup plus 2 tablespoons (150 g) yuzu juice (see sources)

12 large egg yolks

1 cup (200 g) sugar

⅔ cup (150 g) unsalted butter, diced

½ teaspoon (3 g) fine sea salt

GLAZED PETITE CARROTS

24 baby carrots

4 teaspoons (20 g) honey

2 teaspoons (10 g) yuzu juice (see sources)

¼ teaspoon (1.5 g) fine sea salt

PECAN CRUMBLE

1 cup (225 g) unsalted butter, diced

1½ cups (225 g) all-purpose flour

2½ cups (250 g) pecans

¾ teaspoon (4.5 g) fine sea salt

6 tablespoons plus 2 teaspoons (100 g) maple syrup

CARROT SORBET

14 ounces (400 g) Nantes carrots, thinly sliced

1 cup (225 g) carrot juice

Sorbet Base (page 319), as needed

CREAM CHEESE FROSTING

18 ounces (500 g) cream cheese, at room temperature

5 ounces plus ½ tablespoon (150 g) goat's milk butter, at room temperature

1¼ cups (125 g) confectioners' sugar

DRIED GINGER BEER

1⅓ cups (300 g) ginger beer

4 tablespoons plus 2 teaspoons confectioners' sugar

6 grams Methocel F50 (see sources)

8 pieces crystallized ginger, chopped

.5 gram xanthan gum (see sources)

ice bath, and let cool completely, stirring occasionally and replenishing the ice as needed, about 20 minutes. The carrot juice concentrate may be stored in a lidded container in the refrigerator for up to 1 week, or in the freezer for up to 1 month.

YUZU CURD

Put the gelatin sheets in a small bowl of ice water and let soak until softened, about 5 minutes. In a heatproof bowl, combine the yuzu juice, egg yolks, and sugar. Set the bowl over (not touching) simmering water in a saucepan and whisk until the mixture is thick and pale yellow. It should fall in a wide ribbon that slowly dissolves on the surface when the whisk is lifted. Remove the bowl from the pan. Lift the gelatin sheets from the ice water, squeeze out the excess water, and add them to the yolk mixture along with the butter and salt. Whisk gently until the gelatin melts and the butter is absorbed.

Transfer the mixture to a stand mixer fitted with the whisk attachment and whip on medium-high speed until light and homogenized, 5–8 minutes. Pour the mixture into an 8-inch (20-cm) square baking dish and gently smooth the top with an offset spatula to form an even layer about ¼ inch (6 mm) thick. Put the pan in the refrigerator, uncovered, until the curd is set, about 45 minutes. The yuzu curd may be covered and stored in the refrigerator for up to 3 days.

GLAZED PETITE CARROTS

Preheat the circulating water bath to 185°F (85°C).

Put the carrots, honey, yuzu juice, and salt in a vacuum bag and vacuum seal. Cook in the circulating water bath until the carrots feel just tender when gently squeezed through the bag, about 10 minutes. Let the carrots cool in the bag to room temperature, about 20 minutes. The cooled carrots may be stored in the bag in the refrigerator for up to 3 days before using.

PECAN CRUMBLE

Preheat the oven to 350°F (180°C). Line a sheet pan with a silicone mat.

In a bowl, combine the butter, flour, pecans, salt, and maple syrup and mix with a rubber spatula until the texture resembles soft streusel. Spread the mixture in an even layer on the prepared sheet pan. Bake, stirring with a fork every 5 minutes, until dry and golden, about 15 minutes. Remove from the oven and let cool on the pan to room temperature, about 30 minutes. The crumble may be stored in an airtight container at room temperature up to 3 days.

CARROT SORBET

Preheat the circulating water bath to 212°F (100°C), or bring a large pot three-fourths full of water to a boil over high heat.

Put the carrots and carrot juice in a vacuum bag and vacuum seal. Cook in the circulating water bath or the boiling water until the carrots feel soft and break apart when gently squeezed through the bag, about 1 hour.

Remove the carrots from the bag, transfer to the blender, and process until a smooth purée forms. Transfer the purée to a saucepan, place over medium heat, and bring to a boil. Stir the sorbet base into the carrot purée a little at a time until the purée measures between 28 and 30 Brix on the refractometer.

Transfer the purée mixture to a metal bowl set over an ice bath and let cool completely, stirring occasionally and replenishing the ice as needed, about 30 minutes. Cover and refrigerate until very cold, at least 4 hours.

Transfer the chilled mixture to the ice-cream maker and freeze according to the manufacturer's instructions. Transfer to a freezer container and freeze for at least 2 hours to firm up before serving. The sorbet will keep for up to 2 weeks before serving.

CREAM CHEESE FROSTING

In a stand mixer fitted with the whisk attachment, combine the cream cheese, goat's milk butter, and sugar and whip on medium-high speed until light and fluffy, about 5 minutes.

Pour the liquid nitrogen into the Styrofoam cooler, filling it about half full. Using a small ice-cream scoop, carefully drop dollops of the cream cheese mixture into the nitrogen bath and leave for 10–15 seconds. Using a skimmer, retrieve the frozen dollops and transfer them to the clean blender. Process until you have a snowlike texture, adding a spoonful or two of liquid nitrogen if needed to keep everything cold enough to form a powder. Transfer the frosting powder to a covered container and store in the freezer for up to 24 hours before using.

Alternatively, line a loaf pan with plastic wrap. Transfer the whipped mixture to the prepared pan, smooth the top, and cover the pan lightly with plastic wrap. Place in the freezer until frozen solid, at least 4 hours or up to 24 hours. Just before serving, grate the frozen frosting on the small holes of a box grater.

DRIED GINGER BEER

Put the ginger beer in the clean blender and turn it on to low speed. Slowly increase the speed until a vortex forms in the center of the liquid. Sprinkle in the confectioners' sugar, Methocel, and xanthan gum, and process for a full 5 seconds to incorporate completely. Transfer the mixture to a stand mixer fitted with the whisk attachment and whip on medium-high speed until stiff peaks form, 8–10 minutes.

Line a food dehydrator tray or a sheet pan with a silicone mat. Transfer the whipped ginger beer to the mat and, using an offset spatula, spread into an even layer about ¼ inch (6 mm) thick. Sprinkle the crystallized ginger evenly on top. Place in the dehydrator set at 140°F (60°C) or in the oven preheated to 175°F (80°C) until completely dry, about 6 hours. The dried ginger beer is best served fresh, although it may be stored in an airtight container at room temperature for up to 2 days.

THE FROZEN CREAM CHEESE FROSTING IS AN INTRIGUING RIFF ON THE CLASSIC & DISSOLVES WITHOUT LEAVING A SUGARY FILM ON THE TONGUE ALLOWING THE CARROT TO BE THE STAR

SALTWATER FISH

SARDINE
HALIBUT
SABLE FISH
SMELT

This is a huge family. It includes tiny smelts, slightly larger sardines, much bigger halibut, and plenty of shapes, sizes, colors, and flavors in between and beyond. As with freshwater fish and all shellfish, we always consider sustainability first when choosing any saltwater fish. For example, the smelts used here are caught through the ice in coastal New England in wintertime, and the sable fish, or black cod, is from the northern Pacific, where sound management has kept it bountiful. Both recipes also reflect a culinary playfulness that we enjoy exploring as much as possible. The smelts are a riff on the fish sticks in the school cafeterias of our childhood, complete with a delicious replacement for tartar sauce, and the lightly smoked sable fish takes its inspiration from a big platter of Memphis-style barbecued pork ribs.

MAIN INGREDIENTS

9 sardines, filleted (about 8 oz/225 g total weight)

1 tablespoon plus 3/4 teaspoon (22.5 g) fine sea salt

1 teaspoon (4 g) sugar

1/2 teaspoon (3 g) freshly ground black pepper

Finely grated zest of 1/2 lime

Finely grated zest of 1/2 lemon

2 coriander seeds

1 green cardamom pod

Pear and Celery Root Rémoulade (below)

Black Pepper Tuiles (below)

Equipment

vacuum sealer and vacuum bags

Serves 6 as a first course

PEAR AND CELERY ROOT RÉMOULADE

2 shallots, minced

2 tablespoons (28 g) red verjus

2 pears, peeled, cored, and julienned (about 2 cups/235 g)

1 small celery root, peeled and julienned (about 2 cups/125 g)

1 cup (225 g) mayonnaise

Juice and finely grated zest of 1 lemon, preferably Meyer

1 tablespoon (5 g) minced fresh fennel fronds

1 tablespoon (5.5 g) minced fresh tarragon

1/2 teaspoon (3 g) fine sea salt

1/2 cup (100 g) crème fraîche

BLACK PEPPER TUILES

4 tablespoons (56 g) unsalted butter, at room temperature

3 tablespoons (42 g) honey

2 large egg whites

1/2 cup (75 g) all-purpose flour

1/4 cup (28 g) confectioners' sugar

1/4 cup (28 g) cornstarch

1/4 teaspoon (1.5 g) fine sea salt

1/4 teaspoon (.5 g) freshly ground black pepper

BRYAN As a child, I was horrified when I saw Saturday-morning cartoon characters eating sardines out of a can. When I traded in cartoons for a life in the kitchen, I discovered that sardines didn't have to come encased in metal. Here, I have treated the fresh sardines to a citrus-and-herb cure that imparts a complex depth of flavor and paired them with a crisp, full-flavored rémoulade of celery root and pear that promises to banish any thought of their canned cousins.

Cured Sardines, Pear and Celery Root Rémoulade, Black Pepper Tuiles

Line a sheet pan with parchment paper. Inspect the sardines for scales and any bones that may remain from filleting and remove them. Lay the sardines on the prepared pan. To make a cure, in a food processor, combine the salt, sugar, pepper, lime and lemon zests, coriander seeds, and cardamom pod and process until ground to a semifine powder and well blended. Pour the cure over the sardines and turn the fish to coat them evenly. Transfer the sardines and the cure to a vacuum bag and vacuum seal. Place the sardines in the refrigerator to cure for 48 hours.

Open the bag, remove the sardines, and discard the curing mixture. Rinse the fish under cold running water and pat dry with paper towels.

Lay 1 sardine fillet flat on a cutting board so that it forms a straight vertical line. Place a small bundle of pear and celery root rémoulade horizontally across the bottom third of the fish. Roll the fish around the rémoulade so that the salad is completely encircled, then place the bundle on a tray, with the loose end tucked underneath. Repeat with the remaining fillets and rémoulade for a total of 18 bundles. Put 3 sardine rolls in a straight line on each plate. Place 2 black pepper tuiles on top of the sardines, offsetting them. Serve right away.

PEAR AND CELERY ROOT RÉMOULADE

In a small saucepan, combine the shallots and verjus over medium-high heat and bring to a boil. Adjust the heat to maintain a low simmer and cook until the verjus is reduced to a syrup and the shallots are just tender, about 2 minutes. Remove from the heat.

In a bowl, combine the pear and celery root, add the mayonnaise, and mix with a rubber spatula until well blended. Add the shallot reduction, lemon juice and zest, fennel fronds, tarragon, and salt and mix well. Finally, fold in the crème fraîche. Cover and refrigerate for 30–60 minutes before serving.

WHEN I TRADED IN SATURDAY MORNING CARTOONS FOR A LIFE IN THE KITCHEN I WAS PLEASANTLY SURPRISED TO DISCOVER THAT SARDINES DIDN'T HAVE TO COME ENCASED IN METAL

BLACK PEPPER TUILES

In a stand mixer fitted with the paddle attachment, combine the butter and honey and beat on medium speed until smooth, 2–3 minutes. On the second-to-lowest setting, add the egg whites one at a time, mixing well after each addition. When the second egg white is fully absorbed, add the flour, confectioners' sugar, cornstarch, salt, and pepper and mix until a smooth dough forms. Transfer the dough to a bowl, cover, and refrigerate until the dough firms up, at least 1 hour.

Preheat the oven to 300°F (150°C).

Buy or make a stencil of rectangles that measure 1½ by 4 inches (4 by 10 cm). Line a sheet pan with a silicone mat, and put the stencil on the mat. Using a small offset spatula spread a thin, even layer of the dough in each rectangle. You need 12 tuiles for this preparation; extra tuiles make good snacks. Remove the stencil, then remove any excess dough around the edges of the rectangles.

Bake until the tuiles have just begun to puff and are dry to the touch, about 3 minutes. Remove from the oven. Using a ½-inch (12-mm) plain pastry tip, punch out 3 rounds, positioning them slightly offset from one another, in each tuile, leaving the cut circles in place while the cookies finish baking. Return the pan to the oven and bake until the tuiles are set and are a very pale golden brown, 3–5 minutes longer. Let the tuiles cool on the pan on a rack to room temperature. Remove the circles from the rectangles; they are a treat for the chef. The tuiles are best served the day they are made. Store them in an airtight container at room temperature until serving.

MICHAEL Southeast Asia's red curries are the inspiration here. Curries are often so strong that they mask the flavor of the protein that they accompany. To avoid that, I have used a vegetable-juice base, which yields a lighter, more subtly spiced sauce that flavors the delicate halibut flesh without overpowering it. The slightly crunchy texture of the coconut rice, which is steamed, dehydrated, and then deep-fried, provides an interesting contrast to the tender flesh of the fish.

Halibut Cheeks, Red Curry, Coconut Rice

MAIN INGREDIENTS

1 cup (200 g) white miso

5 tablespoons plus 1 teaspoon (80 g) mirin

12 halibut cheeks, each 2–3 ounces (60–85 g)

¾ cup (168 g) unsalted butter, cut into 12 slices, plus 4 tablespoons (56 g)

¼ yellow onion, cut into brunoise

1 kaffir lime leaf

½ cup (100 g) jasmine rice

2 cups (450 g) water

1½ cups (385 g) unsweetened coconut milk

2¼ teaspoons (15 g) Asian fish sauce

¾ teaspoon (4.5 g) fine sea salt, plus more to season

12 green onions, white and tender green tops, cut into 3-inch (7.5-cm) pieces

Puffed Rice (below)

Red Curry Fluid Gel (below)

Coriander blooms

Equipment

thermal immersion circulator

vacuum sealer and vacuum bags

high-speed blender

iSi canister with 3 N_2O chargers (1-quart/.95-l canister)

food dehydrator (optional)

deep fryer (optional)

masticating vegetable juicer

Serves 6 as a main course

››

Put the miso in a bowl. Using a rubber spatula, mix in the mirin to form a spreadable paste with the consistency of jam. Using a pastry brush, generously brush the miso paste on both sides of each halibut cheek, coating evenly. Place the cheeks on a plate, cover, and refrigerate for 1 hour.

Preheat the circulating water bath to 118°F (48°C).

Rinse the halibut under cold running water to remove the miso paste and pat dry with paper towels. Place the halibut cheeks in a single layer in a vacuum bag (or bags), place 1 slice of butter on each cheek, and vacuum seal. Cook in the circulating water bath for 30 minutes. Meanwhile, prepare an ice bath. When the halibut is ready, transfer the bag(s) to the ice bath and let cool completely, replenishing the ice as needed, about 30 minutes. The cooked fish may be stored in the bag(s) in the refrigerator for up to 36 hours before using.

In a large saucepan, combine the onion, lime leaf, rice, water, coconut milk, fish sauce, and ¾ teaspoon (4.5 g) salt over medium-high heat and bring to a simmer. Reduce the heat to maintain a low simmer and cook until the rice is completely soft, about 35 minutes. Discard the lime leaf, transfer the mixture to the blender, and process until a smooth purée forms. Using a funnel, transfer the warm mixture to the iSi canister and, following the manufacturer's instructions, charge 3 times with the nitrous oxide chargers. The charged canister may be held in a pot of simmering water until ready to serve.

Preheat a stove-top grill pan over high heat. Add the green onions to the pan and cook, turning as needed, until seared on all sides, 3–4 minutes total. Transfer the seared onions to a small bowl and season to taste with salt.

Remove the halibut cheeks from the bag and pat dry with paper towels. Heat a large sauté pan over medium-high heat. Add the 4 tablespoons (56 g) butter and swirl in the pan until it melts and begins to brown. Add the halibut cheeks and cook, turning once, until browned on both sides, 3–4 minutes per side. Transfer the browned fish to a large paper towel–lined plate.

PUFFED RICE

1 cup (225 g) water

1½ teaspoons (9 g) fine sea salt, plus more for seasoning

½ cup (100 g) jasmine rice

Canola oil for deep-frying

RED CURRY FLUID GEL

2 tablespoons (28 g) canola oil

1 yellow onion, thinly sliced

6 cloves garlic, crushed

½ lemongrass stalk

2 knobs galangal, about 1¾ ounces (50 g) total weight, peeled and sliced

2½ kaffir lime leaves

4½ teaspoons (6 g) coriander seeds

1½ teaspoons (1.5 g) freshly grated nutmeg

2¼ teaspoons (6.75 g) ground turmeric

1½ teaspoons (3.9 g) sweet paprika

¾ teaspoon (2.1 g) chili powder

¾ teaspoon (1.5 g) ground cinnamon

1 tablespoon (12.5 g) sugar

2½ tablespoons (37.5 g) tomato paste

2 tablespoons (40 g) tamari

1¼ teaspoons (7 g) Asian fish sauce

2 cups plus 3½ tablespoons (500 g) red bell pepper juice (from about 4 large peppers)

Agar (see sources)

Put the puffed rice in a bowl. Extrude the rice cream from the canister over the puffed rice, and fold together with a rubber spatula. Place a spoonful of the red curry fluid gel just off center on each serving plate, and use a small rubber spatula to create a rectangle shape. Put 2 halibut cheeks on each plate. Add a few spoonfuls of the puffed rice–rice cream mixture on and around the fish. Garnish with 2 pieces of seared green onion and coriander blooms and serve.

PUFFED RICE

In a small saucepan, combine the water and salt and bring to a boil over medium-high heat. Add the rice, stir once, reduce the heat to medium-low, cover, and simmer until the rice is tender and the liquid is absorbed, about 20 minutes. Remove from the heat and let stand, covered, for 10 minutes. Line a food dehydrator tray or a sheet pan with a silicone mat. Scoop out the rice in loose clumps onto the mat. Place in the dehydrator set at 155°F (68°C) or the oven preheated to 175°F (80°C) until completely dry, 3–4 hours. The cooled dried rice may be stored in a lock-top bag at room temperature for up to 1 week before continuing.

Pour the canola oil into a deep fryer to the fill line or into a tall-sided saucepan to the depth of 2½ inches (6 cm) and heat to 375°F (190°C).

Carefully sprinkle the dried rice into the hot oil and fry until just puffed, about 5 seconds. Using a skimmer or fine-mesh sieve, transfer to a paper towel–lined sheet pan and season with salt while still hot. The puffed rice is best served the day it is made, but it may be stored in an airtight container at room temperature for up to 48 hours.

RED CURRY FLUID GEL

In a saucepan, heat the canola oil over low heat until it begins to shimmer. Add the onion, garlic, lemongrass, and galangal, cover, and cook until tender, 5–8 minutes. Add the lime leaves, coriander seeds, nutmeg, turmeric, paprika, chili powder, and cinnamon and sauté until the spices bloom and begin to perfume the air, about 2 minutes. Add the sugar and tomato paste and sauté, until the mixture is warm and fully blended, about 2 minutes. Add the tamari, fish sauce, and pepper juice and raise the heat to medium-high. Bring the mixture to a simmer, adjust the heat to maintain a low simmer, and cook for 30 minutes. Remove from the heat, transfer to the clean blender, and pulse until a smooth purée forms. Line a fine-mesh sieve with damp cheesecloth, place over a bowl, and pour the purée into the sieve. Let the purée drip through, undisturbed. Rinse the blender. Weigh the strained purée. Calculate .75 percent of the weight and weigh out that amount of agar. Transfer the warm juice to the clean blender and turn it on to low speed. Slowly increase the speed until a vortex forms in the center. Sprinkle in the agar and process for a full 5 seconds to disperse completely. Transfer the juice to a saucepan, place over medium-high heat, and bring to a boil. Adjust the heat to maintain a low boil and cook for 5 minutes. Pour the juice into a shallow baking dish and let cool to room temperature, about 30 minutes. Refrigerate the cooled mixture, uncovered, until firmly set, about 1 hour. Meanwhile, rinse the blender. Using a rubber spatula, break up the pepper gel into small pieces and scrape it into the clean blender. Purée until smooth. The red pepper fluid gel may be stored in a lidded container in the refrigerator for up to 1 week before using.

BRYAN This dish was inspired by the ribs at Charlie Vergos' Rendezvous in Memphis, which are possibly the best pork ribs I've ever eaten. Charlie is known for the "shake," a super-secret dry rub that he puts on the ribs before they go on the barbecue. This is my version of Charlie's dry rub, here used on rich sable fish, or black cod, from the cold northern Pacific Ocean. The sorghum vinaigrette and tender hazelnuts are nods to the traditional vinegary mop sauce and baked beans, respectively.

BBQ Sable Fish, Hazelnuts, Cornbread, Sorghum Vinaigrette

MAIN INGREDIENTS

½ tablespoon (1.75 g) coriander seeds, ground

½ tablespoon (3.5 g) fennel seeds, ground

½ teaspoon (1.25 g) allspice berries, ground

2 tablespoons plus ¾ teaspoon (40.5 g) fine sea salt

2 tablespoons (20 g) coarsely ground black pepper

Finely grated zest of ½ lemon

1 tablespoon (8 g) sweet paprika

½ tablespoon (2 g) fresh oregano leaves

½ tablespoon (6 g) Espelette pepper

¼ teaspoon (1 g) fresh thyme leaves

¼ teaspoon (.75 g) celery seeds

6 sable fish (black cod) fillet portions, 4 ounces (113 g) each

BBQ Hazelnuts (below)

Cornbread Purée (below)

Sorghum Vinaigrette (below)

Equipment

grill-top smoker and ½ cup applewood chips

plastic squeeze bottle

6-quart (5.7-l) pressure cooker

high-speed blender

Serves 6 as a main course

In a small sauté pan, toast the coriander seeds, fennel seeds, and allspice over medium heat, shaking the pan occasionally, until aromatic, 2–3 minutes. Remove from the heat, transfer to a mini food processor or spice grinder, and add the salt, pepper, lemon zest, paprika, oregano leaves, Espelette pepper, thyme leaves, and celery seeds. Process until all of the herbs and spices are pulverized and well blended. The spice mixture may be stored in an airtight container at room temperature for up to 4 days.

Season the fish generously with the spice mixture, coating each piece evenly. Reserve the remaining spice mixture for preparing the BBQ hazelnuts.

Prepare a fire in a charcoal grill until the coals are white hot, or preheat a gas grill to medium-high. Put the applewood chips in the smoker and set on the grill grate. When you see smoke rising from the smoker, put the fish pieces in the smoker and cook until they feel firm to the touch, about 10 minutes. Or, insert a stainless-steel cake tester into the center of a fish portion, leave for 5 seconds, then withdraw it and press it to your bottom lip. If it feels warm or hot, the fish is done. Gently transfer the fish to a large plate or a sheet pan.

Put a pile of the BBQ hazelnuts in the center of each plate. Squeeze 5 large dots of the cornbread purée around the nuts. Put 1 spoonful of sorghum vinaigrette over each piece of fish, and then carefully put 1 piece of fish on each pile of hazelnuts. Drizzle a spoonful of sorghum vinaigrette around each plate and serve immediately.

BBQ HAZELNUTS

BBQ HAZELNUTS

3 cups (675 g) water

1 cup (150 g) raw hazelnuts

1¼ teaspoons (7.5 g) fine sea salt

2¼ ounces (65 g) Newsom's or other high-quality hickory-smoked slab bacon (see sources), diced

½ yellow onion, minced

1 cup (200 g) diced canned tomatoes

2 teaspoons (4 g) BBQ spice mixture reserved from preparing the fish

4 tablespoons (56 g) unsalted butter

2 tablespoons (30 g) sorghum molasses

Put the water, hazelnuts, and salt in a lidded container and refrigerate for 8–12 hours or up to overnight. Transfer the hazelnuts and water to the pressure cooker. Following the manufacturer's instructions, lock the lid in place, bring the pressure up to high, and cook for 30 minutes. Let the pressure dissipate naturally (to minimize the number of hazelnuts that fall apart), then uncover.

››

CORNBREAD

6 tablespoons plus 1 teaspoon (90 g) unsalted butter, plus more for the pan

1 cup (200 g) sugar

1½ teaspoons (9 g) fine sea salt

3 large eggs

2 cups (520 g) whole milk

2 teaspoons (11 g) honey

2½ teaspoons (12.5 g) maple syrup

2⅔ cups (400 g) all-purpose flour

2 cups (276 g) cornmeal

5 teaspoons (25 g) baking powder

¼ teaspoon (.2 g) freshly grated nutmeg

CORNBREAD PURÉE

2 tablespoons (28 g) unsalted butter

1¾ cups (170 g) diced cornbread (above)

½ cup (130 g) whole milk

1 cup (225 g) Corn Stock (page 96) or liquid from organic canned corn

¼ teaspoon (1.5 g) fine sea salt

SORGHUM VINAIGRETTE

4 tablespoons plus 2 teaspoons (100 g) sorghum molasses

5 teaspoons (27 g) Banyuls vinegar

1 tablespoon (20 g) soy sauce

Drain the hazelnuts, reserving both the cooking liquid and the nuts. Transfer the nuts to a large, shallow bowl and let cool to room temperature, about 1 hour. The hazelnuts and the cooking liquid may be stored in separate lidded containers in the refrigerator for up to 3 days before using.

In a sauté pan, cook the bacon over medium heat, stirring occasionally, until crisp and some of the fat has rendered, 10–15 minutes. Add the onion and cook, stirring constantly, until the onion is translucent and just begins to brown, 5–8 minutes. Add the tomatoes and cook until they are almost dry, 10–15 minutes. Add the reserved hazelnut cooking liquid and the BBQ spice mixture, raise the heat to medium-high, and bring to a boil. Adjust the heat to maintain a low simmer and cook until the sauce is reduced by half and has a syrupy consistency, 10–15 minutes. Add the butter and sorghum molaases and cook gently until smooth. Add the hazelnuts and cook until they are warmed through and glazed with the sauce, 5–8 minutes. Use right away.

CORNBREAD

Preheat the oven to 350°F (180°C). Lightly grease a 13-by-18-inch (33-by-46-cm) sheet pan with butter and line the bottom with parchment paper.

In a stand mixer fitted with the paddle attachment, combine the butter, sugar, and salt and beat on medium speed until the mixture is light and fluffy, 4–5 minutes. Add the eggs one at a time, mixing well after each addition. When the third egg is fully absorbed, add the milk, honey, and maple syrup and mix on low speed until fully incorporated, then stop the mixer. In a bowl, whisk together the flour, cornmeal, baking powder, and nutmeg. Add the flour mixture to the mixer, turn on to low speed, and mix just until fully incorporated. Pour the cornbread batter into the prepared pan and, using an offset spatula, spread it evenly from corner to corner and smooth the surface. Bake until golden brown, 18–22 minutes. Remove from the oven and let cool in the pan on a rack to room temperature.

CORNBREAD PURÉE

In a large sauté pan, melt 1 tablespoon (14 g) of the butter over medium heat. Add the cornbread and cook, stirring gently, until the bread is lightly toasted. Add the milk and corn stock, raise the heat to medium-high, and bring to a simmer. Remove from the heat, transfer to the blender, add the salt, and process until a smooth purée forms.

Pour the purée into a small saucepan, place over low heat, and keep warm until serving, then whisk in the remaining 1 tablespoon (14 g) butter until fully absorbed just before using. Or, the purée may be cooled to room temperature and stored in a lidded container in the refrigerator for up to 3 days. Just before serving, bring the purée to a simmer over medium heat, whisk in the remaining 1 tablespoon (14 g) butter, transfer to the squeeze bottle, and use right away.

SORGHUM VINAIGRETTE

In a small bowl, whisk together the molasses, vinegar, and soy sauce. Use right away, or store in a lidded container in the refrigerator for up to 2 weeks.

MICHAEL Most Americans have sat down to a plate of fish sticks and tartar sauce at least once in their lives, whether in a school cafeteria or at a family dinner table. This recipe, though inspired by that classic pairing, tastes nothing like it. Smelts are great because they are so small you can eat the whole thing, and the creamy, acidic tomato-hazelnut mousse is a welcome alternative to tartar sauce. Open a beer or a bottle of Champagne; either one is a great choice.

Smelt Fish Sticks, Tomato-Hazelnut Cream

MAIN INGREDIENTS

- Canola oil for deep-frying
- One 12-inch (30-cm) white pullman loaf
- 12 smelts or anchovies, about 2¼ pounds (1 kg) total weight, cleaned and heads removed
- 1 large egg
- 2 tablespoons (32.5 g) whole milk
- Fine sea salt
- Tomato-Hazelnut Cream (below)
- Toasted hazelnuts
- Dehydrated Cornichons (below)
- Caper Powder (below)

Equipment

- deep fryer (optional)
- high-speed blender
- food dehydrator (optional)

Serves 4 as a first course

TOMATO-HAZELNUT CREAM

- 2 tablespoons (28 g) extra-virgin olive oil
- 1 small yellow onion, finely diced
- 1 clove garlic, minced
- 1 large celery rib, thinly sliced
- ½ red bell pepper, seeded and thinly sliced
- 5 tablespoons (75 g) tomato paste
- 17½ ounces (500 g) ripe tomatoes, peeled and seeded
- Pinch of saffron threads
- 7 fresh basil leaves
- 3 sheets silver-grade leaf gelatin (see sources)
- Hazelnut oil
- ½ cup plus 4 teaspoons (140 g) heavy cream

DEHYDRATED CORNICHONS

- 2 cornichons

CAPER POWDER

- One 4-ounce (113-g) jar capers in brine, drained, brine discarded

Pour the canola oil into a deep fryer to the fill line or into a tall-sided saucepan to a depth of 2½ inches (6 cm) and heat to 350°F (180°C).

Cut 12 slices each ¼ inch (6 mm) thick from the pullman loaf. Using a rolling pin, roll out each slice ⅛ inch (3 mm) thick. Using a 3-inch (7.5-cm) square plain cutter, cut out the center of each rolled-out slice. Rinse the fish under cold running water and pat dry. In a small bowl, whisk together the egg and milk until frothy to make an egg wash. Place 1 fish along the bottom side of the square of bread with the tail hanging over the edge. Roll the bread and the fish over one turn, then brush the remaining bread with egg wash before rolling the fish over one more turn, and press the bread together. Cut away any excess bread overlapping the edge and put the fish, seam side down, on a sheet pan. Working in batches, add the bread-wrapped fish to the hot oil and fry until golden brown and crisp, 2–3 minutes. Using a skimmer, transfer to a paper towel–lined plate and season lightly with salt. Keep warm.

To serve, trim the head end of each smelt stick so that the tail end can stand upright. Put a quenelle of tomato-hazelnut cream in the center of each plate. Arrange 3 smelt sticks standing up around the quenelle. Using a Microplane grater, grate the hazelnuts over the quenelle. Arrange 5 pieces of dehydrated cornichon around the plate. Sprinkle the caper powder around the outside of the smelt sticks and serve right away.

TOMATO-HAZELNUT CREAM

In a saucepan, heat the olive oil over medium heat until the oil begins to shimmer. Add the onion, garlic, celery, and red pepper and cook, stirring, until the vegetables are tender and translucent, 5–8 minutes. Add the tomato paste and cook, stirring, for 2 minutes. Stir in the tomatoes, saffron, and basil. Cut out a circle of parchment paper that just fits inside the pot rim and press it against the surface of the tomato mixture. Reduce the heat to low and cook, stirring occasionally, until the mixture is very dry, 45–60 minutes.

Put the gelatin sheets in a small bowl of ice water and let soak until softened, about 5 minutes. Remove and discard the basil leaves from the tomato mixture and transfer the mixture to the blender. Process until a smooth purée forms. With the blender running, slowly drizzle in the hazelnut oil, a teaspoon at a time, to taste. Weigh 10½ ounces (300 g) of the purée and place in a bowl. Retrieve the gelatin sheets, squeeze out the excess water, and add the sheets to the bowl. Whisk in the gelatin until it melts. Cover and refrigerate until the mixture has set, at least 3 hours.

In a stand mixer fitted with the whisk attachment, whip the cream on medium-high speed until stiff peaks form. Add one-third of the whipped cream to the tomato mixture and, using a rubber spatula, fold in thoroughly to lighten the mixture. Then gently fold in the remaining cream just until no white streaks remain. The tomato-hazelnut cream may be stored in a lidded container in the refrigerator for up to 1 hour before serving.

DEHYDRATED CORNICHONS

Using a mandoline, slice the cornichons lengthwise about 1⁄16 inch (1.5 mm) thick. Line a food dehydrator tray or a sheet pan with a silicone mat, and spread the cornichon slices in a single layer on the mat. Place in the dehydrator set at 155°F (68°C) or the oven preheated to 175°F (80°C) until crisp and dry, about 3 hours. The cooled slices may be stored in an airtight container at room temperature for up to 2 weeks.

CAPER POWDER

Lay the capers in a single layer on a food dehydrator tray or sheet pan lined with a silicone mat. Place in a dehydrator set at 150°F (65.5°C) or an oven preheated to 175°F (80°C) until the capers are completely dry, about 1½ hours. Grind the capers in a spice grinder to a fine powder. The caper powder may be stored in a lidded container at room temperature for up to 1 month.

SMELTS
ARE GREAT BECAUSE
THEY ARE SO SMALL
YOU CAN EAT THEM
WHOLE
AND THE CREAMY, TART
TOMATO-HAZELNUT MOUSSE
IS A WELCOME
ALTERNATIVE
TO THE TYPICAL TARTAR SAUCE

Staple Recipes

Curry Powder

2 tablespoons (7 g) coriander seeds
1 tablespoon (6 g) cumin seeds
1 teaspoon (2 g) Tellicherry peppercorns
1 teaspoon (2.5 g) yellow mustard seeds
5 whole cloves
1 teaspoon (2 g) whole fenugreek seeds
½ teaspoon (2 g) Espelette pepper
1 teaspoon (3 g) ground turmeric
1 teaspoon (3 g) ground ginger
1 tablespoon (7 g) granulated garlic
1 tablespoon (18 g) fine sea salt
2 tablespoons (25 g) sugar

In a sauté pan, combine the coriander and cumin seeds, peppercorns, mustard seeds, cloves, and fenugreek over medium heat and toast until aromatic, 10–15 seconds. Remove from the heat and let cool slightly, then transfer to a spice grinder. Add the Espelette pepper, turmeric, ginger, garlic, salt, and sugar and grind to a fine powder. Store in an airtight container in a cool cupboard for up to 1 month. Makes about 9 tablespoons (77.5 g).

Garam Masala

1 tablespoon (8 g) caraway seeds
1 tablespoon (4 g) coriander seeds
1½ teaspoons (3.5 g) Tellicherry peppercorns
1½ teaspoons (3 g) cumin seeds
2½ teaspoons (5 g) green cardamom seeds
2 whole star anise
1 tablespoon (3 g) whole cloves
1½ teaspoons (3 g) ground mace
1½ teaspoons (4 g) yellow mustard seeds
1½ teaspoons (4 g) sweet smoked paprika
1½ teaspoons (3 g) ground cinnamon
1½ teaspoons (1.5 g) freshly grated nutmeg

In a sauté pan, combine the caraway seeds, coriander seeds, peppercorns, and cumin seeds over medium heat. Heat, gently shaking the pan, until the spices are toasted and fragrant, 2–3 minutes. Pour onto a plate and let cool. Transfer to a spice grinder, add the cardamom, star anise, cloves, mace, and mustard seeds, and grind to a fine powder. Add the paprika, cinnamon, and nutmegand pulse to mix well. Store in an airtight container in a dark cupboard for up to 1 month. Makes about 6 tablespoons (45 g).

Foie Gras Cure

1 tablespoon (18 g) fine sea salt
1½ teaspoons (6 g) sugar
¾ teaspoon (2 g) freshly ground white pepper
⅛ teaspoon (.9 g) pink curing salt

In a small bowl, mix the sea salt, sugar, pepper, and pink salt. Store in an airtight container at room temperature for up to 6 months. Makes about 5½ teaspoons (27 g).

Pickling Spice

1 tablespoon (8 g) yellow mustard seeds
3 tablespoons (10.5 g) coriander seeds
1 tablespoon (7 g) allspice berries
1 tablespoon (3 g) whole cloves
1½ tablespoons (10.5 g) black peppercorns
1 tablespoon (6 g) red pepper flakes
1 tablespoon (4 g) ground ginger
1½ teaspoons (4 g) mace blades
1 small cinnamon stick
12 bay leaves

In a sauté pan, combine the mustard and coriander seeds, allspice, and cloves over medium-high heat. Heat, gently shaking the pan, until the spices are and fragrant, 2–3 minutes. Pour onto a plate and let cool. Transfer to a mini food processor, add the peppercorns, pepper flakes, ginger, mace, cinnamon, and bay leaves, and grind to a fine powder. Store in an airtight container in a cool cupboard for up to 1 month. Makes about ½ cup (60 g).

Pickling Spice Oil

½ cup (113 g) extra-virgin olive oil
1 teaspoon (3 g) Pickling Spice (above)

In a blender, combine the oil and pickling spice and process on high speed for 1 minute, then let stand for 5 minutes to allow the spices to settle. Carefully pour the oil into a container, leaving the spices in the blender. Discard the spices. Set aside until ready to serve. Makes about ½ cup (116 g).

Pickled Mustard Seeds

1 tablespoon (8 g) yellow mustard seeds
1 tablespoon (11 g) brown mustard seeds
2 cups (450 g) water
¼ cup (70 g) sherry vinegar
2 teaspoons (9 g) evaporated cane juice

In a small saucepan, combine the yellow and brown mustard seeds, water, vinegar, and evaporated cane juice over medium heat. Bring to a simmer and cook until the pan is almost dry, about 45 minutes. Remove from the heat and let cool completely. Store in a lidded container in the refrigerator for up to 2 weeks. Makes about 2 tablespoons (25 g).

Kabocha Squash Preserves

2 pounds (900 g) kabocha squash, peeled, seeded, and sliced ⅛ inch (3 mm) thick
7 tablespoons (100 g) yuzu juice
1½ cups (300 g) sugar
¾ teaspoon plus ⅛ teaspoon (5.2 g) fine sea salt

Bring a large pot of water to a boil over high heat. Put the squash slices into vacuum bags, arranging them in a single layer, and vacuum seal. Cook in the boiling water until very tender, about 1½ hours. Transfer the cooked squash to a blender. In a tall, narrow saucepan, warm the yuzu juice and sugar over low heat and stir until the sugar dissolves. Immediately remove from the heat and pour into the blender, then process until a smooth purée forms. Immediately pour the purée back into the pan and cook over low heat, stirring often, until thick and jammy, about 30 minutes. Transfer to a heatproof container and refrigerate to cool. Store in a lidded container in the refrigerator for up to 1 week. Let stand at room temperature for 30 minutes before serving.

Fish Brine

4½ cups (1000 g) water

5 tablespoons plus 2 teaspoons (100 g) fine sea salt

¼ cup (50 g) sugar

1 lemon, cut into 8 wedges

5 fresh lemon thyme sprigs

5 long peppers

10 coriander seeds

In a large saucepan, combine the water, salt, sugar, lemon, thyme, long pepper, and coriander over high heat. Bring to a simmer and cook for 10 minutes. Prepare an ice bath. Strain the finished brine through a fine-mesh sieve placed over a metal bowl. Set the bowl over the ice bath and let cool completely, stirring occasionally. Store in a lidded container in the refrigerator for up to 3 days. Makes about 4½ cups (1000 g).

Chicken Stock

2 pounds (910 g) chicken feet, rinsed

¾ pound (340 g) turkey necks, rinsed

12⅔ cups (3 l) water

1 carrot, large dice

½ large yellow onion, large dice

1 rib celery, large dice

Put the chicken feet, turkey necks, and water in 6-quart (5.7-l) pressure cooker. Set the cooker over medium-high heat, bring the liquid to a simmer, and use a small ladle to skim the foam and impurities from the surface. Add the carrot, onion, and celery to the cooker. Following the manufacturer's instructions, cook under high pressure for 1 hour. Let the pressure dissipate naturally, then uncover. Prepare an ice bath. Strain the stock through a fine-mesh sieve placed over a large metal bowl and let stand for 10 minutes. Using a large spoon, skim off the fat that rises to the top. Set the bowl over the ice bath and cool completely, stirring occasionally. Store in a lidded container in the refrigerator for up to 3 days. Makes about 5 cups (1125 g).

Vegetable Stock

1 each carrot, yellow onion, and celery root, peeled, and diced

1 cup (85 g) mushroom trimmings or cremini mushrooms, diced

2 each turnips and parsnips, peeled and diced

3 celery ribs, diced

1 bay leaf, split

2 cloves garlic, smashed

2½ tablespoons (50 g) white soy sauce

4 black peppercorns

8½ cups (1913 g) water

In 6-quart (5.7-l) pressure cooker, combine the carrot, onion, celery root, mushrooms, turnips, parsnips, celery, bay leaf, garlic, soy sauce, peppercorns, and water. Following the manufacturer's instructions, cook under high pressure for 15 minutes. Let the pressure dissipate naturally, then uncover. Prepare an ice bath. Strain the stock through a fine-mesh sieve placed over a large metal bowl. Set the bowl over the ice bath and let cool completely, stirring occasionally. Store in a lidded container in the refrigerator for up to 3 days. Makes about 4½ cups (950 g).

Nori–Goat Butter

2 sheets (6 g) nori, ground to a powder

7 ounces (200 g) goat's milk butter, at room temperature

In a food processor, combine the nori powder and butter and pulse until a uniform mixture forms. Scrape the butter onto a sheet of plastic wrap and roll up to form a uniform log. Refrigerate until firm. The butter will keep for up to 2 weeks. Makes about 7 ounces (206 g).

Clarified Butter

1 pound (454 g) unsalted butter, diced

In a small saucepan, melt the butter over medium heat. When it has melted fully and starts to bubble rapidly, reduce the heat to medium-low and cook for 1 minute. Remove from the heat and let stand for 2 minutes to allow the milk solids to settle to the bottom. Using a large spoon, skim off and discard the foam from the surface. Slowly and carefully pour the clear yellow butterfat into a heatproof container, leaving behind the white milk solids and milky liquid. Let the clarified butter cool, then cover tightly. It will keep, refrigerated, for up to 1 month. Makes about ¾ pound (340 g).

Simple Syrup

1 cup (200 g) sugar

1 cup (225 g) water

In a small saucepan, combine the sugar and water. Bring to a boil over medium-high heat, stirring occasionally, and then boil until the sugar is completely dissolved and a syrup has formed. Remove from the heat and let cool to room temperature. The syrup may be stored in a lidded container in the refrigerator for up to 1 month. Makes about 1⅓ cups (360 g).

Sorbet Base

2⅔ cups (600 g) water

¾ cup plus 1 tablespoon (160 g) sugar

¾ cup plus 4 teaspoons (120 g) glucose powder (see sources)

60 grams Trimoline (see sources)

7 grams sorbet stabilizer (see sources)

Prepare an ice bath. Put the water in a saucepan and bring to a boil over medium-high heat. Remove from the heat and, while whisking, rain in the sugar, glucose powder, Trimoline, and sorbet stabilizer until incorporated. Strain the mixture through a fine-mesh sieve placed over a metal bowl. Set the bowl over the ice bath and let cool completely, stirring occasionally. The sorbet base may be stored in a lidded container in the refrigerator for up to 2 weeks.

Sources

Anson Mills
Organic heirloom grains
www.ansonmills.com

Ajinomoto
Activa products
www.ajinomoto-usa.com

Amazon.com
Specialty pantry items such as hydrocolloids, menthol crystals, mesquite flour, risotto rice

Border Springs Farm
Lamb, turkey, poultry
www.borderspringsfarm.com

Broken Arrow Ranch
Free range, all natural game meats, including Axis venison
www.brokenarrowranch.com

The Chef's Garden
Microgreens, oyster blossoms and leaves, shoots
www.chefs-garden.com

The Chef's Warehouse
Specialty pantry items, including argan oil, ice cream stabilizer, leaf gelatin, liquid glucose, sorbitol, Trimoline,
www.chefswarehouse.com

Cherry Glen Goat Cheese Co.
www.cherryglengoatcheese.com

Coleman Family Farm
Fresh produce in Carpinteria, CA
(877) 886-7409

D'Artagnan
Natural and gourmet foods, including foie gras, squab, and truffle products
www.dartagnan.com

Dublin Roasters
Volt blend coffee
www.dublinroasterscoffee.com

Excalibur Dehydrator
www.excaliburdehydrator.com

Fagor Pressure cookers
www.fagoramerica.com

Fresh Origins
Sea beans, saltwort
www.freshorigins.com

Fresh & Wild
Specialty foods, including basil-fed snails, huitlacoche, Minus 8 wine vinegar, Russian corn
www.freshwild.com

Flying Dog Brewery
http://flyingdogales.com

Harry's Berries
www.harrysberries.com

Hudson Valley Foie Gras
www.hudsonvalleyfoiegras.com

iSi
Cream whippers and chargers
www.isinorthamerica.com

Jade Range
Professional cook tops
www.jaderange.com

Jamison Farm
Lamb
www.jamisonfarm.com

JB Prince
Chef tools and equipment
www.jbprince.com

Kenter Canyon Farms
Lettuces, and other produce
www.kentercanyonfarms.com

King Arthur Flour
Baking supplies, including black cocoa powder, flours, nut pastes
www.kingarthurflour.com

Koch Equipment
Vacuum sealers
www.kochequipment.com

Koerner
Hydrocolloids, spaghetti kit, specialty items
www.koerner-co.com

Korin
Bincho charcoal
http://korin.com

La Tienda
Hydrocolloids and other food additives
www.tienda.com

Le Sanctuaire
Hydrocolloids and other food additives
www.le-sanctuaire.com

Mikuni Wild Harvest
Specialty ingredients, including fir needles and microgreens
www.mikuniwildharvest.com

Monterey Abalone Company
www.montereyabalone.com

New England Cheesemaking Supply Company
Vegetable ash
www.cheesemaking.com

Niman Ranch
Humanely and sustainably raised meats
www.nimanranch.com

Polito Family Farms
Citrus
www.politofarms.com

Rational
Professional ovens
www.rational-online.com/US_en

Santa Monica Farmers Market
Organic Produce in Los Angeles
www.smgov.net/portals/farmersmarket/

Seafood.com
Fresh fish and live shellfish

The Stronghold
Denim aprons
www.thestronghold.com

Terra Spice Company
Pantry staples, including agar, exotic salts, coconut powder, malt vinegar powder, tomato powder, Ultra-Tex 3
http://terraspice.com

Tuscarora Organic Growers
Organic produce in the D.C. Metro area
http://tog.coop/

Vitamix high-speed blenders
www.vitamix.com

Whitmore Farm
Heritage breeds, eggs in the D.C. Metro area
www.whitmorefarm.com

Williams-Sonoma
Cooking equipment, specialty ingredients, exotic spices, pink curing salt
www.williams-sonoma.com

Zuckerman's farm produce
www.cuesa.org/farm/zuckermans-farm

Other resources:

For Asian ingredients, visit a local Asian market

For liquid nitrogen, visit a local welding supply company (be sure to wear the proper safety attire when using)

For timothy hay or alfalfa, visit a local organic farm

Index

D

E

F

G

H

I

K

Acknowledgments

FROM BRYAN

I was told by the first chef who gave me a shot in the kitchen, "You will go out there, work for many different chefs who will influence your career, and then you will become yourself, your style, Bryan Voltaggio." Thank you Michael Aleprete for that first shot.

To my wife, Jennifer, who pushed me to succeed, who has always been there through rough times and good ones. You have helped me make the right decisions, and you helped me get back up when I made the wrong ones. I would not be who I am as a chef, husband, and father without you.

People say that rivalry creates foes, but that is not the case with Michael and me. Michael has always pushed me to be a better chef. We both struggle constantly to be the best we can be. We use each other as measurement, resource, and support. I know that we have a special bond and understanding that has helped us become the chefs we are today. Thank you, little brother.

To Charlie Palmer, my mentor, who is a generous teacher. From the first time I walked through the doors at Aureole in Manhattan, I tried to be the best cook I could be and to soak in all of the knowledge and experiences you offered. I continue to tell myself that if I can be half the chef that you are, I will feel a sense of accomplishment in my career and as a family man.

To Gerry Hayden, who hired me as his sous chef at Aureole. You must have seen something in me that made me stand out from the others, because at Aureole they were many great young chefs. You gave me the chance to move to the next step, you encouraged me, you supported me, you taught me. I will always be grateful for the knowledge you shared, and I will continue to mold the next generation of cooks who pass through my kitchen as you molded me.

To my sous chef, Graeme Ritchie, who is my backbone, my friend. Every chef who strives to be regarded among the best has a great team behind him or her and a talented second in command. Thank you Graeme for keeping the machine going, for helping create, polish, and teach.

To my team at VOLT, who have helped me with this project and who have pushed to make the restaurant a success since the first day we opened the doors. I thank everyone who has picked up a knife in my kitchen for his or her dedication and hard work, and I hope all of you will fulfill your dreams.

To Alex Talbot and Aki Kamozawa, for your passion for our craft and for your inspiration and ideas that made this project fun, exciting, and a learning experience. Your *Ideas in Food* taught me a lot, but that was just the beginning. I look forward to sharing ideas with you for years to come.

It is always a good idea to save the best for last. Mom, I love you.

FROM MICHAEL

To Alex Talbot and Aki Kamozawa for their *Ideas in Food* and for helping me edit my own ideas, and to Richard Harvey for believing in the project.

To my father, John Voltaggio, who got me my first job at the hotel where he was head of security and who worked double shifts as a police officer and moonlighted for extra money. Our family never went without, and as I grew older, I understood why: hard work. To my brother, Bryan, the first sous chef I worked under and whose path is the one I continue to follow. And to my little sister, Staci, who served our country in the air force and is now a great mom.

To Michael Aleprete, the raging, ice-carving, hardworking, ball-breaking executive chef who asked if it was Halloween the first day I showed up for work in chef whites.

To Peter Timmins, the philosophical and intimidating Irish master chef who was the head of culinary arts at the famed Greenbrier Resort. On the last day of my apprenticeship, chef Timmins said, "One day you are no longer going to be the student, you are going to be the teacher. Will you be ready for that?" My answer then, now, and forever is no.

To Lawrence McFadden, another certified master chef, who I thought was ignoring me for the first six months I was his sous chef. Instead, I discovered that he was observing and taking notes so that he could one day give me a horrible performance review that pointed out my faults and did not allow me to settle for mediocre. McFadden is the same chef who gave me the honor to train alongside him as he prepared for his biggest professional accomplishment, the master chef examination.

To Sonny Sweetman and Arnaud Berthelier, the two fine-dining chefs at the Ritz-Carlton Hotel in Naples, Florida, where I learned about becoming a professional. They showed me simultaneously that two very different styles can demand the same attention to detail and craftsmanship required to make great food.

To chefs Charlie Palmer and José Andrés, neither of whom need any introduction and both of whom trusted me to execute and represent them and their visions.

To all of the amazing chefs who make their ideas accessible in order to fuel the continuous evolution of our craft. To all of the cooks whom I've worked under and who have worked under me. I have learned and continue to learn so much from all of you every day. You inspire and challenge me with your great ideas and demand that I inspire and challenge you with mine. To the ladies and gentlemen in the front-of-the-houses for composing themselves as such even when I didn't and for tearing down the wall that separated us.

To the two guys who have taken more shit from me than anyone, Cole Dickinson and Adam Cole, both of them my sous chefs, both of them my friends, both of them for having my back, and both of them for holding me accountable while I held them accountable. To the cooks who worked with Bryan and me on the book, Klein Debow, Alex Ramirez, Peter Egan, and more. To Josh Goldman, the most expensive dishwasher we have ever had. To Peter Stougaard for just being cool.

To Tibet, Ryan, Mark, and the rest of my "boys;" we are getting older but we are surviving so far. To my mom, Sharon Mangine, for showing me what strength really is, and to her husband, Bob, for standing beside her while she cheered Bryan and me on. Mom, you are living proof that challenges can be overcome, no matter how difficult.

To my beautiful daughters, Sophia and Olivia, for just being you, and to their mother, Kerri, for raising them so brilliantly in my absence.

JOINT ACKNOWLEDGMENTS

It takes a legion of people to publish a book and we would be remiss if we didn't mention them here: our agents, Matthew Elblonk and Max Stubblefield; our editor, Jennifer Newens; art director Kara Church; designer Tracy White Taylor; copy editor Sharon Silva; the entire staff at Weldon Owen; photographer Ed Anderson; our project managers, Aki Kamozawa and Alex Talbot; and the team at Williams-Sonoma.